Unreal Engine 4 Shaders and Effects Cookbook

Over 70 recipes for mastering post-processing effects and advanced shading techniques

Brais Brenlla Ramos
John P. Doran

BIRMINGHAM - MUMBAI

Unreal Engine 4 Shaders and Effects Cookbook

Commissioning Editor: Kunal Chaudhari
Acquisition Editor: Trusha Shriyan
Content Development Editor: Pranay Fereira
Technical Editor: Diksha Wakode
Copy Editor: Safis Editing
Project Coordinator: Kinjal Bari
Proofreader: Safis Editing
Indexer: Tejal Daruwale Soni
Graphics: Alishon Mendonsa
Production Coordinator: Deepika Naik

First published: May 2019

Production reference: 1240519

Published by Packt Publishing Ltd.
Livery Place
35 Livery Street
Birmingham
B3 2PB, UK.

ISBN 978-1-78953-854-0

www.packtpub.com

`mapt.io`

Mapt is an online digital library that gives you full access to over 5,000 books and videos, as well as industry leading tools to help you plan your personal development and advance your career. For more information, please visit our website.

Why subscribe?

- Spend less time learning and more time coding with practical eBooks and Videos from over 4,000 industry professionals

- Improve your learning with Skill Plans built especially for you

- Get a free eBook or video every month

- Mapt is fully searchable

- Copy and paste, print, and bookmark content

Packt.com

Did you know that Packt offers eBook versions of every book published, with PDF and ePub files available? You can upgrade to the eBook version at `www.packt.com` and as a print book customer, you are entitled to a discount on the eBook copy. Get in touch with us at `customercare@packtpub.com` for more details.

At `www.packt.com`, you can also read a collection of free technical articles, sign up for a range of free newsletters, and receive exclusive discounts and offers on Packt books and eBooks.

Contributors

About the authors

Brais Brenlla Ramos is a passionate Architect, 3D artist, Unreal Engine 4 developer and first-time author based between A Coruña and his place of work in London, UK. His passion for all things 3D-related dates back to when he was playing games as a child, experiences that fuelled his later studies in architecture and computer animation. His entrance into the professional 3D world happened at the same time as his studies were finishing, with initial projects undertaken in the field of architectural visualization for different studios. Since then, he's worked on many different 3D modeling and app development projects, first as a team member, and later as the Unreal Engine 4 lead developer at a company called AccuCities, based in London.

To my friends and family, who got me this far; and to my partner, Tamy, whose support and love carried me throughout.

John P. Doran is a passionate and seasoned technical game designer, software engineer, and author based in Peoria, Illinois.

For over a decade, John has gained extensive hands-on expertise in game development, working in a variety of roles, ranging from game designer to lead UI programmer. Additionally, John has worked in game development education teaching in Singapore, South Korea, and the United States. To date, he has authored over 10 books pertaining to game development.

John is currently an instructor in residence at Bradley University. Prior to his present ventures, he was an award-winning videographer.

I want to thank my wife, Hien, for all of her support over the course of working on this book.

About the reviewer

Deepak Jadhav is a game developer based in Pune, India. Deepak received his bachelor's degree in computer technology and master's degree in game programming and project management. Currently, he is working as a game developer in India's leading game development company. He has been involved in developing games on multiple platforms, such as PC, Mac, and mobile. With years of experience in game development, he has a strong background in C# and C++, and he has developed his skills in platforms including Unity, Unreal Engine, and augmented and virtual reality.

I would like to thank the authors and the Packt Publishing team for giving me the opportunity to review this book.

Packt is searching for authors like you

If you're interested in becoming an author for Packt, please visit `authors.packtpub.com` and apply today. We have worked with thousands of developers and tech professionals, just like you, to help them share their insight with the global tech community. You can make a general application, apply for a specific hot topic that we are recruiting an author for, or submit your own idea.

Table of Contents

Preface

Unreal Engine 4 Shaders and Effects Cookbook aims to take you on a journey of creation and discovery within the Unreal Engine 4 game engine. As the title of the book implies, we'll travel hand in hand to every corner of the engine, performing actions that affect the visuals of our games and apps. We'll do so in an orderly way, starting from the very beginning by covering fundamental topics that will stay with us throughout the rest of the book. Each chapter that follows will expand upon that base, allowing for a gentle progression curve that will allow almost any user to follow along. In spite of that, each entry – or recipe – has been also conceived as an independent unit, letting you tackle it separately from the others in case you are already proficient with the other topics.

We'll start by covering the core concepts behind Unreal Engine's rendering pipeline, such as its physically based rendering approach and post-processing effects. With solid foundational knowledge about those two topics, we'll expand upon them and study different types of materials: opaque ones, translucent ones, and more, such as the different subsurface materials and other shading models. We'll also explore several advanced material creation techniques and tricks that the engine lets us use to create multiple different effects—from mixing materials and blueprints, to instancing and material optimization. There's a whole lot we are going to be covering!

Upon finishing this book, you will have a thorough knowledge about many different material concepts and techniques, both from a practical and a theoretical point of view. You'll be able to use these newly learned concepts in any games, apps, or personal projects that you tackle, with the absolute confidence that you are doing it right. With that said, let's get to it!

Who this book is for

Unreal Engine 4 Shaders and Effects Cookbook benefits from a structure that goes *in crescendo*, covering more difficult topics as we move along together. Thus, the book lends itself to being read by multiple different profiles of user from novice users, to more seasoned ones that haven't yet touched Unreal's material pipeline. Whatever the case, a good understanding of Unreal is definitely a plus, and something that will make your journey throughout this book a much smoother experience.

What this book covers

Chapter 1, *Physically Based Rendering*, starts off this book by going over the fundamental rendering concepts that Unreal relies on, as well as introducing us to the material editor.

Chapter 2, *Post-Processing Effects*, introduces the user to the powerful concept of post-processing in Unreal and explains the different effects that can be achieved through it.

Chapter 3, *Opaque Materials and Texture Mapping*, goes into detail about one of the most common type of materials in Unreal and the different uses that it has.

Chapter 4, *Translucent Materials and More*, covers one of the most exciting type of materials, the translucent ones, as well as many others, including subsurface and emissive materials.

Chapter 5, *Beyond Traditional Material Uses*, goes over different uses that materials can have beyond simply being applied to 3D models, including light functions, UI elements, and displaying videos.

Chapter 6, *Advanced Material Techniques*, talks about some of the most high-end effects that can be created within the material editor by using advanced techniques, such as parallax occlusion mapping and mesh distance fields.

Chapter 7, *Using Material Instances*, discusses how to use the concept of instancing to quickly make tweaks to a material instance, layer different shaders on top of each other, and affect multiple material settings at once.

Chapter 8, *Mobile Shaders and Material Optimization*, goes over various ways to optimize your materials to make them more performant on different hardware where efficiency is important, such as on mobile devices or when working in virtual reality.

Chapter 9, *Some Extra Useful Nodes*, focuses on some of the most useful nodes we can find within Unreal that don't really belong to a collective category of their own.

To get the most out of this book

Any reader will need to have installed a version of Unreal Engine on their computers; the latest version, if possible. Most of the recipes we'll look at should work on different engine versions, but we recommend 4.22 in order to have the latest features installed.

Prior knowledge about the engine is not a must, but having some working experience with Unreal will help the reader enjoy a smoother experience throughout the book. Whilst no coding skills are required, some fluency with the Blueprint visual scripting language would also be of great help.

Download the example code files

You can download the example code files for this book from your account at www.packt.com. If you purchased this book elsewhere, you can visit www.packt.com/support and register to have the files emailed directly to you.

You can download the code files by following these steps:

1. Log in or register at www.packt.com.
2. Select the **SUPPORT** tab.
3. Click on **Code Downloads & Errata**.
4. Enter the name of the book in the **Search** box and follow the onscreen instructions.

Once the file is downloaded, please make sure that you unzip or extract the folder using the latest version of:

- WinRAR/7-Zip for Windows
- Zipeg/iZip/UnRarX for Mac
- 7-Zip/PeaZip for Linux

The code bundle for the book is also hosted on GitHub at https://github.com/PacktPublishing/Unreal-Engine-4-Shaders-and-Effects-Cookbook. In case there's an update to the code, it will be updated on the existing GitHub repository.

We also have other code bundles from our rich catalog of books and videos available at https://github.com/PacktPublishing/. Check them out!

Download the color images

We also provide a PDF file that has color images of the screenshots/diagrams used in this book. You can download it here: https://www.packtpub.com/sites/default/files/downloads/9781789538540_ColorImages.pdf.

Conventions used

There are a number of text conventions used throughout this book.

`CodeInText`: Indicates code words in text, database table names, folder names, filenames, file extensions, pathnames, dummy URLs, user input, and Twitter handles. Here is an example: "Add a `Cheap Contrast` node after the Texture Sample, and connect its In (S) input pin with the output of the previous image"

Bold: Indicates a new term, an important word, or words that you see onscreen. For example, words in menus or dialog boxes appear in the text like this. Here is an example: "Drag a cable out of the original **Texture Sample** and create a new **Multiply** node"

 Warnings or important notes appear like this.

 Tips and tricks appear like this.

Getting ready

This section tells you what to expect in the recipe and describes how to set up any software or any preliminary settings required for the recipe.

How to do it...

This section contains the steps required to follow the recipe.

How it works...

This section usually consists of a detailed explanation of what happened in the previous section.

There's more...

This section consists of additional information about the recipe in order to make you more knowledgeable about the recipe.

See also

This section provides helpful links to other useful information for the recipe.

Get in touch

Feedback from our readers is always welcome.

General feedback: If you have questions about any aspect of this book, mention the book title in the subject of your message and email us at customercare@packtpub.com.

Errata: Although we have taken every care to ensure the accuracy of our content, mistakes do happen. If you have found a mistake in this book, we would be grateful if you would report this to us. Please visit www.packt.com/submit-errata, selecting your book, clicking on the Errata Submission Form link, and entering the details.

Piracy: If you come across any illegal copies of our works in any form on the Internet, we would be grateful if you would provide us with the location address or website name. Please contact us at copyright@packt.com with a link to the material.

If you are interested in becoming an author: If there is a topic that you have expertise in and you are interested in either writing or contributing to a book, please visit authors.packtpub.com.

Reviews

Please leave a review. Once you have read and used this book, why not leave a review on the site that you purchased it from? Potential readers can then see and use your unbiased opinion to make purchase decisions, we at Packt can understand what you think about our products, and our authors can see your feedback on their book. Thank you!

For more information about Packt, please visit packt.com.

Physically Based Rendering

1

Welcome to the first chapter of the book! In the next few pages, we are going to start looking at how to set up a scene in Unreal for visualization purposes—we want to make sure that we nail this first part down before we move any further. Beginner or advanced, no matter what type of user you are, we'll need to make sure to take a look at some of the most critical elements that can make or break a scene in Unreal. Things like taking advantage of the right type of lighting, knowing where to look for the most common material parameters, or learning to measure the impact in performance that the shaders have are vital in any project. With that in mind, we are going to be learning about the following topics:

- Setting up a studio scene
- Working inside the material editor
- Our first physically based material
- Creating some simple glass with the translucent blend mode
- Lighting our scene with image-based lighting
- Checking the cost of our materials

Introduction

Welcome to this in-depth journey through the material creation process in Unreal Engine 4! I think you are going to have a great time if you are excited about the possibilities that this game engine brings to the table in terms of state-of-the-art rendering techniques. And by state-of-the-art I mean a powerful and robust rendering pipeline, where both photorealistic and stylized game art are possible without changing to a different development suite.

The fact that such a flexible system is in place is courtesy of the continuous advances over the years in the field of real-time rendering. We've journeyed from the 2D era into the 3D era, from sprites and flat images to the rendering of polygons and whole worlds.

Each of these changes happened thanks to a combination of new and more powerful hardware as well as increasingly intelligent rendering pipelines and techniques. One of the latest improvements that we can talk about is what we are going to be covering throughout this book—the PBR workflow.

And what does PBR stand for? That would be **Physically Based Rendering**—a particular method that takes into account how light behaves when it comes into contact with 3D objects. In order to represent materials placed in a 3D environment, artists need to specify certain properties for each of the materials that they create—such as what the underlying color should be, how much light they reflect, or how defined those reflections are.

This is significant change from previous workflows, where light propagation and its simulation wasn't taken into account in a realistic way. This meant, for example, that materials couldn't be replicated under different lighting conditions—having, for instance, a night and a day scene using the same assets resulted in them looking substantially different. An artist would therefore need to create different sets of textures or adjust the materials to make them look right for each particular scenario they might be in.

This has changed with the recent introduction of the PBR workflow. Newer game engines, such as Unreal Engine 4, have made this rendering approach their quasi default one—and I say *quasi* as they also allow for older rendering methods to be thrown into the mix in order to give artists more freedom. Materials are coherent under different lighting settings, and knowing how to create content under this pipeline ensures usability under a lot of different circumstances.

However, PBR is not a universally defined convention as far as its implementation goes. This means that how things work under the hood varies across the different rendering engines. The exact implementation that Epic has chosen for their Unreal Engine platform is different from that of other third-party software creators. Furthermore, PBR workflows in real-time applications are slightly different to offline renderers, as efficiency and speed are a must in this industry and things have to be adapted consequently. What we need to take away from these facts is that a physically based approach to rendering has huge advantages (as well as some limitations) that we as artists need to be aware of if we are to use the engine to its full potential.

We conceived the present book with that goal in mind. We aim to present you with a series of recipes that tackle many different functionalities within Unreal, structured in a way where each unit can be read independently from the rest. In order to do so, we'll be taking a look in the following pages at how to get a hold of the engine and how to set up a basic scene, which we'll use to visualize our projects.

Setting up a studio scene

In this first recipe, we are going to create a basic scene that we'll be able to use as our background level throughout this course. This initial step is here just so we can go over the basics of the engine and get familiar with different useful websites from where we can download multiple assets.

Getting ready

Before we actually start creating our basic studio scene, we will need to download Unreal Engine 4. I've started writing this book with version 4.20.3, but don't hesitate to use the latest version at the time of reading.

Here's how you can download it:

1. Get the **Epic Games Launcher** from the engine's website, `https://www.unrealengine.com/en-US/blog`, and follow the installation procedure indicated there.

2. Once installed, download the latest version of the engine. We can do so by navigating to the **UNREAL ENGINE** section of the launcher, in the tab named **Library**. In there, we'll be able to see a + icon (**1**), which lets us download whichever version of Unreal we want. Once we've downloaded it, launch it (**2**) so we can get started:

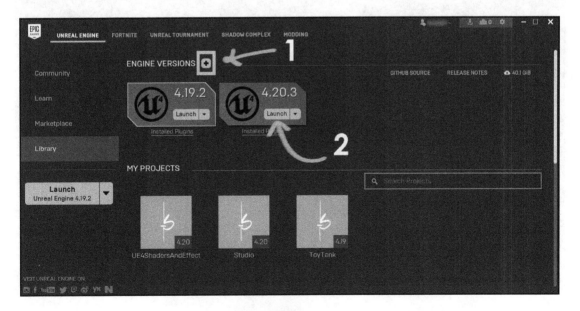

And that's all you need! We now have everything required to get started in Unreal Engine 4. How cool is that? A whole new game engine at our fingertips, completely free, and with a variety of tools within it that would take years to learn and master. It really is a thing of wonder! Next up, we are going to start learning about one of those tools—the materials. And in order to do so, let's start by creating our first project!

How to do it...

Let's start by launching the engine that we have just installed and creating a new project by taking the following steps:

1. Create a **New Project**—give it a name and select the folder where you want it to live. Just as a reference, as shown in the following screenshot, I've decided to start off with a blank blueprint-based project, but it doesn't really matter what we decide to initially include. Nothing special so far! You can choose to add the **Starter Content** if you want, as it comes with several useful resources that we can use later on:

Additionally, you can get more free resources from other different places. You can check the **Learn** tab within the **Epic Games Launcher** to see what freely available examples you can get a hold of, or check the community section to see if there is any new cool content.

Epic has recently collaborated with multiple content creators to make a multitude of different assets available to anyone using Unreal, and you can check them out at the following website: `https://www.unrealengine.com/en-US/blog/new-free-content-coming-to-the-unreal-engine-marketplace?utm_source=launcher utm_medium=chromiumutm_term=forumutm_content=FreeContentutm_campaign=communitytab`.

2. The first thing that we need to do once the editor loads is to go to **File | Save Current As**, just to make sure that the changes we are about to implement get saved. Otherwise, we would just be working on the default untitled map, which wouldn't store any of the changes that we are about to make!

3. Once that's done, we are now ready to start spicing things up. Erase everything from the world outliner—we are not going to be using any of that for our studio scene. Your scene and the world outliner should look something like this:

4. If you haven't done so before, it is now time to include the **Starter Content**. Don't worry if you didn't do it at first! I didn't say it was mandatory only to be able to look at how to include it after starting a new project—just navigate to the content browser and look for the **Add New** option in the upper left corner. Select the first available option in there, named **Add feature or Content Pack**, as shown in the following screenshot:

5. With that included, we can see that the Starter Content includes a blueprint that can be quite useful for setting up the lighting in our scene. You can look for this inside of the **Content Browser** | **Starter Content** | **Blueprints** folder, and it's named **BP_ Light Studio**. Select it and drag it into the scene we have previously created.

The asset called **BP_Light Studio** is a blueprint that Epic Games has already created for us. It includes several lighting settings that will make our lives easier—instead of having to set up multiple lights and assign them different values, it automates all of that work for us so we just have to choose how we want our scene to look. Making a simple studio scene will be something very easy to do this way.

Retaining that level of control over which lights are placed and how we do that is, of course, very important, and something that we'll do later in the book, but for now this is a very powerful tool that we will use.

6. With the **BP_ Light Studio** placed in our scene, we can start tweaking its default values just so we can use it as a lighting studio setup. Select the blueprint from the world outliner and let's tweak several settings.

7. The first one we can look at is the **HDRi** tab inside the details panel for the **BP_ Light Studio**. **HDRi** is short for **High Dynamic Range imaging,** which is a type of texture that stores the lighting information from the place at which the photo was taken. Using that data as a type of light in 3D scenes is a very powerful technique, which makes our environments look more natural and real:

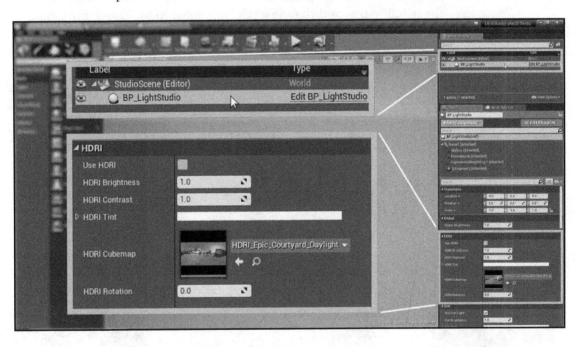

8. However, useful HDRi might be, this lighting method is turned off by default, so make sure to tick the **Use HDRi** checkbox. That will make the texture placed in the **HDRi Cubemap** slot light the scene. Feel free to use any other ones you might have or download one to use throughout the project!

HDRi images are very useful for 3D artists, even though they can be tricky to create as it is usually a lengthy process. There are many websites from which you can buy them, but I like the following one that gives you free access to some very useful ones: http://www.hdrlabs.com/sibl/archive.html.

We will be using the one called **Alexs Apartment**, which is quite useful for interior visualization.

9. You can now untick the **Use Light Sun** and the **Use Atmosphere** option found under the **Sun** and the **Atmosphere** section of the **BP_LightStudio** blueprint if you use an HDRi image. As we said earlier, this type of picture stores lighting information, which renders the use of other lights sometimes optional.

10. Once you've done that, let's create a basic plane on which we can use to lay out our objects. Dragging a plane into the scene from the **Modes** panel will do the job: **Modes | Basic category | Plane**.

11. Let's assign our newly placed plane an interesting default material so we have something to look at—with the plane selected, scroll down to the **Materials** section of the details panel and change its default value to **M_Wood_Pine**. Said material is part of the **Starter Content**, so make sure you have it installed!

We should now be looking at something like the following:

With that out of the way, we can say that we've finished creating our basic studio scene. Having done that will enable us to use this level for visualization purposes, kind of like having a white canvas on which to paint. We will use this to place other models and materials as we create them, in order to correctly visualize our assets.

How it works...

There are at least two different objectives that we can complete if we follow the previous set of steps—the creation of our intro scene being the first one and the second one being getting familiar with the engine. This final task is something that will continue to happen over time—but getting our hands dirty now will have hopefully accelerated that process.

Something that could also speed that up even more is a review process of what we've just done. Not only will we learn things potentially faster, but knowing why we do the things the way we do them will help us cement the knowledge we acquire—so expect to see a *How it works...* section after each recipe we tackle! As the first ever example of the aforementioned section, we'll briefly go over what we have just done before in order to understand how things work in Unreal.

The first step we've taken was to actually create the Unreal Engine project on which we'll be working throughout this book. We've then added the assets present in the Starter Content package that Epic Games supplies, as it contains useful 3D models and materials that we can check later on as we work on other recipes. The most important bit we've done was probably the lighting setup though, as this will be the basis of some of the next recipes. This is because having a light source is vital to visualizing the different assets that we create or add to the scene. Lighting is something that we'll explore more in some of the next recipes, but the method we've chosen in this one is a very cool technique that you can use in your own projects. We are using an asset that Unreal calls a **blueprint**, something that allows you to use the engine's visual scripting language to create different functionalities within the game engine without using C++ code. This is extremely useful, as you can program different behaviors across multiple types of actors to use to your advantage—turning a light on and off, opening a door, creating triggers to fire certain events, and so on. We'll explore them more as we go along, but at the moment we are just using an already available one to specify the lighting effects we want to have in our scene. This is in itself a good example of what a blueprint can do, as it allows us to set up multiple different components without having to specify each one of them individually—such as the HDRi image, the sun position, and others that you can see if you look at the **Details** panel.

Working inside the material editor

Let's get started with the material editor! This is the place where the magic will happen and also where we'll spend most of our time during this cookbook. Better get well acquainted with it then! As with everything inside Unreal, you'll be able to see that this space for creating materials is a very flexible one—full of customizable panels, rearrangeable windows, and expandable areas. You can place them however you want!

Because of its modular nature, some of the initial questions we need to tackle are the following ones: how do we start creating materials and where do we look for the most commonly used parameters? Having different panels means having to look for different functionalities in each of them, so we'll need to know how to find our way around the editor. We won't stop there though—the editor is packed with plenty of useful little tools that will make our jobs as material creators that much easier, and knowing where they live is one of the first mandatory steps.

So, without further ado, let's use the project we have already set up in the previous recipe as our starting point and let's start creating our first material!

Getting ready

There's not much we need to do at this point—all thanks to having previously created the basic blank project. That's the reason we created it in the first place, so we can start working on our materials straight away. Having set up the studio scene is all we need at this point.

In spite of this, don't feel obliged to use the level we created in the first recipe. Any other one will do, as long as there are some lights in it that help you visualize your world. That's the advantage of the PBR workflow, that whatever we create following its principles will work across different lighting scenarios. Let's jump right in!

How to do it...

It's now time to take a look at how the material editor works, at the same time as we create our first material. This editor includes many different tools and functionalities within it, so there are plenty of things to take a look at!

 Remember that you can bring the material editor up by just creating a new material and double-clicking on it.

The first important thing we will be doing is to actually create a material. Of course, this is a very trivial action and there's not much to explain—just right-click anywhere on the content browser and select the **Create Basic Asset | Material** option. What is important is knowing how to name and organize our contents. Even though keeping the **Content Browser** organized is not the main goal of this chapter, I didn't want to pass up on the opportunity to briefly talk about that.

One good way of keeping things tidy is to organize the folder structure in categories (**Materials, Characters, Weapons, Environment...**) and naming the different assets using Unreal's recommended syntax. You can find more about that on several discussion forums or on Epic Games' wiki:

- Unreal Engine 4 style guide: `https://github.com/Allar/ue4-style-guide`
- Assets naming convention: `https://wiki.unrealengine.com/Assets_Naming_Convention`

The second important thing we want to be doing is to make sure that the layout we are looking at is the default one, just so that the images we will be including later on match what you'll be seeing in your monitor. To do that, go to **Window** | **Reset Layout**, as shown in the following screenshot:

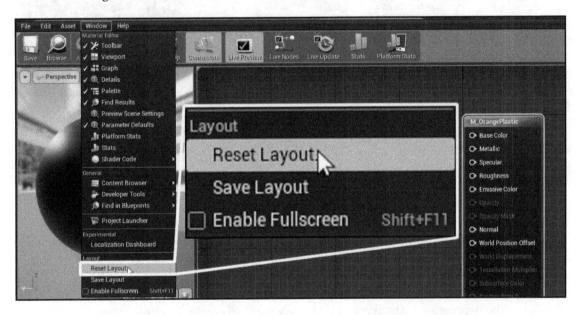

Remember that resetting the layout to its default state can still make things not look perfectly equal between your screen and mine—that's because settings such as the screen resolution or its aspect ratio can hide panels or make them imperceptibly small. Feel free to move things around until you reach a layout that works for you!

Now that we've made sure that we are looking at the same screen, let's turn our attention to the material editor itself and the different parts that constitute it. By default, this is what we should be looking at:

- The first part of the material editor is the **Toolbar**, a common section that you'll find in many other places within the engine. It lets you save your progress or apply any changes that you've made to your materials amongst other things.
- The second panel is the **Viewport**, where we'll be able to see what our material looks like. You can rotate the view, zoom in or out, and change the lighting setup of that window.
- The **Details** panel (**3**) is a very useful one, for here is where we can start to define the properties of the materials that we want to create. Its contents vary depending on what is selected in the main graph editor (the panel numbered **6**).
- The **Stats** and the **Find Results** panels (**4**) is where you can take a look at how costly your materials are or how many textures they are using.
- The **material node Palette** (**5**) is a library of different nodes and functions that we'll use to modify the materials we create.
- The **main graph editor** (**6**) is where the action happens, and where most of the functionality that you want to include in your materials needs to be visually scripted.

Now that we've taken a look at the different parts that make up the material editor in Unreal, we can start creating our own first simple material—a plastic. I find plastics to be a very straightforward type—even though we could make them as complicated as we want to. So, let's explore how we would go about at creating it:

1. Take a look at the main graph. By default, every time you create a new material, you should be looking at a central main node. You will see multiple pins, which are the elements where we want to connect the different elements we will be creating.

2. Right-click on the main graph, preferably to the left of the main material node, and start typing `constant`. As you start to write, notice how the auto-completion system starts to show several options: **Constant**, **Constant2Vector**, **Constant3Vector**, and so on. Select **Constant3Vector**, as shown in the following screenshot:

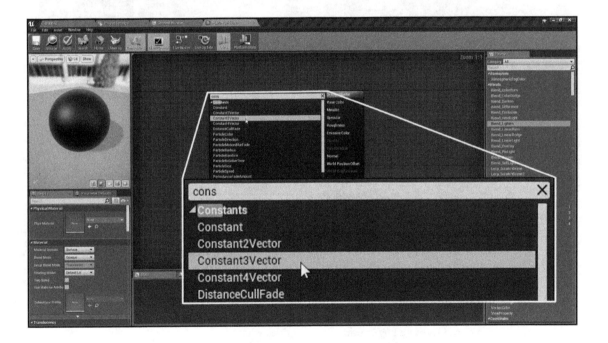

3. Having chosen that option, you will be able to see that a new node has now appeared. You can now connect it to the **Base Color** of the material node. If you are on the constant node, take a look at the **Details** panel and you'll be able to see that there are a couple settings that you can tweak. Since we want to move away from the default blackish appearance that the material now has, click on the black rectangle to the right of where it says **Constant** and use the color wheel to change its current value. I'm going to go with orange:

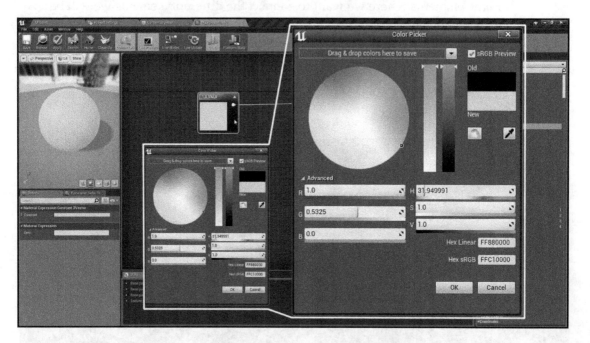

There's more to the base color property than meets the eye! Apart from the different options that are available to select a color, you might be interested to know that the actual value that gets connected to the material slot matters beyond the color choice. Certain materials have a measured intensity to them, and you can check that out on the following website: https://docs.unrealengine.com/en-us/Engine/Rendering/Materials/PhysicallyBased.

It's not something that you should concern yourself with at this stage, but can come in handy in the future!

At the moment, we can see that we have managed to modify the color of our material. We can now change how sharp the reflections are, as we want to go for a *plastic* look. In order to do so, we need to modify the **Roughness** parameter with another different constant. Instead of right-clicking and typing, let's choose it from the palette menu instead.

4. Navigate to the **Palette** section, and look for the **Constant** category. We want to select the first option in there, aptly named like this subsection itself. Alternatively, you can type its name in the search box at the top of the panel:

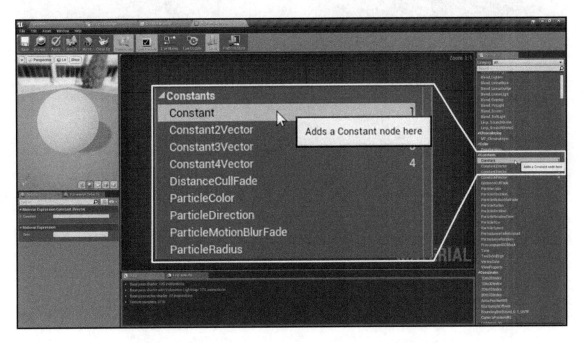

5. A new, smaller node should have now appeared. Unlike the previous one, we don't have the option to select a color—we need to type in a value. Let's go with something low, about **0.2**. Connect it to the **Roughness** pin.

If you look at the preview viewport, you will notice that the appearance of the material has now changed. It looks like the reflections from the environment are much sharper than before. This is happening thanks to the previously created constant pin, which, using a value closer to 0 (or black), makes the reflections stand out that much more. Whiter values decrease the sharpness of those reflections or, in other words, make the surface appear much more rough.

Having done so, we are now in a position where we can finally apply this material to a model inside of our scene. Let's go back to the main level and look at the **Modes** panel, particularly to the **Basic** section. Drag and drop a cube into the main level, and assign it the following values inside of the **Details** panel just so we are looking at the same:

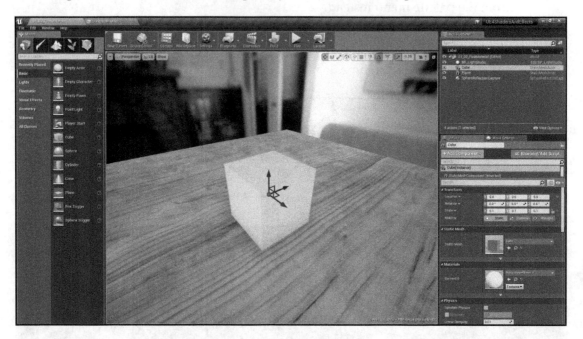

Reducing the size of the cube will make it fit better into our scene. Now head over to the **Materials** section of the **Details** panel, and click on the drop-down menu. Look for the newly created material and assign it to our cube. Finally, click on the **Build** icon located on the toolbar as follows:

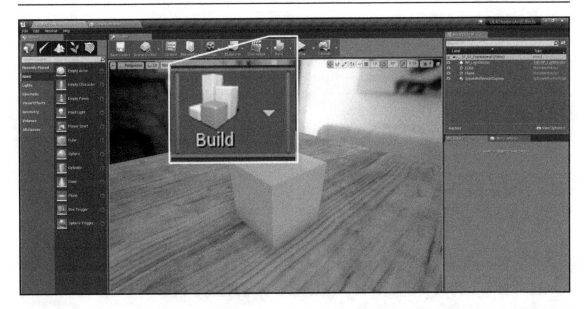

And there it is! We now have our material applied to a simple model, being displayed on the scene we had previously created. Even though this has served as a small introduction to a much bigger world, we've now gone over most of the panels and tools that we'll be using in the material editor. See you in the next recipe!

How it works...

We've used the present recipe to learn about the material editor and we've also created our first material. Knowing what each section does within the editor will help a lot in the immediate future, as what we've just done is but a prelude to our real target—creating a physically based material. Now we are in a much better position to tackle that goal, so let's look at it in the next recipe!

Before moving on though, let's check the nodes that we have used to create this simple material. From an artist's point of view, the names that the engine has given to something like a color value or a grayscale value can seem a bit confusing. It might be difficult to establish a connection between the name of the Constant3Vector node and our idea of a color. But there is a reason for all of this!

The idea behind that naming convention is that these nodes can be used beyond the color values we have just assigned them. At the end of the day, a simple constant can be used in many different scenarios—such as depicting a grayscale value, using it as a brightness multiplier, or as a parameter inside a material function. Don't worry if you haven't seen these other uses yet, we will—the point is, the names that these nodes were given tell us that there are more uses beyond the ones we've seen.

With that in mind, it might be better to think of those elements we've been using in more mathematical terms. For instance, think of a color as an **Red Green Blue** (**RGB**) value, which is what we are defining with that previous `Constant3Vector` node. If you want to use an RGB value alongside an alpha one, why not use the `Constant4Vector`, which allows for a fourth input? Even though we are at a very early stage, it is always good to familiarize ourselves with the different expressions the engine uses.

Our first physically based material

PBR is, at its core, a principle that several graphic engines try to follow. Instead of being a strict set of rules that every rendering program needs to abide by, it is more of an idea—one that dictates that what we see on our screens is the result of a study on how light behaves when it interacts with certain surfaces.

As a direct consequence, the so-called *PBR workflow* varies from one rendering solution to the next, depending on how the creators of the software have decided to program the system. For our case, what we are going to be looking at is the implementation that Epic Games has chosen for their Unreal Engine 4 real-time renderer.

However, we are going to do so in our already established recipe process, that is, by creating real examples of materials that follow the PBR workflow rather than just talking in a general way. Let's get to it!

Getting ready

We don't need a lot in order to start working on this recipe—just the project we have previously created so we don't have to start from scratch. You can continue using the previous section's materials or create new ones, whatever works best for you! Something that would be helpful to have is the scene from the previous recipe open, for instance—that way we already have a 3D model in it that we can use to show our materials on.

We are going to be creating multiple materials in this section, so duplicating and modifying an already existing asset is going to be faster than creating several ones from scratch. To do this, just select any material that you want to duplicate on the content browser and press *Ctrl + W*.

How to do it...

Let's start our journey into the PBR pipeline by creating a new material and looking at the different attributes that define it:

1. Right-click anywhere inside of the **Content Browser** and select the material option in the **Create Basic Asset** section. Name it whatever you want—I'll go with M_PBR_Metal for this particular instance. Double-click on the newly created material to open up the material editor.

2. With the **Material** editor now open, we can start taking a look at the PBR workflow. The first material we are going to create is a metallic one, a particular type that uses most of the attributes associated to this pipeline. With that said, let's focus our attention on the following two different places—the **Details** panel and the main **Material** node itself:

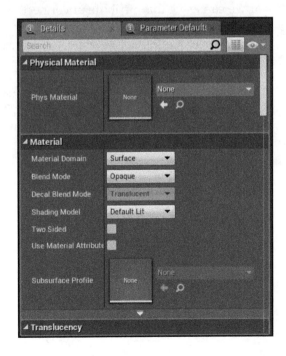

The settings you see here are the default ones for most materials in Unreal, and they follow the PBR pipeline very closely. The first option, the **Material Domain**, is currently set to **Surface**. That tells us that the material we are creating is meant to be used on a 3D model. **Blend Mode**, which has a value of **Opaque**, indicates that it is not a translucent material like glass. Finally, the shading model is set to **Default Lit**, which is the default one for most materials.

This configuration is the default one for most common materials, and the one that we'll need to use to define materials such as metal, plastic, wood, or concrete, to name a few.

3. With that bit of theory out of the way, let's create a **Constant3Vector** node anywhere in the graph and plug it into the **Base Color** input pin of our material. We've used the **Base Color** attribute in the previous recipe, and as we saw, this is the node where the overall color of a material should be plugged into.

4. The next item we will be creating is a **Constant**. You can do so by holding the *1* key on your keyboard and clicking anywhere within the material editor graph. Give it a value of 1 and plug it into the **Metallic** attribute of our material.

The **Metallic** attribute defines whether we are creating a metal or a non-metal material. We should use a value of **1** to define metallic surfaces and a value of **0** for non-metals—or we can leave this attribute unconnected, which would be the same as using a zero. Values between **0** and **1** should only be used in special circumstances, such as when dealing with metals that have been treated—corroded or painted metals and the like.

5. For our next step, let's replicate what we have just done—start by creating another constant and plugging it into the **Roughness** slot. This time, let's not give it a value of 1, but something like 0.2 instead. The final material graph should look something like this:

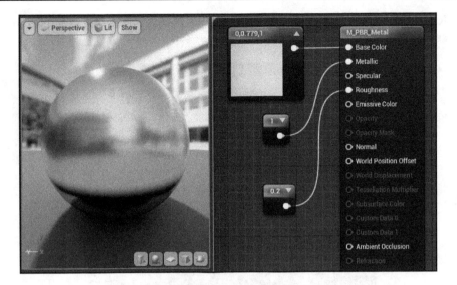

The attribute we are controlling through the previous constant defines how rough the surface of a given material should be. Higher values, such as **1**, simulate the micro details that make light scatter in all directions—which means we are looking at a matte surface where reflections are not clear. Values closer to zero result in those imperfections being removed, allowing a clear reflection of the incoming light rays and a much clearer reflected image.

Through the previous steps, we have taken a look at some of the most important material attributes used to define a PBR material. We've done so by creating a metal, which can be a good example for some of the previous properties. However, it will be good to create another quick material that is not a metallic one—this is because some of the other properties of the PBR workflow, like the specular material attribute, are meant to be used in such cases.

6. Create another material, which we can name M_PBR_Wood, and open the material editor for that asset.
7. Let's plug something into the **Base Color material** attribute—but instead of using a plain value, let's go with an image this time. The **Starter Content** provides multiple textures that can be used for this very purpose, so let's make use of one of those resources.

Right-click anywhere inside of the main graph for our newly created material and search for **TextureSample**, like in the next screenshot:

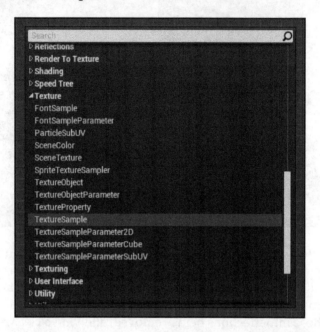

8. With that new node on our graph, click on it to access the options in the **Details** panel. Click again on the drop-down menu found in the **Material Expression Texture Base | Texture** slot and type wood. Select the **T_ Wood_ Floor_ Walnut_ D** asset and connect the **Texture Sample** node into the **Base Color material** attribute as follows:

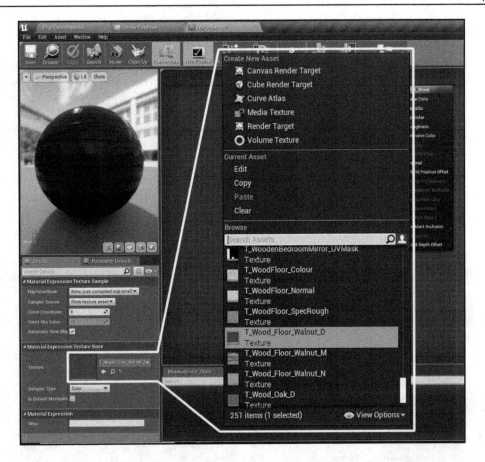

If you want to get hold of more textures online, feel free to browse the internet for more of them. A good place where I like to search for these types of resources is www.textures.com, which allows you to download several samples a day once you create a free account.

With that done, it's time to be looking at another material attribute—the **Specular** parameter. Unlike roughness, this node controls how much light is being reflected by the material and not how clear those reflections are. We therefore tend to modify the specular level when we have small-scale occlusion or small shadows happening across a surface, similar to what would be happening for the texture that we chose before.

9. The seams in between the wood boards are a good place to use a specular map, as those areas will reflect less light. In Unreal, such places are described with values close to **0** (black). Knowing that, drag a pin from the red channel of the previously created **Texture Sample** node into the **Specular** attribute of the main material node.

You might be wondering why we are using the red channel of the wood texture to drive the specular parameter. The simple answer is that even though we could create a custom black and white image to achieve the same effect, any of the original textures' channels are black and white values that contain the information that we are after. Because seams are going to contain darker pixels than other areas, the end result we achieve is still very similar if we use the red channel of the original texture. You can see in the next image our source asset and the red channel by its side:

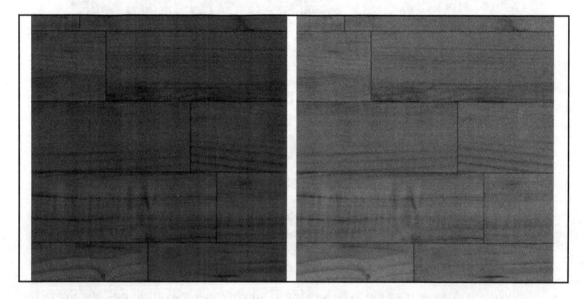

10. Copy the **Texture Sample** node twice, since we are going to use more textures for the roughness and the normal material attribute slots.

11. Just as we did previously, select the **T_ Wood_ Floor_ Walnut_ M** and the **T_ Wood_ Floor_ Walnut_ N** assets on each of the new nodes. Connect the first one to the **Roughness** slot and the second one to the **Normal** node. Save the material and click on the button that says **Apply**. Your material node graph should look something like this:

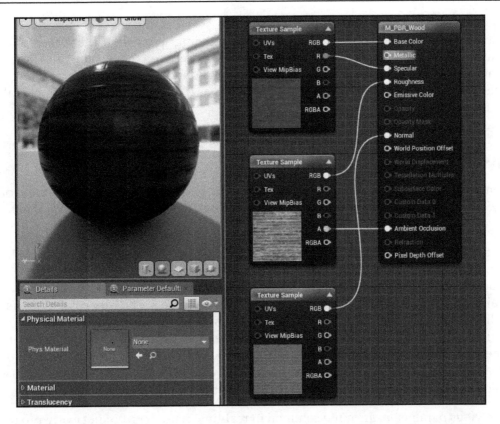

12. Navigate back to the main level, and select the floor plane. In the **Details** panel, scroll down to the **Materials** section and assign the **M_PBR_Wood** material we have just created. Take a look at what our scene looks like now:

Nice job, right? The new nodes we've used, both the specular and the normal ones, contribute to the added details we can see in the preceding screenshot. The specular node diminishes the light that is being reflected in the seams between the wood planks, and the normal map modifies the direction in which the light bounces from the surface. The combined effect is that our model, a flat plane, looks as if it has much more geometrical detail than it really has.

How it works...

Remember how we were talking about each renderer having its own implementation of a PBR workflow? Well, we have just taken a look at how Epic has chosen to set up theirs!

As we have already said, efficiency and speed are at the heart of any real-time application. These are two factors that have heavily influenced the path that the engineers at Epic have chosen when coding their physical approach at rendering. That being the case, the parameters that we have tweaked are the most important ones when it comes to how Unreal deals with the interaction between light and 3D models. The base color gives us the overall appearance of the material, whilst roughness indicates how sharp or blurry the reflections are. Metallic enables us to specify whether an object is made out of metal, and the specular node lets us influence how intense those reflections are. Finally, using normal maps allows for the modification of the direction in which the light gets reflected—a useful technique for adding details without actually using more polygons.

The previous parameters are quite common in real-time renderers, but not every program uses the same ones. For instance, offline suites such as VRay use other types of calculations to generate the final output—physically based in their nature, but using other techniques. This shows us that, at the end of the day, the PBR workflow that Epic uses is specific to the engine and we need to be aware of its possibilities and the limitations.

Throughout the current recipe, we have managed to take a look at some of the most important nodes that affect how the physically based rendering gets tackled in Unreal Engine 4. Base color, roughness, specularity, ambient occlusion, normal maps, and the metallic attribute all constitute the basics of the PBR workflow.

Having seen all of them, we are now ready to start looking into how to build more complex materials and effects. And even though we still need to understand some of the other areas that affect our pipeline, we can do so with the certainty that the basics are covered.

Creating some simple glass with the translucent blend mode

In the previous section, we had the opportunity to create a basic material that followed the physically based approach that Unreal Engine uses to render elements into our screens. By using nodes and expressions that affected the roughness or the metallic attributes of a material, we saw how we could potentially create endless combinations—going from plastics to concrete, metal, or wood.

Those previous examples can be considered simple ones—for they use the same shading model to calculate how each element needs to be rendered. Most of the materials that we experience in our daily lives fall into that category, and they can be described using the attributes we have previously tweaked. In spite of that, there are always examples that can't be exactly covered with one unique shading model. The way that light behaves when it touches glass, for example, needs to be redefined in those cases. The same applies to other elements, such as human skin or foliage, where light distribution varies from that of a wooden material.

With that in mind, we are going to create several small examples of materials that deviate from the standard shading model—starting with some simple glass. This will work as an introductory level, just so we can create more complex examples at a later stage. Buckle up and let's dive right in!

Getting ready

In order to start this recipe, you are not going to need a lot of anything. The sample Unreal project we have previously created will serve us fine, but feel free to create a new one if you are starting in this section of the book. It is completely fine to use standard assets, such as the ones included with the engine, but I've also prepared a few of them that you can download if you want to closely follow this book.

How to do it...

The first example that we are going to create is going to be some simple glass. As before, right-click in the appropriate subfolder of your **Content Browser** and create a new material. Here's how we go about it:

1. Let's name it with a pertinent name, something like M_SampleGlass, as that's what we'll be creating!

2. Open up the material editor, and focus on the D**etails** panel. That's the first area we are going to operate on. Make sure you have the main material node selected—if you haven't created anything else, that's the only element that should exist on the main editor graph:

3. Having the main node selected, you'll be able to see that the second editable attribute under the **Material** section of the **Details** panel is the **Blend Mode**. Let's change that from the default value of **Opaque** to the more appropriate **Translucent** one as follows:

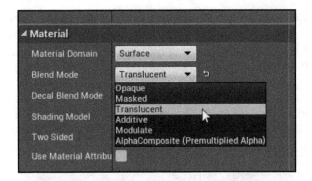

4. After this change has happened, you'll note that several options have been grayed out inside of the main material node. We'll come back to this shortly.

5. Without leaving the **Details** panel, you can now scroll down to the **Translucency** section of the main material node. You should be able to find a drop-down menu named **Lighting Mode**, which we'll need to change from the default value of **Volumetric NonDirectional** to the one named **Surface Translucency Volume**, as shown in the following screenshot:

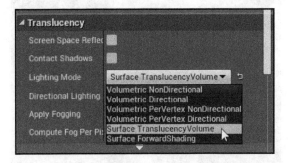

If you hover over each of the options inside of the **Lighting Mode** drop-down menu, you should be able to take a look at their description. You'll note that some of the options are meant to be used with particles, while others are meant for 3D models. That's the reason why some of the material attributes were previously grayed out— some options don't make sense to be used if we are going to be applying the material to a particle, for example, so these are left out.

6. With that out of the way, let's now attach a **Constant4Vector** to the **Base Color** node and give it an interesting value. I'm going with a bluish tone, as we'll be creating a glass and they usually have that kind of tint.

Why a Constant4Vector and not a Constant3Vector, as we used last time? This new type that we are using includes a fourth parameter, which can be used as an alpha value, something very useful for glass-like materials as you'll see for yourself in a moment.

7. Without leaving the Constant4Vector behind, set the *alpha value* to something like **0.5**. Don't go all the way with this parameter! Setting it either as a **0** or a **1** would make our future material fully transparent or opaque, so choose something in between. Plug the value into the **Base Color** material node as follows:

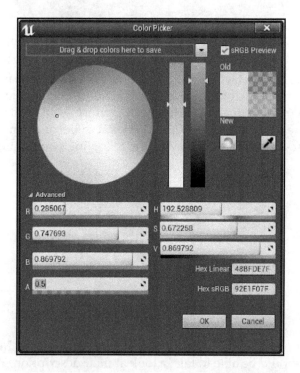

8. Now it's time to plug in the alpha value of our **Constant4Vector** into the **Opacity** slot of our material. Drag from the pin of the **Constant4Vector** into an empty space in the main graph and release the left mouse button. A contextual menu should now appear, and you want to type **mask**. Selecting **ComponentMask** is what we want to be doing now!

9. With the component mask selected, let's take a look at the details panel. In there you'll be able to select which of the four components from the Constant4Vector node you want to use. For our case, as we'll be driving the opacity through the alpha, let's just tick the last option.

10. Finally, connect the mask to the **Opacity** pin. Click on the **Apply** button and save the material. The preview window may take a moment to update itself, but once it does we should be looking at a translucent material like the following:

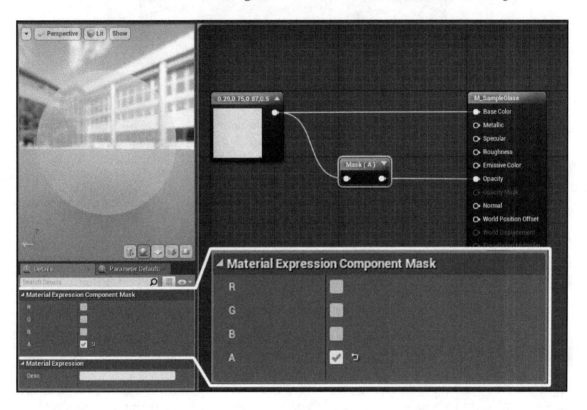

Now that we have our material correctly set up, let's apply it to the model in our scene. If you've opened the level that I've set up for you, **01_ 04_ TranslucentMaterials_ Intro**, you'll see that we have an object called **SM_ Glass**. If you are creating things on your own project, just create a model in which we can apply this newly created material. In any case, the scene should look something like this after you apply the new material:

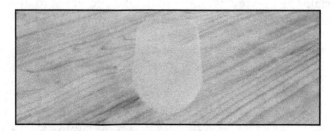

Simple but effective! In the future, we'll be taking a look at how to properly set up a more complex translucent material, with reflections, refractions, and other interesting effects. But for now, we've taken one of the most important steps in that path—actually starting to walk!

How it works...

Translucent materials are really tricky to tackle in real-time renderers—and we are starting to see why. One hint that you might have been able to spot is that we aren't using a different shading model to create glasses. Instead, we are just using a different blend mode. So what are the differences between both of these concepts, and how is driving translucent materials through the latter indicative of their render complexity?

First of all, a shading model is a combination of mathematical expressions and logic that determines how models are *shaded* or painted with light. One such model will describe how light behaves when it comes into contact with a material that uses said shading method. We use as many different models as we need in order to describe the different materials we see on our daily lives—for example, the way light scatters through our skin or the way it does the same on a wooden surface. We need to be able to describe that situation in a way that our computer programs can tackle that problem.

With that in mind, you could think that we should have a different shading model to describe translucent materials. However, things are a bit more complex in real-time renderers as the calculations that we would need to have to realistically simulate that model are too expensive performance-wise. Being always on the lookout for efficiency and speed, the way that Unreal has decided to tackle this issue is by creating a different blend mode. But what is that?

You can think of blend modes as the way that the renderer combines the material that we have applied to a model on the foreground over what is happening on the background. Up until now, we've seen two different types— opaque and the translucent ones.

The opaque blend mode is the easiest one to comprehend: having an object in front of another will hide the second one. This is what happens with opaque materials in real life— wood, concrete, bricks, and so on. The translucent mode, however, lets the previously hidden object to be partially visible according to the opacity value that we feed into the appropriate slot.

This is a neat way of implementing translucency, but there are some caveats that the system introduces we have to be aware of. One such issue is that this blend mode doesn't support specularity, meaning that seeing reflections across the surface is a tricky effect that we will have to overcome later on. But don't worry, we'll definitely get there!

Lighting our scene with image-based lighting

This introductory chapter has so far laid out some of the foundations of the PBR workflow that Unreal introduces. With that pipeline as our main focus, we've already taken a look at several of its key components—namely the different material parameters and shading models.

However, as we've said in the past, PBR takes information from the lights in our scene to display and calculate how everything should look. So far, we've focused on the objects and materials that are being rendered, but that is only part of the equation. One of the other parts is, of course, the light emitters themselves.

Lights are crucial to the PBR workflow. They introduce shadows, reflections, and other subtleties that affect how the final image looks. They work alongside the materials that we've previously applied by giving value to some of the properties we set up. Roughness textures and normal maps work in tandem with the lights and the environment itself. And all of this combined is also an integral part of the pipeline we are looking at in this introductory chapter.

With that as our objective, let's create in this recipe different types of lights and see how they affect some of the materials we have previously created. We'll be taking a look at the all-important **High-dynamic-range imaging (HDRi)** maps, 32-bit textures, which include lighting information in them and that can be used to light up a scene. Let's get started!

Getting ready

You can use the scene we created at the beginning of the book, where we set up a studio environment. We took some time aside in the introduction to this book to set it up just so we could place several objects and visualize them. At that point, we just wanted to create something quick and useful, and one of the things we did was to use one of the already available resources of the Starter Content: the **BP_Light Studio** blueprint. Through that, we've already had access to HDRi lighting, the topic that we are going to be covering in this recipe.

With that in mind, we are now going to explore how to use this type of lighting to its full potential and create a realistic scene through it.

How to do it...

We will start this recipe by placing a reflective object in our default scene and looking at how certain aspects of the environment can be seen reflected in its surface. Take the following steps:

1. Open the map named **01_05_HDRi Lighting**, and take a look at the reflective sphere in the middle of the level:

You can see that I've applied a material to the model, named **M_Chrome**. This is a copy of the material we created in our third recipe, named **M_PBR_Metal**, where we've modified the base color and the roughness value to make it more chrome-looking. Thanks to its reflective properties, we can see the environment clearly. This is happening thanks to the HDRi image we are using. We are now going to replicate this effect without using the blueprint that was already set up for us, and we will instead create our own.

One of the things that we want to move away from in the setup we are going to create is having the environment image visible at all times. You could be thinking that the metal ball is reflecting the image you see in the preceding screenshot and not the actual light—and that would be only natural as you are seeing that image in the background. This is, however, just a visual cue that the blueprint uses to better visualize from where the environment lighting is hitting an object. Having said so, let's start working with the basic building blocks and not with pre-made tools to better understand how things work.

2. **Delete** the **BP_LightStudio** and the **SphereReflectionCapture** and click on the **Build** icon—we should now be looking at a completely dark scene.

3. From the **Modes** panel, navigate to the **Place** tab and to the **Lights** section within it. You should be able to find a **Skylight**, the type of light that we can use to illuminate with HDRi textures. Drag and drop it into the scene as follows:

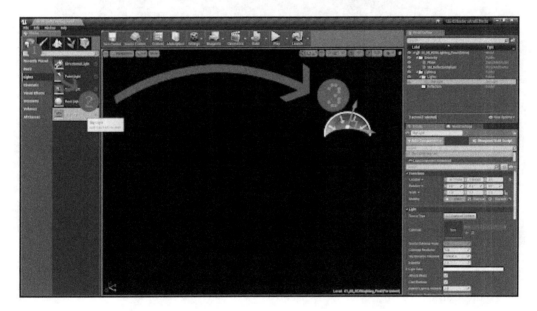

4. With the newly created skylight selected, navigate to the **Details** panel and look at the options under the **Light** section. The first option on the drop-down menu says **SLS Captured Scene**, which uses the already existing scene to create a light. We want to change that value to the other available option, **SLS Specified Cubemap**. Once that's done, select a **Cubemap** from the next drop-down menu—let's go with the one we've used in the past, **HDRI_AlexsApt**, as follows:

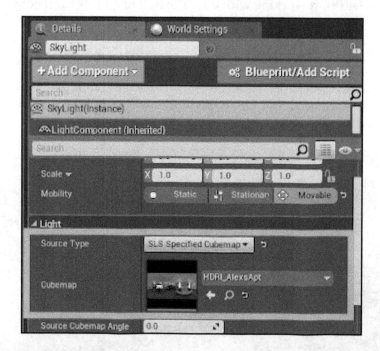

5. After selecting the texture, you will be able to check for yourself that nothing has changed; we are still looking at a black screen. This is because the default type that was spawned was one of the `Static` type and skylights of that type need to get built before we can see them. Click on the **Build** icon again and see what happens:

6. We are now lighting our scene with the HDRi! However, we are still using a static light, which has its inconveniences regarding reflections (as you can see, there are none!). Let's change between static, stationary, and dynamic to see how the scene varies:

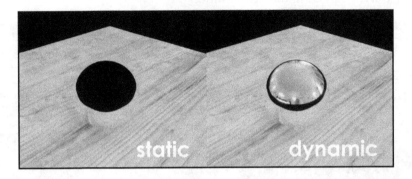

As you can see, going from a static type of light to a dynamic one gets us the reflections back. This is due to the fact that static lights only exist during the light baking process—that is, when we click on the **Build** button. In order to use HDRis to their full extent, we should be aiming for a dynamic or stationary type of light.

Let's focus once again on the metallic ball under this new dynamic skylight that we now have. There might be a bit of a problem, if we look closely:

You can see that there's a black edge going on across the surface of the ball, which is happening because the skylight is by default only using half of a sphere to project the selected texture. This is happening because objects are usually not lit from underneath, and we might be fine with that sometimes. However we can solve that by selecting the next option:

7. As you saw in the previous picture, select the **Skylight** and expand the **Light** section on the **Details** panel. In there you will be able to see that the set **Lower Hemisphere Is Solid** setting is ticked by default—unticking it will make the light use a full sphere to project the HDRi.

You might be inclined to fill your scene with geometry so as to obscure the emptiness that is being reflected in the chrome ball. However, Unreal doesn't render the objects that the camera can't see—so the reflections that should be happening thanks to the objects that would be behind it won't show at all. This is one of the sacrifices that real-time rendering has to make in order to be so efficient, so keep that in mind! We can solve that by placing a reflection capture, as we'll see next.

However useful having a full spherical HDRi skylight lighting our scene might be, it can also introduce some undesired effects that we don't want to see. For instance, we might want to use the actual geometry of our level to affect the lower part of the chrome ball and not the HDRi. If that's the case, tick again the **Lower Hemisphere Is Solid** setting and let's try something different.

8. Place some planes around the level, in a similar fashion to what I'm doing in the next screenshot. This is just to mimic a scenario where we would have more geometry throughout the level, which could be used for reflections, so we don't have that black band across the reflective ball we saw before. Assign those planes a different material—I'm using **M_Basic_Wall** from the Starter Content pack:

9. Place the camera somewhere close to the reflective ball so we can see it clearly. We are still seeing the previous reflections, and not the current ones:

10. In order to fix this, go to the drop-down menu to the right of the **Build** icon and select the option **Build Reflection Captures**:

With that done, you should now be looking at your recently created planes in the reflections of the chrome ball as follows:

How it works...

Throughout the current recipe, we've had the opportunity to work with HDRi lighting. The lights that make use of this technique are usually of the Skylight type in Unreal Engine 4, a particular kind that allows for the input of the necessary textures that contain the photon information.

As we've said before, HDRi images capture the lighting state of a particular scene in order to be able to use that information in a 3D environment. The way they do this is by sampling the same environment multiple times under different exposure settings. Taking multiple pictures this way allows for their combination at a post process stage, where the differences in lighting can be interpolated to better understand how the scene is being lit.

What's important to us it that we need to be on the lookout for the right type of textures. HDRi images need to be in a 32-bit format, such as `.EXR` or `.HDRi`, as each pixel contains multiple layers of information condensed into itself. You might find HDRi images in a non-32-bit format, but these don't contain as much lighting information as the real ones because of the format they use.

Another parameter to take into consideration is the number of f-stops that a given HDRi image is composed of. This number indicates the amount of different pictures that were taken under different exposures to be able to compose the HDRi. A value of five means that the HDRi was created out of five interpolated images, and a value of seven indicates that said number was instead used. More pictures mean a wider range of values and the consequent increase of information. It is a case of the more, the better, as seen in the next screenshot:

These photographs are a sequence of different images that make up an HDRi. HDRi by HDRi labs.

In this recipe, we've taken a look at several key concepts in the PBR workflow—image-based lighting, reflections, and the different mobility types a light can belong to. These elements, while not a part of the material pipeline themselves, are an essential part of the whole physically based approach at rendering that Unreal has at its core. They work hand-in-hand with the materials we create, expanding their capabilities and complementing the base properties we define them to have. Think about it—there's not much use having a highly reflective material if we don't tell the engine how to treat those reflections. Hope you found this useful!

Checking the cost of our materials

In this recipe, we are going to be looking at the impact that our materials have on performance. So far, this introductory chapter has gone over the basics of the rendering pipeline—we've seen how to create a physically based material, understood what the different shading models were, and saw how light played a key role in the overall look of the final image. However, we can't yet move on without understanding the impact that our games or applications have on the machines that are running them.

The first thing that we need to be aware of is that some materials or effects are more expensive in terms of efficiency than others. Chances are you have already experienced that in the past—think, for example, about frames per second in video games. How many times a second our displays are updated by the hardware that runs them directly influences how the game plays and feels. There are many elements that affect performance, but one determining factor in that equation is how complex our materials are.
A different example, if your background is more closely tied to traditional offline renderers such as VRay or Corona, could be how the rendering times vary wildly depending on how complex the materials you are rendering are. Using subsurface scattering, complex translucency, or a combination of multiple advanced effects can take render times from minutes to hours.

The point is that we need to be able to control how performant the scene we are creating is. Unreal offers us several tools that allow us to see how expensive certain effects and materials are, and check where we should be optimizing our assets or where certain things aren't working. With that in mind, let's bring all of the assets we have previously created together and use those tools to check them out.

Getting ready

All we need to do before starting this recipe is to load up the map called **01_ 06_ The Cost Of Materials**. As you can see, it's just the usual scene we have been working with up until now, except that it now has a couple more models in it. Feel free to bring your own meshes and materials, as we are going to be checking them out from a technical point of view. All we care about at this point is having multiple elements that we can take a look at, so having materials that use different blend modes is great in that we will be able to see the difference in performance between them.

How to do it...

No matter if you've opened the level provided with this book or one of your own, we are going to be looking at the rendering cost that materials incur when being displayed. To do so, we'll be taking a look at several different indicators that can help us understand our scenes a little bit better. Take the following steps:

1. Let's start by taking a look at the following scene:

I've included four different objects with their respective materials applied, which should help us understand the cost to performance that each one of them has.

2. Continue by selecting the chrome ball (named **SM_ReflectiveSphere**) and navigate to the **Details** panel, specifically to the **Materials** tab. Double-click on the material that is currently applied to the model to open the material editor.

3. With that editor in front of us, let's take a look at the **Stats** panel:

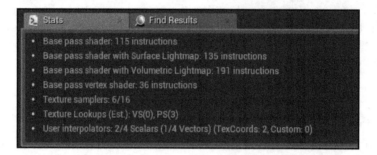

The values we see in there can give us an approximation to how expensive the material is to render. You can see that this **M_ReflectiveSphere** has 115 instructions for the base pass shader, 135 if we are using static lighting, and 191 if we use movable lights. The numbers themselves will be useful if we compare them to other materials.

4. Let's go back to the main scene, and select the object named **SM_Glass**. Open up the material that it has applied just like we did for the reflective ball, and look at the stats panel again:

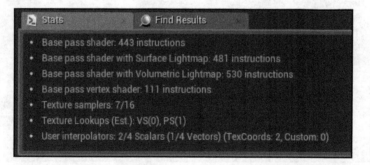

As you can see, the instruction count is much higher than in the last example we saw. This is due to the fact that the complexity of translucent materials is higher than that of opaque ones, and we can see that in here.

5. Another way of looking at the **Shader Complexity** is by navigating to the main viewport and selecting one of the available **Optimization viewmodes**. You can find it in here:

6. After clicking that button, you should be looking at something like this:

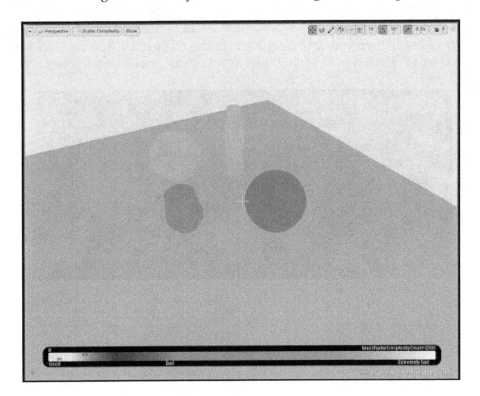

This is a more visually appealing way of looking at the shader complexity. However, it is one that is not 100% accurate, as Unreal only takes the instruction count as a reference to calculate the gradient you are seeing in the preceding image and not the complexity of the material's nodes themselves.

You might see similar values for two different materials that are really not equal in terms of their complexity—for instance, a material that is made out of several textures versus one that uses simple constants might show a similar complexity in this viewmode when in reality using the first is more demanding on the **Graphics Processing Unit (GPU)**.

Now that we've seen one of the *optimization viewmodes*, why stop with just that one? All of them are useful for understanding how our scene is working from different technical points of view. Let's go over them in a quick way to see how they can help us.

7. The first of these modes is called **Light Complexity**. This can serve us to analyze how expensive the different lights we have in our scene are. Toggle that on and let's see how our scene looks.

8. At first you'll see that the whole scene is being rendered in black. This is because we are using a HDRi static type of light—and as the lighting has already been calculated, there's no light complexity at this stage at all. You can only see the object's I've selected being outlined in yellow for reference purposes:

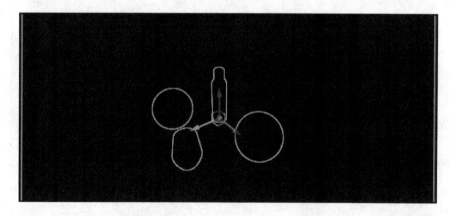

9. If we place a new point light, you'll be able to see how the scene turns blue. This is to indicate that there's some complexity to the scene, but this is just as cheap a lighting method as they come:

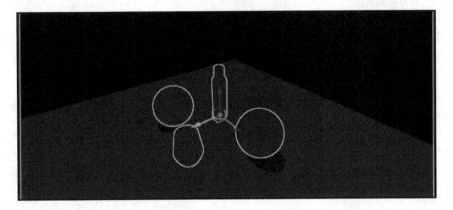

10. Placing more lights will change how your scene looks—getting away from its original blue color. That means that lighting is becoming more complex and costly for our hardware to compute, so keep that in mind! The following screenshot is what our scene looks like in that viewmode with seven different lights:

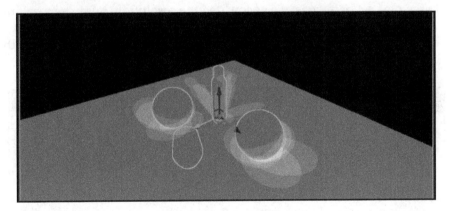

11. Another viewmode related to the previous one is Stationary Light Overlap. If we have multiple stationary lights it will tell us how expensive our scene is to render, in a gradient that goes from green to white.

12. Finally, the lightmap density viewmode shows you how dense the lightmaps are for the objects that occupy your scene. Using static or stationary lights means that static objects will have their shadows baked, and this is the viewmode that lets us see if the settings we've chosen for our models are evenly distributed. Let's take a look at the two following examples.

13. In this first set of images, we've set up the lightmap resolution for both wood planes to a high value of 1,024. That means, as you can see in the first image, that the shadows look correct even across the two surfaces:

14. In the next set of images, we've lowered the resolution, but in a more dramatic way for the vertical wood plane. That means that the vertical plane has much lower quality shadows to the point where they are barely visible, even though they are still there in the horizontal plane:

There are a couple more viewmodes that we haven't talked about, but they deal with the amount of polygons that a model comprises and are not related to the materials we are using. You can take a look at them in the same panel we saw before, and they are called **Quad Overdraw** and **Shader Complexity and Quads**. They can be very useful in order to diagnose our scenes, especially when we have many high poly meshes or semi-transparent models—so keep them on your radar in case you ever need them!

How it works...

As we've seen in previous recipes, materials are not homogeneous entities. And we are not even talking about the ones in real life, but, of course, the ones we have created within Unreal. The mathematics and functions used to describe the different shading and blend modes carry a weight with them that vary from one type to the next. Knowing how heavy each of them is can be a complicated task to burden oneself with, but having an overall idea is key to running a well-oiled application.

In the previous pages, we've taken a look at some examples, which included an opaque material and a translucent one—examples that we've worked on in the past. However, we need to keep in mind that there are more types we can—and will—encounter in the future. Unreal includes the following different shading models, which I will list now in order of how costly they are to render:

- Unlit
- Default lit
- Preintegrated skin
- Subsurface
- Clear coat
- Subsurface profile

(The other shading models—hair and eye—are very specific to characters and we will cover them in the appropriate section.)

Of course, the actual cost of a material depends on how complex we make the graphs for each of them, but that previous order applies to base materials with nothing more applied to them. On top of that, there are options within each type that can make them more or less expensive to render: having a material being two-sided or use a particular type of translucency can increase the cost to the GPU, for example.

On top of this, there are other things to be considered in terms of efficiency that we might want to keep in mind. Epic has created some performance guidelines for artists that highlight where we should be focusing our attention in order to keep our applications running well. You can take a look at them at the following link: `https://docs.`
`unrealengine.com/en-us/Engine/Performance/Guidelines`.

We've used this recipe to take a look at how fast Unreal can process different types of shaders. We've done so by comparing an opaque material against a translucent one, which gives us a good idea about how instruction counts vary and how efficient some shaders are compared to others. Not only that, we've also had the opportunity to see what optimization tools are available for anyone using the engine. All in all, there is a wide variety of options that give the user control over how well their application runs, and now we are in a position in which we know how to use them.

Post-Processing Effects

2

Welcome to the chapter on post-processing effects! Here are some of the things that we are going to be doing in the next few pages:

- Using a Post Process Volume
- Changing the mood of a scene through color grading
- Setting up a cinematic shot using depth of field
- Applying cinematic effects to our games
- Mimicking a real-life camera using Bloom and Lens Flares
- A horror movie pulsating effect with post process materials
- Adjusting anti aliasing and other rendering features

Introduction

As you probably already know, Unreal combines many different pipelines in order to create whatever it is you are after—a video game, an app, an architectural walk-through. From animation to rendering, there are many different fields of study that we could be looking at. However much we would like to do so, the topics are just too wide to be tackled here. But even though we are not going to be looking at all of them, there is one important aspect that we need to pay attention to. It is one that directly affects the material and the rendering pipeline—we are talking, of course, about post-processing effects.

At their core, post-processing effects are a rendering pass that happens after our materials have been constructed but before the whole scene is outputted to the screen. They are like a layer that we can insert between what we have created and what the user experiences, so they are very powerful tools that enable us to modify and correct what we have previously done. Throughout the present chapter, we are going to be covering most of the available functionalities in the following recipes.

The properties we can tweak at that stage are anti-aliasing, color grading, depth of field, bloom, lens flares, vignetting, or screen space reflections. Those are just some of them, but something that they all have in common is that they affect the elements of the scene that are already placed in. Keeping that in mind will help us understand later on what is achievable through those methods and what is better done elsewhere.

Using a post-process volume

In order to access the different post process effects that Unreal has in store for us, we will need to place a specific actor in our level. This actor receives the name **Post Process Volume**, a container in the shape of a box that specifies its area of influence.

Thankfully for us, every setting that we are going to be tweaking in this chapter can be modified using the previous actor. Having all of the post process effects grouped in one place makes our lives easier—so, let's start looking at all of the different options that we can play with!

Getting ready

I've prepared a scene for you to use as you traverse through the different recipes of this chapter—it is a very simple one, but it should help demonstrate the different post process effects that we are going to be using in the next pages. You can locate the file by navigating to the following directory inside the Unreal project we are providing: `Content/UE4ShadersAndEffects/Maps/Chapter02`.

The name of the scene is `02_01_PostProcessEffects`, and as soon as you open it you'll be greeted by the next screenshot:

The purpose behind this little still-life level is to have a custom scene where we can play around the different settings of the post process volume. Feel free to use your own assets if you want, as there's nothing specific in the ones I'm using that would prevent you from gaining the same amount of knowledge out of the following recipes.

 Do you want more models to populate your scenes? Sites such as TurboSquid or CGTrader offer some free assets, so be sure to check them out:
https://www.cgtrader.com/free-3d-models
https://www.turbosquid.com/Search/3D-Models/free

How to do it...

Let's start by opening the scene we've mentioned at the beginning of this recipe, the one called `02_01_PostProcessEffects`. You can find by looking into the content browser: `Content/UE4ShadersAndEffects/Maps/Chapter02`.

If you want to use a custom level that you have created yourself, feel free to go ahead and just use that one instead. We want to have a scene where we have something interesting to look at—after all, we are trying to use post process effects to affect how something already created looks. Once that's done, let's start the recipe by locating the actor we are going to be playing with:

1. Look for the **Post Process Volume** inside the **Modes** | **Place** | **Volumes** panel:

Instead of scrolling through all of the different volumes available in that palette, try typing `Post Process Volume` inside the search bar at the top of that panel. That will single out the element you are looking for!

2. Drag and drop the volume into the level. Place it anywhere you want, but make sure that it is big enough so that it covers all of the visible scene:

3. With our newly placed post process volume selected and positioned, let's take a look at some of its settings. We want to make sure that we are affecting the whole scene and not just the inside of the volume. Scroll down to the **Post Process Volume Settings** and check the **Infinite Extent (Unbound)** setting:

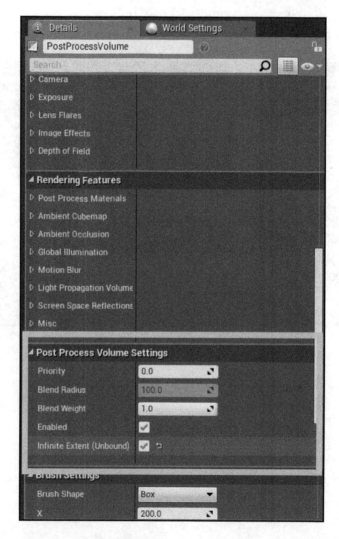

Doing so will make sure that the effect that this volume has is propagated across the entirety of the level.

By now, you will have probably encountered many of the settings that we will be tweaking in the next recipes—possibly when you were looking for the *Unbound* toggle in the previous step. Even though we will look at most of them in greater detail later on, let's see what the basic categories are:

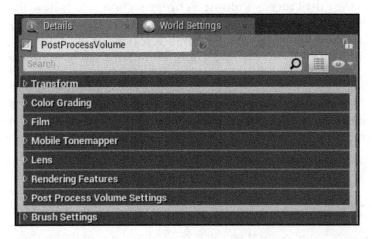

- The **Color Grading** section allows us to modify the color and balance of the scene. Operations such as color correction, creating an intentional mood for the level, or affecting the overall contrast of the scene are performed primarily here.

- The **Film** panel enables the modification of the tonemapper in UE4. The tonemapper in Unreal is there to tell the program how to trick our eyes into seeing a much wider range of color values than our displays can produce. That is the reason it's not meant to be constantly tweaked—it is there to define how that conversion should be happening and not as an artistic resource.

The tonemapper can be a complex topic, so be sure to check the official documentation if you need more info!:

https://docs.unrealengine.com/en-us/Engine/Rendering/
PostProcessEffects/ColorGrading

- **Mobile Tonemapper** is similar to the previous section, but intended for projects that are going to be deployed on mobile hardware.

- The **Lens** tab controls certain camera effects, such as the exposure, the chromatic aberration, bloom or lens flares.

- **Rendering Features** is a panel that controls certain effects that apply to the 3D world. Examples of that are the use of post process materials, the ambient occlusion that is happening across the level, or the quality of the screen space reflections.
- Finally, the **Post Process Volume Settings** section affects how that particular actor behaves in the world. Defining which overlapping volume should be affecting the world when there are multiple ones or the distance in which two different such entities blend are examples of what we have mentioned previously.

As you can see, there are many properties that can be tweaked and adjusted. We will have a look at them in the following recipes, as even though this is just one actor the importance of the different settings is paramount in regard to the final output we are seeing. See you in the next recipe!

How it works...

Something we've seen in the current recipe is how to make sure that our post process volume works across the entirety of the level. This is very useful as we usually want the settings that we tweak within that actor to extend beyond its boundary box. We often do this so that we can forget about the bounding box size for the selected volume in the event that we are only using one.

Convenient as that might be for the purposes of this book, we can't forget that the situation described is not always the one we want to happen. From time to time, especially in complex environments, we will want to place several instances of the post process volume throughout our scene. Think, for example, about a level that contains outdoor areas as well as interior ones—we may want to emphasize the differences between both ambiences by dialing different settings in the post process effects. This is where properties such as the **Blend Radius** or the **Priority** index start to play a bigger role, as they will enable us to merge and change between different volumes.

The first thing that we need to check when working with multiple post process volumes is that the **Infinite Extent** (**Unbound**) setting is disabled. Were that not the case, we would have a post process volume that affects the whole world. Once that's done, the once relatively unimportant **Scale** value comes into play—we need to adjust it so that the whole volume surrounds the area that we want to be affecting. Keep in mind that the volume affects our vision only when the player character is inside of its bounds—so even though you might be applying a specific set of options for a determined area, those won't be visible unless you step inside of it.

This situation can be described in the next image—unless the camera that is rendering the scene isn't inside of the post process volume, this one won't be affecting the final image output:

Apart from that, the other settings are quite intuitive—the **Priority** option enables you to type a number in its adjacent text box, which will in turn be used to calculate which post process volume should be affecting the scene in the event that there are any overlapping ones. On the other hand, the **Blend Radius** allows to specify a value in centimeters, which determines the area around the bounding box in which the settings of the post process volume get blended with any others that might be applied to the scene be they the default ones or those of a different volume.

See also

There is a whole world out there in regard to post processing in Unreal Engine 4, different effects that can be achieved, different techniques that can be used... We will be covering many different examples in the recipes that follow, but here is a link to the official documentation that Epic Games provides: `https://docs.unrealengine.com/en-us/Engine/Rendering/PostProcessEffects`.

Changing the mood of a scene through color grading

After we've taken some time to familiarize ourselves with the post process volume actor, it is now time to start looking at how to use the different functionalities we can find within it.

The first section that we will be covering is also the first one we can find if we look at the details panel for the actor and that is the **Color Grading** tab.

The reason these options exist in Unreal is similar to why they exist elsewhere, like in movies or videos. The end goal is to provide artists with a series of tools that they can use to alter the look of the final image. Similar techniques have been prominent in motion pictures, for example, where the captured footage is adjusted to satisfy a particular need be that the establishing of a stylized look or the ensuring of color continuity. What we are going to be doing in the following pages is exactly that tweaking of the default camera values to modify the look of our scene.

Getting ready

In this recipe, we are going to start with a default scene, where no post process effects are happening at all, and completely change how it feels by tweaking the color grading options in the post process volume actor. As I'm sure it's becoming usual, all you need to tackle this scene is to open up the following level in the Unreal project we are providing: `Content / UE4ShadersAndEffects / Maps / Chapter02 / 02_02_ColorGrading`

You can alternatively choose to continue using your own scene after all, everything you need is a post process volume actor and a nicely crafted environment in which to follow this recipe. Without further ado, let's get started!

How to do it...

Before we start this recipe, let's take a look at how the scene has been set up for you. We are providing the level we mentioned in the previous section as a starting point for you to follow along and you can find it in the following directory: `Content / UE4ShadersAndEffects / Maps / Chapter02 /`.

The name of the scene is **02_02_ColorGrading**, and it includes several elements that are going to be useful for us. At this point, you are probably already familiar with this scene after all, we've used it in the previous recipes to start learning about the post process volume. As we are going to delve a little bit deeper into that same actor, we've also included it in this new level. Additionally, we've decided to add a cinematic camera just so we have a fixed point that we can use to compare the different visual changes we are about to introduce.

Of course, and as should be becoming a bit of a tradition by now, feel free to follow along with any scene you might have created yourself. The key components to include are the post process volume, as always, and perhaps a cinematic camera for a bit of flair. Having an interesting environment in which to test the following steps we are about to perform is always nice, but not essential as we are going to be color grading the whole scene, the visual changes are going to be quite evident. In any case, rest assured, you'll have access to the scene you see if you need it.

Wile we're talking about that camera actor we've included in this level, let's allow ourselves access to its viewpoint. To do so, head over to the upper-left corner on the main viewport – hopefully, you can locate a little button there that, once clicked, shows a dropdown menu that you can use to access the existing camera. The view you will enter is something such as this:

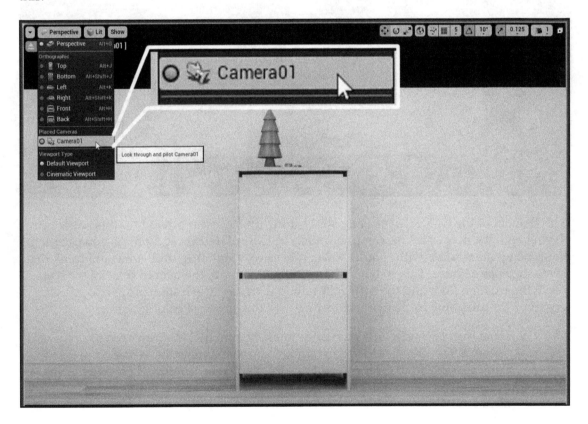

Having access to that camera perspective will enable us to better visualize the changes we are about to make. And all of those changes, as stated, are going to revolve around the **Color Grading** tools inside of the **Post Process Volume** actor. You can find the different settings if you select the appropriate actor and look for the **Color Grading** section within the **Details** panel. You should be looking at something like this:

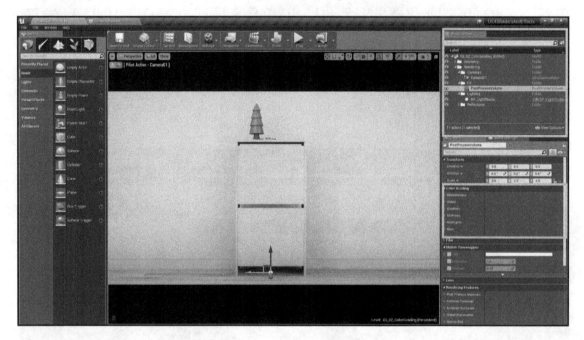

With that out of the way, let's properly start setting up a different mood for this scene by playing with the properties we can find under the **Color Grading** section. As you can see, the scene we are dealing with is quite warm it feels cozy, inviting, and you could think that it was someone's house. This is mainly happening because of the overall color of the scene, where the wooden floor and the soft walls (along with the little festive prop) add to that sensation. We are going to change that feeling with the power of color grading:

1. Head over to the **Details** panel after making sure that the post process volume is selected. The first option we are going to be changing is the **White Balance;** expand that section and tick the **Temp** checkbox, and change the value to something lower. I'm going with the value 4,500, which makes the scene already feel colder.

2. Leave the **Tint** checkbox unticked if you want, as that allows for the modification of the cyan and magenta color ranges. If we decided to use it, we would find ourselves modifying the White Balance temperature tint between those two colors, something we don't want to be doing for this exercise:

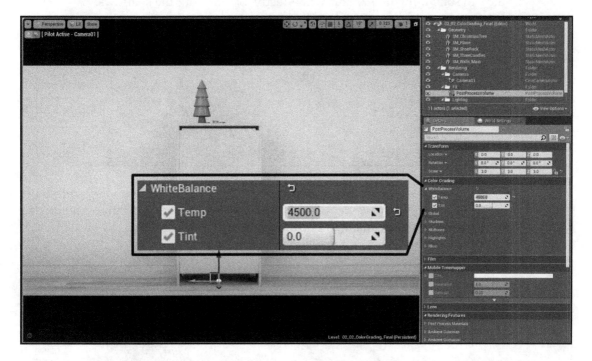

As you can probably already tell by looking at the previous screenshot, the scene feels much colder already. Be sure to check the *How it works...* section to fully understand how modifying the White Balance setting affects our scene. Let's now continue to change the feel of the scene by tweaking a couple more settings.

While still in the **Details** panel, let's take a look now at the following categories within the **Color Grading** tab: the **Global**, **Shadows**, **Midtones** and **Highlights**. All of them control the same properties of the image, but they affect different color ranges. We will be able to change settings such as the saturation of the image or the contrast for each different color spectrum. For instance, modifying the Saturation within the **Highlights** will affect only the brightest values within our image. Doing the same on the **Shadows** section will do the same but on the darker tones.

With that in mind, let's continue to modify our scene:

3. The first operation we will be performing is the adjustment of the shadow intensity. Find the **Gain** property under the **Shadows** category and modify its value to something like **2**. This will effectively wash out the shadows. Now let's change the gain of the shadows:

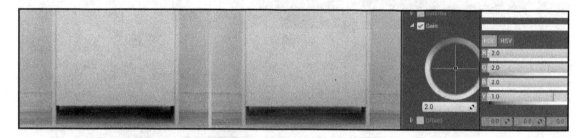

4. We also want to desaturate the image a little bit, just so we move away from the original warmth we were seeing initially. Head over to the **Saturation** section of **Midtones**, where we can apply a lower value than the default 1. I've chosen 0.75 just to make things a bit more pale:

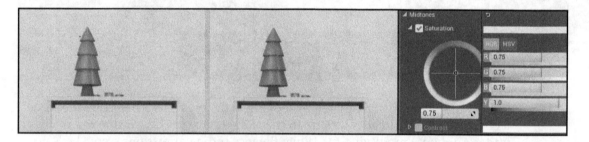

With all of those changes in place, we can now compare the initial scene we were looking at against the current state it is in. If you want to do so, just select the Post Process Volume you have on your scene and uncheck the **Enabled** option under the **Post Process Volume Settings** section inside the **Details** panel. Ticking that box on and off will let you toggle the **Post Process Volume** that is affecting our scene. Let's take a look at the results:

They feel quite different, don't they. The changes might be subtle, but they are definitely there—we are now looking at a much whiter scene, which feels colder overall and is less saturated. While the first image can make you feel warm and cozy, the second one is a bit more neutral. However, let's not stop with the adjustments just yet! Now that we know the basics, let's get a bit crazy. What if we gave the scene a bit of a horror touch?

5. To do so, let's start by cranking up the **Contrast** of the **Midtones** to something like 1.5. That should make the scene pop out a little more:

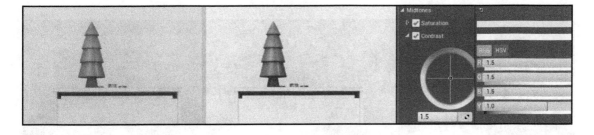

6. Something we can also tweak is the value of the **Saturation** under the **Highlights** section. Let's set that to something really high—I've chosen 1,000 for this particular scene. Doing so should really make the brightest parts of the image stand out in an unnatural way, which could make the viewer feel a bit uneasy and on edge:

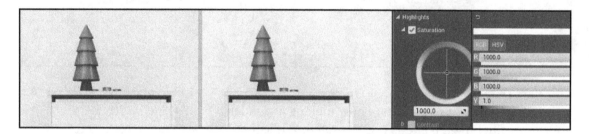

7. Finally, let's apply a color tint to the scene. Horror movies and psychological thrillers often make use of a greenish tint when they want to highlight the fact that something is wrong or just to create a bit of an atmosphere. If you head over to the **Misc** section of the **Color Grading** tab, you will find a setting called **Scene Color Tint**. Changing that to a greenish pastel color should give us the result we are after:

Look at that! With that final touch we've covered most of the settings that we can tweak inside of the **Color Grading** post process category. Now that you have an idea of what they do and what they affect, you may want to play around a little bit more with them to get more familiar and confident. The job of a color grader requires patience, as tweaks and corrections need to constantly be applied until you get to the look you are after. In spite of that, the tools that we have at our disposal are quite powerful and should serve us well. Have fun with them!

How it works...

The color grading tools inside Unreal are quite similar to what can be found in other software packages such as Photoshop or Gimp. They are there to allow the user to modify certain image parameters, most of which we have already seen. In spite of having done so, I would like to take some time aside to further explain what some of the perhaps more obscure parameters affect.

One such example of a setting that might be a bit confusing is the initial **White Balance** we saw and tweaked. That property is controlled via the **Temp** parameter, which is as you've probably guessed short for **Temperature**. This word references one characteristic of the light we see – and that is its color. Saying that a light has a color temperature of 6,500 K means that it has a blueish tint to it. Lower values will start to get closer to a red tint - 3,500 K would be quite yellow and 1,800 is the typical orange from the flame of a candle. Just so we are on the same page, a fluorescent light would have a higher temperature than your typical light bulb, and this one would be in turn higher than a candle.

The reason why we use a temperature value instead of just specifying a color for our lights is that this is the physically correct approach. Feel free to read more about the topic if it isn't clear at this stage, as it can be quite extensive: `https://en.wikipedia.org/wiki/Color_temperature`.

In spite of the preceding, the way the **White Balance Temp** setting works might be a bit counter intuitive compared to what we've just said. According to the previous explanation, lights that have a light color above 5,000 K are considered cold; that is, they have a blueish tint to them. Lower values get us in the range of reds, yellows, and oranges. For instance, a value of 3,000 K would be in the yellow range. That being the case, you can probably infer that the higher the temperature the bluer the light color. However, why did we have to decrease the temp value of the white balance if we wanted to get colder values?

The answer is that we are not tweaking the light color values, but we are defining which one should be the new standard one (which is by default 6,500 K). Imagine that you have a light of 3,500 K because the default white balance is calculated against that value of 6,500 K; that means that your light is quite warm. If we decrease the default of 6,500 to something like 4,500, the value of your light is still lower than the standard, but not by as much as before. That means that it will look closer to white than it previously did. This is how the white balance **temp** setting works.

Something else that I'd also like to mention are the different options that we have on the **Global**, **Shadows**, **Midtones**, and **Highlights** categories. When we looked at them on this current recipe, we only adjusted the overall multiplier that we can find in each subsection. Here's an example to refresh your mind:

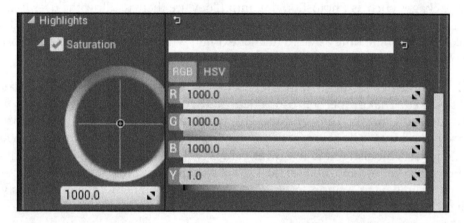

We are usually tweaking the value below the color wheel—that is effectively a multiplier that affects all of the RGB values equally. However, we can have an even finer control if we know that we only want to be affecting a specific channel. Additionally, we can even change between the **RBG** mode and the **HSV** one, which will have us modifying the hue, the saturation or the value instead of a specific color channel.

There's more...

There's something useful we haven't seen yet, as it requires the use of other software apart from Unreal, but I want to mention it before we move on and that is the concept of **Look-Up Tables (LUTs)**, and they are an asset that allow us to match the post process tweaks we make in other software such as Photoshop or Gimp in Unreal.

Think about this – you have an image in Unreal that you want to tweak. You can do so through the methods we've seen before, by modifying and tweaking the post process volume and playing with its settings until you get the effect you are after. However convenient that can be, some users might feel more comfortable taking that image and pasting it in an image editor and adjusting it there. Fortunately for us, this process can be replicated thanks to the LUTs.

The way we would do so is by following the next steps:

1. Export a sample screenshot out of Unreal that shows your scene clearly.
2. Load that sample shot in your image editor of choice, alongside a neutral LUT image. One such asset can be found on Epic's official example, which you can find at the following website: `https://docs.unrealengine.com/en-us/Engine/Rendering/PostProcessEffects/UsingLUTs`. The idea is that all of the changes that you will implement in the next step are applied to both your sample from Unreal and the neutral LUT.
3. Adjust the image however you like change the contrast, the saturation, brightness... Any changes that you make will also affect the LUT texture.
4. Once you are happy with your image, export just the small LUT file. The modifications that the image has suffered are going to enable us to replicate that same effect in Unreal.
5. Import the modified LUT back into Unreal and double-click on it once it is inside the engine. In the **Details** panel for the texture, set the **Mip Gen Settings** to **NiMipmaps** and the **Texture Group** to ColorLookupTable.
6. After that, head back to your post process volume actor and under the **Color Grading | Misc** tick the **Color Grading LUT** checkbox and select your recently imported texture. That should leave you with a scene looking exactly like the one you modified in your image-editing software.

As you can imagine, this technique can be quite useful – especially for those users who are more used to adjusting these types of settings outside Unreal. However great that is, it also has some shortcomings that we should be aware of. Even though we won't cite them all, they all revolve around the notion that LUTs don't translate well across several screens. Even though you might be doing a correction to your particular scene and you might be happy with it, due to the nature of these textures operating in a low dynamic range those changes might not translate well into other displays—especially those using a different color space. Keep that in mind when you work with them!

See also

A useful link to Epic Games' official documentation is due—you might find snippets and a thorough explanation of what each setting does in there. Make sure to look it up if you want to delve deeper! And we'll also include a second link if you want to know more about LUTs.

```
https://docs.unrealengine.com/en-us/Engine/Rendering/PostProcessEffects/
ColorGrading
```

```
https://docs.unrealengine.com/en-us/Engine/Rendering/PostProcessEffects/
UsingLUTs
```

Setting up a cinematic shot using depth of field

In this short recipe, we are going to take a break from the post process volume actor to focus instead on the **Cinematic Camera** one. That doesn't mean we are leaving behind the world of post processing effects, far from it, in fact. The beauty of this recipe resides partially in learning that the previously used post process volume has a companion in the shape of this handy camera. Both of them have access to some of the post processing functionalities that Unreal offers, and learning when to use each one can be quite useful.

The other part that we want to cover as well is the setup of a proper camera, pretty much as we would do if we were working with a real one. This is especially useful as some of the most used visual effects we can introduce directly relate to this actor, so it makes sense to master it before moving forward.

Getting ready

You should really see this coming by now! Yes, we have a scene already set up for you, and you can find it here: `Content / UE4ShadersAndEffects / Maps / Chapter02 / 02_04_CameraDepthOfField`.

Not much has changed from the scenes we have already worked with in the previous recipes; we've just removed some of the work we did at the post processing level and adjusted the position of the cine camera actor. This new camera position will allow us to show some of the cool effects we are going to introduce in this recipe. As usual, feel free to continue to use your own scenes if that's what you prefer to do! If you had something suitable for the previous recipes, chances are that will work here as well. Make sure you have, at least, multiple objects scattered at different positions; this will help us highlight the depth of field effects we are going to be exploring. And that's pretty much it!

How to do it...

Once you open the **02_04_CameraDepthOfField** level, you should find yourself looking at the already familiar level that we are using throughout this chapter. There's nothing new under there! However true that may be, things will start to change if you look through the camera we have in our level. Let's take a look through it:

Wow! You should be able to see that the rendered image is completely out of focus. Getting it back to something more pleasing to our eyes is what our task is going to be, so let's get started!:

1. For our first step, let's take a look at the **Cine Camera Actor** details panel. The name I've given to said camera is **Camera01**, if you want to select it from the world outliner. If you collapse each section in that panel, you should be looking at something such as this:

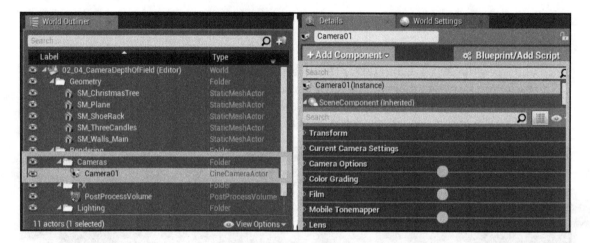

As you can see, many of the different options available to us through this actor are very similar to what we have already seen in the post process volume. In fact, they share almost the same amount of settings except for two main categories. With the camera, we are able to control which type we are using and certain intrinsic settings – the aperture of the lens, the diaphragm blade count or the FStop, among others. With the post process volume, we don't control those exact same settings, but we have access to more specific parameters that determine things the priority of the selected volume or how it blends with any adjacent ones.

2. The first issue we want to solve is the blurriness that we see at the moment in the picture. With the camera selected, open up the **Current Camera Settings** section in the **Details** panel and scroll down to the **Focus Settings** area. Look for the **Draw Debug Focus Plane** and tick the checkbox on:

With that setting enabled, we should now be seeing a purple plane as in the previous screenshot. That element is there as a visual cue for us to know where the focus plane is, that is, the area that is clearly visible. We need to modify its position so that the elements that we want to see clearly are at the same distance as that plane is from the camera.

3. Take a look at the **Manual Focus Distance** entry box and change its current value until it overlaps the candles. A value of 62.5 seems to be working in this case: You can now disable the focus plane if you want, as we've made sure that the area in focus is where we want it to be. That was the most fundamental value we needed to change – let's take a look now at what other options we can play with.

4. As we want the candle to be the protagonist of this shot, let's increase the value **Current Focal Length**. Locate that setting and change the current value of 55 to something like `120`. This should make the candle occupy a bigger space in our screens:

 All we are doing is adjusting certain camera properties. If you want to know more about them, here is a good and quick post about what those properties do in a bit more detail: `https://www.paragon-press.com/lens/lenchart.htm`

As things stand now, we have our main element in focus whilst the rest of the scene has been been blurred. We can play with the aperture of the camera to increase or decrease this effect.

5. Head over to the **Current Aperture** value. As it stands, the value we can find in the adjacent box should be **2.8**. This means that most of the objects that are placed before or after the focus plane will be out of focus—so let's play around with that number to make the effect a bit more subtle. I've chosen a value of **10**, but make sure to set it to whatever you like!:

And having done that we've pretty much covered all of the settings that you need to be aware of in order to manually set up a cinematic camera depth of field effect. The main fields that we need to adjust are the **Focal Length**, the **Aperture** and the **Focus Distance**, much like in a real-world camera. We don't take the ISO into account as we don't have to deal with that problem in Unreal. Something I'd like to mention before we move on is the availability of other post process effects within the camera actor. Even though we've mentioned that before, let's tweak one of these values just to demonstrate how to control them within this actor.

6. Still on the **Details** panel for the **Camera01**, scroll down to the section named **Rendering Features**. Even though we haven't covered this section yet, I feel as if we could enhance the look of this scene by modifying one of the values that can be found within it. In particular, expand the **Ambient Occlusion** category and set the following settings as per the next screenshot:

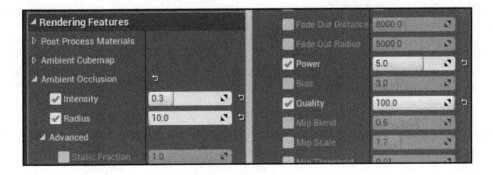

Don't worry for now about understanding how all of the previous settings work—we'll come back to them in one of the next recipes. What we are doing at this stage is showing how different post process effects can be used outside of the post process volume actor. This setting is particularly useful for our cinematic camera, as we are defining the impact that the ambient occlusion has in this particular shot, which might not be the same amount we would like to use throughout the rest of the scene. Let's finally check one last image to see what the difference is after we've applied the effect:

The changes are subtle, but if you look closely at the area where the bottom of the candle and the table surface meet you can see that it's slightly darker than it used to be. This effect, used moderately, can enhance the look of a scene by making it a bit more believable. We'll explore it further later down the road.

How it works...

We've spent most of our time adjusting different post process effects inside the cine camera actor in order to achieve a particular look for the scene. Seeing as we have two different actors that can take care of those effects (the post process volume and the cine camera actor itself), how do we decide when we should be using each one of them?

The answer lies in the specific goals that you want to reach with your project. Sometimes, one of the two actors is more useful or better suited to satisfy one of your needs. We can explore this through different examples.

Think, for instance, that you are playing a multiplayer shooter. If you were to receive any damage, you might be expecting to see some effects pop up on your screen – such as a red tint to the whole image or some other similar visual cue that indicates damage. This situation asks for said effect to be local to the specific player that is suffering said effect, so it makes sense to adjust any post process effects through their player camera.

Another example where we could instead benefit from using a post process volume is when we want to add post process effects to a whole open world game. If we want to artistically tweak how the colors look or modify the look of the scene when the climatology changes we might find a good ally in this type of actor.

There's more...

Something that I'd like to point out with regard to the recipe we've just completed is that it focused on understanding and mastering the use of the depth of field post process effect within Unreal. In order to do so, we've made sure to go over all of the pertinent settings in the Details panel. However, I'd like to point you to a particular setting we haven't tweaked that might be useful in certain circumstances: the **Tracking Focus Method**.

So far, we have spent the current recipe tweaking different settings, and we've done so after we had previously established the **Manual Focus Distance** of the camera. However useful that is, there are other times when we know the specific actor we want to be in focus – and it is on those occasions when the aforementioned **Tracking** method comes into play. Moving away from specifying the actual distance at which we want the focus plane to be, this latest system enables the user to just indicate which actor they want to be in focus. All of the other settings do still play an important role though, as properties such as the aperture or the focal length are still crucial when determining the out-of-focus areas. However, changing to this method when you do know which actor needs to be in focus can save you time from figuring out the distance value you should be inputting. If you want to check it out, be sure to head over to the **Current Camera Settings** section of your camera's Details panel, and look under **Focus Settings** | **Focus Method**.

See also

If you want to have a look at a very detailed explanation of every setting available to you for the cine camera actor, make sure to check out Unreal's official documentation: `https://docs.unrealengine.com/en-us/Engine/Rendering/PostProcessEffects/DepthOfField/CinematicDOFMethods`.

Applying cinematic effects to our games

We took some time aside in the previous recipe to learn about the other type of actors that have access to the post processing effects in UE4 – the cameras. In particular, we focused our attention on the cine camera actor, a specific type that has the potential to use certain cinematic effects. Taking it from there, we will continue to look at some other cinematic techniques available to us while still using that same camera actor. We'll take a look at **Grain**, **Vignetting**, **Chromatic Aberration**, and more.

The reason we continue to use a camera and not the post process volume is because some of the effects we are about to include come from the world of cinematography. While they definitely can be used on the volume as well, it does make sense at this stage to continue to use the camera if only to just replicate how things would also be happening in real life. After all, Unreal bases much of its capabilities in the realm of reality, and these are another set of techniques that come from there.

Getting ready

As usual, we've prepared a scene which you can use to get you started in this recipe. Its name is **02_04_CinematicEffects**, and you can find it inside of the following folder: Content / UE4ShadersAndEffects / Maps / Chapter02.

We are still using the same scene we've previously tweaked, so you are probably familiar with it at this point. All we've done is change the camera position so it helps us better visualize the effects we are about to introduce. Let's begin!

How to do it...

Let's start this recipe by looking through the camera's view; that way, we'll be looking at the same image when we start applying the different effects. Select it, as usual, by clicking on the **Perspective** drop-down button located on the upper left corner of the main viewport. Choose **Camera01** in order to jump to that specific actor. We should be looking at the following screenshot:

The first thing we are going to try is to use several effects to enhance the main focus of the shot; we want to highlight the central area of the image, where the props are located, and direct the attention of the user to said area. We can do so by playing with the vignetting effects:

1. Select the camera in the Content Browser and look at the **Details** panel. If you scroll down to the **Lens** category, you can find within it a section named **Image Effects**. This is where we'll control the **Vignetting** that we want to apply. Tick the box and change the default value of 0.4 to something higher, such as 0.6:

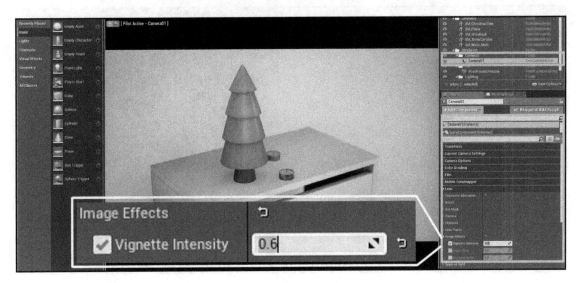

Vignetting is a subtle effect which makes the areas around the center of the image darker than the central ones. It can help highlight the elements that are in the center of the screen if that's our intention, but you can also remove the effect if that's what you prefer.

Vignetting is always applied by default to the scene—the value of 0.4 is always present. It is good to note that you might want to remove the effect sometimes, as it doesn't always fit what you are looking to achieve. If that is the case, make sure to add a post process volume to the scene and check the vignetting box, and giving it a value of 0.

Another setting that is sometimes interesting to use is grain. You might have encountered it in the past in different scenarios; it was originally an effect we could see happening in old movies because of the processing of the photographic film those were recorded in. Nowadays, it is used more as an artistic effect, especially in the video game industry. It can also help hide certain flaws within the rendered image, or introduce granularity in an otherwise flat surface.

2. To use it, take a look at the **Grain Intensity** setting while still inside the **Image Effects** section. In there, tick the checkbox for the **Grain Intensity** setting and give it a value higher than the initial **0. 0.2** seems to work well to demonstrate the effect in a subtle way, but feel free to raise the value to be able to properly see it in action:

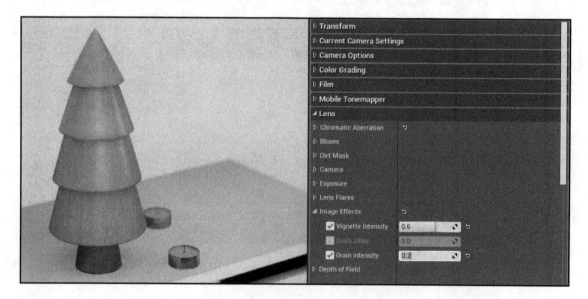

Something else you can also adjust is the amount by which the grain is **jittering**. By default, this value is set to 0, but increasing it will make the grain move more and more:

You might be seeing the grain jitter even though the value is set to 0. This is its default state, and unless you raise the number substantially you probably won't see a lot of difference. We might be used to setting values between **0** and **1** in the previous examples, but feel free to crank this one up to see the difference.

At this point, we've almost covered all of the available settings we could be influencing if we were dealing with a real life camera. We've seen the depth of field features, the aperture, the focal length, the grain and vignetting effects... something we haven't done yet though is tweak the exposure in a manual way. Let's do that now:

3.   Still in the **Lens** category of the **Camera01** Details panel, expand the **Camera** and the **Exposure** tabs. Under **Exposure / Metering Mode** tick its adjacent checkbox and change the default value of Auto Exposure Histogram to **Manual**:

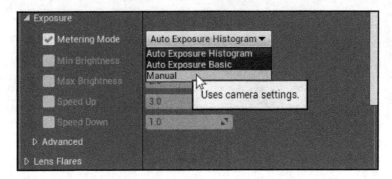

4. We should now be looking at an almost completely black viewport. This is happening because Unreal is no longer taking care of the exposure for us; we are now driving this setting through the camera properties. That being the case, move up a section and look out for the **ISO**, **Aperture** and **Shutter Speed** parameters. Tick the checkboxes next to them:

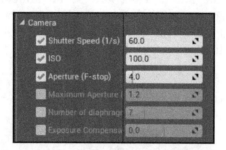

At this stage, we have to start thinking as if we had a real camera in our hands. Thanks to Unreal's physically based approach to rendering, we can feel safe by treating those properties just like we would in real life. Since our scene is too dark at the moment, let's change that.

5. Change the **ISO** to 3200.0 and the **Shutter Speed** to 1. That should make the scene visible again, even though a bit dark. Feel free to raise the ISO or lower the Shutter Speed to make it brighter. This is the final image we should be looking at, as shown in this screenshot:

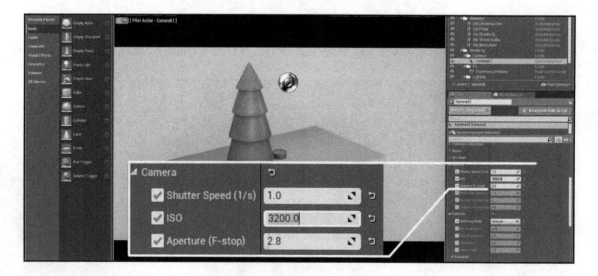

Finally, I'd like to take a look at yet another effect that is wildly used nowadays: the **Chromatic Aberration**. Even though it is a very particular setting, it can have many different uses. It is sometimes used as a substitute for anti aliasing, but more often than not it is seen as a technique that can help with creating a psychedelic feel in our scenes, or just mimicking a real camera by introducing that effect.

6. Focus now on the first parameter within the **Lens** category, aptly named **Chromatic Aberration**. Enable it by ticking the **Intensity** checkbox and giving it a value greater than the default 0. Feel free to crank it up to something that makes it clearly visible, but I'll go with **1** for a subtle effect. The following screenshot will have a value of **5** just to see it clearly:

 In a real camera, this effect is caused by the dispersion of colors as a result of the variation of the refractive index of the camera's lens. It is sometimes associated with a low quality lense, so this effect is also sometimes used when trying to replicate such real-life situations.

7. Finally, check the **Start Offset** box and give it a value of 0.4. What this does is remove the **chromatic aberration** effect from the center of the framebuffer, leaving it on the edges. It can be a good setting to tweak in order to add to the psychedelic feeling:

How it works...

Every setting we've seen so far has been included in the engine in order to give the artist as much creative freedom as possible, and thankfully this is something that happens throughout the engine. However, these tools in particular owe their presence to specific effects that happen in the world of photography or cinematography and as such, we need to be aware of when to use them and how to use them.

Beyond that, I'd like to talk a little bit more about one thing that we've tweaked: the **Manual Exposure** group of settings. Even though we've already seen how they work, it is interesting to note how we can check that the engine behaves in a physically based way through them. If you think about it, changing from the automatic to the manual exposure control is kind of like changing from shooting in automatic or manual in a photographic camera. Because our lighting was a bit dark, (after all, the HDRi we are using was taken in the interior of a house) it makes sense to increase the ISO and make the shutter speed a bit slower since we need the camera to compensate for the lack of light. It is just another nudge that reminds us how everything tries to be grounded on real life, making life easier if we already know how things should behave.

There's more...

Something we saw in one of the last steps of this recipe was the chromatic aberration effect. Even though we used it to emphasize the weird sensation it can cause, it is sometimes used as a cheap alternative to anti aliasing. This is due to the fact that low values for that setting don't introduce a lot noise or strange artifacts; all they due is push the boundaries of the different objects in the scene in a very subtle way. This can create a similar effect to that added by anti aliasing when done in a subtle way.

Whatever the case, all of the previous effects should be used carefully and with taste. Overuse is always a cause for disagreement; some people might like the effect but is usually ends up looking dated given enough time, and it can look like a gimmick. On the other hand, subtlety can go a long way, as even though the effect might not be so evident it still adds to the granularity of the image and can add detail to the scene.

See also

As usual, let me include Epic Games' official documentation for vignetting and exposure settings.

Vignetting: `https://docs.unrealengine.com/en-us/Engine/Rendering/PostProcessEffects/Vignette`

Camera exposure control: `https://docs.unrealengine.com/en-US/Engine/Rendering/PostProcessEffects/AutomaticExposure`

Mimicking a real-life camera using Bloom and Lens Flares

The post processing effects that we are going to covering in this recipe are going to deal with lights. Daily life has probably taught every one of us about the different consequences that light introduces in our vision: as in what happens when we look at a very bright spot or how our eyes adapt to sudden changes in lighting. If you have also dealt with a camera in the past, the chances are you've also seen how certain camera effects can start to show if we have a light source in our sights. This is what we are going to be covering in the following pages: namely, two of them known as **Bloom** and **Lens Flares**. Replicating those effects in Unreal is easy and can add a bit of flavor to your scenes, as long as they are use in a subtle way. Let's take a look at them!

Getting ready

The scene we are going to be using in order to introduce the previous camera effects can be found in the following folder: `Content / UE4ShadersAndEffects / Maps / Chapter02 / 02_05_BloomAndLensFlares`

Albeit similar to the previous levels we've played with, this one introduces a couple of key components that are going to help us in this recipe. The first one is the extra geometry we have placed: having a ceiling and the prop for a downlight will help us to set up the scene. The second important element is the extra light that we have emanating from the ceiling, through which we will be able to showcase both the Bloom and the Lens Flares. Without further ado, let's dive right in!

How to do it...

Let's start tackling this recipe as we always do jump straight into the camera we have placed in the level, the already familiar **Camera01**, and look through its lens. We should be seeing something such as this:

It's the scene we are already familiar with, but seen from a different angle! The light that you see on the ceiling will help us introduce the effects this recipe is going to be covering, so focus your attention on that actor after we tweak the different settings for the bloom and the lens flares. With that said, let's start tweaking our scene:

1. Select the **PostProcessVolume** actor and look inside the **Details** panel. The **Lens** section contains the two effects that we are going to be looking at, separated into their own groups, **Bloom** and **Lens Flares**. We'll start looking at the first of those categories:

Make sure you are looking at the scene in **Gameplay** mode. This viewing setting will let you hide the icons for actors such as the Post Process Volume or the Reflection captures, allowing yo to look at the scene as if you were playing. With the **Main Viewport** as your active panel, you can press the *G* key on your keyboard to toggle this viewing mode on and off.

2. Tick the checkboxes for **Method** and **Intensity**. We are going to be playing with those two values first. Set the Method to **Standard** and bump up the **Intensity** up to 2.5 with those values we should start to see some differences in the rendered image:

The **Threshold** parameter should be left at **-1** if we want all scene colors to contribute to the effect. This is the most physically realistic approach, but feel free to change that value if you are after a specific effect, such as a dreamy scene or something out of the ordinary.

Now expand the **Advanced** section, which is directly underneath the settings we've tweaked in the previous step. In here you will be able to tweak two different type of parameters for the Bloom—the tint and the size of the visible effect.

3. Let's start by adjusting the size, but instead of tweaking each different numbered entry individually we'll focus on the **Size scale** parameter. This is a scale setting for all bloom sizes, so it controls all of them by just applying a multiplying factor. Let's set it to 16.

4. As we want the light to give off a warm sensation, let's tweak the bloom values to something closer to yellow. Modify each of the six tints ever so slightly, going in the yellow direction:

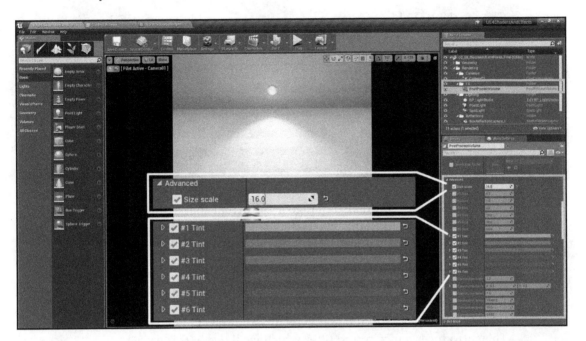

The reason there are six different sizes and tints to be modified is because the Bloom effect is actually made up of six different Gaussian blur filters. Each setting affects one of them, giving you more creative freedom.

Next up, we are going to be looking at the other effect we are going to be adjusting, the lens flares. This is a nice addition to the bloom we've just set up, and I like to work with them in tandem. Let's look at how to set it up:

5. Next up, jump to the **Lens Flares** section, which is a bit further down below the previous **Bloom** category. Tick the **Intensity** checkbox and set its value to something such as **90**, just so the effect is clearly visible.

6. Change the **BokehSize** from the default **3** to something such as **6** in order to make the effect even more visible:

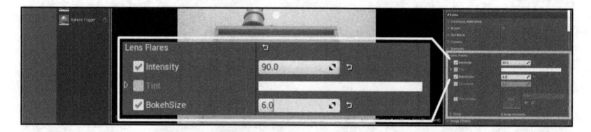

Something else we could also change is the actual shape of the Bokeh effect. The setting named **BokehShape** lets us do just that, so let's take advantage of it as we introduce our last adjustment.

7. Tick the **BokehShape** checkbox and click on the dropdown menu. Click on the **View Options** icon and select **Show Engine Content**; luckily for us, Unreal comes with a couple of different bokeh textures that we can try out. Start typing bokeh to narrow down the search results and select the texture named **Bokeh**. This introduces a nice round filter which we'll use in this case:

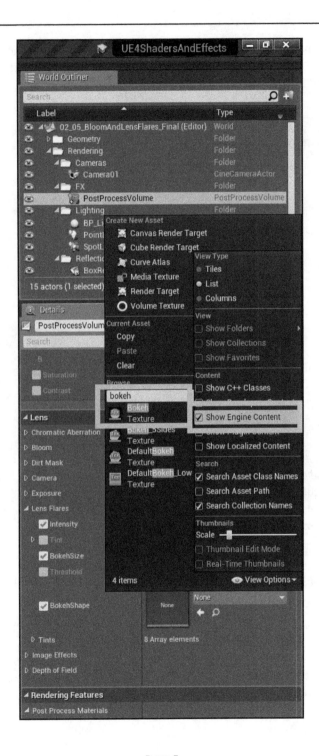

You can also create your own **Bokeh** textures to use in here; just export the ones that the engine includes to see how they created them and play around in an image editor to create something new!

With all of this done, we should be looking at our final image, which should look something like the following screenshot:

As you can see, these are effects that can have a great impact on our scenes, especially when we have multiple light sources. Playing around with the settings until you get to the point where everything feels nice is something that I hope has become easier after this recipe. See you in the next section!

How it works...

The way the bloom and the lens flares effects work is quite intuitive, even though they are slightly different. As we've said before, the first technique is rendered to the screen through six different Gaussian blur passes. Lens Flares, however, is an image based technique that uses textures to simulate the scattering of light through a camera's lens. In the end, what both of those implementations are trying to do is to replicate what can be observed both with our naked eye and through a camera.

As with many other effects we've seen, they are at their best when used in a subtle way. Overuse is always bad, especially with new techniques such as these. Taking care of how those effects impact the scene is an important task for the artist, so make sure to check the effect every so often and under different angles. Best of luck!

There's more...

The specific type of Bloom we've seen in the present chapter is one aimed at video games or real time applications in particular. However, Epic Games has recently introduced a different type that can be considered a bit more high quality, called **Bloom convolution**.

This new effect lets users include their own custom bloom kernel shapes, which is a texture that can depict physically accurate bloom effects as seen through a camera or our eyes. To enable it, just tick the **Method** checkbox in the **Lens** section of our post process volume or camera and change the value from Standard to **Convolution**. Once that's done, we'll be able to change the **Convolution kernel** used as a texture for this effect; again, tick the checkbox with that same name and select any texture that you might desire. By default we'll get an effect similar to this one:

In the previous screenshot, we've also set the **Convolution boost Mult** to 100 in order to make the effect perfectly visible. You can do so if you head over to the **Advanced** section of the **Bloom** category and look for that setting.

See also

As usual, let me include the official documentation for the topics we've covered before. It's a great place to know more about them whenever you feel like exploring a bit more!:

`https://docs.unrealengine.com/en-us/Engine/Rendering/PostProcessEffects/Bloom`

`https://docs.unrealengine.com/en-us/Engine/Rendering/PostProcessEffects/LensFlare`

A horror movie pulsating effect with post process materials

Welcome back to another recipe on post processing effects! I'm quite excited about this one, as we are about to start creating our own personal effects instead of using the ones we already have available through the engine. To do so, we'll take advantage of a particular type of shaders called the **Post Process Materials** that, to be honest, are quite self explanatory. They are the ones to be used when we need to adjust the scene as a whole. They are applied inside the post process volume, and not on a particular 3D model. Because of that, the way we create them is somewhat different to that of a standard material, so we'll be taking a look at how they are structured. This recipe will be the foundation which will let us create more complex effects later on, so let's jump right in!

Getting ready

We are going to start this recipe by loading a specific level, one which might feel familiar. Dive into the following folder and select the specified map: `Content / UE4ShadersAndEffects / Maps / Chapter02 / 02_06_PostProcessMaterials`.

The base scene is one we have already worked with in the past and it's none other than the horror movie-style level we worked on in the color grading recipe. Our goal this time will be to enhance the feel of the shot by introducing a pulsating effect through a post process material, just to make it look a bit more menacing and sinister. As usual, feel free to use any scene you want.

How to do it...

As we said before, this is the exact same scene we worked on the **Color Grading** recipe, and with this as our base, we will continue to expand upon the mood that we had previously created. Make sure to select the **Camera01** actor and look through its lens as we've been doing lately, as that will ensure that the effects we see are the same. With that out of the way, let's start the recipe:

1. Select the **PostProcessVolume** and scroll down to the **Rendering Features** section. The first category we can see should be called **Post Process Materials** be sure to expand that as we'll be using it later on to set up the effects we will be creating. Do also expand the **Array** section and click on the + button, as we will need that at a later stage as well:

2. In order to use any post process materials we first need to actually create one. Head over to the **Content Browser** and create a new material wherever you want; in my case, and following the structure we've been using through the previous pages, I'm creating it in the following directory: `Content Browser / UE4ShadersAndEffects / Assets / Chapter02`. The name I've given it is **M_PostProcessSample**.

3. The first thing we need to do to our material is to specify that it is a Post Process type of shader. To do so, select the main material node and head over to the details panel—the first category inside the **Material** section is called **Material Domain**, and we need to set that to **Post Process**:

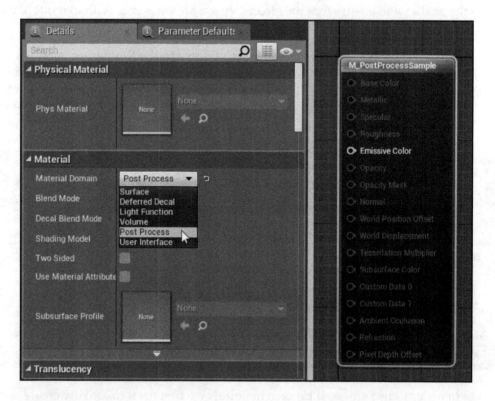

We can start creating the actual functionality after that. The first node we are going to be operating upon is the **SceneTexture**, so let's create it:

4. Right-click in the main Material Graph and look for the **SceneTexture** option. Once created, head over to the **Details** panel and change the default value from **SceneColor** to **PostProcessInput0**. Doing that will let us access the unadulterated color of the scene, which is what we want at this stage, as we'll be modifying it:

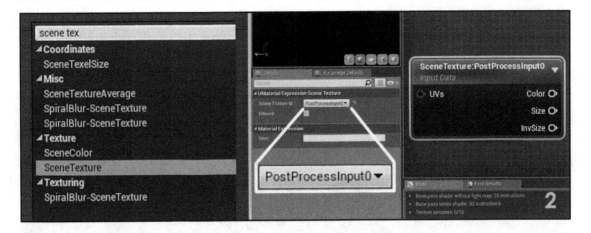

 The **SceneTexture** node is an important concept to grasp in order to understand how Post Process Materials work. Because we are not applying these materials to a 3D model, but instead the scene we are looking at, we need to specify which part of the rendering pipeline we want to be affecting. The **SceneTexture** node lets us do that.

5. Create a **ComponentMask** by right clicking again and typing that same name. Make sure that the **R**, **G** and **B** values are ticked in the **Details** panel for that mask, and connect the **Color** output pin from the **SceneTexture** node to the input pin of our new mask:

The reason we are masking the color of the scene is because we want to play with its RGB values and nothing else. With those two nodes in place we have secured ourselves access to the image that is being rendered, and what we are now about to do is to overlay information on top of that.

6. Create a **TextureSample** node (right-click | **TextureSample**) and assign it the **T_PanningDistortion** asset to it. This image contains a reddish gradient that we will overlay with the base rendered image of the scene:

Alternatively, you can create a **TextureSample** node by holding the *T* key on your keyboard and clicking anywhere within the main graph.

7. Overlay the previous texture with the color of the scene by creating a **Lerp** node. You can do this if you hold the *T* key on your keyboard and click within the boundaries of the main graph or by any other method, such as right-clicking and typing `Lerp` or looking for that node in the palette. Connect to the **A** input pin the output of **Mask**, and the **Texture Sample** into the pin labeled **B**. Finally, Connect the alpha channel of our texture to the **Alpha** input pin for the Lerp:

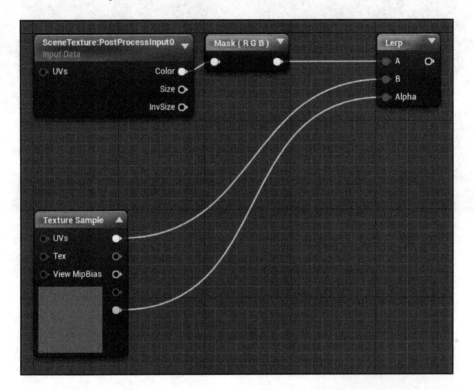

With that done, connect the output of the **Lerp** pin to the **Emissive Color** node on the main material node. Apply and save the material. What we now want to do is to apply the material we have just created as a post processing effect for our scene. Let's get back to the main viewport in order to do so.

8. With the **PostProcessVolume** selected, scroll back to the **Post Process Materials** section we were previously in and select our newly created material as the asset on the Array, like in the following screenshot:

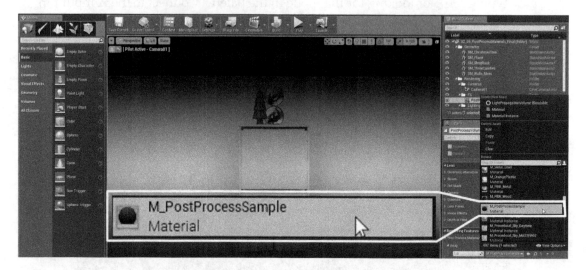

We should be able to see the effect across the screen one that's done. Even though we've technically just created a new material and we are looking at it, I think we can make it a bit more interesting. Let's get back to the material editor and perform a few more tweaks.

The next bit of functionality that we are going to be creating for our material is a time function. What we basically want to do is to animate our texture, just so that the effect we are creating is not static. Let's make it pulsate over time, making our already creepy scene a little bit more eerie.

9. Right-click anywhere within the Material Graph and start typing **Time**. This will allow us to create a new node that will be used to animate the pulsating effect, as the node introduces the concept of time in our material. Pair it with a constant node, which we'll use to affect how fast the effect pulsates, and combine both of the previous nodes in a **Multiply** node. Finally, drag from the output pin of the Multiply node and create another one called **Sine**. The graph should look something like this:

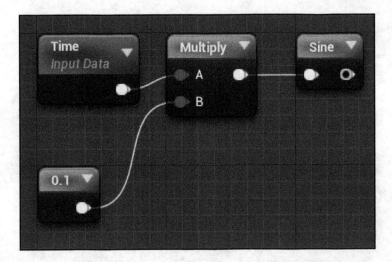

That expression will be driving our future animated material, and we will be able to control how fast it is animated thanks to that constant node we've introduced. The last step in this pipeline is to actually combine the effect we've created with the raw scene color based on this time function:

10. Copy the **SceneTexture** and the **Mask** nodes and past the above the previously created ones.
11. Create a second **Lerp** node, and connect the output of what we created in the previous step to the **A** pin.
12. Connect the output of the initial nodes we had created, the result of the **Lerp** between the scene color and out reddish texture to the **B** pin.

13. Finally, connect the time function to the **Alpha** value of the latest **Lerp** node. The graph should look something like this:

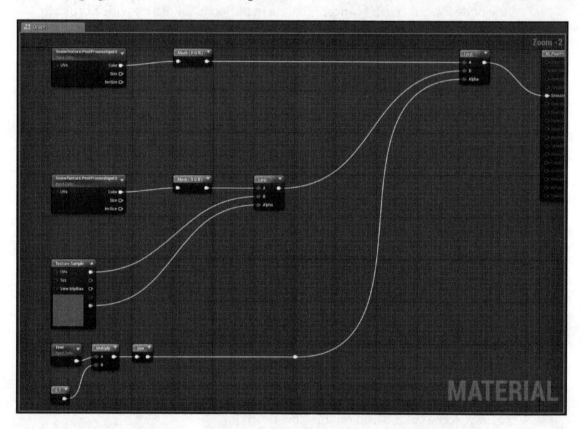

With all of those changes made, we should now be looking at a much more disturbing scene one which blends between the default "greenish" look and a new reddish gradient, which makes things more creepy.

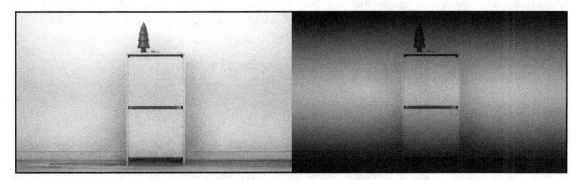

Any other effects would have been possible; the possibilities are almost endless. Be sure to check out further chapters when we'll start to deal with more advanced effects. Until then, see you in the next section!

How it works...

Post process materials are a bit different than the ones we apply to 3D models. Just as we need UVs in our meshes to indicate how textures should wrap around the objects, we need to access a specific bit of information from the scene that is being rendered in order to apply certain effects to it.

Instead of UVs, though, the information that we need from the scene comes in the shape of different scene textures, such as the one we dealt with before named Post Process Input 0. There are many others, and we will use them according to our needs. For instance, we can also access the subsurface color or the Ambient Occlusion pass if we want to. The point is that we have access to many scene buffers and you can use them to create a material that suits your needs.

Of course, using those nodes is not always mandatory and you can create a post process material using only the nodes that you would use on a traditional material. However, don's pass on the resources available to you through the Scene Texture parameter.

There's more...

Before we go, something else that can be of interest is the position in which the **Post Process Material** we create is inserted within the post processing pipeline. If we take a look back at the Details panel for our material, we can see that there are several options if we scroll down to the **Post Process Material** section:

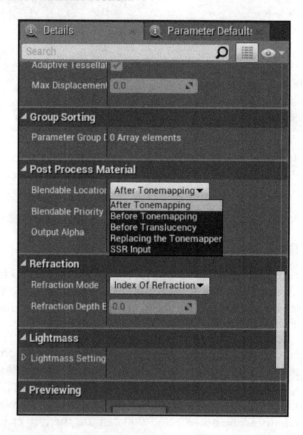

The position in which this happens can be important, depending as always on your particular scene. For instance, selecting the **Before Tonemapping** option means that the effect we are creating happens before the color grading and tone mapping operations happen in our scene. That can be of interest if we need to access the raw values of our level in case any of the corrections we are introducing later is causing issues with our scene. It's always good to take that into consideration, so do have a play with those settings if you are experiencing any issues with the materials you create.

See also

Make sure to check out Epic Games' official documentation if you want a different take on the post process material parameters and a different example of what you can build with them: https://docs.unrealengine.com/en-us/Engine/Rendering/PostProcessEffects/ PostProcessMaterials.

Adjusting anti aliasing and other rendering features

Welcome to the last recipe of this chapter! So far, we've had the opportunity to play around with most of the settings that both the post process volume and the cine camera actor have to offer. We don't want to say goodbye to this topic though without looking at some of the final technical adjustments we can perform on our scenes at a global scale. That being the case, we will focus our attention now on several important values such as the following:

- Supersampling
- Screen Space Reflections
- Ambient Occlusion
- Motion Blur
- Anti Aliasing

All of the previous topics are often viewed more from a technical point of view rather than an artistic one. They can have a great impact on the visual quality and feel of the scene, and we don't want to downplay the part that they have on that regard. However, more often than not, they are values that we have to adjust keeping in mind the performance that we are after. It's not so much a question of whether we want to use supersampling or not, it's more of a case of can we afford to? Let's take a look at the answer then!

Getting ready

As usual, you can find an already prepared scene set up for you in the following folder: `Content / UE4ShadersAndEffects / Maps / Chapter02 /`

The name of the scene is **02_07_AntiAliasing**. Again, feel free to continue using one of your own scenes if you so prefer, as that is completely possible. We will however point out that we are going to be exploring some effects, such as the screen space reflections, which require some highly reflective objects to be placed in the scene in order to be able to see what we are actually modifying, so keep that in mind!

How to do it...

Let's start this recipe by looking through the camera's lens. This is something we have usually done throughout the current chapter, and we've always done that with the hope that certain effects that we are going to use will be better visualized if they are seen from that particular camera location. This is still the case in the current recipe, since we are going to explore screen space reflections and we need to make sure that they are visible. With that said, this is the image we should be seeing once we are looking through the camera:

Having that image as a reference will let us check many of the post processing effects we are about to introduce. Let's start with the first one—choosing the default **Anti Aliasing** method:

1. Head over to **Edit | Project Settings**. In there, navigate to the **Rendering** section under the **Engine** category. Once inside, scroll even further down to the panel called **Default Settings** and look for the anti-aliasing method. Make sure that it's set to **Temporal AA**, which should be by default. You can keep that value throughout the rest of this recipe, or try to change it if you want to see a difference. We'll be exploring this further in the *How it works...* section, but we need to have something at this point for the next steps to happen:

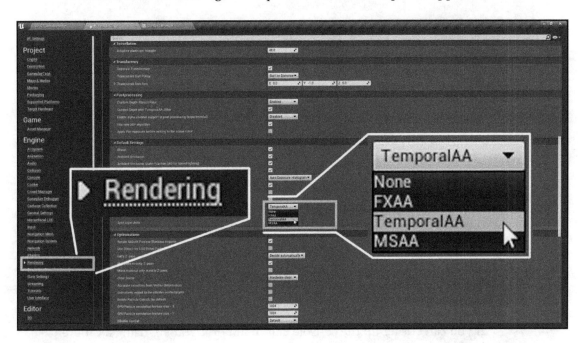

 Even though the anti-aliasing option used to be part of the post process volume actor in past iterations of the engine, they've changed it's location to the one mentioned previously.

The quality of the anti aliasing can be controlled via console commands, both in game and in the editor.

2. Open up the command console by tapping the **tilde** key in your keyboard. Type `r.PostProcessAAQuality 6` to set the quality of the temporal anti aliasing to the maximum the Unreal will allow you to. Feel free to set it up to anything between **0** and **6**, which is the range said command is expecting:

If you can't bring up the console command or if you are using a different keyboard layout other than the English (UK) one, rest assured that you can set a custom key binding to bring it up. Head over to **Project Settings | Engine | Input | Console** to change the default value.

3. Another command you can use to quickly change between the different anti aliasing methods is **r.DefaultFeature.AntiAliasing**. Following that command with a value of **0**, **1** or **2** will toggle between no effect, FXAA or TAA:

As you can see from the preceding screenshot, the difference in the quality of the AA method is really visible if we go from zero to two, or from two to four. Going as high as six doesn't seem to be doing much in our particular scene, but could be useful when heavy aliasing happens in thin objects such as cables. Next up, we are going to be looking at the screen space reflections. With the post process volume selected, head over to the **Details** panel and scroll down to the **Rendering Features** settings.

4. Expand the **Screen Space Reflections** section and tick the **Quality** checkbox. By default this should be set to 50 increase it to 100 instead.

5. While in here, do tick as well the parameter called **Max Roughness**. Its default value of 0.6 might be a bit low for many cases, so let's raise it to 0.8:

We'll explore in further detail what those parameters are affecting in the *There's more...* section, but this setting basically increases the quality of the screen space reflections effect. These can be quite important in some scenes, in particular in those where we have dynamic objects moving around which can cause reflections to update in real time. They are limited in that they can only reflect what is on the screen, so things that are behind the camera or at the very edges of the image won't be picked up. Another rendering feature we can include is the **Ambient Occlusion**. It works on a post process layer by analyzing the scene and determining which areas should be darker according to how occluded they are.

6. Expand the **Ambient Occlusion** section and tick the **Intensity** checkbox, as well as the **Radius** one. Give the first parameter a value of 0.3 and go with 10 for the second one.

7. Expand the **Advanced** section while still within the Ambient Occlusion tab. Check the two tick-boxes where it says **Radius in WorldSpace**. By doing this, we are ensuring that the value of 10 we have previously specified means 10 centimeters in world space units:

If we set the property **Radius in WorldSpace** to true, the Radius we specify takes into account that distance to create the Ambient Occlusion effect. Leaving it on the default false state means that the calculations for the AO happen taking into account the default view space, which is locked to 400 units.

The last setting that we are going to talk about is the **Screen Percentage**. This setting can be found under the **Misc** section of the **Rendering Features** category. What we basically control through it is what you might know as Supersampling; let's try it out.

8. Check the **Screen Percentage** checkbox and increase the default value of 100 to something like 200. Be careful though this has a great impact on performance and you should be careful when choosing a number in this box. You can read more about this in the next section, *How it works...*

9. In order to test this setting we actually need to play the game. As it is a runtime effect, we can't visualize its impact on the main viewport of the Unreal editor; instead, click on the **Play** button at the top of the main **Toolbar**:

Before we go, I'd like to leave you with some images from this scene taken under different **Screen Percentage** settings. They should be representative of the changes in image quality that Supersampling introduces or upscaling, which is the term used when the screen percentage is lower than **100**:

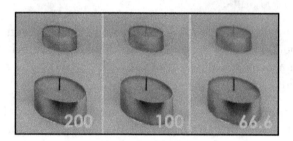

How it works...

Now that we've seen how the previous settings affect our scene, let's take some time aside to go over the theory behind them all. We will start explaining the very last parameter we've tweaked: the **Screen Percentage**.

The specifics behind this technique are quite simple: instead of rendering the scene at a fixed resolution, which would usually match that of our screens, we instead render at a different one. This second number needs to then be transformed back into the initial screen resolution, as that is a fixed variable. We are therefore left with two possible scenarios: if the initial resolution is greater than the one we are rendering the game image at, we would be talking about upscaling. If we are, on the other hand, rendering at a higher pixel density than that of our displays we get what is known as Supersampling.

Upscaling is cheaper to render, as the engine needs to deal with a lower amount of pixels. The resulting image is of a lower quality than what we would if we weren't using this technique. Supersampling, on the other hand, takes advantage of the extra pixel count to create a higher quality image at the expense of being more demanding in terms of performance. It can be used as an anti-aliasing technique, as we are effectively reconstructing the image through this method.

Continuing with the topic of AA, let's focus once again on the different implementations that Unreal has decided to implement. There are four in total: the already-seen Supersampling, Temporal AA, FXAA, and MSAA. This last method is only available when we are using the forward renderer or developing for mobile platforms, which isn't the default state Unreal is targeting. Each method has its strengths and weaknesses, which we'll try to mention next.

FXAA is the cheapest AA method. It is one that was developed by nVidia, and it works on the rendered image that the engine outputs and not on the geometry of our levels. Because of that, it sometimes blurs the textures or operates beyond just the jagged edges we want to tweak so it can introduce unintended consequences. SSAA, or Supersampling anti aliasing, is the technique that we described before we first rendered the scene at a higher resolution and then downsampled it using an averaging filter, which makes the transition between pixels more smooth and greatly reduces jaggies.

MSAA works in a similar way to SSAA, but in an optimized way. Instead of sampling the whole scene by rendering it at a higher resolution, MSAA takes different samples by just focusing on overlapping areas of the level. This saves up on performance while still achieving a great anti-aliasing result.

Finally, Temporal AA is a new actor in the anti-aliasing world. It is the one we use by default in Unreal, and it is a mix of a temporal filter solution, hardware anti-aliasing, and custom algorithms that work throughout the scene. It isn't as cheap to enable as FXAA, but the quality is much better overall. Choosing between one or the other is a matter of what you are trying to achieve with your project.

There's more...

Before moving on, I didn't want to pass on the opportunity of explaining a bit more some of the settings that we tweaked in this recipe. Even though we've covered most of the parameters that define each of the post process effects that we've seen, we haven't had the time to really explain how each setting contributes to the overall effect. Let's do that now:

- The **Screen Space Reflections** are controlled by three different properties: the intensity, the quality and the max roughness. Even though the first two can be quite self explanatory, it's the third one that is a bit more subtle. In simple terms, max roughness is used to specify what roughness value the engine fades the screen space reflections. The higher the number, the more the effect will be seen on surfaces which have a material applied with a high roughness value. This basically means that the effect will be more visible throughout the entirety of the scene.

- The **Ambient Occlusion** has some extra settings that we didn't need to tweak in our example, but which are worth considering when working on a different level. I'd like to mention the **Fade Out Distance**, which is the value that determines up until where this screen space effect is visible in centimeters. Be sure to modify that value if your scene requires it.

- Other settings, such as **Motion Blur**, are quite straightforward; it is enabled by default, and if you want to disable it you need to tick the **Amount** checkbox and set it to 0. The **Max** amount is the maximum distortion that the effect can introduce, and you determine it by specifying a percent of the screen width.

With all of those settings in mind, it will be easy for you to configure the scene to your liking, so make sure to have a go at them!

See also

As usual, the official documentation includes examples and explanations about almost every setting we've seen before—make sure to take a look at them if you want to learn a bit more:

Anti-Aliasing: `https://docs.unrealengine.com/en-us/Engine/Rendering/PostProcessEffects/AntiAliasing`

Screen space reflections: `https://docs.unrealengine.com/en-us/Engine/Rendering/PostProcessEffects/ScreenSpaceReflection`

Ambient Occlusion: `https://docs.unrealengine.com/en-us/Engine/Rendering/LightingAndShadows/AmbientOcclusion`

Screen percentage: `https://docs.unrealengine.com/en-us/Engine/Rendering/ScreenPercentage`

3
Opaque Materials and Texture Mapping

The fact that we have already seen how a material is set up at a basic level should give us the confidence to tackle the present chapter, where we'll expand upon what we have previously learned in order to see more advanced materials and effects. This is what you can expect to see in the pages to follow:

- Using masks within a material
- Instancing a material
- Texturing a small prop
- A plastic cloth using Fresnel and Detail Texturing
- Creating a semi procedural material
- Baking out a material
- Distance-based texture blending

Introduction

Even though we have already exposed ourselves to a material in Unreal Engine 4, that was back in the first chapter. We were toddlers back then! Not really, but that experience was an introductory one. Seeing the inner workings of a PBR material got us close to the material editor and several of its nodes, but we are yet to properly use and master them. And that's what we are planning to do now.

Starting gently—as we always do—we'll begin working on a simple scene where we'll learn how to set up a proper material graph for a small prop. Beyond that, we can also look at how to create materials that are going to be applied on large-scale models, and what clever techniques can be implemented to balance quality and performance. And from there, we will also take a look at a bunch of other interesting resources: material effects driven by the position of the camera, large-scale optimizations, and semi-procedural creation techniques:

Let's get started!

Using masks within a material

Welcome to the first recipe of this third chapter! I think this is a very important moment in our material-creation journey, as we are about to leave the introductory stuff aside in order to focus more on real assets. From now on, everything we do is really real and by that I mean that we are no longer talking about the possibilities or applications of what we are learning, but instead we are doing things that could be part of a real-life project. Hopefully, you'll start feeling like a pro, learning and applying specific techniques that are part of a 3D artist's daily workflow in UE4!

With that in mind, our first goal is going to be the replication of a complex material graph. This is going to be very helpful, as one of the most important steps is to actually decide how our materials should be set up. We'll do that for a small wooden toy tank, which is indicative of many different objects that we might want to texture in the future. We will also take a look at other examples throughout this chapter, but this particular recipe will serve as a nice entry point, as we are about to see.

Getting ready

We've included a small scene that you can use as a starting point for this recipe – its name is **03_01_ComplexShader_Start**, and it includes all of the basic assets that you will need to follow along. As you'll be able to see for yourself, there's a small toy tank that has two UV channels in the center of the level. The first of those channels is the one that Unreal uses by default to understand how it needs to place the textures that we feed to the material the model is using, while the second one is used to generate the lightmaps.

As always, feel free to use your own 3D models and populate your scenes however you like. Something to take into consideration is the need to have well-laid-out UVs, as we are going to be masking certain areas of our models to drive the look of our materials. Make sure that your custom assets follow that rule, as we'll need that to be true for this recipe to work:

 Something that you might want to change now is the camera clipping plane. Unreal's default camera settings aren't really suitable for working with small objects. Head over to the **Project Settings | Engine | General Settings | Settings** section and set the value of the **Near Clip Plane** to something like 1 and remember to restart the editor!

How to do it...

We are going to create our first complex material in Unreal Engine 4! Complex is a word used lightly in this context, as it doesn't have anything to do with the difficulty of creating the asset itself. It's more of a statement: what we are going to be creating from now on are examples that could just as well be real assets in a game studio.

With that said, the first stop in this journey is going to be the laying down of the foundations of the material. We are going to operate on the material graph by organizing and thinking about how things should be put together. Make sure you have the **03_01_ComplexShader_Start** scene open, or any other of your own that you choose, and let's start taking a look at that:

1. Let's start by creating a new material, so that we can change the appearance of the main model to something more exciting. I've created a new asset, named **M_ToyTank**, which will be in the following folder: Content / UE4ShadersAndEffects / Assets / Chapter03. You could use that or also create your own!

2. As the tank has different small parts (the tracks, the barrel, the main body, and so on), chances are that we are going to want to treat those areas differently. To do so, we will need to create masks that fit the selected parts that we want to shade— but before that happens, we need to take a look at how the UVs are laid out. Select **SM_ToyTank** in the content browser, open the asset editor, and click on the **UV button** | **UV Channel 0**. This is what it should look like:

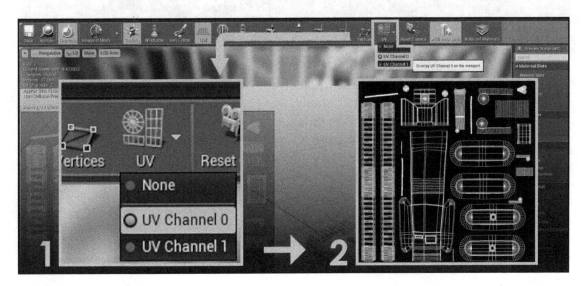

You can export the model from the game engine and alter the UVs in your DCC until you are happy with them. To do this, right-click on the asset within the content browser and select **Asset Actions** | **Export**.

3. There's a small mask that you can use for this example, named **T_TankMasks**, which you'll be able to find in the same folder as the tank. It's basically an RGB image, which you can see in the following screenshot. Drag that resource into the newly created material, as we'll be using it soon:

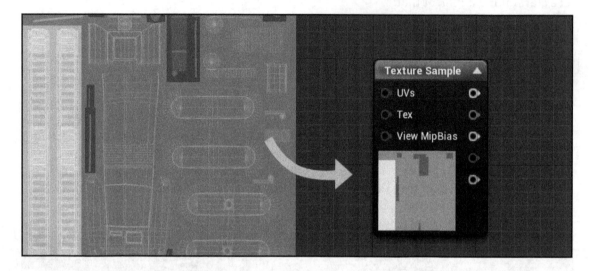

4. Also within the material graph, create two **Constant3** nodes, and select whichever color you want under their color selection wheel. Make sure they are different from one another, though!

5. Next, create a **Lerp** node. That strange word is short for linear interpolation, and it lets us blend between different assets according to the masks that we connect to the **Alpha** pin. Connect the red channel of the **T_TankMasks** asset to that pin of the new node.

6. Connect each of the Constant3 vectors to the **A** and **B** pins of the **Lerp** node.

7. Create another **Lerp** node and a different Constant3 vector. Connect the blue channel of our mask into the **Alpha** of the new **Lerp** and the new **Constant3** vector into the **B** pin. Finally, connect the output of the previous **Lerp** into the A slot. Also, make sure to apply the material to the tank in the main scene! The resulting material graph should look something like this:

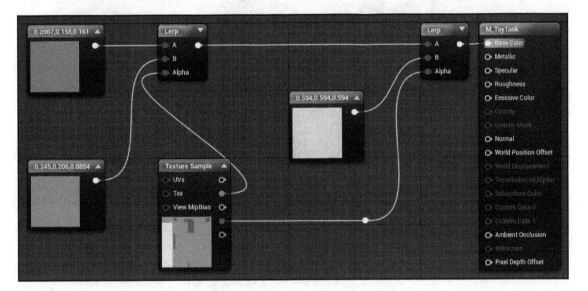

At this stage, we've managed to differentiate certain areas of the model in our material thanks to using masks. We now need to expand this concept to the **Metallic** and the **Roughness** attributes of the material, just so we can also control those independently.

8. Copy all of the previously created nodes and paste them twice—we'll need one copy to connect to the roughness slot and a different one that will drive the **Metallic** attribute.

9. Replace the Constant3 nodes of the new copies for simple Constant nodes. We don't need an RGB value to specify the **Metalness** and **Roughness** properties, so let's tidy that up! The graph should now look something like this:

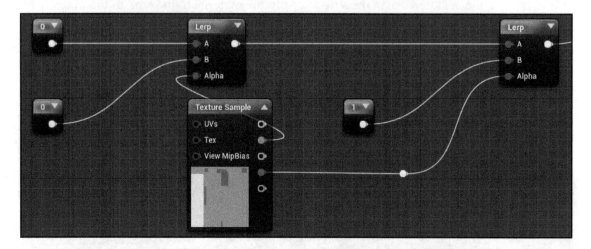

10. Assign custom values for the new constant nodes you have created on the **Metallic** and the **Roughness** attributes. Remember what we saw in the first chapter: a value of 0 for the roughness slot means that the material has very clear reflections, while a value of **1** means the exact opposite. Similarly, a value of **1** connected to the metallic node means that the material is a metal, while 0 determines that it is not. Let's take a look at the final results!

Finally, think about tidying things up by grouping the different sections of the material graph together. This is done by selecting all the nodes that you want to group and pressing the C key on your keyboard. It keeps things organized, which is very important—especially when working with others or whenever you revisit your own work:

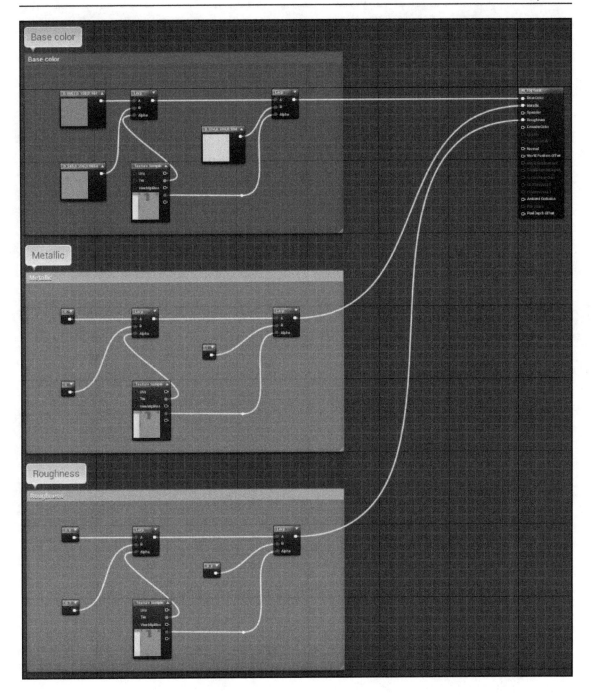

How it works...

Even though we've used masks extensively in this recipe, we haven't had a chance to properly look at how they are set up until now, that is!

In essence, the textures that we've used as masks are images that contain a black and white picture stored in each of the image's RGB channels. As you probably already know, if you were to open up any image in your default photography editing software you would have the chance to take a look at the three individual image channels the picture is composed of the red, green, and blue ones, specifically. There might be an extra one, known as the **Alpha**, depending on the type of file that you are using.

The composition of those file formats is actually beneficial to us, as we can use the separate channels as masks—just like we did in this recipe. The **Lerp** node, as we saw, blends between two inputs according to the values that we provide it. Since those values can be anything from **0** to **1**, or black to white, that means that we have a perfect match in each of the image's RGB (and possibly **Alpha**) channels, since they are each a black and white image if taken separately:

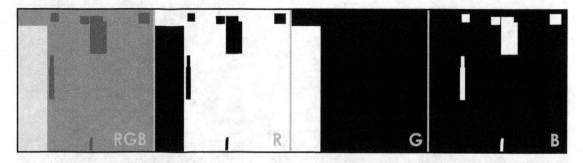

In any case, using masks to drive the appearance of a material is often preferable to using multiple materials per mesh. This is because of the way the rendering pipeline works on the background. Without getting too technical, we could say that each new material makes the whole graphic operation more expensive, and even though we won't start noticing the effects until we have lots of different shaders in the scene, this is something that will eventually happen for almost any project bigger than a small example.

There's more...

We've seen how to use masks to drive the appearance of a material in the previous section. With that said, there's a limitation to that technique with regards of masking—having three or four different channels per texture means that we can have as many masks per image at most. Even though this is sometimes enough, there are always situations where we are bound to want more masks. In those situations, we can either use another image (which would give us three or four extra masks) or use a different technique—color masking.

That last method is one we haven't explored, as it isn't native to Unreal, but it can certainly be useful. The only thing we need to do is have a color texture where each individual color masks an area we want to operate on, as in the following screenshot:

The idea is to color pick from the colored texture the areas that we want to apply a certain effect on. If this is of interest, you can find more information about that at the following link: https://answers.unrealengine.com/questions/191185/how-to-mask-a-single-color.html.

See also

There are more examples of masks being used in other assets that you might want to check out. This is something easy to do, as we've included `Starter Content` in this project, where we can find a couple of other materials that make use of the technique we've just seen.

You can find them in the following folder: **Starter Content | Props | Materials**. Shaders such as **M_Door** or **M_Lamp** have been created according to the methodology explained previously, so be sure to check them out!

Instancing a material

We've seen how to set up the material graph for a small prop in the previous recipe, something that we are sure to be doing multiple times every time we create a new material. Something extra that we can now do is to create an instance of that previous asset: basically, a copy of the previous material that is quicker to edit and that doesn't need to be compiled every time we make a change.

This technique is especially useful precisely because of the removal of that compile time. As you've probably seen by now, every time you make a change to a material, you are then forced to click on the **Compile** and **Save** buttons. This can be a time consuming process in complex materials, especially if we only want to tweak a certain color or a specific value. Furthermore, the lack of compilation means that this specific type of asset can be dynamically changed at runtime, which is quite powerful!

Getting ready

We are going to continue to work on the scene we saw in the previous recipe. This means that, as always, there's not a lot you need to follow along—you can either use the assets we provide or create your own. Either way, we'll be taking a simple model that has a material applied to it and tweak it so that the new shader that we apply at the end of the scene is an instance of the original one. The base level we are going to be working on can be found in the following folder: `Content / UE4ShadersAndEffects/Maps/Chapter03/03_02_MaterialInstance_Start`.

Without further ado, let's get to it!

How to do it...

Let's start by reviewing the material that we have created in the previous recipe—it's a pretty standard one, containing attributes that affect the **Base Color**, the roughness, and the metallic properties of the material. Here's what the part of the graph that affects the metallic material node looks like:

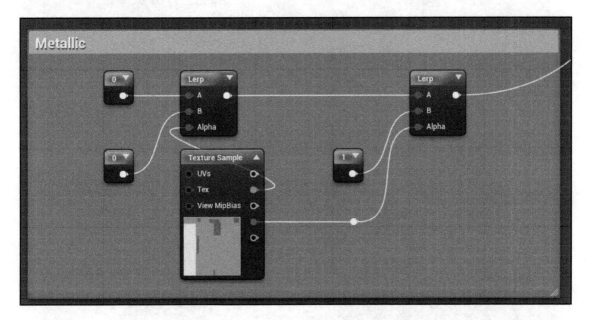

As you can see, there are basically two things happening—we are using Constants to adjust the metalness of the shader and we are also employing texture masks to determine where those values are applied within our models. The same logic applies elsewhere in the material graph both parts of the graph that affect the Roughness and the Base Color properties are almost identical copies of the preceding image.

Even though this is pretty standard, tweaking values this way until we finally have the material look the way we want can be a bit time consuming, especially if we have to compile it every single time we make a change. To alleviate this, we are going to start using parameters and material instances. Let's see how to do this:

1. Open up the material that is currently being applied to the toy tank in the middle of the scene. It should be **M_ToyTank_Parameterized_Start**, or feel free to use one similar to what we used in the previous recipe.

2. Select the constant nodes that live within the Metallic material expression comment (the ones seen in the preceding screenshot) and right-click with your mouse. Select the **Convert to Parameter** option, which will create a **Scalar Parameter**:

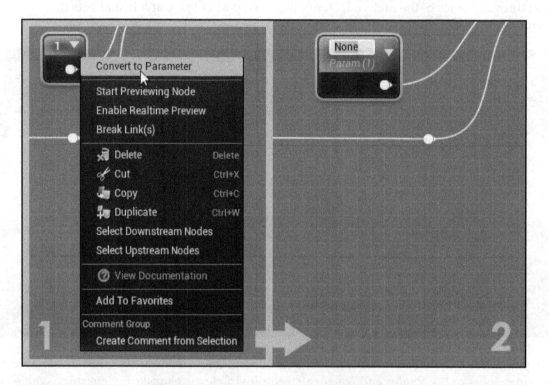

TIP

Instead of doing that, you can also create these type of nodes by right-clicking anywhere within the material graph and searching for scalar parameter. Remember that you can also look for them in the **Palette** panel!

3. With that done, it's now time to give the parameters a name! Judging from the way the mask is dividing the model, I've gone with the following criteria: **Tire Metalness**, **Body Metalness,** and **Cannon Metalness**. Feel free to use your own!

4. Do the same for the constants that can be found within the **Roughness** and the **Base Color** sections and give them appropriate names, just like we did before for the previous nodes. This is how the **Base Color** nodes look after doing that:

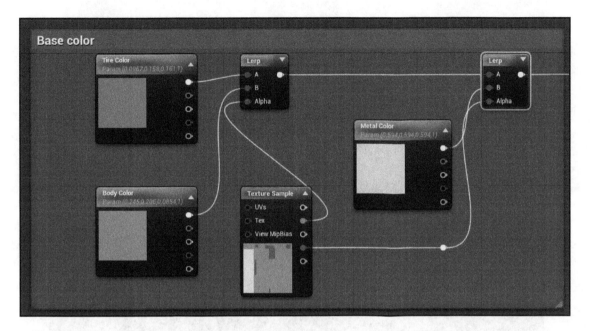

 The type of parameters that will be created from the constant3 nodes found within the **Base Color** section will actually be a different type of nodes from the ones we've seen so far. These new ones are called vector parameters, as opposed to the previous scalar parameters, so keep that in mind when you want to create them from scratch.

Once all of this is done, we should be left with a material graph that looks like what we previously had; but one where we are using parameters instead of constants. This is a key feature that will play a major role in the next steps, as we are about to see.

5. Locate the material you've been operating on within the **Content Browser** and right-click on it. Select the **Create Material Instance** option and give it a name, I've gone with **MI_ToyTank**, since MI is a common prefix for these type of assets:

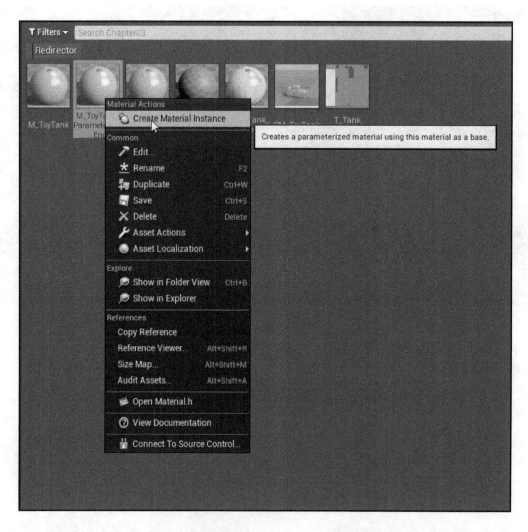

Double-click on the newly created asset to open it up. Unlike with normal materials, instances let us expose the parameters we have created and tweak them—either before or during runtime, and without the need to recompile any shaders.

6. Apply the **Material Instance** to the model, replacing the previous **M_ToyTank_Parameterized_Start**.

7. Tweak the values that you have previously exposed with this new method. First, be sure to **tick the parameters that you want to change** and then modify them to try a different look for the little prop. I've gone a bit psychedelic in the next example, but why not:

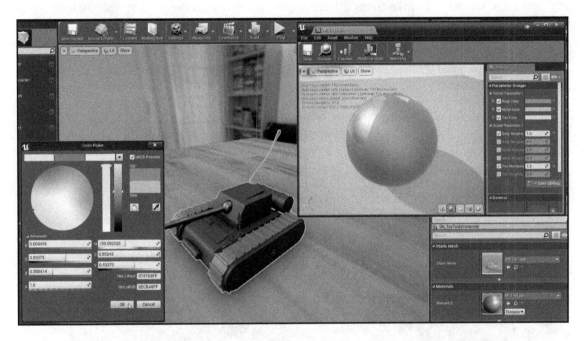

After all of these steps are done, you will have officially created a **Material Instance**. You've already seen the benefits of how modular they can be, and in the next section we'll be also looking at what their benefits are in terms of performance and real-time editability.

How it works...

In this recipe, we've dedicated our efforts to creating a Material Instance. So far, we've seen how to do it, but we haven't yet covered the reasons why they can be beneficial to out workflow. Let's take care of that now.

First and foremost, we have to understand how this type of asset falls within the material pipeline. If we think of a pyramid, a basic material will sit at the bottom layer – this is the basic building block over which the rest of what we are about to be talking about rests. Material Instances are an extension: once we have a basic material set up, we can create multiple instances if we want to modify things like the color, the roughness, or the textures we are using **as long as the basic material graph is the same**. For example, if we have two toy tanks and we want to give them different colors, we would create a master material and then two material instances, which we would apply to each model. That is better in terms of performance than having two master materials applied to each toy.

Furthermore, material instances can also be modified at runtime, something that can't be done using the master materials. The properties that can be tweaked are the ones that we decide to expose in the parent material through the use of different types of parameters, such as the **Scalar** or the **Vector** types that we have seen in this recipe. These materials that can be modified during gameplay receive the distinctive name of **Material Instance Dynamic**, as even though they are also an instance of a master material, they are created differently. We'll see one method that we can use to create them in the next few steps:

1. Create an **Actor Blueprint** and assign a **Static Mesh** to it.
2. In the **Construction Script**, add the **Create Dynamic Material Instance** node and hook the static mesh to its **Target** input pin. Select the parent material that you'd like to modify in the **Source Material** drop-down menu, and store this material as a variable:

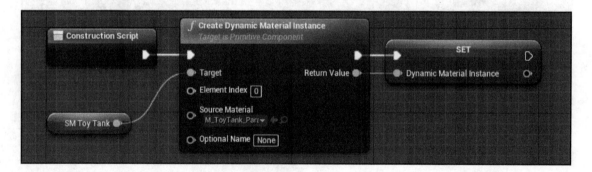

3. Use a **Set Vector Parameter Value** node in conjunction with a custom event to drive the changing of the material parameter that you'd like to trigger. Remember to type the exact parameter you'd like to change and assign a value to it:

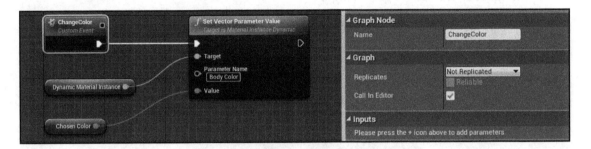

I'll leave the previous set of steps as a challenge for you, as it includes certain topics that we haven't covered yet, such as the creation of **Blueprints**, which you'll need to be a little bit familiar with if you want to tackle it. However, if you'd like to see an example for yourself without having to complete the challenge, rest assured that you'll be able to do so. I've left something for you in the Unreal Engine project examples we include alongside this book: a blueprint called **BP_ChangingColorTank** that you can open to see for yourself how it's been set up.

There's more...

Something we didn't do in the recipe is group the different parameters we created into groups. If you remember, when we had to edit the different options within the material instance, those were all grouped under two different categories: **Vector Parameter Values** and **Scalar Parameter Values**. The names are only representative of the type they belong to, and not what they are affecting. That is something that we can fortunately modify by going back to the parent material.

If we go there, and select each of the parameters we had created, you'll be able to see that there is an option named **Group** in the **Details** panel. Giving it a name different to the default **None** is what will appear instead of the previous vector or scalar parameter values in the **Material Instance**. You can put several nodes into the same group, which might help to keep things tidy. Be sure to give it a go:

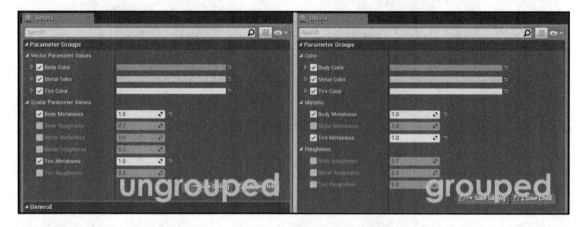

See also

As always, and before we move on to the next recipe, I'd like to leave you with the official documentation on this topic, as written by Epic Games: `https://docs.unrealengine.com/en-us/Engine/Rendering/Materials/MaterialInstances`.

Texturing a small prop

In this recipe, we are going to take a look at how to properly work with textures within a material. The word properly is the real key element in the previous sentence – for even though we've worked with images in the past, we haven't really manipulated them inside the editor or seen what tricks we can use on them to enhance the look of our materials. It's time we did that, so let's take a look at it in this recipe!

Getting ready

I'm almost sure you know what I'm about to say by now, having read similar *Getting ready* sections elsewhere in this book. So, before doing that, let me say: "hello to you Sir/Madam, nice to see you here again! " Apart from that, you can follow along if you open up the following level from the UE4 project we are providing: `Content /UE4ShadersAndEffects / Maps / Chapter03 / 03_03_TexturedMaterial_Start`.

We'll be using assets that are also part of the project we provide or from the Starter Content, so make sure to include those ones as well if you haven't done so yet. If you want to follow along on your own personal project, know that the only thing you'll need is a small 3D model that you can get a hold of and some textures. We are going to be using wood images for this example, but the principles we are going to be looking at really work across any kind of texture, so include whatever suits your tastes. See you in the next section!

How to do it...

So far, we've used simple colors in our toy tank material – and even though they can look good depending on the type of visuals that we are after, we are going to use realistic textures this time. As usual, the assets we'll be using can be found in either the Starter Content package or the ones that we are providing with the book. Let's start:

1. Duplicate the material we had previously created in the first recipe of this chapter, which was **M_ToyTank**. This is going to be useful, as we don't want to reinvent the wheel so much as expand a system that already works. Having everything separated with masks and neatly organized will speed things up greatly. Name the new asset however you like I've gone with **M_ToyTank_Textured**.
2. **Open up** the material graph by double-clicking on the newly created asset and delete the constant3 node that can be found inside of the **Base Color** section.

3. **Create** a new **Texture Sample** node and assign the following texture to it: **T_Wood_Pine_D**. Link that to the **B** pin of the **Lerp** node where the output of the recently deleted constant3 node used to be connected to drive the appearance of the main body of the tank:

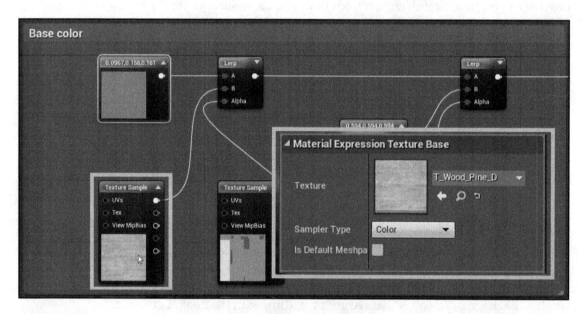

Remember that the shortcut for the **Texture Sample** node is the *T* on your keyboard. Hold it and left-click anywhere within the material graph to create one!

There are a couple of extra things that we can do to this texture—firstly, we can probably adjust the tiling so that the wood veins are a bit closer to each other. Secondly, we might want to rotate it just to modify the current direction of the image. Even though this is an aesthetic choice, it's useful to get familiar with these nodes, as they are often quite useful.

4. **Add a texture coordinate node** and give it a value of 3, for instance, or adjust it until you are happy with the result. There's a keyboard shortcut for this node as well, and it's the *U* key. Hold it and left-click with your mouse to make it appear!

5. Next, create a **CustomRotator** node and before the recently created **Texture Coordinate** one. Plug the output of that texture sample into the **UVs (V2)** input pin of the **CustomRotator**, and connect the **Result Values** output node to the UVs of the **Texture Sample** where we have the wooden texture.

6. Create a simple **Constant** node and plug it into the **Rotation Angle (0-1) (S)** node of the **CustomRotator**. Give it a value of **0.25** if you want to rotate the texture 90 degrees:

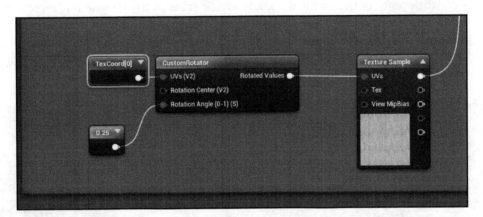

You might be wondering why a value of **0.25** equates to a rotation value of **90** degrees. This is because the **Rotation Angle** expects a value in the range between 0 and 1, which it then translates into a 0 to 360 degree range. With that in mind, **0.25** is the value that corresponds to 90 following that same logic.

Next, let's add a little extra variation to other parts of the material. I'd like to focus on the other two masked elements—the tires and the metallic parts, and make them a little bit more interesting, visually speaking.

7. Change the color of the rubber constant3 vector to something that better represents that material. At the moment, we've been using a blueish color, so something closer to black would probably be a better match—even though white can be quite cool as well. Make it your own!

8. Create a **Multiply** node right after that constant3 vector and hook its **A** input pin to the output of the same constant3. Give the **B** value something like 0.5, which can be done in the **Details** panel without the need to create a new Constant.

9. **Lerp** between the default value of the constant3 and the result of the previous multiplication. We'll be feeding the **Alpha** in the next steps.

10. Create a **Texture Sample** and assign the **T_Smoked_Tiled_D** asset to its texture slot.

11. Connect a **Texture Coordinate** node to the just created **Texture Sample** and give it a higher value than the default 1. I've gone with 3, just so we can see the effect this will have more clearly in the future.

12. Drag a pin out of the **Texture Sample** node for the new black and white smoke texture and create a **Cheap Contrast** node.

13. Create a constant and connect it to the **Cheap Contrast** node. This will increase the difference between the dark and white areas of the texture it is affecting, making the final effect more obvious.

14. Connect the result of the **Cheap Contrast** node to the **Alpha** of the new **Lerp** node you created in *step 9*, and connect the output of that to the original **Lerp** node that is being driven by the texture mask:

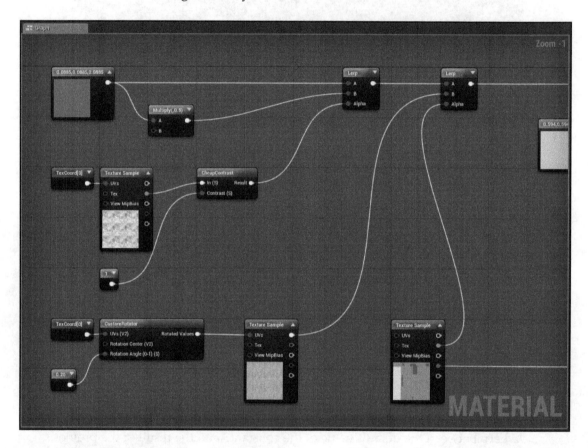

We've managed to introduce a little bit of color variation thanks to the use of the smoke texture as a mask. This is something that we'll come back to in future recipes, as it's quite useful when you want to create non-repetitive materials.

Clicking on the teapot icon in the **Material Editor Viewport** whichever mesh you have selected on the **Content Browser** as the visible asset. This is useful for previewing changes without moving back and forward between the material editor and the main viewport.

Finally, let's introduce some extra changes to the metallic parts of the model in a very similar way to what we've done with the rubber. To do that, head over to the Roughness section of the material graph.

15. Create a **Texture Sample** parameter and assign the **T_MacroVariation** texture to it. This will serve as the **Alpha** for a new **Lerp** node we are about to create.
16. Add two simple constants and give them two different values. Keep in mind that these will affect the **Roughness** of the metallic parts when choosing the values.
17. Include a **Lerp** node and plug the new constants into the **A** and **B** input pins. Remember to also plug in the red channel of the **Texture Sample** to the **Alpha**.

Why are we connecting the Red channel into the **Alpha** of the **Lerp** node? Each individual channel of an image offers a black and white picture, in contrast with the RGB output, which gives us a color texture.

18. Finally, replace the initial constant that was driving the **Roughness** value of the metallic parts with the node network we have created in the three previous steps. The graph should now look something like this:

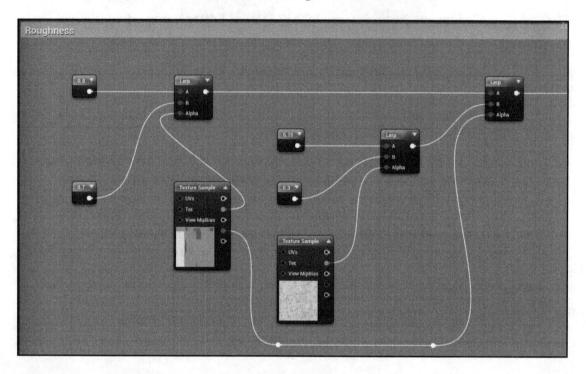

And after doing that, let's now... oh, wait, I think we can call it a day! After all of those changes have been made, we will be left with a nice new material that is a more realistic version of the shaders we had previously created. Furthermore, everything we've done constitutes the basics of setting up a real material in Unreal Engine 4. Combining textures with math operations, blending nodes according to different masks, and taking advantage of different assets to create specific effects are everyday tasks that many artists working with the engine have to face. And now you know how to as well! Let's check out the results before moving on, and see you in the next recipe:

How it works...

We are at a point where I feel it's pertinent to talk about the importance of correctly laid-out UVs. Everything we've used so far relies on them—starting with the Texture Samples we've placed to the masks that drive the position of the different material effects we are using. They map where these different nodes are placed across the surfaces of our models, but they are also a part of the 3D modeling process that I feel doesn't receive enough attention.

This is partly because 3D models are created in a wide variety of computer programs. Some of them allow for UV editing, and they tend to be the most 3D oriented packages: Max, Maya, C4D, Blender. However, other useful programs that can also create these type of assets don't allow you to edit the UVs of the models, and this is something that limits what can be done inside of Unreal. If that's your case, you might want to consider taking your models to a program that lets you create and edit the UVs. For instance, Blender is a freely available package that you can try to use to do just that as well as many more things. The point is, UVs are quite important in the context of Unreal and this should be noted before moving forward.

There's more...

The material we've created in this recipe isn't a particularly complex one—it has some basic math thanks to us using the **Lerp** node, and it also includes a couple of Texture Samples that drive the appearance of the final shader. Even though this isn't something very demanding, I didn't want to pass over the opportunity of introducing certain limitations that arrive when working with mobile platforms. Better to talk about them now, while we haven't encountered any issues, rather than wait until we hit a wall.

The first thing to talk about when mixing textures and mobile platforms is the maximum size these type of assets can have. It's 2K, or 2048 by 2048 pixels. There are other quirks though: for example, the images we use need to be a power of two, preferably square (64 x 64), but definitely at least complying with that first requirement (512 x 64 would also be accepted).

Apart from this, which is something to get right from the beginning, it is also recommended to leave the **Compression** settings as either the **Default** or the **Normal Map** option, as they require the least amount of memory. Following that logic, using as few textures as possible will help to keep the memory demands of your project low and the number of texture requests from memory at a nice point.

Now that you know a bit more about this topic, test yourself by going back and changing the different parts of the material that we've created. Changing the textures that we've used, playing with the rotation values, or modifying the roughness and metallic properties will make you more confident in your skills, so make sure to give it a go!

See also

I wanted to leave you with the official documentation that Epic Games provides for using Textures in Unreal Engine: `https://docs.unrealengine.com/en-us/Engine/Content/Types/Textures`.

They provide a thorough look at that type of asset within the engine, even going so far as giving guidelines for importing different images, best practices, and how to create some more complex textures such as normal maps. Don't hesitate to check it out!

A plastic cloth using Fresnel and detail texturing

We've started to use textures extensively in the previous recipe, and while at it we also had the opportunity to talk about certain useful nodes, such as the **Cheap Contrast** one or the **CustomRotator**. Just like those two, Unreal includes several other ones that are there for a number of reasons, sometimes to improve the look of our models or to create specific effects in a smart way. Whatever the case, learning about them is sure to improve the look of our scenes.

In this recipe, we'll be taking a look at some of those useful nodes to create a velvety effect, something that would be more difficult without them. Let's take a look at them!

Getting ready

The scene we are going to use is similar to one we worked on in previous recipes from `Chapter 2`, *Post Processing Effects*, but it includes a new element that is going to be the focus of our work. The name of the level is **03_04_AdvancedTechniques_Start** and it can be found in the following folder: `Content / UE4ShadersAndEffects / Maps / Chapter03 / 03_02_MaterialInstance_Start`.

If you want to follow, know that we'll be creating a velvet-like material. You can use your own 3D model and scene if you want, as the only thing you'll need is an asset that is properly UV-mapped to start. All of the assets that we'll be using are part of the **Starter Content**, except for one texture that we are providing with the Unreal Project.

How to do it...

Here is an screenshot that highlights what we'll be doing in the following pages:

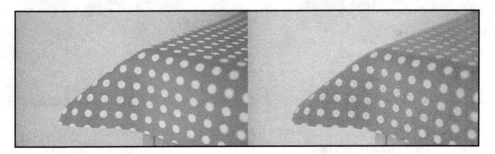

We are going to take a simple material and enhance it thanks to some of Unreal's material nodes, which will help us—with very little effort on our side—to improve its final appearance. First of all, open the level **03_04_AdvancedTechniques_Start** and open the material that is being applied to the tablecloth, named **M_TableCloth_Start**, as we are going to be working on that one. As you can see, it only has a single **Texture Sample** applied, being driven by a **Texture Coordinate** node that is adjusting the tiling of the asset:

1. Create a **Constant3** vector and give it a soft red color, similar to the one being displayed on the existing Texture Sample. I've chosen values of **R = 0.90**, **G = 0.44**, and **B = 0.44**. We'll use this to drive a future effect with it.

2. Add a **Lerp** node after both the original **Texture Sample** and the Constant3 vector, and connect the two nodes to its **A** and **B** pins.

3. It's not time to introduce a new node. Right-click anywhere within the material graph and type `Fresnel`, and create that node.

4. Connect the output of the **Fresnel** node to the **Alpha** of the **Lerp**. This is the material graph we should now be looking at:

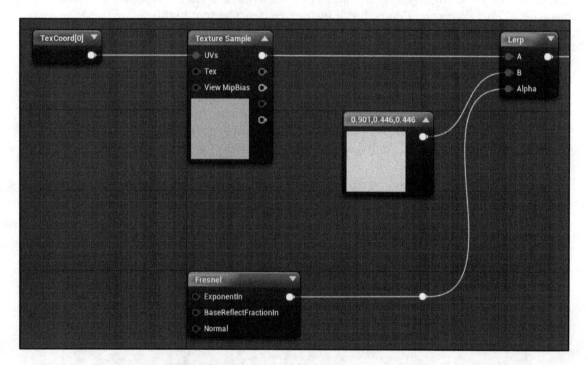

The **Fresnel** effect node modifies the value of a given pixel depending on the angle from which it is being viewed by the camera. When the normal of the surface you are viewing points directly at you, the value will be zero, whilst when the surface normal is perpendicular to the camera, a value of **1** will be in place. This creates a black and white gradient that varies according to the camera position and the surface the node is affecting, something quite useful in different circumstances. In our case, where we are dealing with a cloth-like material, we can use it to simulate the light dispersion on velvety surfaces, as the pixels that face the camera will be seen differently to those that are directed elsewhere.

5. Select the **Fresnel** node and head over to the **Details** panel. Set the **Exponent** parameter to something lower than the default, which will make the effect more apparent. I've gone with **2.5**, which seems to work fine:

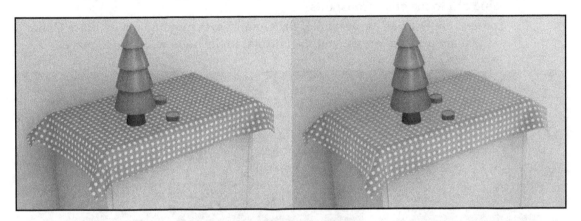

Next up, we are going to start using another new different node: the **Detail Texturing** one. This node allows us to use two different textures to enhance the look of a material. Its usefulness resides in the ability to create highly detailed models without the need for large texture assets. Of course, there might be other cases where this is also useful beyond the example I've just mentioned. Let's see how to set it up.

6. Right-click in the material graph and type `Detail Texturing`. You'll see a new node appear, the one we want to use.

7. In order to work with this node, we are going to need some extra ones as well create three constants and two **Texture Samples**.

8. Connect the constants to the scale, diffuse intensity, and normal intensity input pins. We'll give them values later.

9. Set the **T_ground_Moss_D** and the **T_ground_Moss_N** as the assets in the **Texture Samples** we have created. They are part of the **Starter Content**, so you should have them with you already.

Using the **Detail Texturing** node presents a little quirk, in that the previous two **Texture Samples** that we've created will need to be converted into what is known as a **Texture Object**.

10. Right-click on the two **Texture Samples** we've created and select the second option, **Convert to Texture Object**.

11. Give the first constant, the one connected to the **Scale** pin, a value of **20** and a value of **1** to the other **Constants**.

12. Connect the **Diffuse** output pin of the **Detail Texturing node** in the **Base Color** of the main material graph, and the **Normal** to the node with the same name:

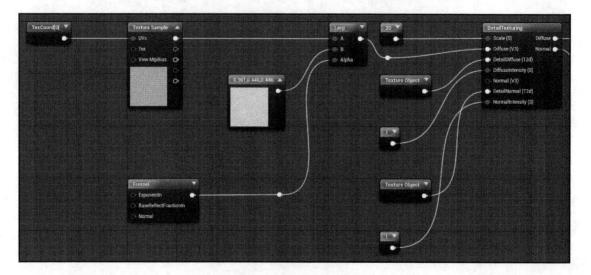

With that out of the way, we are pretty much done. However, let's use the Fresnel node before we go once again to drive the **Roughness** parameter of the material. The idea is to use the **Fresnel node** again, but this time to specify the Roughness values. We want the parts that are facing the camera to have less clear reflections than the parts that are perpendicular to our vision, see let's do that!

13. Create two constants, and give them different values. I've gone with **0.65** and **0.35**: more rough if we are looking directly at the surface, less so around the areas that don't face us.

14. Add a **Lerp** node, and connect the previously created Constants to its **A** and **B** pins. The rougher value (**0.65**) should go into **A**.

15. Drag another pin from our original **Fresnel** node and hook it to the **Alpha** of the new **Lerp**. The final graph should look something along these lines:

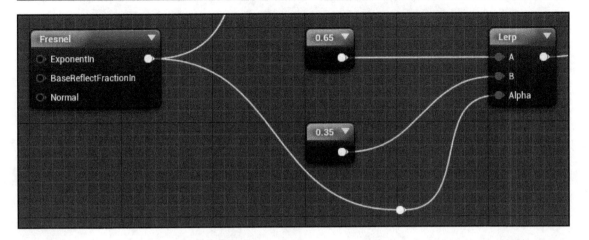

Finally, all we need to do is to click on the **Apply** and **Save** buttons and assign the material to our model in the main viewport. I'll leave you with a final image of what we've created, compared to what we used to have:

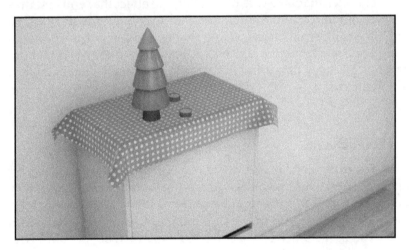

See you in the next section!

How it works...

Let's take a minute to go over how the **Fresnel** node works once again, as it can be tricky to grasp at first. As we've already mentioned, this effect consists of giving a different value to each pixel depending on the direction the normal at that point is facing. However, there are certain settings we haven't yet gone over the parameters it takes, specifically.

There are three in this version of the node: **ExponentIn**, **BaseReflectFrctionIn**, and **Normal**. The first of them controls the falloff of the effect, and higher values will make it only visible on the parts of a surface that are perpendicular to the camera. The second attribute specifies, put technically, "the fraction of specular reflection when the surface is viewed from straight on". This basically specifies how the areas that are neither facing the camera nor perpendicular to it behave. The **Normal** parameter lets us input such a map to modify the effect.

Detail texturing is also a handy node to get familiar with, as seen in this example. But even though it's quite easy to use, we don't really need it to blend and use at the same time two textures or assets. As with pretty much everything else in Unreal, this task can be done thanks to the use of a series of logically connected nodes, as we are about to see. So, how does detail texturing work?

The answer can be found if you double-click on the node itself. Doing that will open up a material function called **DetailTexturing**, which comes bundled with Unreal as part of the Engine Content; more about this in the There's More section, next. This material function contains a bunch of nodes that take care of creating the effect that you end up seeing, and you can check them out inside of the editor. Because they are normal nodes, you can copy and paste them into your own material. Doing that would remove the need to use the **Detail Texturing** node itself, but this also highlights why we use Material Functions in the first place they are a nice way of reusing the same logic across different materials whilst keeping things organized.

There's more...

Just as the Detail Texturing node is part of the content that comes bundled with the engine, so are plenty of other functions and assets. Accessing them is not a straightforward operation, and for good reason—it's often best to leave these assets alone if you don't know exactly what you are doing. However, we can find many examples from which we can learn, just like we did in the preceding section. Not only that, but certain assets (such as specific textures or models) are also hidden as part of that content, so accessing it is always useful. If you want to do so, make sure to check the **View Options** icon situated in the lower right-hand corner of the **Content Browser** and tick the checkbox for **Show Engine Content**:

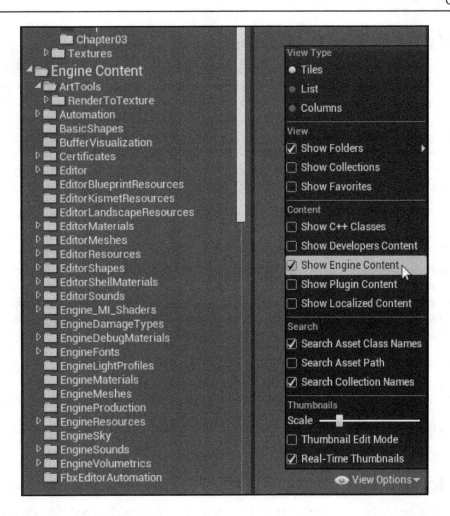

That's all you need to do!

See also

You can find more documentation about the Fresnel and the Detail Texturing nodes through Epic's official documents:

https://docs.unrealengine.com/en-us/Engine/Rendering/Materials/HowTo/Fresnel

https://docs.unrealengine.com/en-us/Engine/Rendering/Materials/HowTo/
DetailTexturing

Creating a semi procedural material

So far, we've worked on examples of materials that were applied to relatively small 3D models, where a single texture or color was enough to make them look good. However, that is but one case from the many different ones that we can encounter in a real-life project. Sometimes, we will face other scenarios where we have to deal with bigger meshes, making the texturing process not as straightforward as we've seen so far. In those circumstances, we are forced to think creatively and find ways to realistically shade that asset. Thankfully, Unreal provides us with a very robust material editor and several ways of tackling this issue, as we'll see next.

Getting ready

We are about to use several different assets to semi-procedurally texture a 3D model, but all of the resources that you will need come bundled by default with Unreal Engine 4. Be sure to include the **Starter Content** if you want to follow along using the same textures and models I'll be using, but don't worry if you want to use your own everything we are about to do can be done with very simple assets that you can get on the web.

As always, if you have the Unreal project that we are providing you alongside this book you can open the level named **03_04_SemiProceduralMaterial_Start**, which you can find in the following folder: `Content / UE4ShadersAndEffects / Maps / Chapter03`.

See you in the next section!

How to do it...

Let's start this recipe by opening up the **03_04_SemiProceduralMaterial_Start** level and looking at the problems that we have to deal with when working with large-scale surfaces. As you can see, I've placed two cameras in the scene, just so we can better understand what we are dealing with. The geometry is quite simple, as we only have a plane, but that will be enough for this case. Let's take a look through the cameras:

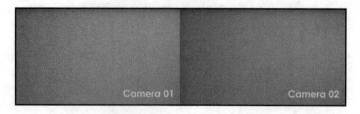

As you can see, the first image is actually quite nice we have a concrete floor that looks like a concrete floor! However, things start to get messy once the camera gets farther from the ground. Even though it's difficult to notice, the repetition of the texture across the surface is starting to show up, and the overall look is quite bland because of that. This is what we are going to try to fix in this recipe: creating materials that look good both up close and far from the camera thanks to semi-procedural material creation techniques. Let's dive right in:

1. Open up the material being applied to the plane, which is **M_SemiProceduralConcrete_Start**. You should see a lonely Texture Sample (**T_Concrete_Poured_D**) node being driven by a **Texture Coordinate**, which is currently adjusting the tiling. This will serve as our starting point.

2. Add another Texture Samples, and set the **T_Rock_Marble_Polished_D** texture from the **Starter Content** as its value. We are going to blend between these first two images thanks to the use of a third one, which will serve as a mask.

Using multiple similar assets can be key when creating semi-procedural content. Blending between two or more textures in a random pattern helps to alleviate the visible tiling across big surfaces.

3. Create a **Texture Coordinate** node and give it a value of 20 both in the **UTiling** and the **VTiling** sections of the **Details** panel. Hook the output node to the **UVs** input pin of the previous two texture samples.

The next step would be to create a **Lerp** node that we could use to randomize between the first two images. However, if we want to fully mix the two initial assets, we need to have a black and white image as a mask, and even though we've selected one, it doesn't completely work as it currently is. Let's take a look at it:

As you can see, it's more of a gray and white image rather than a black and white one. Even though that is great to blend between two textures (after all, gray values sample from the two assets), we still want to see fully white or black areas every now and then. If we do that, we would be ensuring that the black parts of the mask show **Input A**, the white parts show **Input B**, and the gray areas display a mixture of both. That's the ideal scenario, as we would get both textures and a soft blend between them in certain areas. We can achieve that effect if we increase the contrast of the image used as a mask.

4. Create a new **Texture Sample** and assign the **T_MacroVariation** resource to it.

5. Create a **Cheap Contrast** node after this last **Texture Sample** and hook its input pin to the output of said texture (**T_MacroVariation**).

6. **Add a Constant** and connect it to the contrast slot in the **Cheap Contrast** node. Give it a value of **0.5**, so that we achieve the desired effect we mentioned before:

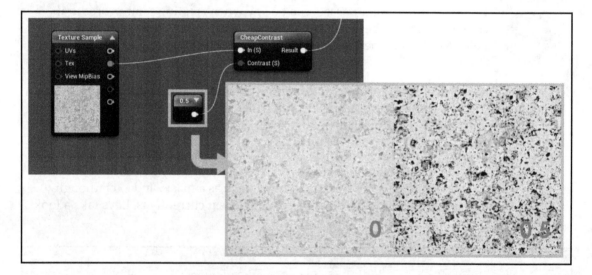

If you want to preview how a certain node is affecting the material graph, you can do so by right-clicking on the desired node and selecting the **Start Previewing Node** option.

7. Create a **Lerp** node, which we'll use to combine the first two texture samples according to the mask we've created in the previous step.

8. Connect the output nodes of the first two textures
(**T_Rock_Marble_Polished_D** and **T_Concrete_Poured_D**) to the **A** and **B** input
pins of the **Lerp** node, and connect the **Alpha** to the output of the **Cheap
Contrast** node. The graph should now look something like this:

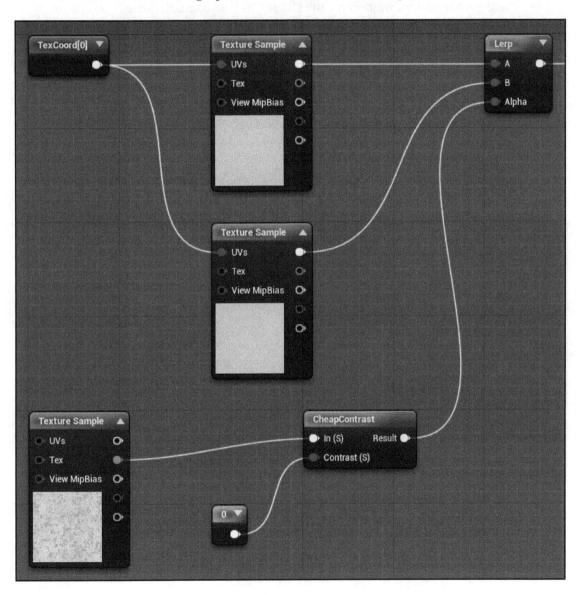

We've managed to add variety and randomness to our material thanks to the graph we've created in the previous steps. In spite of that, there's still room for improvement, as we can take the previous approach one step further and improve upon what we've created. We will now include a third texture, which will help to further randomize the shader, as well as teach ourselves how to further modify an image within Unreal.

9. Create a new combo made out of a **Texture Coordinate** and a **Texture Sample**. Assign the **T_Rock_Sandstone_D** asset as the default value of the **Texture Sample**, and give the **Texture Coordinate** a value of 15 in both the **U** and the **V** tiling fields.

10. Add a **Desaturation** node and a **Constant** one right after that last **Texture Sample**. Give the **Constant** a value of 0.95 and connect it to the **Fraction** input pin of the **Desaturation** node.

11. Connect the output of the last created **Texture Sample** into the main input node of the **Desaturation** node:

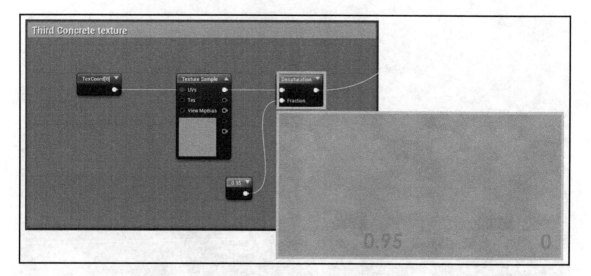

Following these steps has left us with a texture quite similar to the other ones we've been using as concrete lookalikes, which will enable us to further mix it with the rest without it looking too out of place. Let's create the final blend mask!

12. Add a new **Texture Sample** with the **T_MacroVariation** asset as its selected texture.

13. Include a **Texture Coordinate** node giving it a value of 2.

14. Add a **CustomRotator** node, and hook it to the previously created **Texture Coordinate** one.

15. Create a **Constant** and feed it to the **Rotation Angle** input pin of the **CustomRotator**. Give it a value of **0.167**, which will mean a rotation of 60 degrees.

 Why does a value of 0.167 equate to a rotation value of 60 degrees? Just like we saw two recipes ago, the Custom Rotator node maps the 0 to 360 degree range to a range of 0 to 1. This makes 0.167 roughly 60 degrees - 60.12 degrees, to be precise!

16. Hook the **Custom Rotator** into the **Texture Sample**.

17. Create a new Lerp node, and feed the previous **Texture Sample** into the **Alpha** input pin.

18. Connect the **A** pin to the output of the original **Lerp** and connect the **B** pin to the third concrete texture. We are now finished creating random variation for this material!

If you have any doubts about the final graph, be sure to check the material we are providing as an example **M_SemiProceduralConcrete_End**. Our end result will be visible in this final image:

As you can see, the final shader looks good both up close and far away from the camera. This is happening thanks to the techniques we've used, which help reduce the repetition across our 3D models quite dramatically. Be sure to pay attention to these methods, as they are quite awesome!

How it works...

The principles behind this technique are quite simple—just introduce enough randomness as you can so you can cheat the eye into thinking there's no one texture repeating endlessly. Even though the principle is simple to grasp, tricking the eye is no simple task and as the surfaces you work on increase in size, so will your challenge as an artist.

Choosing the right textures for the job is part of the solution—be sure to blend gently between different layers, and don't overuse the same masks throughout the entirety of your projects. Doing so could result in the eye knowing what's going on. In general, this is a method that has to be increasingly tested. Keep that in mind!

There's more...

In this recipe, we've created what could be considered as semi-procedural materials through the use of several black and white gradient noise textures. However, they are limited in that they too repeat themselves just like the images we were using as the base color. Thankfully, we have access to the **Noise** node in Unreal, which gets rid of that limitation:

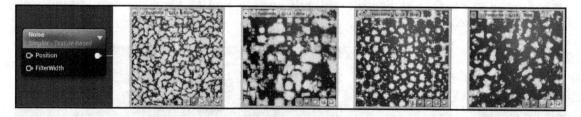

This node is exactly what we are looking for in order to create fully procedural materials. As you can see, it creates random patterns that we have a great deal of control over through the settings in the **Details** panel, and the resulting maps are similar to the ones we've used in this recipe.

The reason why we didn't take advantage of this asset is because it is taxing on the performance of our apps, so it's often used to create nice looking materials that are then baked. We'll be taking a look at that in the next recipe, so be sure to check it out!

See also

Before we go, you can find an extensive article on the **Noise** node at the following link: `https://www.unrealengine.com/en-US/tech-blog/getting-the-most-out-of-noise-in-ue4`

It's also a great resource if you want to learn more about procedural content creation, so be sure to give it a go!

Baking out a material

Materials are a type of asset that can be sometimes simplified without losing any quality. Think, for example, about the shader we created in the previous recipe—we made use of several nodes to make sure that it looked good both on close-ups as well as when the camera was far from the object the material was being applied to. Creating materials that way can sometimes be expensive for the GPU, especially if the object that is being rendered is very far from the screen or at a point where we can no longer make out the subtleties on its surface.

For those cases, Unreal offers us the possibility of baking out a material into another one, a more simplified version of our initial asset. What we'll be doing now is reducing the complexity of the original material graphs by baking out simple textures that behave just like the more complicated original material graphs we had previously set up. Let's go!

Getting ready

The scene we will be using throughout this recipe is the level named **03_06_BakingAMaterial_Start**, located in the following folder: `Content / UE4ShadersAndEffects / Maps / Chapter03`.

We will be using the same scene we saw in the recipe called Simulating velvet through Fresnel and Detail Texturing, as it includes several assets that we will be able to merge or optimize. If you want to follow on your own, there might be some considerations to take into account, such as the following:

- The 3D models need to be correctly UV-unwrapped.
- The UVs need to stay in the 0 to 1 UV space.

- There need to be no dynamic effects happening within your base materials, such as vertex animation or panning textures.
- Only Static Meshes; Skeletal Meshes are not supported.

With that in mind, let's get to it!

How to do it...

In this recipe, we are not only going to be looking at materials and textures, but also at **Blueprints!** If you are using Unreal, you are bound to come into contact with them – they are basically the **Visual Scripting** language that Unreal uses, a helpful way for artists to create functionality without the need to learn how to program. We will be creating a very simple Blueprint to help us bake a material, so let's start with that:

1. Create a Blueprint anywhere in the **Content Browser**. I'm creating mine in the same folder where all of the assets for this Chapter live, inside **Content** | **UE4ShadersAndEffects** | **Assets** | **Chapter03** | **MaterialBaking**. I've named mine **BP_MaterialBaker**:

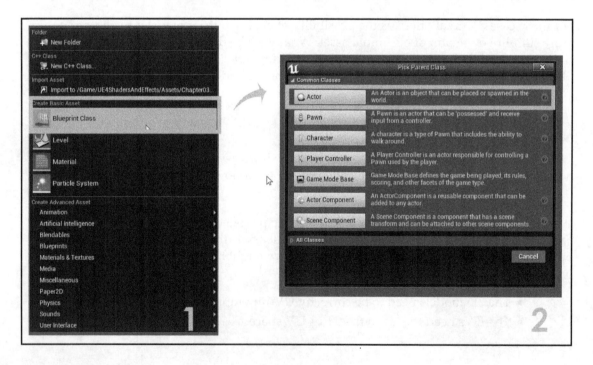

2. Apart from the **Blueprint**, we'll also need a **Render Target**. You can create one by right-clicking in the same folder as before, and choosing **Materials & Textures | Render Target**. I've named it **RT_TextureTarget**:

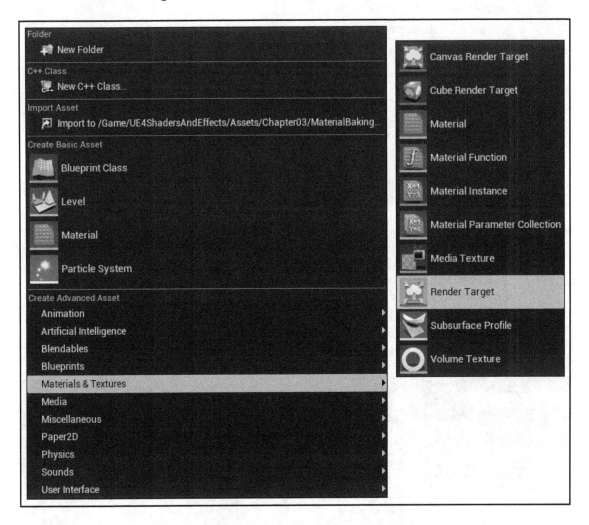

Even though this is just the first time we've used Render Targets so far, they are quite straightforward. Think of them as a white canvas in which you can store image information that you want to render. They are, in a way, the opposite of textures, in that we don't read info from them as much as we store data inside.

3. Open up the **Blueprint** you've just created and select all of the nodes that exist on the Event Graph. Delete them all! If you don't know your way around the Blueprint editor, check the *How it works...* section of this recipe. They are quite straightforward!

4. Create a **Custom Event** and give it a name—I'll go with **OnBake**. To create one, just right-click anywhere within the Event Graph and start typing Custom Event—it will eventually appear before you.

5. Drag a line from the execution pin of the Custom Event node and create a **Draw Material To Render Target** function.

Every time that you drag a line from a pin and then release the left mouse button, you'll be immediately prompted to create a new node, just as if you clicked with the right mouse button. The advantage of this is that the nodes that you'll be able to create will be context sensitive, meaning that you'll only see the nodes that make sense to be created according to the one where you are coming from!

6. Again, drag a line from the **Texture Render Target** and the **Material** pins of the just created **Draw Material** To **Render Target** node. Select the **Promote to Variable** option in both cases. Give them appropriate names, like **RenderTargetTexture** and **MaterialToRender**.

7. Make the variables **Public**. You can do so by clicking on the Eye icon to the right of their names in the Variables section of the **MyBlueprint** panel. The Even Graph should now look something like this:

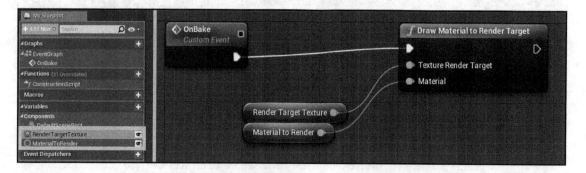

Let's now head over to the **Construction** script, where we'll be calling the Custom Event, which we've just created.

8. Drag from the pin of the **Construction** Script and start typing `OnBake` as soon as you release the mouse. That will let you create a node that will trigger the functionality that we created before.

9. Click on **Save** and **Compile**:

With that done, we have almost everything we need to bake out our materials. But before we do, we need to slightly modify the base materials that we are about to bake. Because of that, let's follow the next steps:

10. Create a copy of the material that you want to bake. I'll do so with the **M_TableCloth** one, which I'll rename **M_TableCloth_Baking**.

11. Open it up and set the **Shading Model** to **Unlit**.

If you open **M_TableCloth_Baking**, you'll be able to see that I've removed certain parts of the graph, especially the **Fresnel** node. This is because the material baker can't process screen space effects or dynamic nodes, so keep that in mind!

The next steps are going to be quite important—we are going to be exporting one texture at a time, so we need to hook up each section of the graph that we want to export into the **Emissive Color** pin of the main material node. In other words, each cable that we were connecting into the **Base Color** or the **Roughness** nodes previously will now be connected into the Emissive one. As it only accepts one line, we'll do it as many times as we need to.

12. Connect the **Diffuse** output pin from the **DetailTexturing** node into the **Emissive Color** pin of the main material graph.

13. Drag and drop the **BP_MaterialBaker** blueprint from the Content Browser into the scene, and place it wherever you want.

14. Assign the appropriate render target and material that you want to bake in the **Details** panel. After that, move the blueprint around (this is needed for the **Render Target** texture to update):

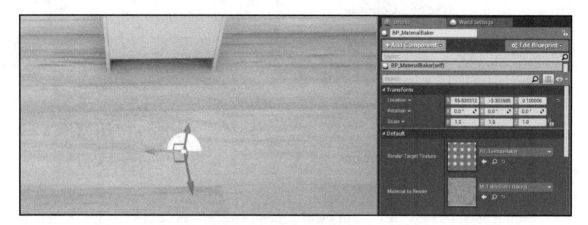

Once all of these steps are done, the render target should have created a new texture containing the information of the diffuse color for the material that we've specified. Because that information lives inside of the render target, and we don't want to lose that data, we need to create a texture out of it.

15. Select the render target (we called it **RT_TextureBaker**) within the Content Browser and right-click on it. Select the **Create Static Texture** option.

16. Rename the newly created asset something unique, such as **T_TableCloth_Baked_D**. Remember that for every different texture that your original material contains, you will have to repeat *steps 12* to *16*. Now that we have a new baked texture, let's create a new material and replace the original one to compare the results.

17. Create a new material and drag the newly created texture into it. Connect it to the **Base Color** node.

18. Replace the material that is being applied to the **SM_ShoeRackRug** model with the new one:

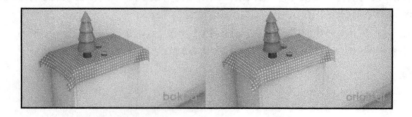

As you can see, both the original material and the newly baked one look identical, but we have an increase in performance using the first one.

How it works...

Something we need to talk about briefly is the Blueprint Editor. Even though we've used it lightly in this recipe, it might be a good idea to go over it if we want to get the most out of Unreal. Before we jump into it, let's remind ourselves how to create a Blueprint; just right-click anywhere in the **Content Browser** and select the **Blueprint** option. Once we have something to work upon, double-click on it and let's take a look at the Blueprint editor:

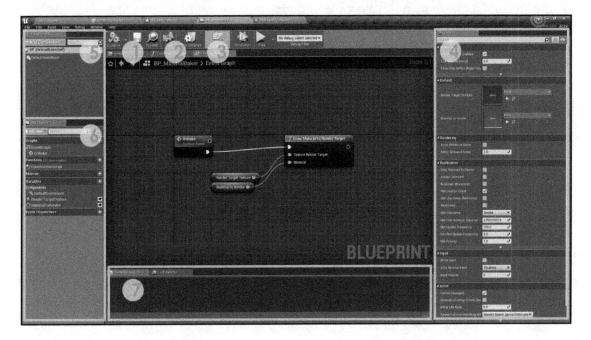

1. **Viewport**: This is where you can see the assets that can be part of the Blueprint, if any. Things such as static meshes would appear in here.
2. **Construction Script**: The place to code the functionality that happens before runtime, whilst you are on the editor.
3. **Event Graph**: This is the section where we code different functionalities through Visual Scripting.
4. **Details panel**: Similar to other sections we've seen elsewhere, this offers context-sensitive information.
5. **Components tab**: A window that display the hierarchy of the Blueprint.

6. **My Blueprint**: Section of the asset that displays all of the available meta assets, such as the graphs, functions, variables, and components.
7. **Compiler results and find results**: A handy place to see if everything we are doing plays nicely with the editor or if there's something we should worry about.

Those are the basic sections, and we've used several ones in this recipe—the Event Graph and the Construction Script specifically. We are sure to be coming back to it later on!

There's more...

Before we go, I'd like to mention a couple of things that were left unsaid. First of all, the resolution of the render target. You can change it according to your needs, and doing so is quite simple: just double-click on the asset itself to open up the texture editor, and focus on the **Details** panel. Size X and Size Y determine its resolution, so set it to whatever you need!

Something else that you might want to check out is the **Merge Actors** tool. You can find it under **Window | Developer Tools**, and it allows you to do something very similar to what we've done in this recipe. Even though it can also merge actors, you can use it on a single model to create a simpler version of the material that is being applied. Make sure to check the **Use Specific LOD Level** under the **LOD Selection Type** settings to enable the material baking part of the tool, and then play with the options under **Material** settings to create the material you want. It's quite a straightforward process, so be sure to check it out!

All of those techniques are really helpful in multiple game development scenarios, especially during the late stages of development. Think, for instance, about a level where you've crammed in multiple different assets. Performance might be an issue, especially on low-end devices that don't support as many materials at the same time onscreen. Using these techniques can help reduce the number of draw calls, as well as the complexity of the shaders themselves. Keeping those elements in line can be helpful whenever you struggle maintaining an even level of performance, hence their importance.

See also

This functionality is based on a tutorial from Epic, which you can find here: `https://www.youtube.com/watch?v=WaM_owaUpbE`.

You can read a little bit more about the topic on the following website: `https://docs.unrealengine.com/en-us/Engine/Actors/Merging`.

Distance-based texture blending

We are now going to learn how to blend between a couple of different textures according to how far we are from them. Even though it's great to have a complex material that works both when the camera is close to the 3D model or far from it, having a complex material graph operating on a model that only occupies a small percentage in our screens can be a bit too much. This is especially true if we can achieve the same effect with a much lower resolution texture.

With that goal in mind, we are going to take a look at another useful node available in the material graph that will make our lives easier. Let's get started!

Getting ready

If we take a look back at one of the recipes that we've tackled in this chapter, you will probably remember about the semi-procedural concrete we created a couple of recipes ago. While it wasn't an overly complicated material, it did make use of several nodes and textures. This serves us well to prove what we want to show in the following pages: a material that makes use of simple textures to create a similar effect to our original complex shader. We will thus start our journey with a very similar scene to what we have already seen, and you can find it in the following folder: Content / UE4ShadersAndEffects / Maps / Chapter03 / 03_07_DistanceBasedBlending_Start.

Let's now take a look at it and start improving things in there!

How to do it...

Right before we start this recipe, I'd like to mention that I've created another texture for you, named **T_DistantConcrete_D**, which we'll be using in the following steps. The curious thing about this asset is that it's a baked texture from the original, more complex material we used in the **Creating a Semi Procedural Material** recipe. So, we are actually using two different things we learner in previous lessons—a baked texture and a semi-procedural asset. This is top-tier stuff!

With that said, let's start taking a look at how to achieve our goal of distance blending two textures:

1. Create a new material, which I've called **M_DistanceBasedConcrete**, and apply it to the plane in the center of the level. This is the humble start of our journey!
2. Add two **Texture Samples**, and choose the **T_Concrete_Poured_D** and the T_**DistantConcrete_D** resources as the selected assets.
3. Include a **Texture Coordinate** node and plug it into the first of the two Texture Samples. Give it a value of 20 for both fields in the **Details** panel, UTiling, and VTiling.
4. Finally, place a **Lerp** node into the graph and connect its **A** and **B** pins to the previous created Texture Samples:

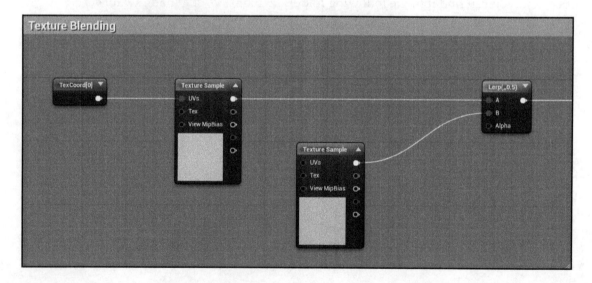

So far, everything we've done is a simple mixture of two textures, one of which we had previously used in a different recipe as our base image. The idea is to create something very similar to what we previously had, but more efficient. The part that we are now going to tackle is the **Distance Based** calculations, as we'll see next.

5. Add an **Absolute World Position** node by right-clicking anywhere within the content browser and typing `World Position`. Be careful not to type `Absolute`, as that will prevent the search box from finding the node.

6. Create a **Camera Position** node, in a similar fashion to what we've seen before for the **World Position** node. Similarly, even though you can type **Camera Position** when looking for the node, the actual name is **Camera Position WS**. The WS stands for world space.

7. Include a **Distance** node after the previous two and connect it to them. **Absolute World Position** should be plugged into the **A** input pin, and **Camera Position** should connect to **B**:

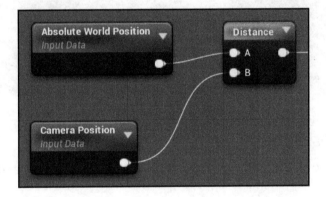

8. Next, add a **Divide** and a **Constant** node. It should appear if you just type that, as there are no other similarly named nodes. Give the constant a value of something like 256.

9. Connect the constant to the **B** pin of the **Divide** node, and connect the A to the output of the previous **distance**.

The Constant we have just created will drive the distance at which the swapping of the textures will happen. Higher numbers mean that it will be further from the camera, so feel free to play around with several values.

10. Add a **Power** node after the previous **Divide**, and connect the **Base** input pin it to that.

11. Create another **Constant** to feed the **Exp** pin of the Power node. The higher the number, the softer the transition between the two textures. Sensible numbers happen in the range from **1** to **10**, so set it to something like **4** or **5**.

12. Finally, throw a **Clamp** node into the mix at the end, right after the final Power node, and connect both. Leave the values at their default, with the 0 as a minimum and 1 as the max.

The final node we have created does what it says, because it clamps whatever range of values we feed it to a 0-to-1 range. This is precisely what we need, as the **Lerp** node expects such values. The resulting graph should look something like this:

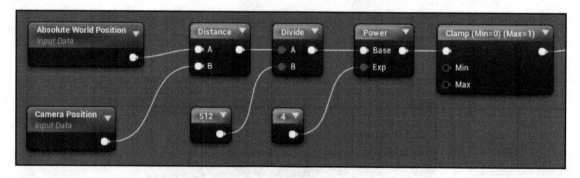

At this point, remember to connect the output pin of the **Clamp** to the **Lerp** that is blending between the two original textures.

With all of the previous steps done, we should now have a material that can effectively blend between two different assets according to the distance the model is from the camera. Of course, this approach could be expanded upon to make it so that we are not just blending between two textures, but as many as we want—it's just a matter on how far you want to take things.

One of the most useful things we can use this technique for is to reduce the cost of previously expensive materials, such as the semi-procedural concrete we used in one of the previous recipes. I'll leave you with an image that highlights the results both up-close and far away from our level's main plane using the new material, comparing it with the previous semi-procedural one we had.

Here is a close-up comparison:

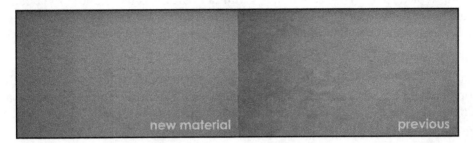

And here it is, as seen from far away:

How it works...

Let's now focus our attention for a little bit on what exactly is going on across the Distance Blend nodes we've previously created. Even though we took the time to place them in the graph, it's always good to know why we are doing the things we are doing. Plus, I promised we would take a closer look, didn't I? I like to keep my word! First, let's refresh our memory by bringing up the picture of the part of the graph that controls how we blend between the two textures according to how far away the camera is:

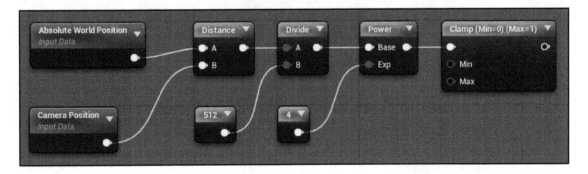

The first node, **Absolute World Position**, gives us the position of the vertices we are looking at in world space. The second one, **Camera Position**, tells us about the position of the camera in the same coordinate system as before. With those two values, we can get the distance by creating a third **Distance** node and plugging the first two nodes into its input pins.

After that, we include a fourth node that will help us control the distance at which the transition between one texture and the other happens. Its name is simply **Distance**, and we add a **Constant** node into its **B** input pin for control purposes. Higher numbers will make the fade effect happen further from the camera and vice versa.

One of the last steps is to use a **Power** node to affect the distribution of the effect across the surfaces. This is similar to what we were seeing in the **Fresnel** node, in that higher numbers will make the effect more visible beyond the central areas of the model we are looking at.

Finally, we add a **Clamp** node to get our values in the 0 to 1 range, precisely what the Lerp node we are feeding all of this sequence into is expecting.

There's more...

Sometimes, it's useful to group these nodes together. There can be plenty of reasons to do this, but I can think of two immediately: to quickly reuse them across different materials and to keep things tidy. So how do we do that?

First, create a **Material Function**. I'll name mine **MF_DistanceBlending**. You can do so if you right-click on the content browser and then select **Materials & Textures | Material Function**:

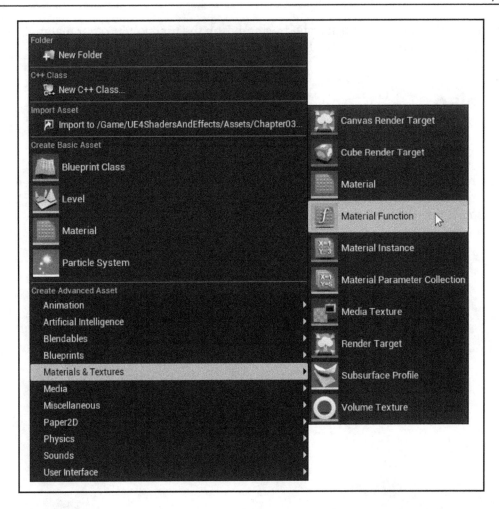

After that, copy the nodes that are driving the distance blend (the ones before the **Lerp** node in the original material) and paste them inside the function. Click on **Apply** and **Save**:

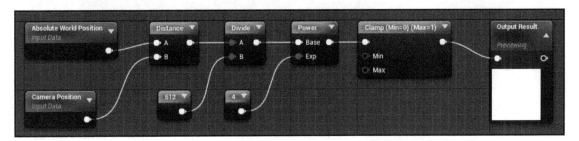

Once all of that is done, we can simply drag and drop the function into our material, replacing the nodes that were there before. Neat!

See also

You can find extra information about some of the nodes we've used, such as the **Absolute World Position**, in Epic Games' official documentation: `https://docs.unrealengine.com/ en-US/Engine/Rendering/Materials/ExpressionReference/Coordinates`. Not only that, but that reference material provides access to some extra nodes that can be quite useful to create other cool effects. We'll see some of them in future recipes, but be sure to check it out in case something catches your eye!

4
Translucent Materials and More

The previous chapter saw us dealing with multiple different materials, and, even though they were all unique, they also shared a common attribute: they all made use of the **Opaque Blend Mode** and the **Default Lit Shading Model**. In this chapter, we are going to explore other examples of materials that differ from at least one of those two attributes—so get ready to talk about translucency, refraction, subsurface shaders, and planar reflections. This is the place where we will start looking at those cases.

In this chapter, we will be covering the following topics:

- Creating a candle material with SSS
- Setting up a truly transparent glass
- A different type of translucency – holograms
- Achieving realistic reflections
- Mastering refraction by creating a pool water material
- Water caustics
- Animating a sea shaders

Let's dive right in!

Introduction

Now that we know how to properly set up and control a material in **Unreal Engine 4** (**UE4**), it's time that we get out of our comfort zone and start exploring other areas. We have a basic toolkit at our disposal, which is everything we learned in Chapter 3, *Opaque Materials and Texture Mapping*, about material masks, texture coordinate nodes, and other useful functions that we can apply within the material graph. It's now time to venture out into the wild with that knowledge and learn about other non-opaque material cases, with the final goal of mastering every possible material that we can image:

Creating a candle material with SSS

One of the first materials we'll explore outside the opaque blend mode realm is going to be wax. Wax! I think that this can serve as a good first example in this journey we are about to start, as it is a nice bridge between the Chapter 3, *Opaque Materials and Texture Mapping*, and some of the further recipes you'll find in this one. Why? Well, we'll be using the SSS shading model in order to build up this material, and that is neither too different from the previous opaque model nor too similar to some others that we'll be seeing in a few pages.

Getting ready

You can follow along by opening the `04_01_Subsurface_Start` map located inside the `Content / UE4ShadersAndEffects / Maps / Chapter04` folder. As always, all of the assets that you'll be seeing in the next few pages can be found in there—but what if you want to use your own?

You'll need a couple of things, as you did in previous chapters—the first being a basic scene setup with some lights so that we can see the materials that we are about to introduce. The second element you'll need to have is some type of model where the subsurface effect can be seen, such as a candle, an ear, a human head, or a patch of snow or ice. Even though we can apply a material that makes use of SSS to any mesh, the effect will be more obvious if it's applied to an object where it would also be visible in real life. Take the following image of the model that we'll be using as an example:

As you would expect, the thinner areas of that candle are the places where the effect will be the most visible. You might want to take that into consideration when choosing your own objects.

How to do it...

At the time of writing, Unreal offers several possibilities in terms of SSS rendering – two main ones with the **Subsurface Profile** and **Subsurface** options, and some other more specific ones, such as the pre-integrated skin method. In this section, we'll be exploring the first implementation, but we'll talk about the others in the *How it works* section. Let's start by creating the material that we'll use in this recipe:

1. Create a new material, and, assuming you've opened the previous level we mentioned in the *Getting ready* section, assign it to the `SM_Candle` static mesh in the scene that we have opened. I've named mine `M_CandleWax_SSS`. Double-click on it once created to open the Material Editor.

   If you are using your own assets, just assign the material to the model on which you want to see the subsurface effect happening.

2. Drag and drop some of the textures that we have created for you into the
    material you've just created. I've included three, named `T_ Candle_`
    `ColorAndOp`, `T_ Candle_ AORM`, and `T_ Candle_ Normals`, which you can
    see as the three texture samples here. Connect them to the appropriate nodes, as
    seen in the following screenshot:

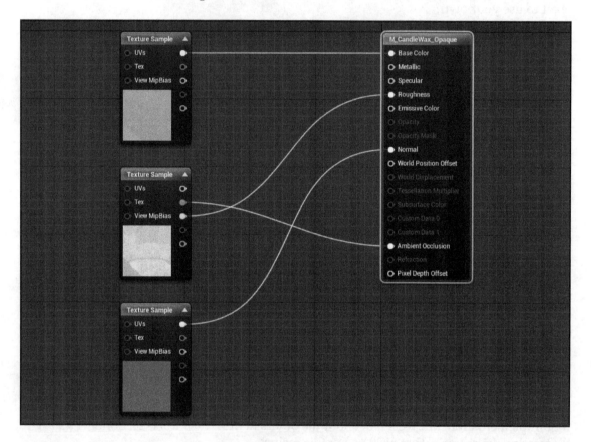

 Instead of using the textures I've mentioned before, feel free to create your
own or use simple constants to drive the appearance of those basic
properties of the material. The important stuff is what comes next: setting
up the subsurface properties of the shader.

Before we go any further, it's time to create the asset that we'll be using in the next
few steps: the **Subsurface Profile** one. We are going to need it very soon, so let's
create it now.

3. Go back to the **Content Browser** and create a new **Subsurface Profile** object. You can find the right type if you right-click and look in the **Create Advanced Asset** category: **Materials & Textures | Subsurface Profile**. I've named mine SSP_Wax:

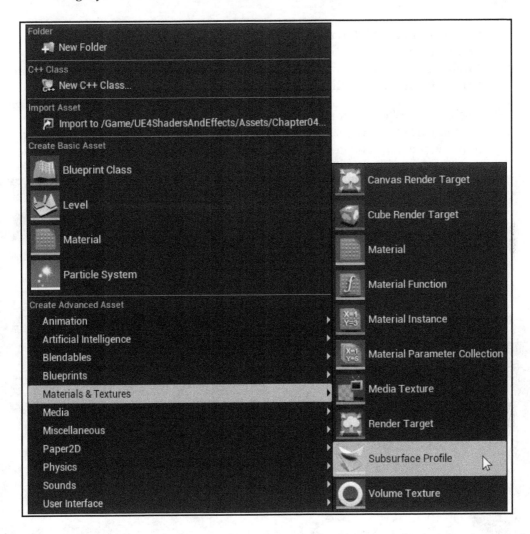

Now that we have it, we can set it up properly. Before we do that, however, let's assign it to the material that we have applied to our candle.

Not having a **Subsurface Profile** object defined for our material means that Unreal will assign it the default one, tailored to the visualization of Caucasian human skin.

4. Once back in the **Material** editor, and with nothing selected in the material graph, let's look at the **Details** panel and focus our attention on the **Shading Model** category. The default value should be **Default Lit**, but we want to change that to **Subsurface Profile**.

5. Assign **SSP_Wax** (or whatever you named your subsurface profile asset!) to the **Subsurface Profile** section of the material. You can find this category right after the previous one in the **Details** panel, as seen in the following screenshot:

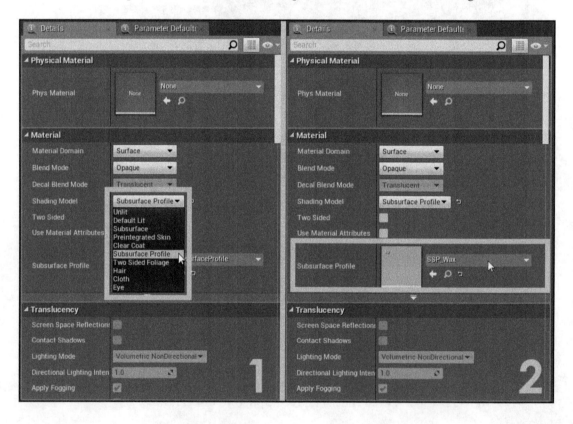

With that done, we have finally told the Unreal Engine that the material we are working with is going to behave like wax or human skin. The next steps are going to deal with tweaking that effect until it looks like what we are after, and, to achieve that, we'll need to head back to the **Subsurface Profile** object that we created and tweak its parameters. Let's do that!

It's good to have the **Subsurface Profile** object applied to the material before tweaking its properties as we are about to do, since this will enable us to check how they affect the model in real time.

6. Open the previously created **Subsurface Profile** object by double-clicking on it in the **Content Browser**. Having it open at the same time as the main viewport will help you see how the candle material changes in real time.

7. The first parameter we can change is the **Scatter Radius**. This controls the distance that the engine uses to perform the scattering effect in centimeters, which has an obvious impact on the appearance of the material. I've chosen a value of **30** so that the effect is easy to notice.

8. The next option we can tweak is the **Subsurface Color**, which acts as a control mechanism for the overall effect. You can think of it as the intensity of the effect, with a black value negating it and white acting as the opposite. Choosing a non-grayscale value, similar to the diffuse color, can give you a more interesting result, and that's what I've chosen for this category.

9. The third option we'll be talking about is the **Falloff Color**. If you change this, you'll quickly notice how this parameter affects the color of the areas where the scattering is happening the most—those where we can see the light trapped inside the material. Be sure to play with this setting until you get the result you want:

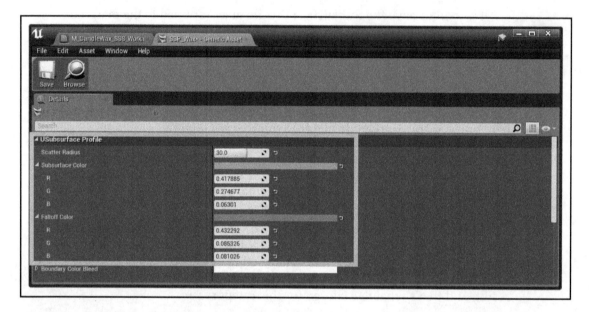

You'll note that there are some extra parameters that we haven't explored and there's a reason for that. Subsurface profile is an asset that can be used to define the subsurface behavior of many different materials, and the options that we haven't talked about were created to serve other use cases. We might come back to some of them eventually, but you can learn more about them in Epic's official documentation, available at `https://docs.unrealengine.com/en-us/Resources/Showcases/DigitalHumans`.

With all of these changes in place, there's one further interesting element that we can look at before moving on. Apart from modifying the different settings within the **Subsurface Profile** asset to get the results we want, there's also the option to make use of the **Opacity** channel within the material graph. Through this, we have the ability to change how the subsurface effect works across the entirety of our models. Going back to our candle example, we want the scattering effect to happen on the main body of the object, but not on the wick. We can set this up by plugging a mask into the **Opacity** input pin of the main material node, as seen in the following screenshot:

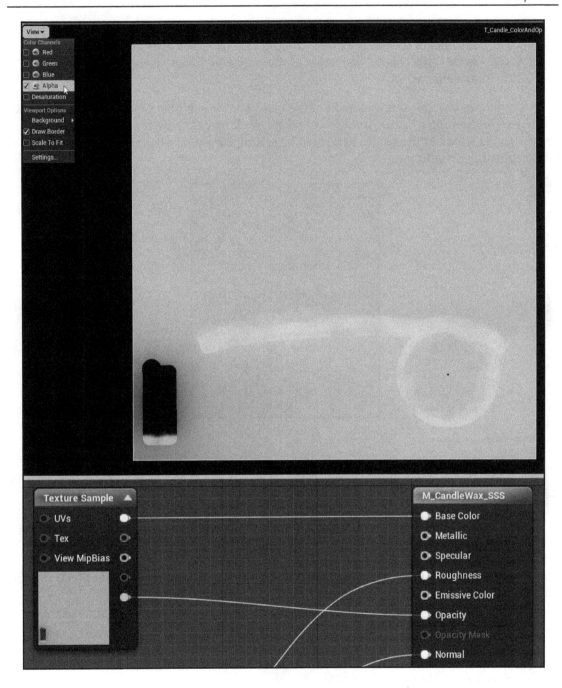

In the preceding screenshot, you can see that we've connected the **Alpha** channel of the color texture into the opacity input pin of the main material node. This channel is shown as the grayscale image at the top of the screenshot.

With all of those changes implemented in the material, we can now say that we've achieved our objective: creating a candle made out of wax. We'll leave it here for the moment, but not before having a look at the result. You must be feeling confident now about your ability to tackle subsurface shading:

From left to right: no SSS, SSS radius of 1, and SSS radius of 30; bottom: the final result

How it works...

In the previous section, we looked at the implementation of the subsurface profile shading model inside UE4. This is quite a powerful rendering technique, one that makes a huge difference when we are dealing with materials that exhibit properties such as wax or skin. But how does it work under the hood? First of all, we need to understand that this is not the only way we can enable the subsurface effect in our materials. In total, there are four shading models that can do so:

- The standard subsurface model
- The preintegrated skin model
- The subsurface profile model
- The two-sided foliage model

Each of these is geared toward achieving a specific goal, and we'll be exploring some of them in later recipes. For now, let's focus on the one we know, which is aimed for use in high-end projects.

The subsurface profile shading model works as a screen space technique, similar to what we saw with ambient occlusion or screen space reflections back in Chapter 1, *Physically-based Rendering*. This is a different implementation from what the other three methods offer, and this is the key difference we need to be aware of when working with it. While the standard subsurface shading model is cheaper and can run faster overall, using the subsurface profile model offers several advantages in terms of quality. The different settings we can modify, some of which we've already seen in the previous pages, such as scatter radius or color, help us to realistically define the effect that is applied throughout the material. Other settings, such as the ones found under the **Transmission** tab in a **Subsurface Profile** asset, help to define how light scatters from the back of an object.

I would also like to point out the difference in functionality of some of the nodes that make up a **Subsurface Profile** material. If you look at the main **Material** node in the **Material** graph, you'll see that the **Opacity** input pin is no longer grayed out, unlike what happened when we were using a **Default Lit** type of shader:

As you can see in the previous screenshot, the **Opacity** input pin is now available for us to use. However, it can be a bit counter-intuitive as to what it does—it affects the strength of the subsurface effect in our model, as we saw in this recipe, and not how opaque the 3D mesh is actually going to be.

Something else that we need to note is the limitation with regards to the **Metallic** input pin. If we plug anything into that slot, the subsurface effect will disappear; this is because that material channel has now been repurposed in shading model to accommodate the subsurface profile data. Keep that in mind!

There's more...

You might remember that the material for the candle that we created was being driven by several textures placed within the material graph. We used three main ones: `T_ Candle_ ColorAndOp`, `T_ Candle_ AORM`, and `T_ Candle_ Normals`. I'd like to talk a bit more about the first two, as we are doing something smart with them that we haven't seen before.

As you already know, some material attributes can be driven by the grayscale values. That being the case, we find ourselves in the situation where we can use the RGB channels (as well as the alpha channels) of a texture to drive certain material input. That's exactly what we are doing with the `T_Candle_AORM` asset; we store the ambient occlusion, the **Roughness**, and the **Metallic** textures into each of that image's channels (hence the **Ambient Occlusion, Roughness, and Metallic (AORM)** suffix). You can see this in the following screenshot:

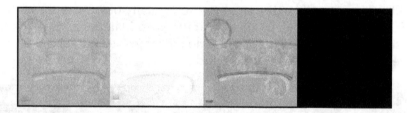

See also

Epic Games is continuously updating their documentation on this topic, so be sure to check it out at `https://docs.unrealengine.com/en-us/Engine/Rendering/Materials/LightingModels/SubSurfaceProfile`.

Setting up a truly transparent glass

After having played with a material that didn't make use of the Opaque blend mode for the first time in the previous recipe, it is now time to go a little bit further. As we just saw, a material that makes use of the subsurface profile shading model treats light differently than the examples we created in earlier chapters. The next shaders we create will follow suit; starting with a realistic glass material in this recipe, we are about to see how we can deal with these type of surfaces. Let's take a look!

Getting ready

Let me get the easiest part out of the way without delay: the scene we'll be using is called 04_02_Glass_Start, and it can be found in the Content/UE4ShadersAndEffects/Maps/Chapter04 folder.

We'll use a very similar scene to the last one, as you'll be able to see this for yourself if you want to use the same assets I'll be using. However, unlike in the previous recipe, there's no special consideration in terms of the geometry we'll employ. Where SSS is happening, models are at their best if they exhibit some of the traits their real-life counterparts show, such as the variations in thickness seen in human ears and noses. If we don't have a similar model, the effect might be more difficult to spot. Glass, on the other hand, is quite obvious – so no worries at this stage!

How to do it...

As we've seen in some of the previous recipes, we have to focus on at least two different places any time that we want to set up a new material. The first one is where most of the logic is coded, the so-called main material graph, where many of the parameters that specify what our material looks like are placed. The second one is the **Details** panel for the material itself, where we can find the options that define how that material behaves at a more intrinsic level. That is going to be our point of entry for this new recipe:

1. Create a new material for the glass located in the center of the screen and apply it to that element. This is what we'll be working on over the next few pages. I've called mine M_Glass, and this can be found in the same folder as the static mesh I'm applying it to.

2. Open up the material editor for the new asset we've created, and, with the main **Material** node selected, switch your focus to the **Details** panel. There are several things we'll want to modify here:

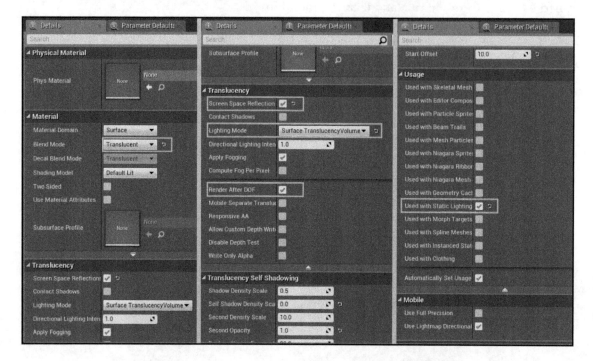

The preceding screenshot will help you identify the locations of the different settings we are about to change. Even though there aren't that many that need to be tweaked, they are scattered throughout the panel.

3. The first parameter we want to change is the **Blend Mode**, which is the second setting we can change under the **Material** category within the **Details** panel. Select **Translucent** instead of the default **Opaque** option.

4. Scroll down to the **Translucency** section. There are three parameters that we want to change in here: check the checkbox next to **Screen Space Reflection**, change the **Lighting Mode** to **Surface Translucency Volume**, and check the **Render after DOF** box.

5. Search under the **Usage** category for the checkbox next to **Used with Static Lighting**. We want to be sure to check this one, as this is the type of lighting we'll be using.

Having implemented all of those changes in the main material node, this has effectively changed the way the surface we apply the material to reacts to the light that hits it, and how it deals with other things, such as transparency, reflections, or the depth-of-field calculations. Be sure to check out the *How it works* section to learn more about this topic, as this is quite important and sometimes confusing for translucent materials.

Next up is the actual creation of the material logic. We'll start in a gentle way, playing with parameters we already know, only to introduce new concepts, such as view dependent opacity or refraction, later on.

6. Create a `Vector` parameter, which we'll use to feed the **Base Color** node of the material. This will act as the main color of the glass, so choose something with a blueish tint. Remember to also give it a name!

 Remember Vector parameters? We've used them in the past to create Material instances, and that is what we are going to be doing in this recipe as well. That will enable us to quickly change the material without needing to recompile it.

7. Throw a **Scalar** parameter into the mix, give it a value of `0.9`, and plug that into the **Metallic** node of the material. Even though assigning a metallic value to a glass is a questionable thing to do, it makes the final image a bit more vibrant and closer to the real thing.

So far, so good! The next bit we are going to be doing is the part that gets interesting. Since we are dealing with glass, we also need to tackle reflections, the refraction of light, and the opacity of the material itself. All of these are going to be viewing-dependent—reflections on the glass are most notorious when our view is parallel to the surface of the object. That being the case, we'll need to call our old friend, the Fresnel function, to do the job.

8. Right-click within the material graph and start typing `Fresnel`. You can create the basic node that we've used in previous recipes, but feel free to select **Fresnel_Function**, especially if you are using your own custom meshes. It is a bit more complex to set up than the simple one, but it also gives you more control over the different parameters it contains.

9. Add a **Scalar** parameter right before **Fresnel_Function** and name it Power, since that's the input pin we'll be connecting it to on the newly created function. Give it a value of 3:

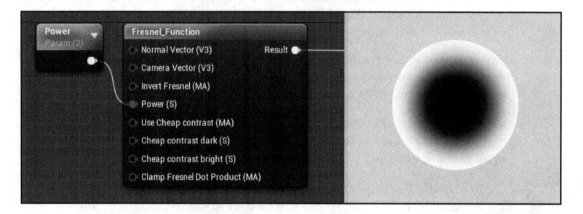

The previous two nodes will allow us to drive the appearance of the material in terms of those three parameters we mentioned: the **Reflection**, the **Refraction**, and the **Opacity** parameters. We'll be using the previous Fresnel function to drive the linear interpolation of two values in those categories, so let's create six scalar parameters for that purpose two per category.

10. Add two scalar parameters to control the reflections and name them appropriately, such as Reflection front and Reflection side. After that, create a **Lerp** node and plug each parameter into the **A** and the **B** pins (**A** for the front reflection, **B** for the other one).

11. Repeat the same operation as before, creating two other scalar parameters and the **Lerp** node, but give them names such as Opacity front and Opacity side.

12. Repeat the same sequence for a third time, naming the new parameters **Refraction front** and **Refraction side**, and **Lerp** between them once more.

In total, we should have three sets of two scalar parameters, with the corresponding **Lerp** nodes after each set, as you can see in the next screenshot. By the way, the reason I've named them **Reflection front** instead of **Front reflection** is because they will be easier to read once we create a material instance out of this one. It's quicker for the eye to read, but feel free to use your own nomenclature:

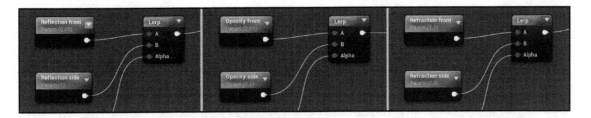

Apart from creating those parameters, remember to give them values! I didn't want to say it before as we'll be able to interactively change them once we create a material instance, but if you want something that works, go with the following:

- 0.05 for **Reflection front**
- 1 for **Reflection side**
- 0.05 for **Opacity front**
- 0.2 for **Opacity side**
- 1.2 for **Refraction front**
- 0.8 for **Refraction side**

13. Connect the **Result** output node of the **Fresnel_Function** into the **Alpha** of the last three **Lerp** nodes we created.
14. Plug the output pin of said **Lerp** nodes into the **Roughness**, **Opacity**, and **Refraction** input pins of the main material node.

This is what your material should now look like if applied to the glass in the scene:

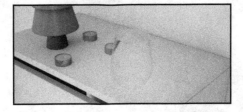

Looking good, right? But we are not yet finished! Something that I like to adjust is the opacity in the upper edges of the glass, which is difficult to achieve by default in Unreal. If you take a look at anything made out of this material, you'll be able to see that the bits where you place your mouth to drink are usually more opaque or darker than the rest of the body. This usually happens as an optic effect, one that is difficult to mimic inside the engine. However, something we can do is fake it, which we'll do next.

15. Create a texture sample node close to the scalar parameters we created for the opacity. Assign the texture named **T_Glass_OpacityMask** in the **Details** panel.

    T_ Glass_ OpacityMask is a custom texture that we've created for the model that we are using in this recipe, which will mask out the rim of the glass. What if you are using your own models, you say? You'll have to create a mask of your own, which can be easily done in a program such as Photoshop or Gimp. Since the last of those two is free, we'll leave a link to it in the *See also* section. Remember that the only thing you'll need to do is to create a black and white image, where the white part matches the rim of your object that you want to be more opaque than the rest.

16. Create another scalar parameter, and name it **Opacity Rim** or something similar. Give it a value of 1.

17. Add a **Lerp** node after these two new ones we've just created, and plug the **Opacity rim** into the **B** input pin. Connect the **Opacity** mask to the **Alpha** pin, and finally connect the output of the original **Opacity Lerp** node to pin **A**. The sequence should look something like this:

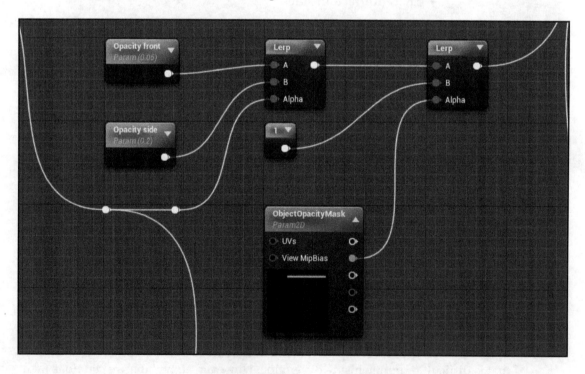

Once we implement the preceding steps, we'll end up with a glass that has a much more opaque edge, which should look nicer than before. These type of adjustments are often made to materials such as glass, where we can't just rely on the engine's implementation of translucency and we need an artist to tweak the scene a little bit:

How it works...

Glass! It can be a complicated thing to get right in real-time renderers for sure, and even though we've come a long way in recent years, it still has its hurdles. Because of that, we'll need to talk about these issues in order to fully understand what we've just created.

Most of the issues that we might experience when working with translucent materials often boil down to how this effect is actually tackled by the engine. Whenever we have an object that makes use of this type of material, such as the glass in the current recipe, Unreal needs to know how it affects the objects that are behind it. Not only that, it also needs to know whether the image has to be distorted, how much light can pass through its surface, or the type of shadows that the object is casting. Some of these problems are solved by adopting smart rendering methods that can provide affordable solutions to hard computational problems, which can sometimes introduce little errors for the sake of performance.

One such example of this balance between realism and performance is the implementation of refraction within the engine. Unreal has introduced two different solutions to the problem: one physically-based, which uses the index of refraction to calculate the effect, and another one more that is artistic in nature, named **Pixel Normal Offset**. Even though the first one relies on a real-world measurable value, the second one is sometimes better in order to achieve the desired effect. This is because the refraction method takes the scene color into account to calculate the distortion, which can cause undesired artifacts, especially in big translucent objects.

There's more...

Before we finish, let's talk about a couple of things that we have just covered briefly before, but are actually quite important in this recipe. The first thing I'd like to mention is the already-familiar material instance asset—a tool that can save us quite a bit of time when working with translucent materials.

You might have noticed that the material took a while to update itself every time that we changed any of its settings. Creating an instance out of the material once we set it up can greatly speed up this process—that way, we'll be able to modify every exposed parameter on the go, without having to wait for our shader to recompile.

The second item we should talk about is the Refraction parameters we have chosen as our default values. We chose **1.2** and **0.8** as the **Refraction Front** and **Refraction Side**, respectively, and even though the real-life **index of refraction** (IOR) for glass is closer to **1.52**, those looked better in the viewport. Something that also works well and that you can try is to combine the following nodes: two constants, one with a value of **1** and another one with the real IOR value, hooked into a **Lerp** node being driven by a Fresnel one. This is usually closer to the real-life appearance than using just the real IOR value.

See also

There are lots of useful and interesting official docs that cover this topic, so be sure to read them if you are interested!

- Transparency: https://docs.unrealengine.com/en-us/Engine/Rendering/Materials/HowTo/Transparency
- Index of refraction: https://docs.unrealengine.com/en-us/Engine/Rendering/Materials/HowTo/Refraction
- Getting Gimp: https://www.gimp.org/

A different type of translucency – holograms

Now that we are familiar with translucent materials, why don't we spice things up a little bit and see what other cool effects we can create using the same blend mode? An interesting one that comes to mind is **holograms**—the ever-so-sci-fi, cool-looking effect that we can see in futuristic movies. This can be quite an interesting technique to implement, as not only are we going to deal with transparent surfaces, but also with animated textures and light-emitting properties.

All in all, holograms are going to enable us to revisit certain topics we already know something about while discovering new features of the material editor, which will come in handy not just in this recipe, but in any animated material we want to create in the future. Let's see what it's all about!

Getting ready

You'll probably remember from previous recipes that we always provide you with the same assets you see throughout the pages of this book. This is, of course, so you can easily follow along. This time won't be any different, but you'll probably start to see that sometimes, we won't even need any type of models or textures to tackle a specific topic. As we get more and more proficient with the engine, we'll sometimes start to make use of procedural and mathematical approaches to material creation. This allows us to expose some very powerful material creation techniques, as well as freeing ourselves from the need to use resolution-dependent textures.

With that said, you can expect a lot of math nodes and smart techniques in the following pages. The binary assets, models, and textures are provided as always by us, and you can find them in the following folder:

- **Assets:** Content / UE4ShadersAndEffects / Assets / Chapter04
- **Maps:** Content / UE4ShadersAndEffects / Maps / Chapter04

The name of the map we'll be working on is **04_03_Hologram_Start**, so make sure to open that one up if you want to use the same resources. If you prefer to use your own, you'll only need a 3D model either created by you or one found in the **Starter Content**. With that said, let's get the ball rolling!

How to do it...

Let's start by taking a look at the scene we'll be working off:

As you can see from the previous picture, the tree in the center of the screen is the 3D model we are going to operate on—it's similar to one we've seen in the past, but tweaked to make it look more sci-fi once we start implementing the material on it. If you select it, you'll be able to see that it has two material slots: the first one with a material called **M_ChristmasTree_ Base** and the second one named **M_ ChristmasTree_ Hologram**. This is the one we'll be operating upon, so make sure to open it up! Let's get started:

1. Open up the second material, named **M_ ChristmasTree_ Hologram**, and delete everything but the main material node.
2. With the main material node selected, head over the **Details** panel and look for the **Blend Mode** and the **Shading Model** sections.

3. Change the default values from **Opaque** to **Translucent** and from **Default Lit** to **Unlit**, as seen in the next screenshot:

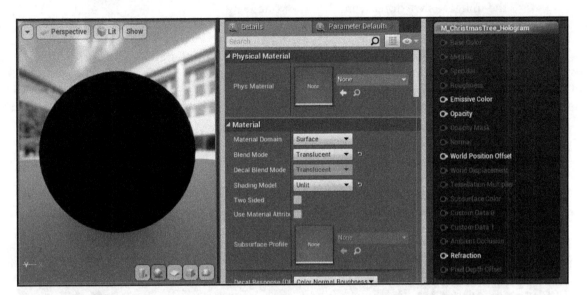

There are two materials applied to the same model because they each make use of a different **Shading Model** and **Blend Mode**. Unlike with metallic and non-metallic objects, which we can mask apart, surfaces that require a different shading model have to make use of their own unique material.

The preceding step has ensured that the material we create is not going to be affected by any scene lighting, which is quite common for light-emitting materials such as a hologram. Changing the **Blend Mode** to **Translucent** has also enabled that see-through quality that most sci-fi holograms have. All in all, we are now ready to start adjusting the look of our material.

4. Add a **Texture Sample**, a **Constant**, and a **Cheap Contrast** node. We are already familiar with the first two items, and the third one is easily accessible by right-clicking anywhere in the material graph and typing its name.
5. Select the **T_ ChristmasTree_ D** texture in the **Details** panel of the **Texture Sample**. We will use this asset as a holographic reminder of what the prop once looked like with a different shader.

6. Plug the **Red** channel of the **Texture Sample** into the **In (S)** input pin of the **Cheap Contrast** node. This means that we are using a black and white version of the image, as we don't want the color one.

7. Assign a value of 0.2 to our constant, and plug it into the **Contrast (S)** input pin of the **Cheap Contrast** node. This will make the brighter areas a little bit whiter, and the darker areas lean more toward black values.

8. Add a **Multiply** node and a **Constant**. Hook the output pin of the **Cheap Contrast** node into pin **A** of the **Multiply**, and our new constant into pin **B**.

9. Give the **Constant** a value of **2**. Right-click on the **Multiply** node and select the **Start Previewing Node** option. That will let you see what the graph would look like up until that point:

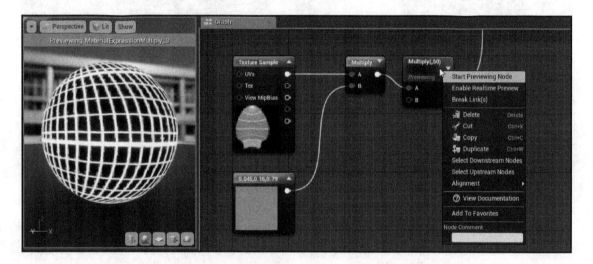

As you probably already know, holograms are usually tinted, and, more often than not, they are given a blueish color. We can easily achieve that if we do the following.

10. Create a new **Multiply** node and place it after the previous sequence.

11. Add a new **Constant3** vector and give it a blueish value. I've gone with the following: **0.52**, **0.55**, and **0.74** in the RGB values.

12. Plug the result of **Constant3** into pin **B** of the new **Multiply** node, and hook pin **A** to the output of the previous **Multiply** node.

13. You might want to add a third **Multiply** node, if only to control the overall brightness of what we've created. I've connected the **A** pin to the output of the second **Multiply** node and given the **B** pin a value of **0.5**:

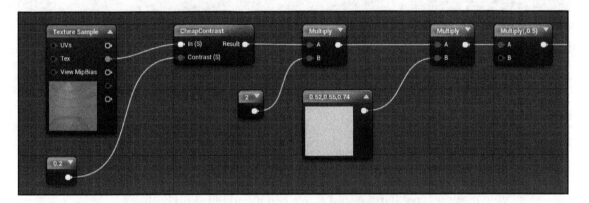

(We'll call the previous nodes part A, and we'll come back to them in *step 18*)

All of what we've done so far has left us with a washed-out, blueish wood-ghost material, which we'll use later on. If this were a cookbook, we would now put what we've made aside to focus on other things. For organizational purposes, let's call what we've created part A. The next part we are going to be looking at is the creation of a wireframe overlay, which will give us a very sci-fi look—we'll call this part B, as we'll need to merge both parts.

14. Create a **Texture Sample** node and assign the **T_ChristmasTree_UVs** asset to it.

15. Add a **Constant3** node and give it a blueish color, brighter than the one we created in *step 11*. RGB values of **0.045**, **0.16**, and **0.79** would be a good starting point.

16. Multiply both assets.

17. Create a new **Multiply** node after the previous one and connect pin **A** to the output of the first Multiply. The **B** value will decide the brightness of the wireframe, so feel free to give it a high value. I've gone with **50**:

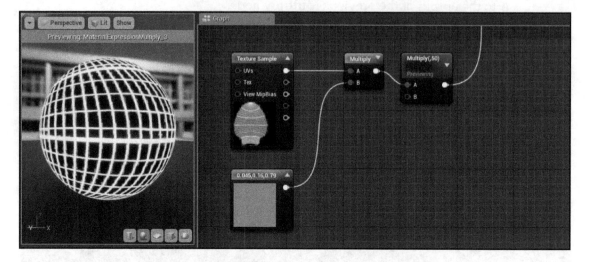

Now that we have Parts **A** and **B**, we can blend between both.

18. Create a **Lerp** node and place it after both parts A and B.

19. Connect the result of part A (the output of the last **Multiply** node of the wood-ghost effect) into pin A of the new **Lerp** node. Do the same with pin **B** and the last **Multiply** node of part B (the wireframe part).

20. Add a new **Texture Sample** node and select the **T_ ChristmasTree_ UVs** image as its value. Connect the **Alpha** node to the **Alpha** input pin of the **Lerp** node.

Having done that will see us almost finished with most of the nodes that we are going to be connecting to the Emissive Color input pin of the main material node. However, we are not finished with this section yet, as there's a small addition we can implement. Some holographic implementations have a Fresnel quality to them—this is, they are brighter around the edges of the model than they are in the center of it. Let's implement that.

21. Create a **Multiply** node and give it a high value, such as 10. Place it immediately after the last **Lerp** node we had created that was interpolating between the previous Parts **A** and **B** of the graph.

22. Introduce a **Lerp** node after this last **Multiply**. Hook pin **A** to the output of the previous **Lerp** and pin **B** to the previous **Multiply**.

23. Add a **Fresnel** node to work as the **Alpha** for the last **Lerp**. If you click on it and look at the **Details** panel, you'll be able to modify its default values. I've chosen **8** as the **Exponent** and 0.01 for the **Base Reflect Fraction** value:

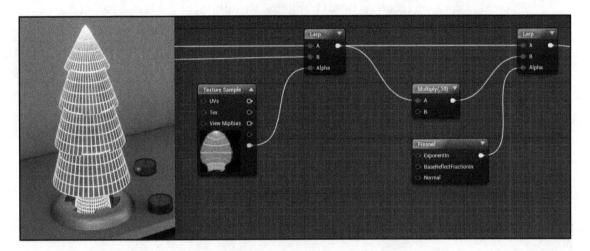

With those last changes, we can say that our material looks like a proper hologram! However, a nice addition to the current setup would be the introduction of some varying levels of opacity. Most holograms we see in movies are translucent objects, as we can see what's behind them. Furthermore, some holograms flicker and get distorted with time—this is often done to emulate how a hypothetical technology that allows the holograms to even exist would work. Think of it like an old TV effect, where the scan lines get updated from one side of the screen to the other every frame. That's what we'll be trying to replicate next.

 Some of the nodes that we are about to use change the way textures get projected into our models. This is useful whenever we want to have an effect working independently from the UVs of the object, like we are about to see.

24. Head over to an empty plot in our material graph and add a **Texture Sample**. Select the **T_ ChristmasTree_ Scanlines** texture as the default value—we will use them to drive the opacity of the material.
25. The texture can't be applied as-is to the object, as it doesn't match the UVs of our model. Create a **BoundingBoxBased_0-1_UVW** node in order to use a custom projection for the previous texture. If you right-click and start typing that name, the node should appear. Place the node a little bit before the previous **Texture Sample**, as we'll be driving its UVs through it.

26. Create a **MakeFloat2** node after the previous **Bounding Box** one. Connect the **R** value of the bounding box to the **X** of the **MakeFloat**, and the **B** value to **Y**.

27. Add a **One Minus** node after the **MakeFloat** one. This will invert the previously-created content. Hook its input pin to the **Result** pin of the Make Float node.

28. Include a **Multiply** node that will act as a scale control for the texture this array of nodes is affecting. Connect pin **A** to the output of the **One Minus** node, and assign a value to pin **B**—I've gone with 3.

29. Create a **Panner** and plug the result of the previous **Multiply** into its **Coordinate** input pin.

30. Select the **Panner** and look at the **Details** panel. As we want the scan lines to be moving upward, leave the **Speed X** at **zero** and increase the value for the **Speed Y** setting. I've chosen **0.025** to give it a nice, slow effect.

31. Connect the output of the **Panner** node to the **UVs** input pin of the **Texture Sample** scan lines.

This is what the previous part of the graph should look like, which for reference we'll call part C:

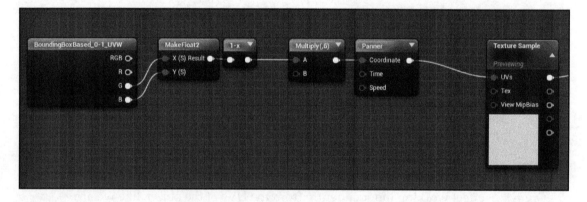

Now let's add a little bit of variation to this scan-line effect, and finally plug it into the opacity channel of the main material node.

32. Copy the graph we've just created and paste it immediately under the previous one. We should have two identical bits of visual scripting code, one on top of the other, which we can refer to as part C and part D.

33. Head over to the **Multiply** node of the copied graph (part D) and change its previous value of 3 to something such as 6. This will make the scan-line effect in this section smaller than the previous one.

34. Combine both effects by creating an **Add** node and hooking its **A** and **B** pins to the output of the **Texture Sample** in part C and D, respectively.

35. Add two **Constant3** vectors after the last **Add** node. Give the first of them a value of **0.2** in each of its channels (**R**, **G**, and **B**) and assign the second **Constant3** node a value of **1** on each channel as well.

> We'll use those **Constant3** vectors to drive the opacity of the material. We need them to be that specific type and not simple constants to match the texture we'll be using as the blending mask, the scan lines, which are a 3 vector as well.

36. Create a **Lerp** node and connect its **A** pin to the first of the **Constant3** vectors, and pin **B** to the second one.

37. For the **Alpha** value, use the output of the **Add** node where we combined both scan lines.

The resulting graph and effect should be similar to the one seen in the next screenshot:

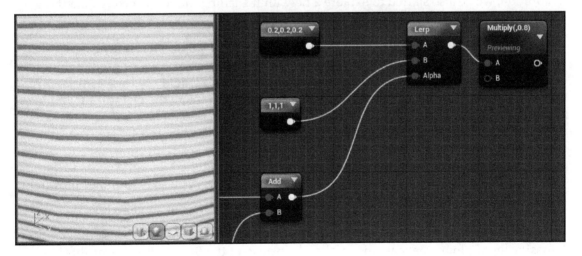

Connecting the output of the previous **Multiply** node to the **Opacity** input pin of our material will give us the final look we were trying to achieve: a nice holographic material based on a small wooden tree prop:

And there you go! We've finally achieved the look we want, while also learning about some new useful nodes. Like in many of the other recipes, sometimes the most useful lessons we learn are snippets of information that we can then apply elsewhere. Hope you've learned something new!

How it works...

The holographic material we've been dealing with made use of the **Translucent** blend mode, something we dealt with when we created the glass material in the previous recipe. In addition, we've also started to explore a new unlit shading model, which is something completely new to us at this point.

Even though we are just starting to explore this new type of shader, it is quite easy to understand the way it works by just comparing it to the other types we've used in the past. In essence, a shading model is a function used to describe how light affects the surfaces of the objects within Unreal. So far, we've explored a couple of them: the **Default Lit** and the **Subsurface Profile** in particular. The former is meant to be used on types of objects that reflect light in a similar way to opaque objects, such as wood, iron, or concrete. The latter was explored in the recipe where we created a candle, and is very helpful when part of the light that reaches a certain object gets absorbed by it and scattered underneath its surface. This new shading model, the unlit one we are now dealing with, also determines how light interacts with objects that make use of it. However, the main peculiarity, in this case, is the lack of interactivity between the light and the materials altogether—that is, lights in our scene are not going to affect our models at all. That's one of the reasons we use the **Emissive** input pin on the main material node instead of the **Base Color** one, as this is a property that doesn't get affected by the existence of lights throughout our levels.

There's more...

The emissive property of our materials is a powerful resource when we want to fake lights or actually create them. Even though this is not the standard procedure to add a new light, setting up material to make use of the emissive node can replace them under certain conditions. So what options do we have when we work with these type of assets?

First of all, we have two basic choices: we can use the emissive property to give the impression that our material is casting light, or we can set it up so that it actually affects the world by emitting photons. The way the engine deals with the faking part is by actually using the emissive node of the material to affect its contribution to the bloom effect and give the impression that you are looking at a bright light. If we don't want this technique to just be an illusion, but to actually affect the shadows in our scene, we also have the option to do that. The way we achieve this is by selecting the model that the emissive material is being applied to and looking at its **Details** panel. Under the **Lighting** tab, we should be able to find an option named **Use Emissive for Static Lighting**. Turn that on, click on the **Build** button to calculate the shadow maps, and you're good to go!

Something to note at this point is the type of light that the materials can emit, as they are always going to be of the static type. You'll have to keep this in mind in case you want to achieve any type of real-time effect, as that's not currently possible.

See also

You can find more information on the unlit shading model and the emissive material input pin in Epic Games' official documentation at `https://docs.unrealengine.com/Engine/Rendering/Materials/HowTo/EmissiveGlow`.

Achieving realistic reflections

Reflections are a very interesting and powerful effect, and one that can often make or break a scene. They are amazing when used to their full potential, since their inclusion alone adds a layer of realism that can be difficult to fake. So far, we've made use of two reflection methods in the previous recipes: the standard **Screen Space Reflections** that is enabled by default in the engine, and the **Reflection Captures** we've always had around in our scenes. Even though we only set them up in the Chapter 1, *Physically Based Rendering*, both of these methods have been implemented in the scenes we have provided.

With that covered, it is now time to deal with other additional reflection techniques that can enhance the look of our models even further, such as **Planar Reflections**. The methods we've used so far have worked great with the assets that we were dealing with, but some of the materials that we are going to be exploring in the immediate future will benefit from more precise reflection techniques. They are going to play an important role in future recipes as well, so let's see what's so special about them!

Getting ready

Want to follow along using the same assets? Then just open up the level called **04_04_AccurateReflections_Start** located in the `Content / UE4ShadersAndEffects / Maps / Chapter04` folder.

The scene you'll be greeted with is a simple one, using some of the assets we've seen in the past, but arranged in a way where we can get nice reflections happening in the surface of the central mirror. This is very simple to replicate using your own assets and scenes, as there's nothing special you need—not even a specific type of model. If you wanted to, you could use the standard assets that come bundled by default with Unreal Engine. Just make sure that you add a plane that can act as a mirror, and a highly reflective material with a low roughness value. Let's get started:

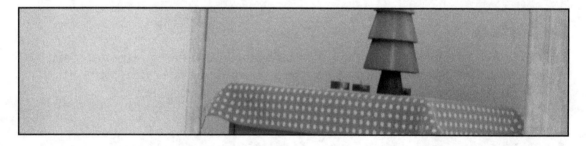

How to do it...

Something we've had to do in some of the previous recipes was enable certain settings within the engine in order to turn on specific functionalities. We saw this when we were working with translucent materials, as we had to enable screen space reflections on those type of shaders since they weren't switched on by default. Something similar will happen next—as we are about to work with Planar Reflections, there is a certain Project Setting that we have to enable first:

1. Open the Project Settings by heading over to **Edit | Project Settings.** Click on **All Settings**, and type **clip** on the **Search** box.
2. Under **Engine | Rendering | Lighting**, you'll be able to see a certain parameter named **Support global clip plane for Planar Reflections**. Check the checkbox by its side and restart the project when prompted:

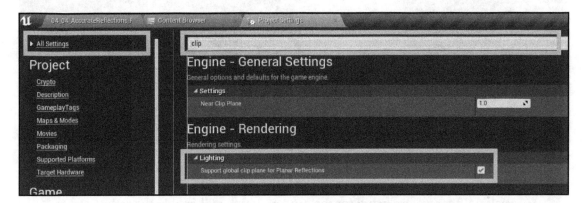

Doing that will enable us to use the **Planar Reflection** actor. You'll be able to find it within the **Place** tab of the **Modes** panel, provided that you type `Planar Reflection` in the search box. If you don't want to type, know that it can be also found under the **Visual Effects** section of the same panel.

3. Drag and drop the **Planar Reflection** actor into the scene.
4. With said actor selected, rotate it until it is perpendicular to the floor. We want to place it parallel to the mirror in our scene, so keep that as a reference.

Planar actors can be a bit frustrating to work with, as they are only visible in the editor if you are not in **Game View**. Remember that you can enter and exit **Game View** at will by pressing the *G* key on your keyboard while the main viewport is in focus (it won't work if you are on the World Outliner, for example).

The next screenshot shows how to add a **Planar Reflection Actor** from the **Modes** panel:

With that done, we can start tweaking the different settings of the **Planar Reflection** actor. Before we do so, however, remember that you can inspect the material that we are using for the mirror, which will enable the reflections to work.

5. Select **SM_WoodenBedroomMirror** and check the material that is being applied to the model in the **Details** panel. Open it up to see what it's made of.

6. Once inside of the material graph, feel free to play around with the roughness value for the mirror surface. That setting can be controlled by selecting the **Lerp** node and changing the value of **Const A** in the **Details** panel:

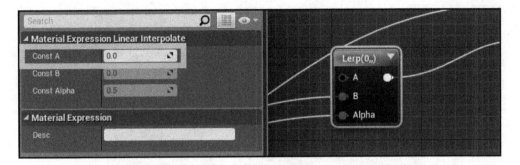

As you can see, the material is a simple one. We are using two textures: one that connects to the **Base Color** and another that stores the values for **Ambient Occlusion**, **Roughness**, and **Metalness** of the material as grayscale masks. Even though most input are directly connected, the **Roughness** gets treated differently—to make sure that the mirror surface is perfectly clean, we isolate that area using the metallic value as a mask and we give a 0 value to ensure we have a smooth surface.

With that out of the way, we can now start to play with the **Planar Reflection** properties to achieve the desired look.

7. Select the **Planar Reflection** actor and look at the **Details** panel. Set the **Normal Distortion Strength** to 100, decreasing it from the default 500. This will make the reflections appear more realistic in our tilted mirror, but feel free to play with this setting if you are using your own models.

8. Set **Distance from Plane Fadeout Start** and **Distance from Plane Fadeout End** to 600 and 700, respectively. This will ensure that the objects that are supposed to be reflected are in fact displayed in the mirror.

9. Uncheck the **Show Preview Plane** option, just so that it doesn't bother us whenever we are in **Game View**.

10. Expand the **Planar Reflection** category of the same actor to find some extra settings we want to tweak, then focus on the **Screen Percentage** option. Change it to 100, which will increase the quality of the reflections:

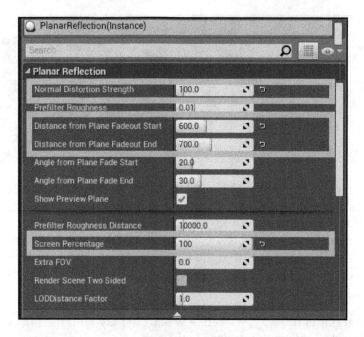

Having performed the preceding steps will give us a nice planar reflection in our mirror, which we can compare to the existing previous one:

Even though we now have a reliable way of achieving realistic reflections, this is a method that can be quite expensive—as we are basically rendering the scene twice. With that in mind, we will be looking at a different system that can also generate nice, detailed reflections in a cheaper way, which will be the **Scene Capture** technique.

This second method that we are going to explore presents some benefits as well as some potential inconveniences, and we need to be aware of them! The benefits? Well, this time we don't need to render the scene twice every so often to achieve the desired results, as this new technique for capturing reflections consists of baking our scene into a texture that is then fed to the objects where we want those reflections to show. This can present a bit of a problem, as we'll need to manually tweak and position the baked environment in order to ensure that it blends well in our scene.

11. Delete the previous **Planar Reflection** actor so it doesn't affect our scene anymore.
12. Head over to the **Place** tab of the **Modes** panel and search for a **Scene Capture Cube** actor. Drag and drop it into our scene:

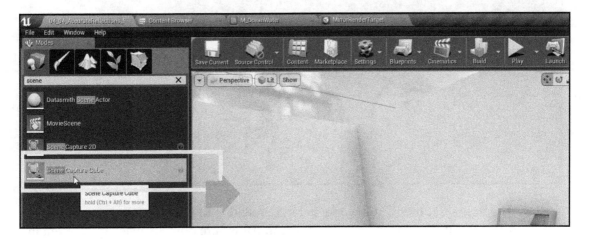

13. Place the previous **Scene Capture Cube** actor close to the mirror in our scene. You can take a look at the next screenshot for reference purposes:

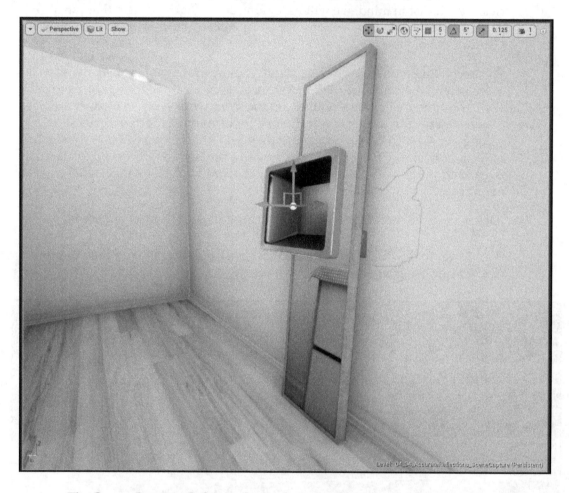

The **Scene Capture Cube** works in tandem with a **Render Target**—a texture where we'll store the view from the actor. All we are doing is placing a camera in our scene, which will create a photograph of the level for us to use as a reflection value.

14. Create a **Render Target** texture by right-clicking in an empty space of the **Content Browser** and browsing inside the **Materials & Textures** section.

15. Give it a name you'll remember and double-click on it to access its **Details** panel. You'll find a parameter named **Size X** under the **Texture Render Target Cube** category. Assign it a value of 2048 (**2K**):

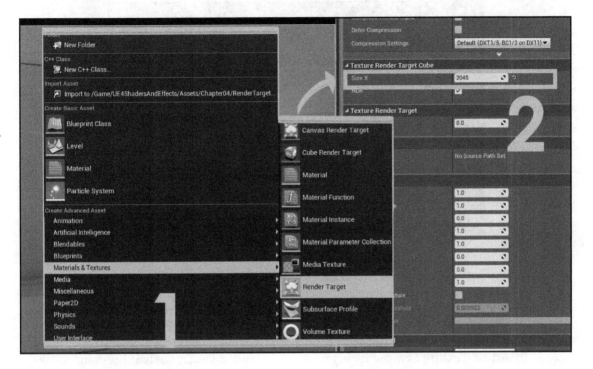

16. Head back to the main viewport and select the **Scene Capture Cube** we placed in *step 13*. Look at its **Details** panel and set the previously-created **Render Target** in the **Texture Target** category.

17. There's another setting a little bit further down, named **Capture Every Frame**. Disable this to increase performance.

18. Move the camera around slightly. This should update the contents of our **Render Target**, which you'll be able to check if you double-click on it again:

Now that we have that texture, we can use it within our mirror material. With that goal in mind, let's create a new material where we can put that in motion.

19. Create a new material, and apply it to the mirror in our scene (replacing the previous one). I've named mine **M_ WoodenMirror_ CaptureReflection**. Open the new asset in the **Material Editor**.

20. Add a **Texture Sample** node and set the **Render Target** we had previously created as its value.

Even though we now have that texture inside our new material, we need to affect the way we look at it based on the position of the camera. This will give the impression that the reflection gets updated as we look at the mirror. Thankfully, Unreal has a handy node that allows us to do just that.

21. Right-click within the material graph and start typing Reflection Vector WS. This will give us what we need to make our **Render Target** work as intended. Connect its output to the UVs input pin of the previous **Texture Sample**.

22. Connect the output of the **Texture Sample** to a **Multiply** node, and set the value for the **B** parameter to something like **5**. This will brighten up the reflection we see once we apply and save the material, so make sure to play around with this until you are happy.

All of the previous steps have created a reflection texture that we can see no matter where we are with regards to the mirror object. We now need to blend that with the other parts that make up the mirror, such as the wooden frame.

23. Add three texture samples and assign the following textures to them: **T_ WoodenBedroomMirror_ AORM**, **T_ WoodenBedroomMirror_ UVMask**, and **T_ WoodenBedroomMirror_ BaseColor**. All of them will be needed in the following steps.

24. Create a **Lerp** node, which we'll use to mix between the texture that will act as the reflection and the wood color.

25. Connect the result of the **Multiply** node we created in *step 22* to pin **A** of the new **Lerp**.

26. Connect the **T_ WoodenBedroomMirror_ BaseColor** texture to its B input pin.

27. Connect the **Alpha** to the green channel of the **T_ WoodenBedroomMirror_ UVMask** asset. Remember to connect the **Lerp** to the **Base Color** of the material as well.

Performing the previous steps has given us the color, let's now tackle the roughness value.

28. Connect the red channel of **T_ WoodenBedroomMirror_ AORM** directly into the **Ambient Occlusion** input pin of the main material node.

29. Create another **Lerp** node, which we'll use similarly to the one we needed to drive the color values, but that will work for the roughness this time.

30. Connect the green channel of the **T_ WoodenBedroomMirror_ UVMask** texture into the **Alpha** input pin, and assign pin **A** a value of 1. Connect pin **B** to the green channel of the **T_ WoodenBedroomMirror_ AORM** asset.

31. Plug the result of the previous **Lerp** node into the **Roughness** channel of our material.

Here's what the material graph should look like, all things considered:

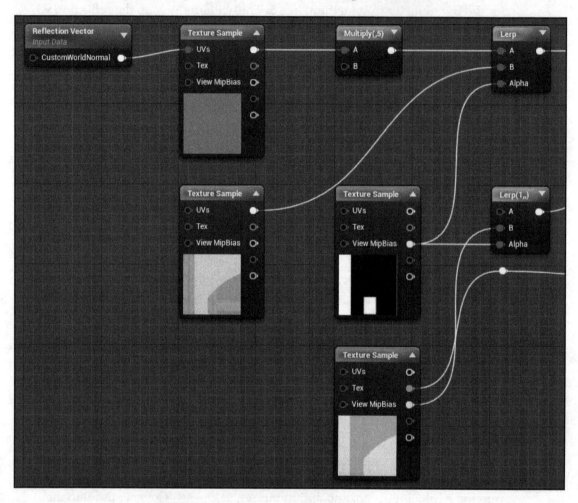

With these last changes, we have effectively finished our intervention in the material, and we can finally check the results if we go back to the main viewport. You'll notice that the effect is far from perfect in this case, but it does work at certain angles and it works according to plan. You might want to test the effect on other surfaces to see the results, as this method tends to work best with objects larger than our mirror. However, it still is a powerful technique that can add life to our scenes and limit the impact on performance that other methods can have. Be sure to test it on different types of surfaces and materials!

How it works...

Every actor in our level can be affected by a **Planar Reflection** asset, even though this effect will be most obvious in those materials that have a low **roughness** value. Such is the case of the mirror in our scene, as you saw in this recipe. Other surfaces, such as the walls or the rest of the props inside of the level, didn't get affected as much since their roughness settings didn't allow for that.

The way that the Planar Reflection affects our scene is tied directly to the settings we specify in its **Details** panel. The first of the bunch, the normal distortion strength, determines how much the normals of the affected surfaces distort the final reflection. This is especially useful if we have multiple actors that we want to be affecting at the same time that are not facing in the exact same way—instead of creating multiple planar reflections that are parallel to each individual rotated object, we can adjust the normal distortion strength to allow for varying rotation angles.

Other useful settings to remember are the distance from the plane fade out start and its twin, the end one, as they control the region where the effect is happening. However, maybe one of the most important ones is the one labelled **Screen Percentage**, as that controls the quality of the overall effect and the rendering cost of the effect.

There's more...

The **Scene Capture Cube** actor is a very cool asset, as it allows us to create similar effects to what we've seen in this recipe that can be used in a myriad of places. Continuing with the topic of reflections, we know that they can be costly to render in real time. The technique that we've studied can be effective when dealing with materials where real-time reflections are too much of an overhead. One such example would be glass or water materials, where enabling screen space reflections on those shaders increases their instruction count and thus the complexity of the materials. Instead of doing that, we can disable that SSR effect in the **Details** panel of the material and fake the reflections by using the same technique we saw in this recipe instead.

Of course, the way we would apply the texture wouldn't be exactly the same; instead of completely replacing the color info like we did in the previous pages, we might want to overlay it a little bit or just mix it in the right amount so that we don't lose the underlying image. There are many different options in which we can apply that technique, so be sure to play around with it!

See also

Let me leave you with with some links to the official documentation regarding planar reflections and render targets:

- https://docs.unrealengine.com/en-us/Engine/Rendering/ LightingAndShadows/PlanarReflections
- https://docs.unrealengine.com/en-us/Resources/ContentExamples/ Reflections/1_6
- https://docs.unrealengine.com/en-us/Engine/Rendering/RenderTargets

Mastering refraction by creating a pool water material

Water is cool, pool water is cooler, but apart from studying it for that reason, it's interesting to see how to deal with different bodies of water in UE4. We are going to be looking at two different types: a see-through implementation, and a rough sea shader. This recipe will deal with the first type, which is going to allow us to check a different refraction implementation within the engine that works well with large surfaces. We'll check out the sea shader in a later recipe.

Apart from that, we are also going to be able to tackle different interesting nodes, such as the **Depth Fade** one, which we'll talk about more later. With that in mind, let's see what you'll need to get started!

Getting ready

Since we'll be trying out different effects, we'll need to actually set up the scene in a way that allows for them to show up. First of all, we'll need a plane onto which we can apply the water material we'll be creating. Apart from that, we'll also need something to act as a container for the water—I'm going to use a 3D model of a bath tub, so something similar will do. Having something opaque wrapping around the water plane is actually quite important, as we'll be using nodes that detect the intersection of several geometries. Those two things would be the basics, but we'll probably want to add a small prop just so that we can check the refraction in the water body—a rubber duck can work!

As always, we'll be providing you with everything you need if you want to use the same assets. Open the **04_ 05_ StillWater_ Start** scene, located in Content / UE4ShadersAndEffects / Maps / Chapter04, and you'll find everything you need to follow along:

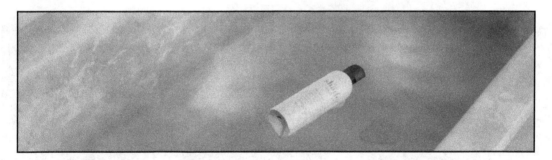

How to do it...

As we are about to create a new type of translucent material, it's always good to think about what we want to achieve before we begin. We've dealt with different types of translucent surfaces in the past, but this time things won't be as straightforward as before. The reason for that lies within the specific asset that we want to create: water. Unlike glass, water is a material that is rarely found resting perfectly still. Its condition as a fluid means that it is almost always in motion, and that introduces certain conditions that we need to take into account, such as how the normals of the material are going to be animated, how the direction of those affect the color of the material, and how the opacity changes across the body of water. We will explore all of those conditions next:

1. Create a new material and name it whatever you like—I've gone with **M_BathtubWater**, as that's what we'll be creating.

2. Change the Blend Mode to **Translucent**, and check **Screen Space Reflections** checkbox found a little further down on the **Details** panel, in the **Translucency** section.

3. Change the **Lighting Mode** to **Surface Translucency Volume** and check the **Render after DOF** checkbox. Scroll down to the **Usage** category, look for the checkbox next to **Used with Static Lighting ...**, and check it:

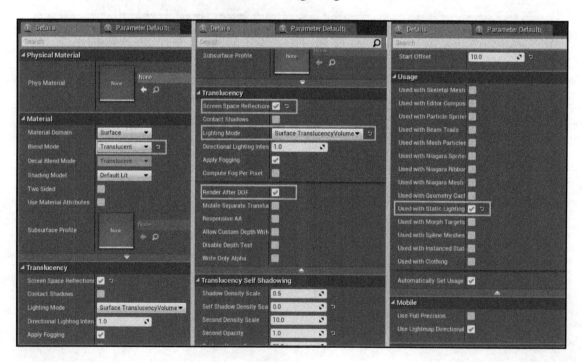

So far, these are the same steps we had to follow when creating the glass material, so the previous screenshot will just act as a reminder. The first bespoke modifications we are going to introduce deal with the way we assign the opacity and the color values to our material. Since we have water in a bathtub, you'll note that the surface tends to lose its see-through properties the deeper we go, in real life, that is. We'll replicate this with a handy node, called **Depth Fade**, which performs that calculation for us.

4. Start by adding a **Depth Fade** node into the material graph. You'll find it either in the **Palette** menu or by right-clicking and typing its name.
5. Look at the **Details** panel and modify the two properties you'll find in there. Leave the **Opacity Default** with its default value of **1** and set the **Fade Distance Default** to **10**.
6. Try hooking that node up to the **Base Color** of the material and see what it looks like back in the main viewport. To do that, remember to apply the new material to the **SM_ BathTub_ Water** model that lives in the center of the scene:

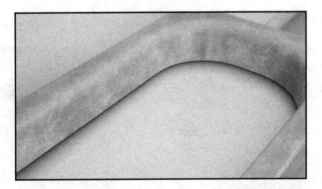

As you can see, the areas of the model that are closer to the walls of the bathtub are displayed in black, fading gradually to white as we get away from them. This will act as a mask, which we'll use to drive the color and the opacity of the material.

7. Drag from the output pin of the **Depth Fade** node and create a **Clamp** node at its end. Leave the new node as is, with the default values of 0 and 1 as the minimum and maximum. This ensures every value from the **Depth Fade** node is constrained to that range.
8. Create a **Lerp** node, and connect the output of the previous **Clamp** to its **Alpha** input pin.

9. Add two **Scalar Parameters**, which will act as the opacity controls for our material. Name them and connect them to the **A** and **B** pins of the previous **Lerp** node. Hook the output of the **Lerp** node into the **Opacity** pin in the main material node.

I've named the two previous parameters **Edge opacity** and **Default opacity**, as the first one controls the value at the edge of the bathtub and the other one adjusts the rest. The values I've gone with are **0.3** and **0.65**, but feel free to play with them. You can also wait and create a material instance later to test how they look interactively!

You'll need to feed something into the Lerp node's **Alpha** pin be it a grayscale value or a constant. Whatever it is, it can be described as a black and white value, and the **A** and **B** input pins will get blended according to that. As a rule of thumb, you can associate **A** and **B** with black and white pin **A** will show in the black areas and pin B will appear on the white ones.

The following screenshot shows the nodes we have previously created:

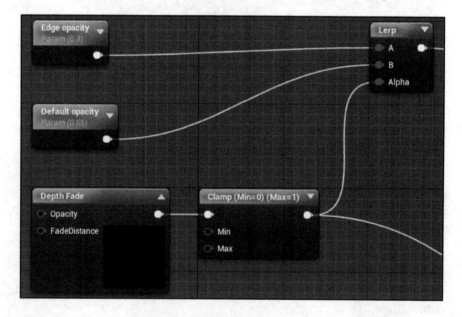

The next steps are almost going to be an identical copy of what we've just done, as we'll be driving the color of the material through the same **Depth Fade** node.

10. Create a couple of **Vector Parameters**, and assign them a name and a value. I've gone with **Edge Color** and **Main Color**, choosing a whitish value as the first one and a slightly bluer variant for the main part.

11. Add a **Lerp** node after the two previous parameters, and connect them to pins **A** and **B** of this new node.

12. Drag another cable from the **Clamp** located after the **Depth Fade** node and connect it to the **Alpha** of the new **Lerp**, just as we did for the opacity. Connect that to the **Base Color** pin of our material.

We now need to address the roughness, the normal, and the refraction of the material, which will rely on an animated water texture. Before that, let's introduce a simple modifier for the **Metallic** property of the material, which can help our water look a bit nicer.

13. Create a **Constant** vector and give it a value of **0.9**. Connect it to the **Metallic** input pin on the main material node:

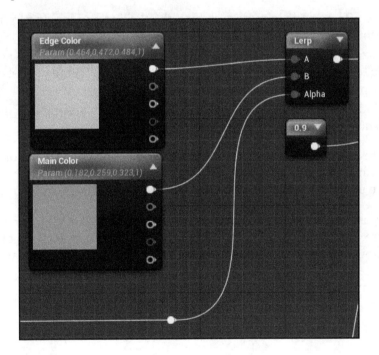

Here are the previously-created nodes—note that the **Alpha** on the **Lerp** node is being controlled by the **Clamp** after the **Depth Fade** node.

As we said, it is now time to animate a normal texture so we can do a couple of different things: we'll use it to drive the roughness of our water body, and to affect the normals and the refraction to create the illusion of a moving surface.

14. Create a **Panner** node, which we'll use to animate the water normals. For this node to work, we need to give it some values: it needs to know the coordinates it is going to be animating and the time and speed at which it's going to operate. Let's define those.

15. Create a **Texture Coordinate** node and a **Scalar Parameter**. This last node is going to control the scale of the pattern we'll be applying, so let's name it sensibly. I've gone with **Wave** scale and given it a value of **3**.

16. **Multiply** those two nodes and connect the output to the **Coordinate** pin of the previous **Panner**.

   That was the part that feeds into the **Coordinate** input pin of the **Panner**. Let's now focus on the time and speed.

17. Create a **Time** node in our graph by right-clicking and looking for that name. This introduces the concept of time to the material.

18. Create a **Multiply** node and hook its **A** pin to the previous **Time** node. Set the **B** value to `0.03`, either by adjusting that setting in the **Details** panel of the **Multiply** node or by creating and connecting a **Constant** vector.

19. Hook the output of the previous node into the **Time** input pin of the **Panner**. Let's now take care of the **Speed** section.

20. Create a **Scalar Parameter** and connect it to the **Speed** input pin of the **Panner**. We want to be able to modify this node in case we create a Material Instance, hence us choosing that specific node. A value of `0.5` here can work well!

   The reason we created this part of the node network is to affect or animate a texture. With that said, it becomes obvious that we need to create one! Let's do that now and select one that can fulfill the role of the water normals.

21. Create a **Texture Sample** node and assign the texture named **T_ Water_ N**. It's part of the **Starter Content**, so make sure you've included that!

With that last node created, we now have a fully-functioning **Panner** system. For the sake of simplicity, and because we'll come back to this section multiple times, let's give this set of nodes a name—we'll call it part A. Let's review what we've got so far in the next screenshot:

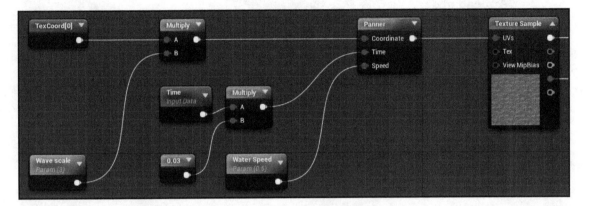

We'll now branch off this node multiple times, hence the need to be able to quickly refer to this part as we'll come back to it—to the **Texture Sample** node in particular. This is the basic building block where the refraction, the normal, and the roughness stem from. The first element of the triad we'll tackle is the Refraction bit.

22. Drag a cable out of the **Texture Sample** we created in *step 21* and create a **Component Mask**. Select the red and green channels.

23. Drag again from the end of the **Component Mask** and create a **Multiply** node. Set it to **2**.

The previous nodes are quite a powerful technique. By taking the red and green channels of the normal texture, where the actual values that define this type of textures are stored, and increasing their intensity, we make the effect more noticeable.

24. Create an **Append** vector and connect the result of the previous **Multiply** node to its **A** pin.

25. Go back to part **A**, drag a cable out of the blue channel of the **Texture Sample** that contains our original water normals, and connect it to pin **B** of the previous **Append** node.

Doing this has given us a more intense version of the normal map we are using for the water, which we can almost immediately use to drive the Refraction of the material.

26. Click on the **main material node** and head back to its **Details** panel. Scroll all the way down to the **Refraction** tab (it's one of the last ones) and set the **Refraction Mode** drop-down box to the **Pixel Normal Offset** option. We'll see how this works in the *There's more* section.

27. Head back to the **Append** node we created in *step 24* and connect it to the Refraction input pin of our main material node:

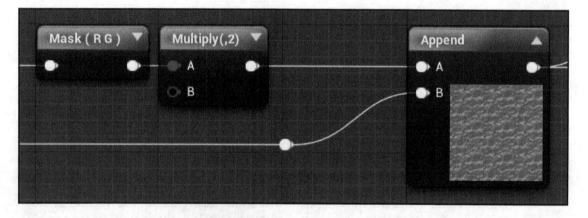

The preceding screenshot shows a part of the material that we'll copy later on, so let's refer to it as part B. Apart from using the previous nodes to drive the refraction, we can also modify the roughness of the water through them.

28. Add a **Fresnel** node and connect its **Normal** input pin to the output of the previous **Append** node. Set the **exponent** to `1.5` and the **Base Reflect Function** to `0.1` in the **Details** panel.

29. Include a couple of **Scalar Parameters** in order to drive the different roughness values. I've created one called **Parallel roughness** and another one called **Perpendicular roughness** so that it helps me to identify the viewing direction at which those values are supposed to show.

30. Create a **Lerp** node and connect the three previous nodes to the **A**, **B**, and **Alpha** input pins. Connect that in turn to the **Roughness** material input pin.

 Even though the roughness of the water should really be the same value as long as there's no oil or other substances in its surface, we've decided to modify it a little bit as there's usually other surfaces apart from water in a bathtub, such as soap.

The last bit we need to tackle is the actual **Normal** input pin of the material, which we haven't yet connected. Instead of using the previous normal we created, we will blend between different intensities of the same one according to a random texture. This will help us to introduce further variation in the material so there's no repetition.

31. Copy part B of the material a couple of times.

32. Adjust the **B** value of the **Multiply** node on each. Set the first one to `0.1`, and the second to `0.2`.

33. Connect pin **B** of the two new **Append** nodes back to the blue channel of the **Texture Sample** in part A. The **Component Masks** should be connected to the general output of that same texture, just like what happened in part B.

34. Create a new **Texture Sample** and assign it the **T_Smoke_Tiled_D** texture.

35. Add a **Cheap Contrast** and connect it to that last Texture Sample, and connect a Constant with a value of **1** to the **Contrast** input pin.

36. Throw a **Lerp** node and connect the output of the two previous **Append** vectors to the **A** and **B** pins. The **Alpha** should be connected to the output of the **Cheap Contrast** node. Feed the output of the **Lerp** node into the **Normal** input pin of the material:

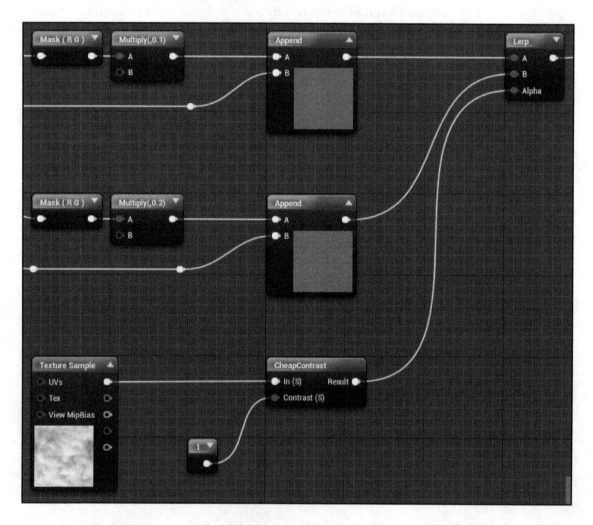

All of the previous changes have left us with the final material we'll apply to the bathtub water. Be sure to check out how it looks, and feel free to tweak the different parameters we've set up. Creating a Material Instance can be especially useful in this case, since it will allow us to quickly modify the material without having to wait for the compilation process:

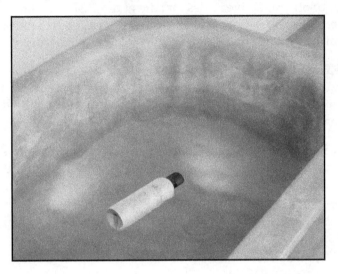

How it works...

We introduced a couple of new concepts in this recipe, and I'd like to go into a little bit more detail on one of them: the **Pixel Normal Offset** refraction mode. We used this technique instead of the traditional IOR, which we saw in the second recipe of this chapter, because it tends to work better on large and/or flat surfaces. Even though we might think that the IOR method is closer to real-life refraction mechanics, the implementation that Unreal has chosen for this system is not always our best option when trying to mimic reality. Without getting too technical, their IOR implementation makes some assumptions that can introduce artifacts in the type of models that we mentioned before. To counter this, Epic has also introduced the Pixel Normal Offset Refraction method as an alternative.

This new refraction model works by using the vertex normal data to calculate the refraction offset that you see. This is possible by computing the difference between the per-pixel normal against that of the vertex normal, offering the results that you see onscreen, which match the real world better than the IOR method.

There's more...

Another useful node we employed is the **Depth Fade** one, which allowed us to mask an area according to the distance to the shore. Beyond its actual usefulness, it helps to highlight a number of other creative nodes that are at our disposal and that make the material-creation process a very powerful and versatile one. I'd like to leave you thinking about some of them, as they might help you realize your material ideas later on.

One of them is the **Pixel Depth** function. This expression assigns a value to the rendered pixels that is tied to their distance to the camera. This can be used in different ways and to achieve a multitude of effects—one of them being a manual depth of field effect, where we might blur areas that are far from the camera or closer to it.

The second one we'll cover is the **Scene Depth** node. It is very similar to the previous node, except that the depth values it gives us are sampled at any location of the scene and not just on the pixels currently being drawn. This is a useful node to use in conjunction with the previous one, as we can create interesting effects by comparing both nodes.

See also

As always, make sure to read Epic Games' official documentation if you want to learn more about the subject available at `https://docs.unrealengine.com/en-us/Engine/Rendering/Materials/PixelNormalOffset.`

Water caustics

Nailing down the right look for a water surface can greatly increase the realism of our scenes, especially when dealing with tricky materials, such as the ones that make use of translucency. Getting those nice reflections to show up, the refraction working in the right way, and the animation to feel believable is something we tackled in the previous recipe. On top of that, we can add an extra effect that is often seen in bodies of water: caustics.

This technique, which tries to mimic how the refracted envelope of light rays that the surface of our water body is projecting onto another object works (the bathtub, in our case), is difficult to calculate in real-time renderers. That being the case, we usually rely on approaches that try to fake the effect rather than realistically show it. We'll be exploring one such method in the following pages.

Getting ready

Since this recipe is going to follow in the footsteps of the previous one, there's nothing new that you'll need. All of the same considerations we took into account some pages ago still apply here: we'll need a plane that can act as a body of water and a model that acts as its container. With regards of the new bits that we'll be using, all of them are provided as part of the **Starter Content** so make sure to include that!

If you want to follow along using the same assets, you can find the map we'll be using as the starting point in the Content / UE4ShadersAndEffects / Maps / Chapter04 / 04_06_WaterCaustics_Start folder.

See you in the next section!

How to do it...

As we said before, caustics are usually faked within the engine rather than computed in real time as there's no current method that allows for that operation to run at a high refresh rate. As such, we'll fake them with something called a light function, which is a type of asset that is applied to lights in UE4. With that in mind, let's first place the light that will support this technique:

1. Add a **Spot Light** to the scene. This type of light is quite helpful when dealing with caustics, since it has a couple of parameters (the **Outer Cone Angle** and the **Inner Cone Angle**) that allow us to have a nice area where the light isn't fully on or off.

2. Place the **Spot Light** slightly above the water plane and tilt it a little bit, like in the following screenshot:

Just as a reference, I've used a rotation value of **90**, **-60**, **-60** in the **X**, **Y**, and **Z** axes.

3. Set the type of light to **Movable**.

4. Play a little bit with the values for the light—weak the **Intensity**, adjust the **Inner** and **Outer Cone Angles**. I've set the values to **2.3** for the first of those settings, **22** degrees for the **Inner Cone Angle** and **42** for the **Outer** one.

5. Scroll down to expand the available settings under the **Light** section of our **Spot Light** actor and focus on the **Lighting Channels** section. Uncheck **Channel 0**, which should be on by default, and check **Channel 1**.

6. Select the **SM_BathTub** actor and head over to the **Lighting** section in the **Details** panel. At the bottom of that section, you will have the opportunity to check **Channel 1** as well. Leave both channels checked on this occasion:

Lighting Channels for the **Spot Light** and the **Bathtub**.

Assigning a specific **Lighting Channel** to a mesh means that said model will only be affected by lights that make use of the same **Lighting Channel**. Keep that in mind when you want to create special effects that only affect certain surfaces.

With that out of the way, we can finally dedicate our efforts to build the light function through which we are going to emulate the caustic effect. We'll start this process by heading over to the **Content Browser** and creating a new material.

7. Create a new material and perform the usual steps—give it a name, save it, and so on. I've named mine `M_ WaterCaustics`.

8. Open the new asset in the **Material** editor and head over to the **Details** panel. Change the **Material Domain** to **Light Function**.

9. Assign the new material to our **Spot Light**. To do so, head back to the main editor and select the spot light. Look at its **Details** panel—there's a section there called **Light Function** that you'll find if you scroll down enough:

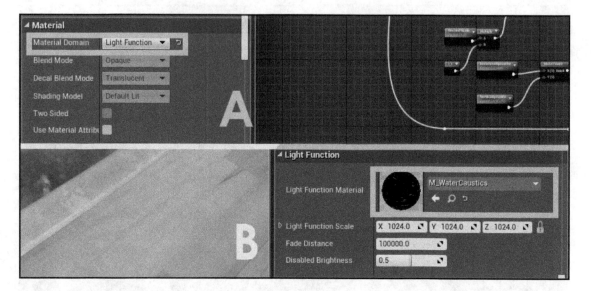

A / B : Set the **Material Domain** to **Light Function** and assign the material to the **Spot Light**.

Having the material applied to the light will allow us to see the changes as we make them and save them. Let's start modifying it!

10. Create a **Texture Coordinate** node as we need one of these whenever we want to alter the size or the position of our textures.

11. Add a **Multiply** node after the previous **Texture Coordinate** one, and connect the output of that one to the pin **A** of our new node.

12. Somewhere under the **Texture Coordinate**, create a **Scalar Parameter**. We will use this to change the tiling of the **Texture Sample** we'll create later instead of the **Texture Coordinate** node, simply because Scalar parameters can be tweaked in Material Instances, unlike **Texture Coordinate** nodes. Set it to **1**.

13. Connect the **Scalar Parameter** to the pin labelled **B** of the previous **Multiply** node.

For organizational purposes, let's call the previous steps we've performed part A. This will help us to remember what we have to connect where.

14. Create a couple of **Scalar Parameters**; name one **Horizontal Speed 01** and the other **Vertical Speed 01**. Feel free to give them whatever name you want, but know that's what we'll be using them for to define the speed at which a future texture is going to move. Set them to `0.01` and `0.025`, respectively.

15. Create a **MakeFloat2** node. As this is a new node, know that you can do so if you right-click anywhere within the **Material Graph** and start to type that name.

16. Connect the scalar parameter that affects the horizontal speed to the input pin named **X (S)** of the **MakeFloat2** node, and the one that affects the vertical speed to the pin labelled **Y (S)**.

17. Drag a line from the **Result** pin of the **MakeFloat2** node and create a **Multiply** node at the end of it. It will automatically connect itself to pin **A**, and leave pin **B** with the default value of **1** at this stage, since it will come in handy later on.

We can call these last few steps part B. With these two parts under our belts, we can create the next bit, which is going to tie things together.

18. Add a **Panner** node (right-click **Panner**).

19. Connect part A to the Coordinate pin of our **Panner** and then connect part B to the Speed pin of the same **Panner** node.

This is what our graphs should look like now:

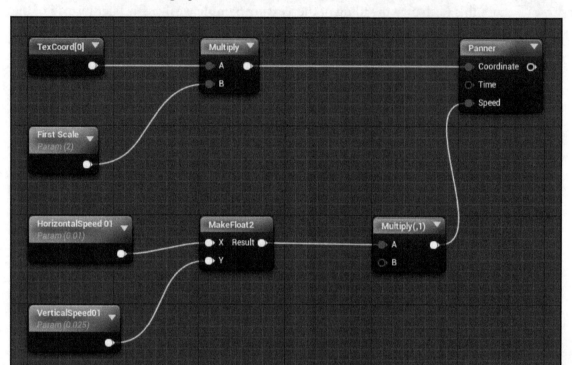

Feed the Speed pin with a 2D vector! That's why we used the
`MakeFloat2`— to control the Speed in X and Y independently. Had we
only used a Constant, we would be tweaking both speeds with just one
value, resulting in a diagonal movement.

20. Drag a cable out of the output pin of the **Panner** node and create the **Texture
Sample** that the whole sequence we created is going to be affecting.

21. Select the **T_Water_M** texture as the value for our new **Texture Sample**. This
asset is part of the **Starter Content**, so be sure to include it if you haven't done so.

Every step we've performed so far now has left us with a node network that we could use to drive the appearance of the material. Thanks to the texture we just selected, which contains a similar pattern to that of water caustics, the light function could just as well work. In fact, if you click on the **Apply** and **Save** buttons, you'll be able to see what it looks like on our scene. However, we want to do something more caustics are a type of pattern that usually wraps around and moves fluently on the surfaces where it appears, and that's what we are going to replicate next. And those things we are going to create in just a second are going to be quite similar to the ones we now have, so let's call the node network we have already created section A before we move on:

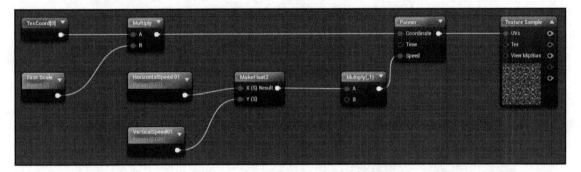

22. Duplicate section **A** and place it below the first instance of section A. We'll call this part section B, where we'll be operating next.

23. Change the names of the scalar parameters located within section B. I've gone with **Second Scale, Horizontal Speed 02**, and **Vertical Speed 02** to reflect what they'll be doing.

24. Apart from changing the names, feel free to play around with the values of the previous parameters as well. Making them similar but different to the ones in *Section A* will work well, as our intention is to create a slightly different pattern. I've gone with the following values: `1.5` for the scale, `-0.008` for the horizontal speed, and `-0.0125` for the vertical one.

> The values on those fields can change drastically depending on the type of surface that you are working on and how its UVs are laid out. Feel free to experiment with them if you are using your own assets.

Having this duplicate of the original node network will let us mix both in a nice, subtle way. With this as our objective, let's create a node that can do that.

25. Add a **Lerp** node after both of the previous sections. Connect the output of section **A** to pin **A**, and the output of section B to pin **B**. Leave the **Alpha** as it is by default, with a value of **0.5**, which will create a 50% blend between both input.
26. Include a **Multiply** node right after the last **Lerp**.
27. Create another **Scalar Parameter** and name it Overall Intensity. We'll use that to control the strength of the light function.
28. Connect the output pin of the **Lerp** node into pin **A** of the Multiply, and the last **Scalar Parameter** into the **B** pin.
29. Plug the result of the **Multiply** node into the **Emissive Color** pin of our main material node.

Even though we are almost finished, we can still add one more scalar parameter to control the overall speed of the effect. Do you remember that we left an unconnected pin on the **Multiply** node in section **A** after the **MakeFloat2**? We'll take care of that now.

30. Create a **Scalar Parameter** with a value of **1** to control the overall speed at the beginning of the graph. Name it **Overall Speed**.
31. Hook its output pin to pin **B** of both the Multiply nodes located in sections A and B (the ones that are placed right after the **MakeFloat2** nodes).

32. Compile and save your work:

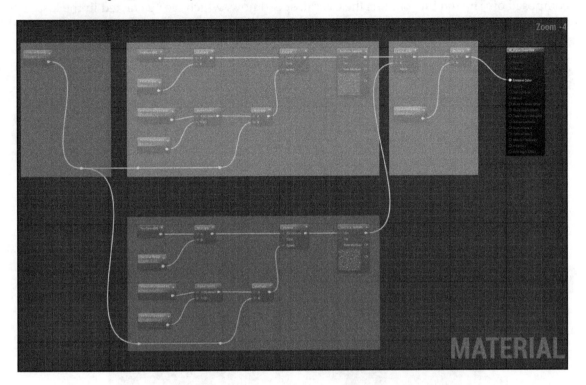

We've included the previous screenshot as a reminder of what our node graph should be composed of. The red bit contains the overall speed now, which we've created in the last steps to control that property of the material. The orange and blue rectangles match what we've called sections A and B, with the green bit at the end blending between both and adjusting the intensity. With all of those changes in place, this is what our scene should now look like:

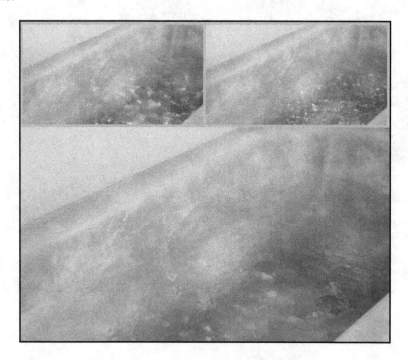

How it works...

Light functions are great! You already knew that, but the way we've used them in this recipe really highlights Unreal's versatility. Think about it: we've used a light. However, this light doesn't cast shadows, as we've disabled that. The light that it emits doesn't affect any other surface apart from the one we want to affect, as we used the lighting channels Unreal provides to take care of that. Pretty uncommon behavior as far as lights go!

This type of versatility is something that we should exploit more and more as Unreal users, as it only offers us benefits in the long run. We become more familiar with the engine, know what the possibilities are, and where the limits lie.

There's more...

Before we finish, let's talk about realistic water caustics. If, for some reason, you wanted to create a more realistic version of the water caustic effect, instead of faking it, there's an option that you might want to explore, even though, all being said, it's not 100% accurate either.

Something you could do is record the animation of the water plane you are going to be using from a top-down perspective, and render that sequence of images into a video. Of course there's no use in us rendering the color, we would need to render the height map, but that's something we can do in other 3D editing software packages or if we visualize our scene through the Scene Depth buffer and we then adjust the values to create a height map.

All in all, the point is to record an animated height map that matches the real movement of an animated water plane—the same one that we'll use, to be precise. This animation can then be fed into the light function, and if we align it correctly and play with it, we'll have a much more realistic water caustic!

See also

You can find more info about light functions and lighting channels here (official Epic Docs, as always!):

- https://docs.unrealengine.com/en-us/Engine/Rendering/
  LightingAndShadows/LightFunctions
- https://docs.unrealengine.com/en-us/Engine/Rendering/
  LightingAndShadows/LightingChannels

Animating a sea shader

Even though we've worked on water before, I couldn't pass up the opportunity to talk about large-scale ocean shaders in UE4. I'll admit it: this is one of my favorite subjects in computer rendering, and achieving great results is completely possible thanks to the methods we are about to see. However, this is not going to be a mere expansion of any of the previous topics. Instead, we are going to continue to learn new techniques and apply new concepts throughout the following pages—so buckle up, there's no time for rest in our journey!

Getting ready

Big changes for this recipe but everything you'll need is, as always, provided either by us, included in the **Starter Content**, or part of the engine. Since we are going to be working on a large ocean material, it made sense to move from the familiar interior scene we've been working on to a large outdoors environment. The level we'll be working on is called **04_07_SeaShader_Start**, and you can find it in the folder for this chapter: `Content / UE4ShadersAndEffects / Maps / Chapter04`.

But what if you want to apply what we'll be learning on your own projects, you say? In that case, here are the basic building blocks you'll need: a subdivided plane and the **BP_LightStudio** blueprint (that comes provided with the **Starter Content**). Basically, a plane that has enough subdivisions so that we can fake the motion of the waves and a light to see it. That's it!

How to do it...

Working with oceans usually means working with large-scale surfaces. In our industry, and unlike in real life, those surfaces could actually be very small but for the purposes of this recipe, we are going to force ourselves to deal with big areas. Doing so allow us to learn how to tackle them, as their scale usually comes with certain challenges. The main one we'll face is something called tiling, which is a word we use to refer to the visible repetition of a texture across a model. Even though that's something we dealt with in Chapter 3, *Opaque Materials and Texture Mapping*, when working on concrete surfaces, we'll expand upon that by adding interesting effects and techniques that we couldn't apply there. One of them is the addition of sea foam depending on the height of the waves we create – something extremely useful as it introduces dynamic changes in our materials.

1. With your scene already set up—either by opening the one we provide or after creating yours—add a new material in the **Content Browser**. I've named mine **M_OceanWater** which is self-explanatory!

   As one of our main worries will be to hide any repetition that may become obvious in our material, we'll start by defining two set of randomly-generated waves—one smaller and one larger in scale. We'll call this first bit part A, dedicated to the creation of the small waves.

2. Create a **Material Function Call**, either by holding the *F* key and left-clicking in an empty space of the material graph or by right-clicking and typing its name.

3. With the new node selected, look at the **Details** panel and expand the drop-down menu for the material function. Search for and select the one called **Motion_4WayChaos_Normal**.

   This handy function will create a randomized animated motion based on a normal texture we'll use as input. Let's set the parameters up.

4. Pop an **Absolute World Position** node in. Remember to just type World Position, as starting with **Absolute** will give you no results.

5. Throw two scalar parameters into the mix. The first one, which I've named **Water Scale (1)**, will be used as a general control for the scale of our ocean. The second one, named **Small Wave Scale (256)**, will control the specific scale of the smaller waves.

6. Add a **Multiply** node and connect its **A** and **B** input to the previous two scalar parameters.

7. Create a **Divide** node and place it after the **Absolute World Position** one. Connect its A input pin to the output of the **World Position**.

8. Connect pin **B** of the new divide node to the output of the previous Multiply node.

9. Place a **Component Mask** after the **Divide** node. Select the **Red** and **Green** channels in the **Details** panel.

10. Connect the output of that network of nodes to the **Coordinates/UVs** input pin of the original **Material Function**:

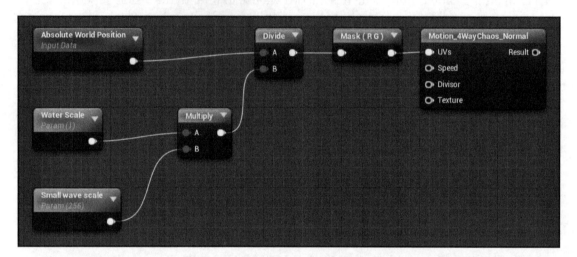

This first part that is feeding into the UVs input pin of the Four-Way Chaos function defines how it will project itself onto the surfaces we apply this material to. On the one hand, the World Position gives us a projection that doesn't rely on the UVs of the model. We affect the scale of this projection through the two scalar parameters we created, and we finally mask the red and green channels as we need a two-coordinate vector to feed into the final input pin. With the coordinates under control, let's now affect the Speed and the Texture pins.

11. Create a couple of scalar parameters, one which we'll call **Small Wave Speed (0.2)** and one called **Water Speed (1.5)**. This is the same approach we took when we created the scalar parameters that affected the scale of these small waves—except now we are controlling the speed instead.

12. Multiply both by creating one such node and connecting the previous scalar parameters to it.

13. Connect the output of that **Multiply** node to the **Speed** input pin of the Four-Way Chaos function.

14. Include a **Texture Object Parameter**, assign the **T_ Water_ N** texture to it, and connect it to the Texture input node of our previous function.

    We are creating so many scalar parameters and texture object parameters because we want to create a Material Instance at the end of this process and be able to edit all of those things in real time, as going one by one and compiling every change would take a lot of time.

    With that done, we are almost finished with this section of the graph (part A). We still need to create a couple more nodes in order to finish it, so let's do that.

15. Create two **Constant3Vector** nodes. Assign the first a value of **0,0,0** and the second one a value of **1,1,0.2**.
16. Create a Scalar Parameter and name it **Small wave amplifier**, with a value of **0.5**.
17. **Lerp** between the first two vectors according to this last parameter.
18. Add a **Multiply** after the Four-Way Chaos function and connect that to the A input pin of the new node. Connect pin **B** to the output of the previous **Lerp**.

    Implementing all of the previous steps will see us finished with part A of the material, which controls the scale, speed, and magnitude of the small scale waves:

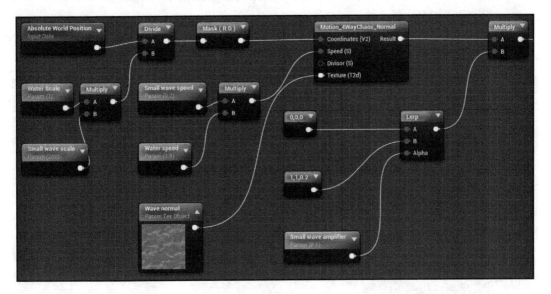

This will enable us to quickly duplicate the contents we've just created and generate the second set of waves, which will be larger in scale hence the name we'll be giving them, **Large Scale Waves**. We'll start to do that now, but just as a reference, we'll call this section of the graph part B.

19. Copy all of the nodes that we've previously created, what we've called part A, and paste them a little bit further down the material graph. This is going to be called part **B**, which will control the scale, speed, and amplitude of the large-scale waves.

20. Rename things, as the names of the scalar parameters need to be adapted for this large-scale section of the graph. **Small Wave Scale**, **Small Wave Speed**, and **Small Wave Amplifier** should change the word **Small** to **Large** in all of them.

21. Other scalar parameters need to be renamed so that they match their original names. That will ensure that we are using the same parameters across the whole material. Pay special attention to **Water Scale** and **Water Speed**, as they've slightly changed their names after the copy/paste process.

22. Change the values of **Large Wave Scale**, **Large Wave Speed**, and **Large Wave Amplifier**. The new values should be something like 1024, 0.05, and 0.9. Also, change the values of the Constant3 Vectors that feed into the **Lerp** being driven by the **Large Wave Amplifier**, the new values should be **1,1,3** and **1,1,0.1** in the **A** and **B** pins.

23. As a small addition, include a **Rotator** node between the Component Mask and the Four-Way Chaos function in this part B of the material. This will spice things up a little bit as we would otherwise end up with just a larger-scale version of the previous texture.

24. Feed the **Time** input pin of this rotator with a simple constant, which I've given a value of **1.342**:

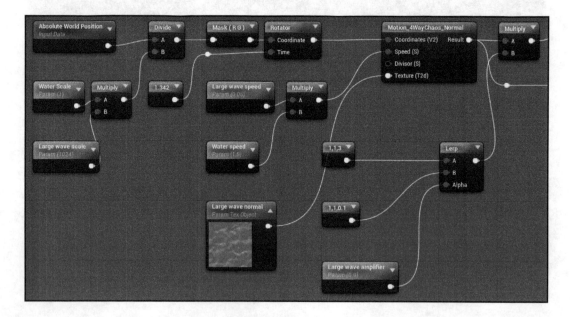

The previous changes have left us with a functional part B of the graph, identical to part A except for the different scalar parameters and values we've applied. This means that we now have two functions that are creating two wave patterns of different sizes, animated at different speeds and that have a different normal intensity. Let's see what this means by connecting the output of each part into the **Base Color**, one at a time:

As you can see, this is creating a nice wave pattern. However, the reason we've created two different ones is so we can blend between them to remove the repetition we see. This will be useful to drive other elements of the material, as we are about to do. However, there's something that we can do straight out of the box at this stage, which is to connect the blend of both parts into the Normal input of the main material node:

25. Create an **Add** node after both parts A and B and connect each of them to the input pins.
26. Connect the output of the previous **Add** node into the **Normal** input pin of the main material node.

    Those actions have taken care of the normals for the material. We still need to address its **Base Color**, the **Displacement**, and many of the other properties that define the look of our shaders. We can start this process by tackling the displacement of the plane on which we are applying the material.

27. Copy part B of the material and paste it under the original part B. We'll call this other section part C, which we are about to modify as well.
28. Delete the **Multiply** located after the 4 Way Chaos function, along with the **Lerp**, the two Constant3 vectors, and the scalar value that are feeding its **B** input pin.

29. Select the **Motion_4WatChaos_Normal** function and change it to the one called **Motion_4WayChaos**. Be careful with the name, as they are very similar but are meant for different purposes.

30. Change the texture being fed to the **Texture Object Parameter** to the one named **T_Water_M**. This is a heightmap version of the previous one, included with the **Starter Content** as well. While you're at it, change the name of this parameter to **Large Wave Height**.

31. Rename the rest of the other scalar parameters to match those found in part B.

32. Add a **Power** node after the function, and connect the **Result** pin of that to the **Base pin of the new node**:

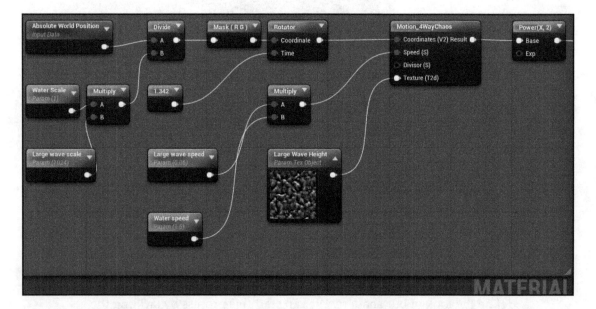

All of the previous actions will have left us with part C of the material graph. As you can probably tell by now, this is going to be a complex shader! Part C basically does the same as part B; it defines the scale and speed of the large waves. However, instead of calculating the normals, we are calculating the height, which is going to be useful in order to drive the displacement of our model as well as the location of the foam in the shader.

At this stage, we are going to branch off part C, as we'll need this to drive the location of the sea foam and the displacement of the material. The displacement can be used almost as-is, so let's focus on that for the time being.

33. Add a **Scalar Parameter** and name it **Luminance bias** to control the intensity of the height-map. Give it a value of **0**. This will control how high or low it is in our world. Create an **Add** node and connect this to the **Luminance Bias** and to the output of the **Power** node from *step 32*.

34. Mask the red channel with a **Component Mask**. This will give us a grayscale texture that we can then store in a different channel. We'll want to put it in the blue one in particular, or the **Z** one as it is sometimes known.

35. Create an **Append** node and a **Constant2 Vector**. Give the vector a value of 0,0, and connect it to pin **A** of the **Append** node. Connect the previous mask we created into pin **B** of the Append node. This will effectively create a three-component vector and store the height map as the **Z** value.

36. Throw a **Multiply** node to increase the intensity. Multiply it by 5.

37. Create another **Multiply** node and a **Scalar Parameter**. This latest parameter will control the displacement, so name it just that and give it an initial value of something like **10**. Connect the new scalar parameter and the output of the previous multiply node to the new one.

38. Right-click and create a **Vertex Normal** vector. This will give us the world space value of the vertex normals our material is applied to, which will let us displace the model in turn. Add that node to the previous **Multiply** by creating a new **Add** and doing just that.

39. Hook the result of the **Add** node into the **World Displacement** input pin of the material:

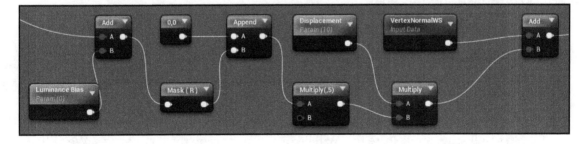

Now we can take care of the water color; the first step in that journey is going to be the creation of the **Sea Foam** texture. Let's do it.

40. Copy part C and paste it between parts B and C. Create space in between if you don't have any at the moment.

41. Rename some of the scalar parameters; we should have **Seafom scale** instead of Large wave scale, and **Seafoam speed** instead of Large wave speed.

42. Set the **Water_d** texture as the **Texture Object Parameter** default value.

Before we continue, let's introduce a small difference. If we were to join the result of the **Component Mask** to the **Coordinate** input pin of the **Motion_4WayChaos** function, we would be effectively populating our material with sea foam all over the place. However, we want this texture to appear linked to the large waves (part B). Here's how we can take care of that:

43. Include an **Add** node between the **Component Mask** node and the material function of the sea foam. The **Component Mask** should be fed into one of the input pins of the **Add** node, and the output of that connected again to the material function.

44. We should now have an empty input pin on the latest Add node. We'll come back to this in a few steps, so keep this in the back of your head.

45. Go back to part B of the large wave section, and drag another cable out of the material function (**Motion_4WayChaos_Normal**). Create a **Component Mask** and select the **Red** and **Green** channels.

46. Continue to drag another cable, out of the output pin of the new mask, and create a **One Minus** node.

47. Create a **Multiply** node.

48. Add a **Scalar Parameter** and name it **Foam distortion**. Hook it into pin **B** of the previous Multiply.

49. Connect the output of the **One Minus** node in pin **A**.

50. Connect the result of the **Multiply** node back into the original Add node from *step 43*.

Steps 40 to 50 will be referred to as part D. Those steps have enabled us to include a small sea foam texture that will be driven in part by the large waves. We will use this to modify the appearance of our material. It is now time to tackle the **Base Color** of the shader a process that will involve several steps. The first of them will see us trying to mimic the effect that we see when we look at the ocean: the color seems to change according to the position and movement of the waves, where surfaces that are pointing toward us seem darker than those that are parallel to our vision:

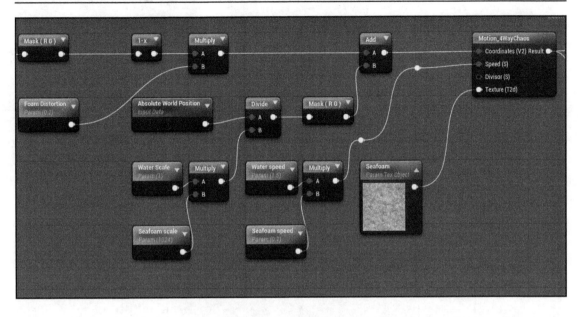

51. Drag a cable from the **Add** node we created in *step 25* (the one that combines parts A and B).
52. Create a **Normalize** node at the end of it. This expression takes the vector values we give them and returns the unit vector back to us (a vector with a length of **1**).
53. Add a **Transform Vector** after the **Normalize** node, which will take the tangent space values that we are inputting and output them according to the world space.
54. Create a **Fresnel** node, and hook the previous **Transform Vector** into its **Normal** input pin. With the node still selected, set the **Exponent** to 5 and the **Base Reflect Fraction** to **0**.
55. Throw a **Clamp** node after the **Fresnel** and leave the **Min** and **Max** values with the default **0** and **1**:

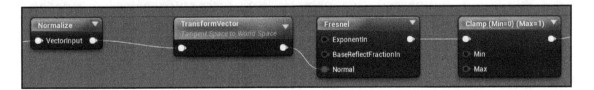

We'll call the previous part of the graph part E for future reference. All of those nodes have given us a mask that treats the areas of the material that aren't facing the camera differently to those that are and what's even more useful, taking the waves into account. We finally have something that can help us drive the appearance of the different water parts. Next, we'll create the colors of the water, which we'll call part F.

56. Create two vector parameters. Name the first something like **Water color** and the second **Water side color**, and give them values that you think would work well with such a material. You can give them wildly different colors if you want to see the effect in action in a more obvious way.

57. **Lerp** between those two vector parameters using the output of part E as the **Alpha**:

At this point, all we need to do is to merge this color with the sea foam we previously created. To do so, we still need to implement a little bit of code.

58. Go back to the **Power** node in part C (where we calculated the Large wave height), which we created in *step 32*, and drag a pin from it in order to create a new **Power** node at the end.

59. Create a **Scalar Parameter**, which we'll use to control how much foam we can see. I've named it **Seafoam Height Power** and given it a value of **2**. Connect it to the **Exp** pin of the previous **Power** node.

60. Create a **Multiply** node, and connect its **A** pin to the output of the Power node.

61. Create another scalar parameter, which will control the tolerance at which the sea foam will be placed. I've named it **Seafoam Height Multiply**, and given it a value of 2,048. Connect it to pin **B** of the previous **Multiply** node.

62. Create a **Component Mask** out of the **Multiply** node and select the **Red** channel as its only option.

63. **Clamp** the output of the previous mask between **0** and **1**:

We'll refer to the previous set of nodes as part G. They control the height at which the foam is going to be positioned, so they are bound to come into play soon.

64. Drag a wire out of the output pin of the **Lerp** node in part F, the one that interpolates between the water colors.

65. Create a **Lerp** node at the end of that wire, which should automatically connect itself with the output of the previous **Lerp**.

66. Connect its **B** pin to the output of the **Motion_4WayChaos** material function from part D, where we created the sea foam.

67. Create a **Component Mask** with the Green channel selected after that same **Motion_4WayChaos** function. Connect that to the **Alpha** pin of *step 65*.

The previous steps have enabled us to interpolate between the normal water color and the sea foam texture, according to the motion of the large waves. We also need to introduce a final requirement so that the foam only shows on the highest parts of the large waves, which we've calculated in part G.

68. Drag another wire from the **Lerp** node in part F, and create another **Lerp**.

69. Connect the output of the **Lerp** in *step 65* to the B pin of the new **Lerp**.

70. The **Alpha** pin should be hooked to the output of the **Clamp** node from part G.

71. Hook the output of this final **Lerp** into the **Base Color** of the **material** node.

The only thing we now need to do is to create a couple of constants to define the **Metallic**, the **Specular**, and the **Roughness** of the material. We can create three such **scalar parameters** and give them values of 0.1 to define the metalness, 1 for the specular to really boost the reflections, and 0.01 on the **Roughness** slot, since we want to see the details reflected in the surface of our water body. Make sure to create a material instance after doing that, and tweak the values until you are happy with the result. As a final image, here's what it should look like once you adjust the color values to something natural:

How it works...

We did a lot in this recipe. And I'm sure things will take a while to settle and become clear, but let's see whether we can expedite that process in the next few sentences.

At the end of the day, it's always useful to think about any complex materials in terms of what we are doing instead of the individual steps we are taking. If you break it down into small pieces, such as the different Parts we've mentioned, things can become clear. Let's review our work.

Parts **A** and **B** are quite straightforward: we are creating an animated wave pattern, one small and one large in scale, thanks to a material function that the engine includes. We also introduced a small variation in the large wave pattern by introducing a rotator node.

Beyond that, we used part D to create a sea foam texture. Unlike the **A** and **B** sections, which were completely independent, part C relies on the large-scale waves as we only want the foam to appear on their crests.

Part C calculated the height map for the large waves, and part H used that information to drive the displacement of the waves. Part G also relied in the height map from part C to define which areas should have sea foam in them. Everything came together as we merged the water color and the sea foam according to these calculations.

That's pretty much it! I know it's still a lot to take in, and the best way to tackle this kind of complexity is by reviewing the graph and making sure everything makes sense.

There's more...

I don't want to finish this chapter without mentioning a very useful technique that can help us review our graph. This is especially useful in complex materials such as this latest one, as it's easy to lose track of what we are doing. The tool I'm talking about is the **Start Previewing Node** option within the material graph. To enable it, just select the node of your graph that you want to check and right-click on it. **Said** option should become apparent as one of the first ones—just click on it and look at the material viewport, which should now show the results. Remember to right-click and select the **Stop Previewing Node** option to cancel that effect.

Note that some effects are difficult to visualize by just clicking the **Start Previewing Node** option. This is especially true with techniques that rely on screen space calculations, as they will only show in our viewport. Effects such as the **Depth Fade node**, which we used when creating the bath tub water a couple of recipes ago will by affected by that circumstance, for example.

See also

One of the things we used the most in this recipe was the 4 Way Chaos material function. Even though we've used several useful nodes in the past, functions are kind of new to us and going back to Unreal Engine's official docs can be a great way to learn more about them: https://docs.unrealengine.com/en-us/Engine/Rendering/Materials/Functions/Overview. Additionally, we all know that this last recipe has been a bit on the long side but the different parts we've tackled are actually very important and quite advanced stuff! As an assignment, try to test yourself and go over the different steps we've reproduced by creating a similar material once again, introducing your own tweaks. You'll gain a lot of knowledge and hands-on experience when doing so!

Beyond Traditional Material Uses

5

All of the materials and techniques we've seen so far had one thing in common: they were designed to affect the look of our scenes. Many shaders fall under this category, and it seems logical given the real-world definition of what a material is. However, they can also be useful in many ways other than the one described when working with real-time applications. In this chapter, we will look at the following recipes:

- Using an emissive material to light the scene
- Playing a video from the internet on a screen
- Creating a CCTV camera feed
- Highlighting interactive elements within our game
- Creating a video game compass
- Creating a mini map

As you can see, there are other interesting uses for materials that can help game or app development. Let's explore them in the next recipes!

Introduction

Try to think for a moment about any game or app you've played in the past – that could be your favorite childhood video game or a recent one that you can't stop thinking about. I'm sure that the first thing you'll remember will be tied to a specific experience you had while playing the game, something that impressed you at the time. It could be the way the world was crafted within the game, or a specific sequence of events that happened in it. In any case, we can probably agree that apps and games aren't just made out of static components, such as models and materials, but the interactions and the magic that happens when everything works together.

In this recipe, we'll take a look at some of those elements within the realm of materials that add interactivity and functionality to our real-time experiences. As we said before, shaders have the ability to be interactive as well, and thanks to that and the logic that we write, we can create powerful assets that make our levels that much more interesting. Let's take a look at them!

Using an emissive material to light the scene

One of the first examples that we'll explore is a material – a lamp, to be precise – that is being used outside of its traditional *comfort zone*. This light-emitting object isn't going to rely on a light asset derived from one of the many different engine classes that are available to us—instead, we'll use a good, old material to do the job. We won't stop there though, as creating the material is actually not the difficult part. What's going to be tricky is getting the right results out of the light baking process, so we'll explore which settings we need to tweak there. All in all, we'll have access to a powerful way of faking and computing light which will come in handy in many different situations.

Let's start exploring one of them! Take a look at the following screenshot:

Getting ready

Even though we are going to be using some custom 3D models and textures in this recipe, this is just so we have something pretty to look at. If you want to use your own assets, know that there won't be many requirements in terms of what you'll need to produce. You'll want to have a simple mesh where you can apply the emissive material we'll be creating and a small scene where you can test the results of the light-baking process we'll be tackling. Even using the assets provided as part of the engine can work in here!

If you, however, want to use the assets we'll be providing, feel free to open the level named **05_ 01_ EmissiveAsStaticLighting_ Start** located inside the Content Browser / UE4ShadersAndEffects / Maps / Chapter05 folder.

How to do it...

The first step we'll need to take before starting this recipe deals with the scene setup. No matter whether you've opened the same level we started with or your own, we want to have quite a dark scene so we can clearly see the effects of what we are about to create. If you've opened the scene we provided, make sure to do the following:

1. Select the **BP_LightStudio** blueprint asset within the **World Outliner** and look at the **Details** panel. The third visible category, named **HDRI**, has an option called **Use HDRI**. Make sure that box is *unchecked* so we can better appreciate the results of the next steps we'll be enabling.

Even though we should have no lights at this point, you might need to click on the **Build** button just so that the engine can rebuild the lighting. Once that's done, you should be looking at an almost completely black level.

Don't worry if, at this point, you still see some light on certain objects—those are reflections present in very reflective surfaces, such as candles or certain parts of the wooden floor. It's interesting to note that they are there, however, as it gives us an idea about how the engine composes the final render output. Refer to the following screenshot:

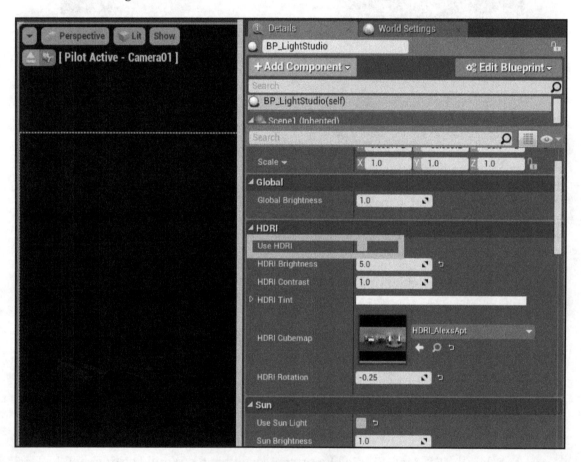

2. Create a new material within the content browser; one which we'll use as the light caster. Name it whatever you like—I've gone with M_LightBulb.

3. Select the main material node and change the shading model from **Default Lit** to **Unlit**. You can do so in the **Details** panel of the selected node, as we've seen in previous recipes.

    We'll be ready to start creating the material logic once we've performed the previous couple of steps. Creating an emissive light is simple, so we'll try to spice things up along the way. The first bit that I want to make you aware of is that we'll try to stay close to the original look of the lamp, which you can check by looking at the first image in this recipe or once you open up the starting scene. We'll use the same textures to achieve that.

4. Create a `Texture Sample` node, and assign it the **T_Lamp_Color** texture. We've included that asset in the `Assets` folder for this chapter.

5. Add a `Cheap Contrast` node after the previous **Texture Sample**, and connect its **In (S)** input pin with the output of the previous image.

6. Include a **Scalar Parameter** and name it something like `Contrast Intensity` – since that's what it will control. Connect it to the **Contrast (S)** input pin of the **CheapContrast** node, but not before assigning it a value (something such as **2** works well).

    The previous set of nodes has taken a regular texture and created a contrast-adjusted black and white version of it. This will let us mask certain areas of the lamp, so that some of them emit more light than others. Take a look at the following screenshot:

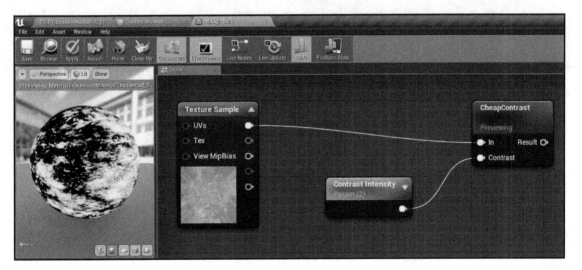

The preceding screenshot of the graph so far, previewing the results of the **CheapContrast** node.

7. Include a **Multiply** node right after the **CheapContrast** one. Connect the result of the contrast to its **B** input pin and the output of the texture sample to pin **A**. Doing this will color the lighter areas of the white and black image with the original texture's color.

8. Add a second **Multiply** node after the previous one, and connect that to pin **A**. Pin **B** will be connected to a parameter that will control the intensity of the lighter areas.

9. Create a **Scalar Parameter**, which we'll use to feed into pin **B** of the previous **Multiply** node. As this will control the brightness of the lighter areas, name it accordingly. Remember to also assign a value, something high, such as **500**.

The previous node sequence has left us with an emissive material that is only casting light on the lighter areas of our original texture. The darker parts aren't emitting at the moment, which is something we'll want to change.

10. Drag a cable out of the original **Texture Sample** and create a new **Multiply** node.

11. Add a new **Scalar Parameter** and name it something like `Dark area brightness`, as we'll use it to control the emissive intensity in those areas.

12. Add a **Lerp** node after both this latest **Multiply** node and the one we created in *step 8*. Connect that **Multiply** to pin **B** of the new **Lerp**, and connect the node created in *step 10* to the **A** input pin.

13. Connect the **Result** pin of the **CheapContrast** node to the **Alpha** of our new **Lerp**.

14. Connect the output of the **Lerp** node to the **Emissive Color** input pin of the material:

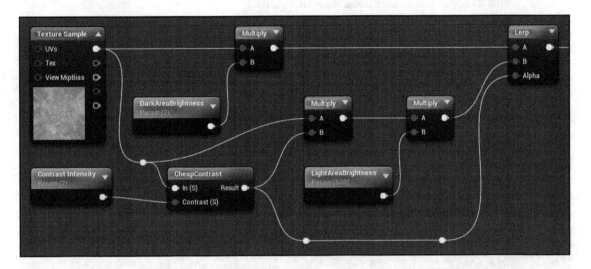

We are left with an emissive material that we can apply to the lamp in our scene. We'll still need to do a couple more things before we see the results though, as there are some settings that need to be enabled.

15. Select the lamp from the **World Outliner** and look at its **Details** panel. You'll be able to find an option called **Use Emissive for Static Lighting** if you scroll down to the **Lighting** section of that panel. Check the checkbox at its side.

16. Apply the material we created to the model. If you are using the model we've provided, you can do so by looking in the **Materials** section of the **Details** panel and assigning it under the **Element 1** panel:

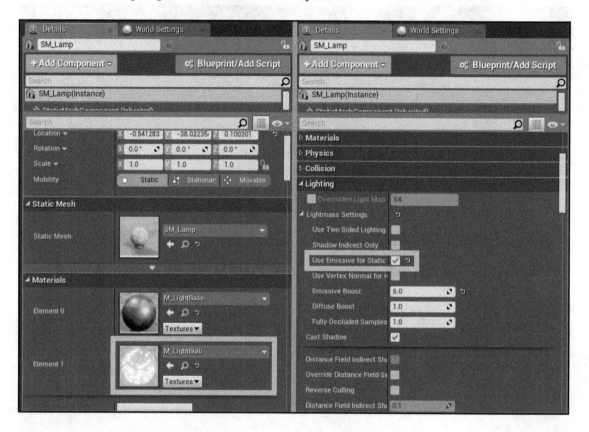

We are ready to build the lighting and start checking out the results. Don't worry if the initial tests are a bit messy—in order for this type of lighting to work well, we'll need to tweak certain **Lightmass** properties. Let's see how things look if we just use the default values though:

It worked! But as we said, the results aren't as clean as we would like. We need to adjust the **Lightmass** settings if we want to increase the quality of the render output. **Lightmass** properties can be accessed through the **World settings** panel. If you don't know where to locate this panel, head over to **Window | World Settings** to find it. The default values that you'll find in the **Lightmass** category will be shown now, with the adjusted ones that I'll be using to increase the visual fidelity of the image by their side and in bold:

- **Static Lighting Level Scale**: 1.0/0.3
- **Num Indirect Lighting Bounces**: 3/30
- **Num Sky Lighting Bounces**: 1/7
- **Indirect Lighting Quality**: 1.0/5.0
- **Indirect Lighting Smoothness**: 1.0/3.0

Apart from that, it can be also useful to check the checkbox next to the **Use Ambient Occlusion** option.

Finally, and before we build the lighting once again to show the final results, I'd like to make you aware of a couple of extra options that can be useful for controlling how this emissive material affects the bloom in the scene. This is especially useful as objects that use the emissive output to cast light can become very bright, and we don't usually want that. If you want to change that, make sure to select the **Post Process Volume** in your scene and look at its **Details** panel. You can adjust the **Bloom** intensity there, which we have changed to **0.1** in this particular example as it works better than the default value.

Something else you can do is to adjust the **Emissive Boost** property in the **Details** panel for the object that is casting light to achieve a similar effect:

How it works...

So, how does it all work? What are the principles that govern the light-emitting properties of the emissive materials? Those might seem like big questions, but they are actually not that difficult to answer. First of all, you can think of using emissive materials for light-emitting purposes in a similar way to static lights. You need to calculate the lighting pass in order for the results to show, and you need to pay attention to certain Lightmass settings to achieve your desired result.

Using this method is actually quite cheap on our machines. The material is lighter to render than most of the other ones we've seen so far, as it uses the Unlit shading model. The light itself is also very simple and won't drain resources away from our computers, as it's basically of the static type. This means no dynamic shadows, and it also means that we have to build the lighting of our level if we want to use it.

The most demanding aspect we need to pay attention to is the Lightmass settings we use when building the light, as that process can take a long time depending on the size of our level and its complexity. Other than that, feel free to use this method as much as you want, as it can be a cheap way to add lighting complexity to your scenes. Many artists use this technique to fake detail lighting, where they would have real lights that define the overall look of the scene but they use this baked method to highlight certain areas. Be sure to test this yourself!

There's more...

As we just saw, using the emissive property in our materials to illuminate a scene is similar to employing a static light. We need to know that, if we want to get good results, we need to tweak the indirect lighting settings in the **Lightmass** panel in order to increase the final quality. That being the case, I'd like to leave you with more examples on this topic, provided for free by Epic Games. If you want to take a look at them, all you need to do is head over to the Epic Games launcher and download the **Content Examples** project. To do so, look under the **Unreal Engine** tab and inside the **Learn** category. You can then download that project and explore the maps dedicated to the indirect lighting topic! Refer to the following screenshot:

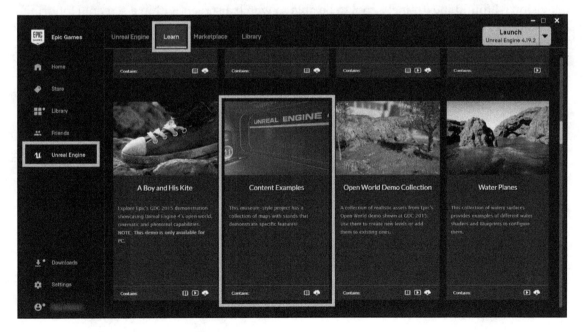

Once you create the project, you'll be able to find the appropriate maps by looking inside **Content Browser | Maps | Lighting Section**. Be sure to give it a go!

See also

Check out Epic's official documentation on emissive materials if you haven't done so yet: `https://docs.unrealengine.com/Engine/Rendering/Materials/HowTo/ EmissiveGlow`.

Playing a video from the internet on a screen

Something we talked about in the introduction of this recipe was the fact that games are able to produce magical moments by combining different interactive elements and putting them together. What those *magical moments* actually are will vary depending on who you ask, and you'll probably get as many different answers as people you question. To me, something that kept me amazed in the early days of 3D games was looking at an in-game television – I found it extremely cool to be able to watch a screen within a screen! Honoring that memory, we'll tackle how to create an interactive display and how to link any videos that you might want to play in it. I hope you find it as useful as I find it entertaining! Take a look at the following screenshot:

Getting ready

We usually say that you don't need a lot to follow these recipes. While that is mostly true, we're at a point where we'll actually need to create one of the assets we'll be using – the TV screen—in a specific way. Be sure to check out the *There's more...* section if you are planning on using your own models! Apart from that, you can get your hands dirty straight away if you want to use the assets we provide. As always, you can open the level named **05 02 VideoStreaming_ Start** located inside the `Content Browser / UE4ShadersAndEffects / Maps / Chapter05` folder and you'll have everything you need to follow along!

How to do it...

Our main goal for this recipe is going to be streaming a video over the internet – sounds easy, right?! It will be, I promise! However, something that we'll need in order to play said broadcast is a display. If you are using the same assets as we are, this can be the **SM_TV_Screen** static mesh that comes bundled with the project. If you are using your own models, bring something that can act as a display and make sure to take into consideration some of the things that we'll cover in the *There's more...* section. Whatever you do, we won't be able to use either of those two models as they are—we'll need to create a Blueprint out of them, as follows:

1. Right-click in the **Content Browser** and create a `Blueprint` asset of the `Actor` type. Give it a name; something such as `BP_TVScreen_Video` will work!
2. Double-click on this new asset to open the Blueprint editor. This is where we'll be operating throughout most of the recipe.
3. Drag your static mesh for the TV display model into the blueprint. You can do this by dragging and dropping the static mesh from the **Content Browser** into the **Blueprint** or by selecting the **Add Component** option in the Blueprint itself and selecting a **Static Mesh** component from the drop-down list.

4. Make the new imported TV screen the default root of your blueprint. You can do this by dragging and dropping the name of the static mesh component into the **Components** panel above the **Default Scene Root** one:

At this point, with the blueprint containing the model for the TV Screen, feel free to replace the existing static mesh of the TV in the main level with this new blueprint if you started using the same level as I am!

Before we go back to the blueprint Editor to continue to implement different layers of functionality, we'll need to create a number of assets that will enable us to stream a video from the internet and play it in our app.

5. Create a `Media Player` asset. You can do this by right-clicking in the **Content Browser** and looking under the **Create Advanced Asset** tab and then the **Media** tab. Remember to give it a name!

6. As soon as you create that **Media Player**, it should give you the option to create a **Media Texture** as well. Know that you can also create one such asset by looking in the same category as before if that doesn't happen.

7. Include a `Streaming Media Source` asset, which can be created just like we did with the **Media Player**.

 Just as a reminder, since the video that we want to play is going to be streamed over the internet, we'll need an active internet connection in place when testing this technique.

Refer to the following screenshot:

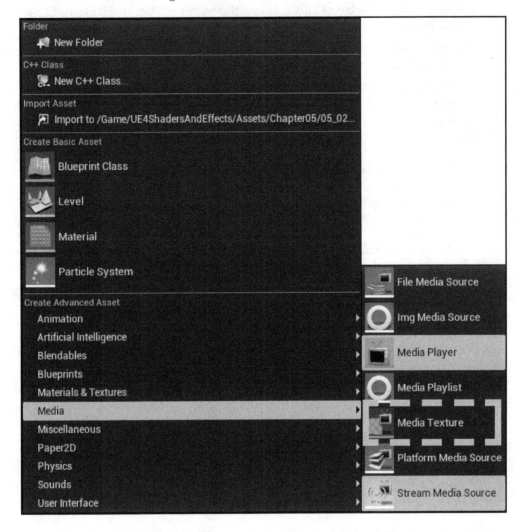

8. Open the new **Media Player** and look at its **Details** panel. There should be an option called **Loop** and a checkbox at its side—make sure to check it so that our video loops when we play it.

Once all of the previous assets have been created and edited, we can get back to our TV blueprint and continue implementing the different bits of functionality.

9. Create three new variables inside our TV blueprint.

10. The first of those variables should be of the `String` type, and it should be public. Name it something like `Media URL`.

11. The second of those variables can be named `Media Player`, and it should be of the **Media Player Object Reference** type.

12. The last variable has to be of the `Stream Media Source Object Reference` type. You can name it `Stream Media Source`, for example. The point is to have recognizable names for when we get these variables in the event graph!

You can quickly make a variable `Public` by clicking on the closed-eye icon to the right of the variable's name. This will allow you to edit it in the editor without having to double-click and enter the blueprint graph.

Now that all of those variables have been created, we need to assign them some default values that match the previous assets we created.

13. Select the **Stream Media** variable and assign the `Stream Media Source` asset we created in *step 7* to it. You can do so by looking at the **Details** panel and choosing said element from the available drop-down menu.

14. Do something similar for the `Media Player` variable, selecting the `Media Player` asset we created in *step 5*.

15. Select the string we created and type the following URL, where I've uploaded a video that you can use to check this functionality: `https://www.dropbox.com/s/sd80rzatl05rhwm/SampleVideo.mp4?dl=1`.

You will need to **Compile** and **Save** your blueprint in order to be able to assign the default values to the different variables you create. Keep that in mind!

If you want to upload or use your own videos, know that we've got you covered. All you need to do is to head over to the *There's more...* section and read all about that topic that way, you'll be able to use your own video links!

We now have all of the basic ingredients that we need to implement the functionality within the Blueprint's **Event Graph**. Let's jump over there and start coding it.

16. Get a reference to the `Stream Media Source` variable in the graph.
17. Drag a wire out of the output pin of our `Stream Media Source` reference and start typing `Set Stream URL` to create that node.
18. Drop the `Media URL` variable that is, the string that contains our URL reference and connect it to the **Stream URL** input pin of the previous Set Stream URL node.
19. Drag a wire out of the **Event Begin Play** node and connect it to the input execution pin of the **Set Stream URL** node.
20. Get a reference to the **Media Player** and drop it after the last node.
21. Create an **Open Source** node by dragging a wire out of the **Media Player** node and typing that name.
22. Connect the `Stream Media Source` reference to the **Media Source** input pin of the previous node.
23. Wire the execution output pin of the **Set Stream URL** node to the execution input pin of the **Open Source** node.
24. Copy the **Media Player** reference once again and paste it after all of the previous nodes.
25. Drag a wire out of it and look for the **Play** node. Wire its input execution pin to the output execution pin of the **Open Source** node.

The graph should now look something like this:

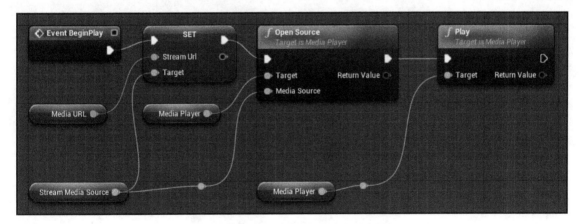

Once you complete the graph, you'll be ready to test out whether it works!

Once you hit **Play**, give the game a couple of seconds to load the video from the web and you should be ready to go. Videos downloaded from Dropbox links aren't the only ones that work though, and you might want to experiment with other URLs to see what works and what doesn't for you. Whatever the case, be sure to stay tuned for the next section, where we'll explain how to get a Dropbox link working in the first place—spoiler: they don't always!

How it works...

I highly recommend having a look at Epic Games' official documentation about their media framework to learn more about which formats are supported across different platforms. I say that because different devices might support different video formats, so we need to be aware of that! Whatever the case, I'd like to put some time aside to talk about some specific considerations you need to take into account when hosting one of your videos online in a `Dropbox` folder, for example.

If you want to do that, the first step will be to actually upload the video to your desired folder. Next, you'll need to generate a link – a step that is quite easy, as you only need to click on the **Share** button next to the video's name and follow the instructions you will be shown. The tricky part is the modification of the URL the system gives you by default, as more often than not the direction will end in something like this: `.....mp4?dl=0`. The zero at the end of that link is the part that we need to correct by replacing it with a `1`. This will allow Unreal to download the file and play it back in our apps, so change it to look something more like this: `.....mp4?dl=1`.

There's more...

Something we need to mention is how to set up the UVs of your TV display in case you want to use your own assets. Here's how you can do it:

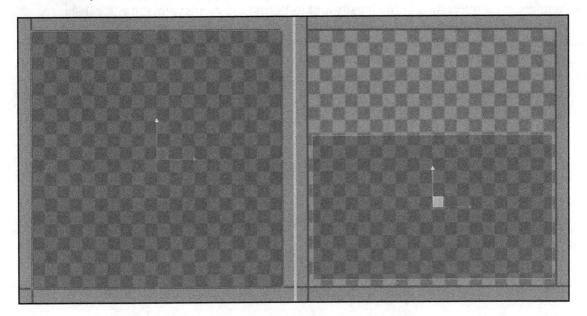

What we'll do is quite simple, even though it can be counter-intuitive—especially if you've unwrapped UVs in the past. Instead of trying to lay out the UVs so that they match the shape of the object, such as in the image on the right, we want them to occupy the entirety of the 0-to-1 UV space. This will ensure that whatever image comes our way gets shown across the entirety of the display, which is our main goal—something you can see in the image on the left. Make sure to follow the same guidelines!

See also

You can find a lot of other related information about Unreal's media framework in the official docs: https://docs.unrealengine.com/en-us/Engine/MediaFramework/HowTo/en-us/Engine/MediaFramework/TechReference.

Creating a CCTV camera feed

Getting a video from the internet is cool, but wait until you capture your own scene in real time! This is something that has many different potential applications, and I think all of them are quite interesting both visually and in terms of gameplay. Imagine, for instance, that you were trying to escape from a monster and you needed to rely on CCTV surveillance footage to plan your escape. The technique we are about to see can help you realize that vision – and more! The potential uses go well beyond that, as I'm sure you'll start to see for yourself once we start working on this. Capturing a scene in real time can have many other applications, such as creating portals and enhancing reflections. Let's start to look at what they are all about!

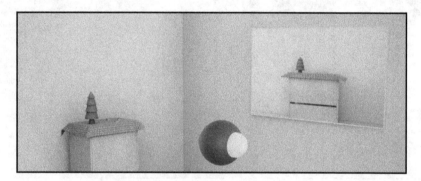

Getting ready

Most of the assets we'll be using are part of the engine, especially the ones that will enable us to capture the scene. We've also included some extra ones that will act as props which, as always, are included as part of the project we'll be providing you with. They can be found in the `Content Browser / UE4 Shaders And Effects / Assets / Chapter05` folder. If you want to start using the same map as well, remember to head over to the appropriate section within the **Content Browser** for the current chapter.

If you prefer to use your own levels and assets, know that this time it's just a matter of having a scene populated with some props and with some lighting going on. The only thing that would literally not work would be a completely blank scene, so anything beyond that would probably serve you well!

How to do it...

Let's kick things off by taking a look at how we'll tackle the current recipe, since there are many possibilities we could explore. Capturing a scene can be done to achieve multiple aims, but we've decided to center our strengths on a CCTV feed. That being the idea, what elements do you think are needed in such a system? Having an idea about that will help us visualize the whole process, as there are going to be multiple phases. If we think about it in real-life terms, we'll probably need at least a *camera* than can capture the scene, a *display* where we can play the video back, and some sort of *storage unit* or transfer mechanism in order to move the data between the camera and the display. As you'll see, those same actors will also be needed in Unreal as well, so let's start by creating them:

1. Create a new Blueprint anywhere within the **Content Browser** and give it a name that denotes it's a capturing device—following the theme of the scene, you can probably go with something such as `BP_WebCam`. Incidentally, that's kind of how the static mesh we'll be using looks!

2. Open up the blueprint editor and create a **Static Mesh** component by selecting one from the `Add Component` drop-down menu.

3. Look for another type of component in the same panel as before – this time, we'll need to look for **Scene Capture Component 2D**:

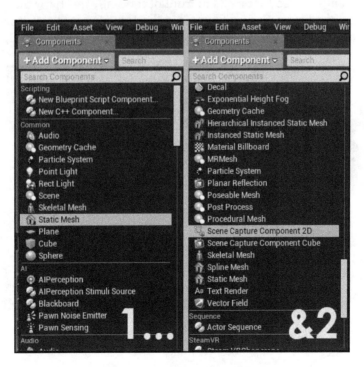

With those assets in place, it's time to assign them some default values.

4. Make **Static Mesh** the root component of this blueprint. You can do so by dragging and dropping its name into **Default Scene Root** on the **Components** panel.

5. Select **Static Mesh** and look in the **Details** panel. The section named like the component will let you assign the model you want to use if you want to use the same one I'll be using, select the SM_WebCam asset.

6. Before we can assign anything to the **Scene Capture Component 2D**, we need to create a different asset that works with that. Go back to **Content Browser** and right-click anywhere you want to create the new asset in look for the **Render Target** resource under the **Media & Textures** section.

7. Give a name to the previous created asset, something such as RT_WebCam.

8. Go back to the blueprint and select **Scene Capture Component 2D**. Look in its **Details** panel, scroll all the way down to the **Scene Capture** section, and assign the previously created **Render Target** to the **Texture Target** category.

9. Make sure the **Capture Every Frame** option is ticked, which you can find a little bit below the previous setting.

10. With a **Scene Capture Component 2D** selected and while in the **Viewport** tab, move it a little bit so that it sits in front of the static mesh for the webcam. This will allow the **Scene Capture** to record the scene properly, as it would otherwise look black if we didn't move it (as it would be inside the camera!):

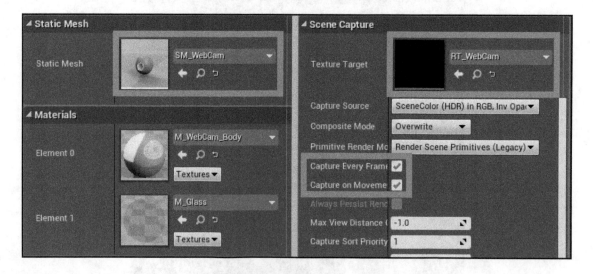

If we leave things as they are for this blueprint, we could already create something with which we can work—however, we would be looking at a still image since the webcam blueprint doesn't have any logic that makes it move. Let's take care of that by adding a looping motion to the camera that will make it rotate between two defined angles. To do that, head over to the **Event Graph** section of the blueprint.

11. Create a **Timeline** in there, right after **Event Begin Play**. You can do so by right-clicking and selecting the **Add Timeline** option.

12. Connect both of those nodes together—the output of the execution pin of the **Begin Play** to the **Play** input pin on the **Timeline**.

13. Double-click on the **Timeline** node to open up its **Curve Editor**.

14. Add a **Float Track** by clicking on the **f+** button located on the upper-left corner of the new window.

15. Give it a name, something such as `Camera Rotation` can work!

16. Give it a **Length** by typing a number in the appropriate entry box, located a few spaces to the left of the previous `Add Float Track` button. Set it to `10`, and check the **Loop** checkbox a little bit to the right as well.

17. Create the different points that make up the curve: start by right-clicking in the main section of the editor and selecting **Add key to....** A new point will appear.

18. Set the **Time** to **0.0** and the **Value** to **0.25**. You can modify those two properties once you have the point selected, as two small editable boxes will appear in the upper-left corner of the screen.

19. Create two more points, and give them the following values: **Time** of **5** and **Value** of **-0.25** for the first, and **Time 10**, **Value 0.25** for the last one:

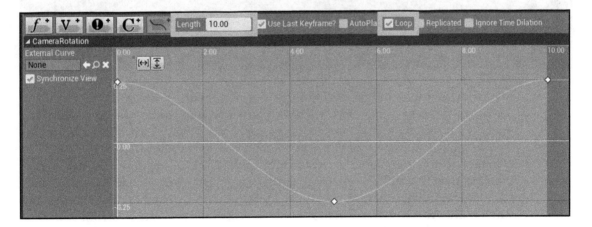

You can find more info on Timelines in the *There's more...* section.

Now that we have that timeline with us, let's put it to good use! Let's go back to the **Event Graph** and create a node that will enable the web cam to rotate thanks to the node we just created.

20. Drag a reference to the **Static Mesh** of our blueprint into the Event Graph.
21. Create an **Add Relative Rotation** node by dragging a wire out of the previous reference to our **Static Mesh** and typing the name of the new node.
22. Right-click over the **Delta Rotation** input pin and select the **Split Struct Pin** option. You'll have access to each axis that determines the movement individually now.
23. Connect the output float pin of the timeline (which should have the name of the Float Curve you created in *steps 13* and *14*) and connect it to the **Delta Rotation Z (Yaw)** input pin of the **Add Relative Rotation** Node.

Our graph should now look something like this:

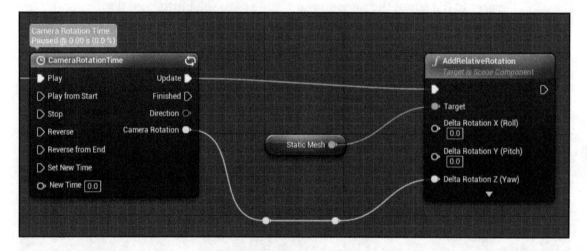

Even though we are only applying the movement to the webcam's static mesh, the **Scene Capture** component will also follow the same motion as it is a child of that. As a result, there's no need for us to apply any other nodes in the graph. Also as a quick summary of what we've achieved so far, know that we've managed to create an animated value that drives the rotation of our model. The timeline asset is a tool we can use to animate a given value, such as a float in our case, by specifying different values at different times. Hooked to the Yaw rotation value of the **Add Relative Rotation** node, it will make the camera swing both ways at a fixed period.

It will first turn one way, stop, and then rotate in the other direction, thanks to the way we've defined the curve. On top of that, it will constantly loop, giving the appearance of a non-stop motion.

Having the blueprint in place means that we can store the camera's view to the **Render Target** and use it within a material to drive the appearance of the display on the TV screen. The last part that we need to put in place to realize this vision is the material itself—which, as we are about to see, is fairly simple.

24. Create a new material anywhere you like within the **Content Browser**, and give it an appropriate name. I've gone with M_ TV_ WebCamDisplay.
25. Open up the material editor and *drag and drop* the previously-created **Render Target** into the graph.
26. Connect the output of the **Render** target to the **Emissive Color** input pin of our material.

And that's as far as we'll go with the material! We don't need to do anything else, as those previous steps have already taken care of showing the captured scene through the **Emissive** input of our material. Using that input makes it look like a proper TV display, giving the illusion that it's also emitting light. The next bit we need to take care of is the part where we actually assign the material to the model, and then we'll be pretty much done:

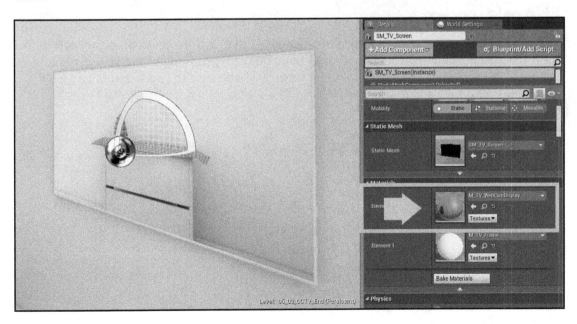

You can now hit Play and see the image on the TV screen update as the webcam blueprint rotates. Just make sure to include the new blueprint in the scene, the TV with the updated material, and you should be good to go!

How it works...

We might have gone over all of the steps that were necessary to create the previous recipe, but it's always good to review the overall logic we've implemented. If we think about it from a high level, all we did was set up a webcam that captured the scene and passed that information to a texture that could then be reused by another actor in our level. Knowing how to tackle the problem can help us think about the assets that we'll need to achieve that and as we saw, there were a few.

The first of them was the webcam—a blueprint that incorporates both a static mesh and a scene capture 2D. We need the first to give the user a visual cue of what they are looking at, and the second to actually do the capturing work. This scene capture in turn works with a **Render Target** to store the information it captures, acting as a tape. As a result, we can feed that tape into a material that is driving the appearance of the TV screen, giving us the final look we are after!

There's more...

As promised, here's some more info about Timelines that aims to get you up to speed with this topic in case you've never encountered them before. Additionally, we've left a link to Epic's official documentation in the *See also* section—so be sure to check that out as well! Refer to the following screenshot:

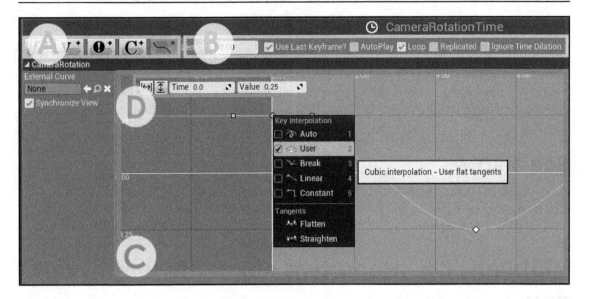

The screenshot is broken down into the following parts:

- **Part A**: This series of five buttons will allow you to create different types of timelines. We've used one based on the float type, which allows us to specify several values and times. Others types can be selected, and you'll choose them whenever it makes sense for your project. For example, we have access to **Vector** tracks, useful for defining positions for objects; **Event** tracks, which provide us with a different execution pin that triggers at certain frames that we can define; and **Color** tracks, useful for animating colors. We can also select an external curve we might have in our **Content Browser** to use that instead.

- **Part B**: This part of the editor grants us access to several important properties that control the behavior of the curve, such as its length, whether it should loop, or whether it should be replicated over the network. One important setting is called **Use Last Keyframe?**, which automatically adjusts the length of the timeline to match the position of the last key created. This often matches what we want, so make sure to check this box!

- **Part C**: This is the main window of the curve editor, where we can create the different keys and give them values. If we right-click on the key frames themselves, we'll be able to modify the interpolation between them.

- **Part D**: Located in this corner are important buttons for daily work with Timelines. Things such as framing the graph to the selected keys or the overall length/width, or assigning the values to the different keys, can be located here. Something to note is the context-sensitive nature of certain panels, such as the **Time** and **Value** ones, which will only show if a certain key is selected.

Having covered all of these different parts, make sure to play around a little bit with all of them in order to get comfortable and know what everything does! It will boost your confidence when working with Timelines, which can be initially a bit confusing when something isn't working as expected and you don't know why. One important setting I'd like to point out again is **Use Last Keyframe?**, which if left unchecked will make you define the length of the animation. This is something easy to forget, so keep that in mind!

See also

Here's some extra documentation on the Timelines provided by Epic Games: `https://docs.unrealengine.com/en-us/Engine/Blueprints/UserGuide/Timelines`.

Highlighting interactive elements within our game

So far we've had the opportunity to work with various materials; some of them more traditional in nature, as seen in previous chapters, and some others more disruptive, as we are just starting to see. Continuing with the theme of the present section, adding interactivity and functionality to our real-time experiences, we'll now take a look at a different type of shader that can contribute to that goal. We are talking about the **Post Process Material** – a type of asset that taps into the post-processing pipeline that Unreal has in place, enabling us to create some very cool and interesting effects. We'll explore one such example in the following pages, and we'll use it to highlight interactive elements within our games and apps. Take a look at the following screenshot:

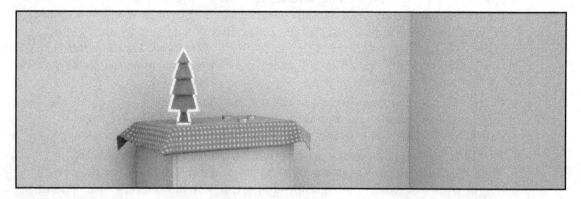

Getting ready

You'll soon find out that the material we are about to create relies heavily on custom math nodes and scripting, which means that there are not a lot of custom parts, such as textures or other assets, that we'll need. As a consequence, it's easier than ever to apply the knowledge of this recipe to any custom level that you might have already with you! However, and as always, we'll be providing you with a map that you can use to test the functionality we are about to introduce. Its name is **05_04_OutlineEffect_Start** and you can find it in the `Content Browser / UE4ShadersAndEffects / Maps / Chapter05` folder.

How to do it...

As we said in the last few lines, we'll be creating a new material of the post-process type, which will let us highlight certain key gameplay elements. We'll explain everything as we go along in terms of the nodes that we'll be using and the effects that they bring, but we also recommend heading over to the *How it works* section as that will cover the logic behind our actions in a more thorough way. Post-process materials are inherently different to the ones we've used so far, and the techniques we are about to implement are better understood when seen from a technical point of view. Don't be afraid though, as I know this can sound a bit daunting! But do remember to head over to the aforementioned section, as it contains some nifty information. With that said, let's dive right in:

1. Create a new material, as this is what we'll be using to highlight different elements in our scene. We can call it `M_EdgeOutline`, as that's what the shader is going to be doing!
2. With the main material node selected, we need to focus on the **Details** panel as there are a couple of things we need to change. The first of them is the **Material Domain**—select the **Post Process** option instead of the default Surface one.

3. Adjust the **Blendable Location** of the material. You can find this option within the **Post Process Material** section of the **Details** panel for our material, almost in the same place where we were before except a little bit further down. Make sure to change that setting from the default **After Tonemapping** to **Before Tonemapping**. Refer to the following screenshot:

The previous option is one that is available to this type of material, as they get inserted into Unreal's post-processing pipeline and we have the ability to decide at which point this happens. You can check out the *There's more...* section for more info about this process.

With that done, we can now start to create the logic within the node graph. Since we'll want to outline the shape of certain objects, the first bit we'll have to calculate is the part that deals with edge detection. This is done in a similar way to many other image-editing programs, and it is based on the convolution operation. Just like we said before, feel free to have a look at the *How it works...* section to find out more about the logic behind this process!

4. Create four different **Constant 2 Vectors**—we'll use these to sample between different pixels in order to be able to detect the edges of our models. Given a known pixel, we'll want to compare it to the one on the top, to the right, to the left, and to the bottom, so that's going to give us the values for the new Constant 2 Vectors we have just created.

5. Give the previous vectors the following values: (-1,0), (1,0), (0,-1), and (0,1). This will let us sample the left, right, top, and bottom pixels.

   The next bit of code that we need to have in place to actually sample those pixels is going to be repeated multiple times, and we can use this as an excuse to use **Material Functions**. These assets are basically chunks of the material graph that can be reused inside any other material where we want to have that functionality, without the need to copy-paste the same nodes over and over multiple times.

6. Head back to the **Content Browser** and create a new **Material Function**. This can be done by right-clicking inside the browser and looking under the **Materials & Textures** section. Name it `MF_PixelDepthCalculation`.

7. Open up the new function and create your first node here, which will be a **Function Input**. This will let us have an input in our function once we place it inside the main material we were previously creating.

8. With that new node selected, head over to the **Details** panel and change the **Input type** to **Function Input Vector 2**. You can also give a name under the **Input Name** section, such as **Offset**, as the values that get connected to that pin are going to be used for that. Check the **Use Preview Value as Default** checkbox as well.

9. Include a **Multiply** node and connect one of its pins to the previous **Function Input**.

10. Add a **Scene Texel Size** and connect it to the other pin of the previous **Multiply** node.

   The **Scene Texel Size** is a handy node that enables us to take into account the different resolutions under which our app might be running. As we will be calculating pixel offsets, using a fixed value wouldn't work and we need to grab hold of this node to help us with those calculations.

11. Create a **Texture Coordinate** node above the previous group.

12. Include an **Add** node after it, and connect its **A** input pin to the output of the **Texture Coordinate**. Connect pin **B** to the output of the **Multiply** node from *step 9*.

13. Add a **Scene Depth** node after the **Add** and connect it to it.

14. Wire the output of the previous node to the **Output Result** node:

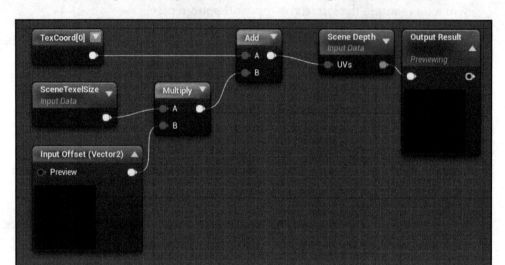

 Don't worry if you see a red warning that says **Only transparent or postprocess materials can read from scene depth**, as that's where we'll be using this function.

Once we finish placing the last of those nodes, we will be finished with this new Material Function. Using it back in the main material we were previously creating means that we only need to include a small function call that will perform the preceding bit of code, making things neater for us.

15. Create a **Material Function Call** inside of the main **M_EdgeOutline** material. With the new node selected, head to the **Details** panel and assign the previously-created material function (`MF_PixelDepthCalculations`) in the selection slot.

16. Copy it four times, positioning each instance at the side of the original Constant 2 Vectors we created in *step 4*. Leave some space between those nodes.

17. Copy it for a fifth time and place it below the other four.

18. Create a **Scalar Parameter** and place it before the Constant 2 Vectors. This will allow us to control the width of the outline effect, so let's give it an appropriate name. I've gone with `Line Width`.

19. Create four **Multiply** nodes, and place them between each of the four Constant 2 Vectors and the material functions. Connect pin **A** to the Constants, and the output to the material functions.

20. Connect every **B** pin of the **Multiply** nodes to the output of the **Scalar Parameter** we have just created that controls the line width:

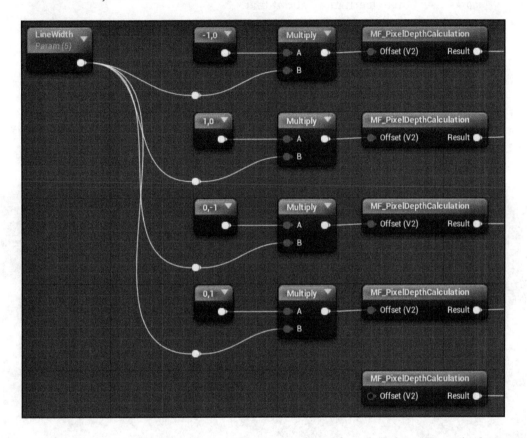

Having those nodes in place will let us perform the edge-detection calculation on the pixels on every side of the current one we are analyzing, but not before we actually combine them! Let's take care of that now.

21. Create and **Add** node, place it after the first two material functions, and use those as the input.

22. Do the same by creating another **Add** node and combining the two following material functions.

23. Include a **Multiply** node right after the fifth material function, and connect that to the **A** input pin.

24. We'll need a **Constant** connected to the **B** pin of the previous **Multiply**, so create one and assign it a value of −4.

   The reason behind using that number as a constant is directly related to the convolution operation we are performing, so be sure to head over to the *How it works...* section to learn more about that.

25. Throw a couple more **Add** nodes into the mix, which we'll use next.

26. Connect the first of them to both of the previous two add ones we created in *steps 21* and *22*.

27. Wire the output of that first one to the second **Add** node we just created, and connect its **B** pin to the result of the previous **Multiply** from *step 23*.

28. Create an **Abs** node, which will give us the absolute value of anything we have up until this point. We need this to ensure that every value from now on is positive:

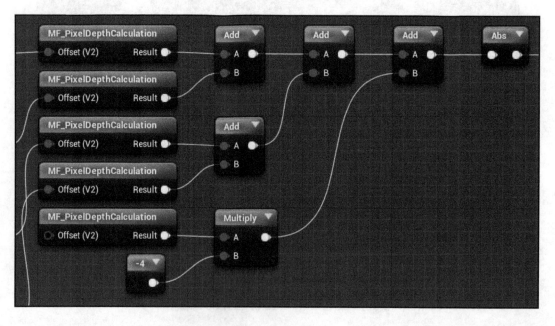

   We use the absolute node here because we only care about the values that we get out of the previous operations, as it will help us determine whether what we are looking at is an edge. You could think of this as looking at the module of a vector – we don't care about whether it is negative or positive, but we do want to know how big it is.

Now that we have created the first part of our edge-detection system, we need to refine it a little bit more. It's not perfect in its current state, as we would get more lines than desired were we to apply it as is. This is because we are not taking into account the differences in depth of the computed image as seen from the camera – we'll take care of that now.

29. Create an **If** node and place it after the previous **Abs** node, connecting its **A** pin to the output of that. This will create a conditional branch that we will populate accordingly.

30. Create a **Scalar Parameter** and connect it to the **B** pin. Name it something such as Threshold, as it will control that.

31. Create two **Constants**, one that connects to the **A > B** pin and the other one which will need to be wired to the **A < B** pin. The first one should be given a value of **1**, and the second one a value of **0**. Refer to the following screenshot:

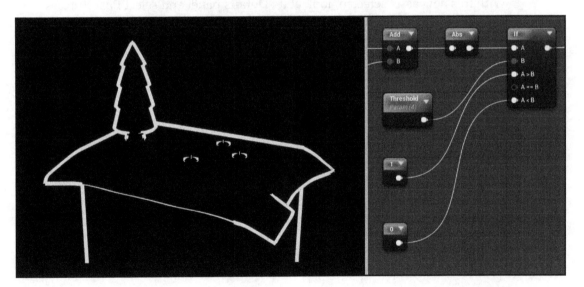

The previous operation implies that when the absolute value of the initial convolution operation is greater than the threshold we set, the detected edges of the model will show. Otherwise they won't! We are now at a point where all of the major steps we wanted to introduce have been completed, and we finally have an edge-detection system in place. You can check this out if you apply the material to the post process volume in the scene.

32. Exit the material editor for a moment, go back to the main level, and select **Post Process Volume**. Looking at its **Details** panel, scroll down to the **Rendering Features** section and expand the category named **Post Process Materials**.

33. Click on the + icon next to the **Array** word.

34. In the drop-down menu that will appear after clicking the + button, select **Asset**.

35. Select the material we are creating to see how it is impacting the scene so far.

    The black and white image that you see should be representative of most of the edges that we have in our scene, and we'll use this binary output as a mask to create a highlight effect in some of the objects in our scene. Let's do that now!

36. Go back to the post-process material and create a **Lerp** node. Connect its Alpha channel to the output of the **If** node created in *step 29*.

37. Create a **Scene Texture** node and connect it to pin A of the previous **Lerp** node. With this new asset selected, look at its **Details** panel and select **Post Process Input 0** as the **Scene Texture Id**. This is a pass that we can use to get hold of the scene color, which means how the base scene looks without this new post-process material applied.

38. Add a **Vector Parameter** and name it something such as `Outline Color`, as this is what it's going to be used for. Assign it the color that you want to use for that effect.

39. Include a **Make Float 4** node and connect each of its pins to the RGBA channels of the previous vector parameter.

40. Get ahold of a **Multiply** node, place it right after the previous **Make Float 4**, and connect it to the input of that.

41. Introduce a **Scalar Parameter** and name it `Outline Intensity`, since it's going to work as a multiplier for the chosen outline's color intensity. Start giving it a value of something such as **5**. Connect it to the free available pin of the previous **Multiply** node.

42. Connect the **Multiply** node from *step 40* to the **B** input pin of the **Lerp** created in *step 36*.

    The previous set of nodes can be seen in the next screenshot. The Outline Color vector parameter will control the color of the effect, and the **OutlineIntensity** will control the brightness of that original color:

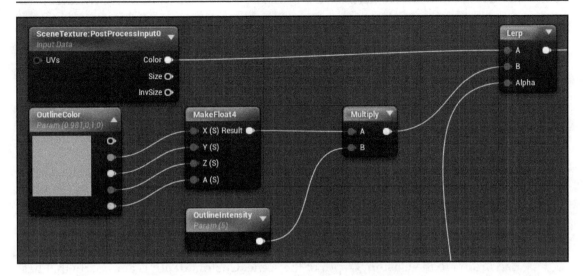

Completing these steps and applying the material like that to the scene will give us a level where every object has a noticeable outline effect, like in the following screenshot. While we are definitely on the right track, this is not exactly what we want—we need a way to control which objects get affected and which ones don't. This is going to be the last thing we tackle in this material, so let's get to it!

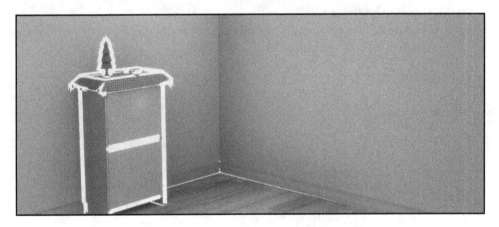

43. Create a new **Lerp** node and add it everything we've done before. Connect its **B** input pin to the output of the previous **Lerp** created in *step 39*.

44. Copy the **Scene Texture** we created in *step 37* and paste it again close to the **A** input pin of the new **Lerp** node, as that's where it's going to be connected. Wire it up now!

45. Create another **Scene Texture**, but select the **Custom Depth** option as the **Scene Texture Id**.

46. Connect that to a new **Multiply** node that we can now create, and choose a low value for the **B** input pin. 0,01 works well in our level.

47. Throw a **Frac** node after the previous **Multiply**. This asset outputs the fractional portion of the original values we feed it, useful in this case as we really need a very low value and we wouldn't be able to type it without Unreal rounding up to 0.

48. Connect the output of the previous **Frac** node to the **Alpha** input pin of the **Lerp** created in *step 43*, and connect that to the Emissive Color of our material. That's everything we need to do to this material!

In the previous steps, we blended the original scene (which we get as a render pass through the **Post Process Input 0** scene texture node) and the outline effect according to the **Custom Depth** of the scene. **Custom depth** is a property that has to be activated for each model we have in our scene, allowing us to determine which meshes we want to see. This can be done in many different ways, and it lends itself to be tweaked interactively via blueprint commands. The final step we need to take is to actually set up the objects that we want to see highlighted.

49. Select the object that you want to apply the effect to and scroll to the **Rendering** section of its **Details** panel.

50. There should be a setting called **Render Custom Depth Pass**. Check the checkbox next to it and see the magic happen:

And that's it! You can control the **Custom Depth** property through the blueprint functionality, by calling a reference to the specific objects through the level blueprint, for example. This is something that can enhance any of your projects, so make sure to give it a go!

How it works...

Things didn't make much sense? This is where we make sense of it all! Usually when you read a recipe, you'll be able to find the explanations of why we are doing what we are doing alongside the different numbered steps. Even though that is still partially true here, we are basing most of the logic in an established edge-detection operation called **Convolution**. Since that is the case, it's better if we tackle what that is at this point, instead of boring you with the details while you are trying to complete the recipe.

First of all, convolution is the name given to an operation performed on two groups of numbers to produce a single third one. In image-based operations, those two groups of numbers can be broken down like this: we have a grid of defined values, known as the **kernel**, acting as the first group. The second one is going to be the actual values of the corresponding pixel to the previous grid. The size of that grid is often a 3 x 3 pixel matrix, just a little thing where the center pixel is the protagonist. The way we use it to calculate the third value that is, the result is by multiplying the values of the kernel by the values of the pixels underneath and adding all of them to produce a final number that gets assigned to the center pixel. By moving and applying this multiplication across the image, we get a final result that we use for different purposes, depending on the values of the kernel grid: to sharpen edges, to blur them, or to actually perform the edge detection like we did in this recipe. The kernel values we can use in that case are the ones we saw in this recipe, which follow the **Laplacian** edge-detection system, and which are the following:

The whole concept was performed in this recipe in the initial stages, roughly from *steps 4* to 27. We did it in different places—first, we got the left, right, upper, and lower pixel of the grid by creating the Constant 2 nodes and using those as input for the material functions, where we multiplied the values of the kernel by the pixel underneath. After that, we got the value of the center pixel by multiplying that by the value of the kernel, the **-4** constant we created in *step 24*. Finally, we added everything together to get the right result. There was no need for us to calculate the pixels in the corner as the kernel uses 0 values in those regions.

There's more...

Before we finish, I'd like to leave you with some additional thoughts that can be helpful to understand how post-process materials and the post-process pipeline work in Unreal Engine 4. So far, we've had the opportunity to become familiar with many different types of shaders—opaque ones such as wood or concrete, translucent ones such as glass or water, and things in between, such as wax. One of the ways we can define them all is through their interaction with the lights in our scene, as we can sort them depending on how that happens. This is because those types of materials are meant to be applied on the objects that live within our levels, just so that the renderer can calculate the final look of our scenes.

This is not true for post-process materials, because they are not meant to be applied to 3D models. They are there to be inserted into the engine's post-process pipeline, contributing to the scene in a different way, mainly by operating on any of the different render passes. Unreal, as a rendered, stores the information of the scene in multiple layers, such as the depth of field, the temporal anti-aliasing, the eye adaptation, the tone mapper. Having access to those multiple render passes can be very helpful in order to achieve certain effects, just like we've done in the present recipe. This is very powerful, as we are affecting how the engine works at a fundamental level—giving us the ability to create multiple visual styles and rendering effects. The possibilities are almost endless!

See also

A couple of links before we finish: one that goes in depth about different types of outline effects and one that explains Unreal's render passes. Both of them are very informative, so be sure to check them out:

- https://www.raywenderlich.com/92-unreal-engine-4-toon-outlines-tutorial7
- https://unrealartoptimization.github.io/book/profiling/passes/

Creating a game compass

Continuing with our search for new spaces where materials can enhance the functionality of our apps and games, let's explore a place that we haven't been before: the User Interface, or UI. I'm sure you are already familiar with these interfaces, as they are part of our everyday life – be it in any computer program that we use, an app, or any other piece of software with which we interact. Many of the elements that make up these assets are the familiar buttons, drop-down menus, and logos that we often see on our screens. However, materials also have a big role to play, especially in a game engine such as Unreal where they can help to further enrich the UI experience. We'll take a look at this by creating an in-game compass that will help us orient ourselves within the game world:

Getting ready

Since we'll be creating a compass material to use in the UI for this recipe, what better setting to use as a backdrop than the ocean?! We'll be revisiting the level we created in the previous chapter as it kind of thematically fits our goal, but there are no more requirements in terms of level constraints that we need to be aware of in case you want to use your own creations. Something we will need is a couple of textures in order to drive the appearance of the compass, which you'll be able to find in the following folder: Content Browser / UE4ShadersAndEffects / Assets / Chapter05 / 05_05.

The textures themselves are quite simple, and we've shown them in the following screenshot for you to see in case you want to create similar ones. There are two: one that will always remain in the same position, acting as a marker: and one that contains the cardinal directions and that will be panned according to the player's rotation:

And one that contains the cardinal directions and that will be panned according to the player's rotation:

As an extra requirement, remember to assign an Alpha channel to those textures that matches the pixel information found in them—that is, leave the background transparent!

How to do it...

As we were saying at the beginning of this recipe, the material we are about to create is going to work as a UI element. That being the case, the first step is the creation of our first-ever User Interface! If you haven't dealt with UIs before, make sure to check how they work in the *There's more...* section of this recipe:

1. Head over to your favorite spot in the **Content Browser** and create a new User Interface. These types of assets can be created thanks to the **Widget Blueprint** resource, so select that when right-clicking and look under the User Interface category.

2. Open the new widget and select a **Scale Box** from the **Palette** tab. Drag it into the main viewport (you'll find it by looking inside the **Panel** subsection or by typing its name into the **Search Palette** search box).

3. Select an **Image** from the **Palette** tab of the UI editor and drag it into the main viewport. Name it something such as T_Compass.

4. Look at the **Hierarchy** panel, which will show you all of the elements that currently make up our UI. Make the Scale Box the parent of the Image by dragging and dropping it into the Scale Box.

5. Select the Scale Box and look at the **Details** Panel. Select the upper-middle anchor in the **Anchors** drop-down menu.

6. Type in the following settings for your Scale Box: **Position X** left as **0.0**, **Position Y** changed to **75.0**, **Size to Content** turned on, and **Alignment** set to **0.5** in the X and 0 in the Y value. Our goal here is to place the scale box in the upper-middle of the screen in a centered position. Refer to the following screenshot:

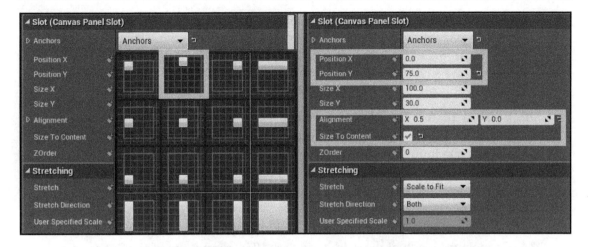

Again, be sure to check out the *There's more...* section if you've never dealt with the UI editor before. Completing all of the previous steps will take care of almost every setting we need to tweak within the UI itself, but we'll still need to assign a material to the image to work as a compass. Let's do that now.

7. Create a new material within the **Content Browser** and give it an appropriate name, something such as M_Compass. Open up the material editor and let's start tweaking it!

8. Select the main material node, look at its details panel, and change the **Material Domain** property from the default **Surface** option to the **User Interface** one. That's all we need to do in order to have our materials available to be used as part of other UI elements!

9. Change the blend mode from **Opaque** to **Masked**. This will let us use the alpha channel of the images in our UI material to control what is and isn't visible:

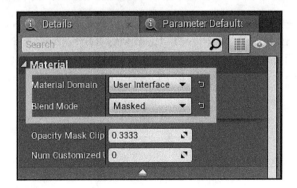

Let's start creating the actual functionality within the material. Something we need to take into consideration is how the compass will look like in the end – we'll have an animated texture that will show us the cardinal directions as the player rotates, and another fixed image working as a maker. We've already seen both of those textures in the *Getting ready* section, so let's implement them now.

10. Create a **Texture Coordinate** node and add it to the graph.
11. Create a **Panner** node and feed the previous **Texture Toordinate** to the **Coordinate** input pin of this new node.
12. Create a **Scalar Parameter** and give it a name similar to `Player Rotation`, as we'll use this to get the current rotation of the player.
13. Include an **Add** node right after the previous **Scalar Parameter** and connect them both. Choose **0.25** as the value for the **B** input pin.
14. Connect the result of the **Add** node to the **Time** input pin of the **Panner** node.

Why are we including that **0.25** constant in the previous **Add** node? This is because we need an initial offset due to the way the image we will be using later was created. As you can see, the North indicator is in the middle of that image, and we need to offset it a little bit to match Unreal's real North position.

15. Add a couple of **Constants** and assign them a value of **1** and **0**.
16. Include a **Make Float 2** node and connect the previous two Constants to it. Make sure that the **1** is connected to the **X** input pin and the **0** to the Y one.
17. Wire the result of that previous node into the **Speed** node of the **Panner**.

We are using the **1** and **0** constants to ensure that the texture will pan along the *X* axis at a constant speed, and not in the *Y* axis. The actual amount by which we'll perform the panning operation will be driven by the Player Rotation scalar parameter, which we will dynamically link to the player later on.

18. Create a **Texture Sample** and connect its UVs input pin to the output of the previous **Panner** node. Assign **T_Compass_Directions** to it.
19. Create a **Vector Parameter** and give it a name similar to **Directions Color**, as we'll use it to affect the shade of the movable part of this material.

20. Multiply the previous two nodes by creating a **Multiply** node and connecting its input pins to the output of the previous **Texture Sample** and **Vector Parameter**:

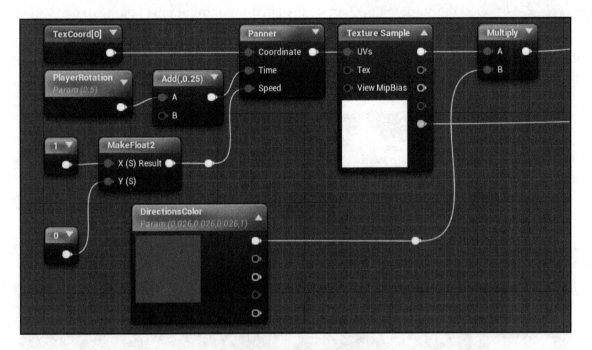

Even though we have something that we could already use as an animated compass, we still need to add the static marker to help indicate the direction the player is facing, so let's do that now.

21. Add a **Texture Sample** node and assign it the **T_Compass_Fixed** asset to it.
22. Include another **Vector Parameter** and name it something such as `Marker Color`, as that's what it'll do.
23. Create a **Multiply** node and connect the output of the previous two nodes to its input pins.

    The previous steps will let us tint the fixed part of the compass material when we create a material instance. We'll now add both sections together and define the **Opacity Mask** of the material.

24. Throw a **Lerp** node after the previous **Multiply** and connect that node's output to our new one's **A** input pin.
25. Connect pin **B** of the **Lerp** node to the output of the **Multiply** node we created in *step 20*.

26. We'll use the **Alpha** channel of the **Texture Sample** created in *step 18* for the Alpha input pin of the **Lerp** node.

27. Connect the output of the **Lerp** to the **Final Color** input pin of our material.

28. Create an **Add** node just before that the **Opacity Mask** input pin of our material and connect both.

29. Wire the **Alpha** channel of both **Texture Samples** into the **A** and **B** input pins of the previous **Add** node:

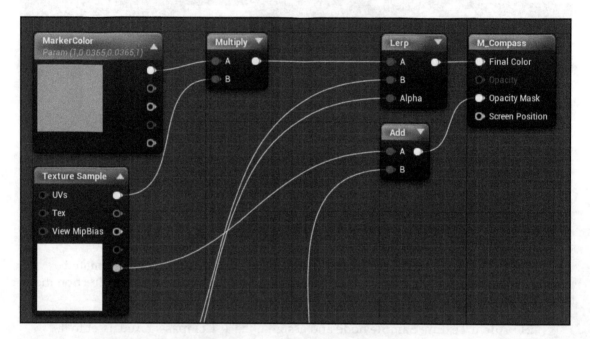

All of those steps will have left us with a working material, so let's now create a **Material Instance** out of it and apply it to the UI!

30. Right-click on the material we created in the **Content Browser** and select the **Create Material Instance** option.

31. Tweak the different editable settings however you like, especially the **Directions** and **Marker Color**, so that they look good on your end.

32. Head back to the UI we created and select the image in the **Hierarchy** panel. Looking at the **Details** panel, expand the **Brush** option and assign the material instance as the image's image.

33. Set the image's size to 1,532 and 24 or something that clearly shows the compass at the top of your screen. This can vary depending on your screen's resolution, so make sure it looks like in the image at the end of this section:

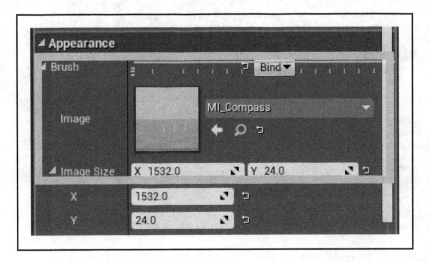

We are now in a position where we can feed the player's rotation to the scalar parameter we set in the material and drive the appearance of the compass through it. Let's jump to the Event Graph to do that!

34. Drag and drop the **T_Compass** variable into the main event graph.

35. Drag a wire out of the **T_Compass** node and start typing **Get Dynamic Material** after releasing the left mouse button.

36. Connect the main execution input pin of that new node to the output execution pin of the **Event Tick** node.

37. Create a **Get Player Controller** node.

38. Drag a wire from the previous node and search for **Get Controller Rotation**.

39. Pull another cable out of the previous node and look for **Break Rotator**.

40. Out of the **Z (Yaw)** output pin of the previous node, we'll want to create a **float/float** node. Set the divisor to 360.

41. Drag a wire out of the **Return Value** output pin of the **Get Dynamic Material** node and start typing **Set Scalar Parameter Value**.

42. Type the name of the **Scalar Parameter** created in *step 12*. Make sure it is the same name, otherwise the whole thing won't work:

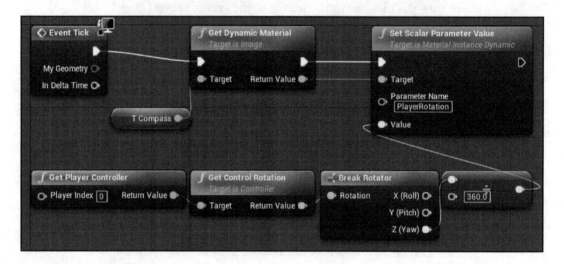

With that done, let's show the UI in our screens by adding some logic to the Level Blueprint.

43. Open the Level blueprint (**Toolbar** tab | **Blueprints** | **Open Level Blueprint**).
44. Drag a wire out of the **Event Begin Play** and create a **Create Widget** node.
45. Create a **Get Player Controller** node and wire it to the **Owning Player** input pin of the previous Create Widget node.
46. Choose the right widget in the **Create Widget**'s drop-down menu.
47. Pull a wire out of the **Return Value** of the Create **Widget** node and add an **Add to Viewport** one.

With that done, you should be able to see the results for yourself once you hit play! Having the ability to know where North is can be very helpful, especially in certain types of games and apps. Think, for example, about recent hits in the video game industry, such as Fortnite, where the user is presented with a world where certain navigational tools, such as a map and a compass, are almost essential. With this new tool at your disposal, you already know how to tackle this problems, so make sure to put them to good use!

How it works...

As usual, let's recap what we did in this recipe just to make sure that everything makes sense. The core of the functionality of this recipe lies in the logic we created within the material graph for the compass material, so let's make sure we review that carefully.

The first and most crucial component of our material graph is probably the **Panner** and all of the accompanying nodes. This is the where we are specifying how much to pan the texture, which will impact what appears to be the North once the material is properly set up. We are relying on a scalar parameter named **Player Rotation** in order to know how much to pan the texture, but the actual amount provided by this node won't be known until we implement the functionality within the event graph of the UI. The other nodes that feed into the Panner, such as the **Texture Sample** and the nodes that affect the Speed, are there to provide a custom value we are setting everything to a value of 1 in all of those fields except for the speed in the Y direction, which needs to be 0 as we are only planning on panning along the X axis.

The rest of the material graph should be more familiar to us, as we are doing things we've already done in the past setting the colors of certain textures by multiplying them times a color we set as a variable, adding the results of our calculations together thanks to the Add and Lerp nodes. The next bit of interesting code comes in the shape of the event graph we set up as part of the UI, where we actually modify the value of the Scalar Parameter we defined within the material. We do that by getting a reference to the dynamic material that is being applied to the image, which is the Material Instance we previously created, and passing a reference to the **Player Rotation** scalar parameter. The values we send are calculated attending to the Z value of the player's rotation, which gives us where it is looking at in the world. Simple as that!

There's more...

In case you haven't dealt with UIs before, let's take a quick look at how to work with them now. This is going to be especially useful in this recipe; if you are not familiar with how they operate, make sure to read the following helpful tips!

The first bit we need to know is how to create them to do that, just right click anywhere within the appropriate folder of the content browser and select the **Widget Blueprint** option that you'll find in the *User Interface* section:

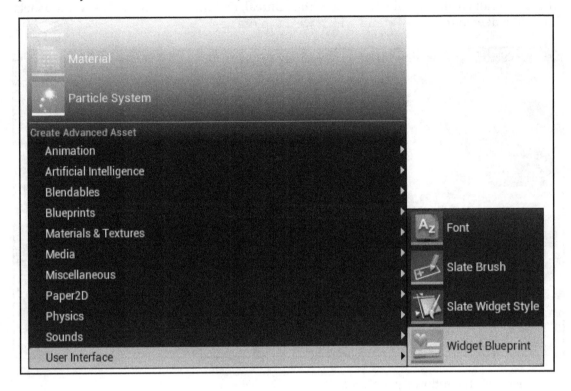

The next bit we need to talk about is the UI editor itself. There are two parts to this: the **Designer** and the **Graph** tabs. The second one is similar to the **Blueprint** Graph we are already familiar with, but things are a bit different in the **Designer** panel. This is an editor where you can create any UI you want within Unreal, and therefore includes several panels that will make your life easier and which we'll explore next:

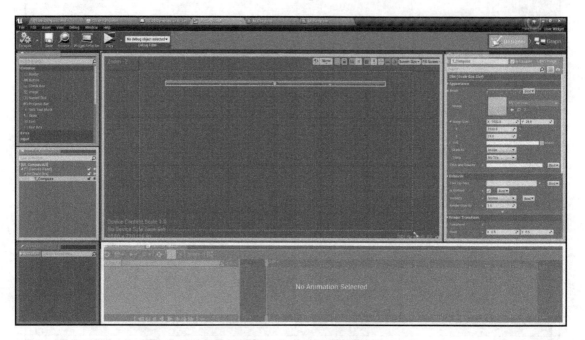

Let's check out the following features:

- **Palette:** This is the place where you can select from the different elements you have at your disposal to create your UI. Buttons, images, vertical boxes, or safe zones are just a few examples of the available elements, and each has some unique features that make them more suitable for certain situations than others. Getting familiar with this section is very useful, and this is where we'll select all of the different assets we want to add to our widget.

- **Hierarchy:** The hierarchy panel is a very important one, as the different elements that we can create tend to expect a certain structure. For instance, different assets from the **Palette** tab can accept a different amount of children and this is important to know in order to properly organize our UI. A button, for example, only accepts a single child, whereas a Vertical Box accepts many. This is the place where we can parent and child different components to each other so that we get the functionality that we want out of them.

- **Animations:** If you want to create little animations on your UI, this is the place to be. Imagine you want to create a nice fade-in effect when you load the app, just so that the UI doesn't load in an abrupt way—this is the place where you would create the different animations.
- **Designer:** The designer is where you can arrange and check the different elements that you create. All of them will appear in here, and you'll be able to visualize what you are doing in real time.
- **Timeline/Compiler results:** If the **Animations** panel was where we created the animations, the **Timeline** is where we want to be to actually work with them. This is where we assign keys and values to our animations, so we'll spend most of the time when creating such assets.
- **Details:** If you have something selected, chances are you are going to look at the **Details** panel to see or change how that specific element looks or works.

Something to note is how the panels you see here can change positions according to the resolution of your screen or the ones you have selected. If you want to add or remove certain ones, feel free to look under the **Window** setting and select all of the ones that you need!

Now that you know where to locate each element within the UI editor, you should be able to complete the current recipe. Have a play within the editor itself for a little bit, get comfortable with the different panels, and you should be ready to go in no time. See you in the recipe!

See also

The UI editor can be a daunting experience, but believe me, it wants to be your friend! Even though it can be scary at first, the possibilities and the potential within it are enormous, so much so that not exploring it would be a shame. From the ability to create nice button functionality to conveying the idea behind your app better, the UI editor is there to help you realize your vision. Make sure to read more about this tool in Epic's official docs: https://docs.unrealengine.com/en-us/Engine/UMG.

Creating a mini map

Now that we are familiar with dynamic UI elements, let's continue exploring this topic by creating a mini map! This can be a nice extension to the compass we just created, as both elements often appear side by side in games and apps. Furthermore, it will add a new layer of interactivity between what's happening in game and its visual representation on the UI. Let's see what this is all about:

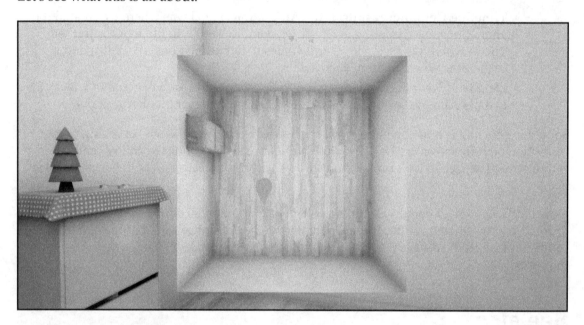

Getting ready

You'll need a couple of things this time, which, as always, are provided by us if you want to follow along using the same assets, but using your own resources will be completely fine. The basic building blocks you'll need if you want to go solo come in the shape of a couple of textures that will act as a map and as the player's position locator. Luckily for us, we don't need to create them in an external piece of software if we don't want to – we can find perfectly valid solutions thanks to the already-included engine content and a couple of tricks I'll show you later. If you want to use the same assets I'll be working with, rest easy as they are included in the project we provide you with and can be found in the `Content Browser / UE4ShadersAndEffects / Assets / Chapter05 / 05_06` folder. You can also open the same level we'll be using by looking inside the Maps folder and searching for **05_06_MiniMap_Start**.

How to do it...

No matter whether you open up the same level I'll be working on or one of your own, the first step we'll take in this recipe is to get hold of the textures we'll need. You should already know that we'll provide you with every asset you'll need in order to complete this recipe on your own. However, if you prefer to use your own levels or textures, feel free to check out the *There's more...* section as that will provide you with useful tips on how to produce some of the necessary textures we'll be working with. With that said, let's start working on our minimap!

As usual, the first steps in our journey will involve creating the assets with which we'll be working. The first of those will be the UI, which will host the minimap itself. Instead of creating one, we can **duplicate** the one we created for the Compass and expand upon it:

1. Search for the UI we created in the previous recipe, named **UI_Compass UI**, and duplicate it. You can find that widget in the `Content / UE4 Shaders And Effects / Assets / Chapter 05 / 05_05` folder.

2. Give the new widget a different name, something such as **UI_Minimap And Compass**.

3. Open the new widget by double-clicking on it and add a second **Scale Box**. Set its anchor point to be in the middle of the screen.

4. Set its **Alignment** to 0.5 in both the **X** and **Y** fields, and check the **Size To Content** checkbox:

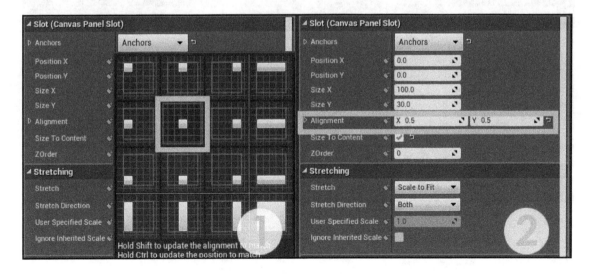

So far, we've taken care of creating a new UI and adding a **Scale Box** that will constrain the position of the mini map within our widget. The next steps are going to deal with the creation of the textures that will drive the appearance of the minimap itself.

5. Create an **Overlay** and child it to the previous **Scale Box**. This asset will allow us to stack multiple widgets, which is perfect since we basically want to have multiple layers in our minimap—one for the base map, and a second one that indicates the player's location.

6. Check the checkbox next to the **Is Variable** text at the top of the **Details** panel of the **Overlay**. We'll need this to access its properties at run time.

7. Create two **Images** and child them to the previous **Overlay**.

8. Rename the first of them to something such as **I_Minimap** and assign the mini map texture to it. If you are using the asset we'll be providing, called **T_Minimap**, you might want to resize it a little bit so it looks good within the UI. A value of 800 x 800 pixels works well in our case, instead of the default 1,024 x 1,024.

9. The second image will be the icon for the player location, so rename it accordingly and select the icon that you like best. I've gone with the name of **I_Player Location** this time, and we are using the texture **T_ Minimap_ Locator**:

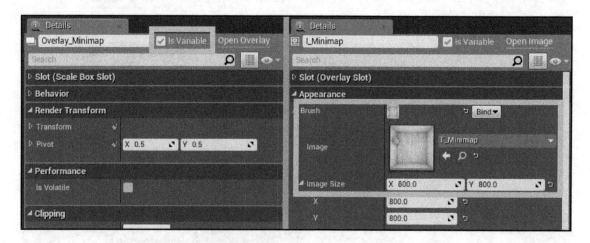

Check the **Is Variable** checkbox for the **Overlay** and assign the right textures to the images.

Even though we are providing an asset called **T_Minimap_Locator**, know that you can find another one provided as part of the Engine Content, named "Target Icon", that will also do the job.

With all of the previous elements added, we can now start to implement the logic that will drive the behavior of our mini map. Unlike in previous recipes, where we built the logic within a material, we'll do that now in the graph editor of the UI itself. This is because we don't need a material in this instance, so let's take advantage of that! With that in mind, let's open up the **Graph Editor** of the UI and continue from where we left off in the previous recipe, at the last node of the Compass functionality. This should be the **Set Scalar Parameter Value** we had previously created, so keep that in mind as the next bit of functionality will continue from there. Alternatively, in case you have created a new UI from scratch, just remember to use the **Event Tick** node as the source of your execution wire.

10. Let's start by creating a couple of new variables of the **Vector** type. You can do so by clicking the + icon in the **Variables** section of the **My Blueprint** panel.
11. The first of those two new assets should be called something such as **Lower Right World Position**, and the second one **Upper Left World Position**. These are going to be the physical coordinates of the corners of the texture that is visible on the mini map—so let's measure that data next.

12. In order to know the coordinates of the map bounds, you can simply create a temporary actor and manually place it in the world on those two positions we mentioned. Look at the details panel and write down the coordinates! If you are following along using the same assets as I am, the values should be **X** = 350, **Y** = 180, **Z** = 0 for the **Lower Right World Position** vector and **X** = −15, **Y** = −180, **Z** = 0 for the other one:

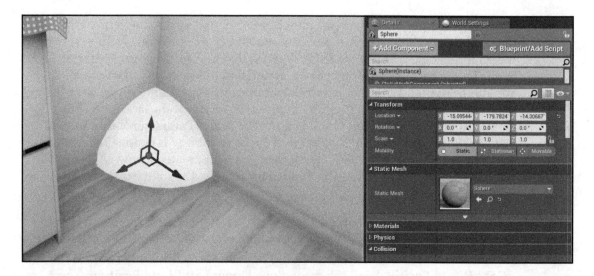

Place a dummy actor in the appropriate location and write down its coordinates from the **Details** panel.

Just so we are on the same page, you'll need to write down the position of the Northwest and Southeast corners of your map. This will work as long as the upper edge of your custom texture is facing North.

With those coordinates written down and assigned to the previous vector variables, we can now continue to grow the logic in the Event Graph.

13. Drag both of the previous vector variables into the UI graph.
14. Create a **Vector/Vector** node after them, and set the **Lower Right World Position** as the Minuend and the other vector as the Subtrahend.
15. Right-click on the vector output pin of the **Vector/Vector** node and select the **Split Struct Pin** option, as we'll need access to the **X** and **Y** coordinates.

16. Create a couple of **Float/Float** nodes and place them to the right of the previous nodes. Position one above the other.

17. Connect the **X** and **Y** float output from the previous **Vector/Vector** node to the divisor input pin of each of the Float/Float node.

18. If we checked the **Is Variable** checkbox back in *step 6* for the Overlay panel, we should now have access to it via the variables category inside the My Blueprint tab. Get a reference to it on the UI graph.

19. Drag a wire out of the output pin of the **Overlay** node, then select the **Get Desired Size** node. Right-click over the **Return Value** output pin and select the **Split Struct Pin** option just like we did on the **Vector/Vector** node.

20. Connect the **Result Value X** output pin from the previous **Get Desired Size** node to the dividend of the **Float/Float** node created in *step 16*.

21. Do the same with the **Result Value Y**, wiring it to the other **Float/Float** node:

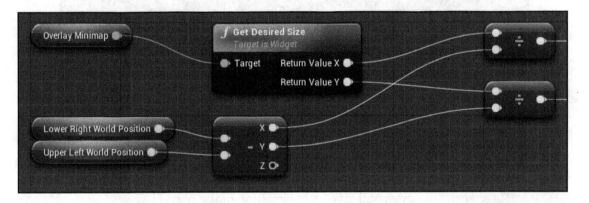

I'd like to say something before things start to get messy: every float operation we perform in this recipe will only involve one axis. If you look at the previous example, you'll be able to see that we are dividing the output of the Return Value X between the X coordinate of the **Vector/Vector** node. Likewise, we are operating on the Y values on the other **Float/Float** node. Just as in that example, all of the following nodes we'll create will follow that rule. I think this is pertinent to say at this stage as we are about to create a large number of nodes and we could get confused as to what goes where. When in doubt, make sure that you are not mixing X and Y values in your graph.

22. Duplicate the **Upper Left World Position** vector and place it a little bit further down the graph, to the right.

23. Right-click somewhere below the Upper Left World Position vector and look for a **Get Player Camera Manager** node.

24. Drag a wire out of that last node and create a **Get Actor Location** node.

25. Subtract that from the **Upper Left World Position** node created in *step 22* by creating a **Vector/Vector** node and wiring things appropriately.

26. Just like we did with the **Vector/Vector** node in *step 14*, right-click on the vector output pin and select the **Split Struct Pin** option.

27. Create a couple of **Float/Float** nodes and add them after that last node. Leave 0 as the minuend of both nodes and wire the subtrahend to the X and Y outputs of the previous **Vector/Vector** node:

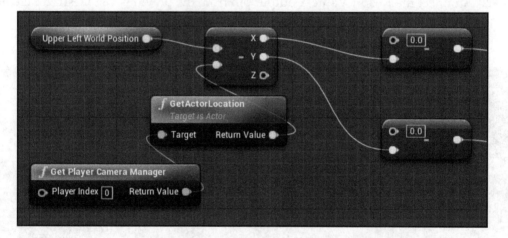

Those series of nodes will give us the position of the player, which will be able to compute where the texture icon should be placed on top of the mini map.

28. Create one **Multiply** node, and connect the first of its input pins to the result of the **Float/Float** node that is dividing the **Return Value X** of the **Get Desired Size** node between the X float value of the **Vector/Vector** operation from *step 16*.

29. The second input pin should be connected to the output of one of the Float/Float nodes we created in *step 27*, the one where we are subtracting the result of the X from 0.

30. Create a second **Multiply** node, and in a similar way to what we did before, connect the first of its input pins the result of the **Float/Float** node that is dividing the **Return Value Y** of the **Get Desired Size** node between the Y float value of the **Vector/Vector** operation.

31. The second input pin of that latest **Multiply** node should be connected to the output of the other **Float/Float** node we created in *step 27*, the one where we are subtracting the result of the **Y** from **0**.

32. Create a couple of **Float/Float** nodes and place them after the previous two **Multiply** nodes.

33. Connect the result of each of the previous Multiply nodes to the **Minuend** of the last **Float/Float** nodes, following the rule of not mixing the X and the Y paths.

34. Set the **Subtrahend** to be half the resolution of our player icon's resolution, which should be **64** if you are using the same assets I am.

35. Create a couple of **Clamp (float)** nodes. Set the value input pin to be the result of the previous **Multiply** nodes—one for the wire connected to the **X** and the other for the Y.

36. Don't connect the **Min** input pin. Instead, use the number **-64** in that field (or the negative value of half of the texture resolution you are using for the player's icon):

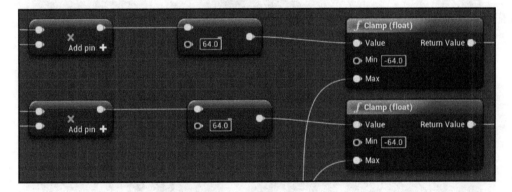

Everything we've done so far is a comparison between the real-world bounds of our level and the widget's dimensions. All of this in order to know where we need the player icon to be in widget space to match the position of our player. We now need to complete this logic by feeding the last values into the previous **Clamp** nodes.

38. Include another set of two **Float/Float** nodes and place them somewhere after the **Get Desired Size** node we created in *step 19*.

39. Connect the **Return Value X** and **Return Value Y** output pins of the **Get Desired Size** node to the minuend of the previous two **Float/ Float** nodes.

40. Set the **Subtrahend** of the **Float/Float** nodes to half the resolution of our player icon resolution. If you are using the assets we are providing with this project, that number should be **64**.

41. Connect their output to the **Max** input pin on the **Clamp** nodes we created in *step 36*.

42. Get a reference to the player location's image into the Event Graph.

43. Drag a wire out of that last node, then start typing `Set Render Transform` to create a node.

44. Right-click over the **In Transform** input pin and select the **Split Struct Pin** option.

45. Wire the results of the previous **Clamp** nodes into the **In Transform X** and **In Transform Y** input pins.

46. Connect the main execution pin to **Set Render Transform**:

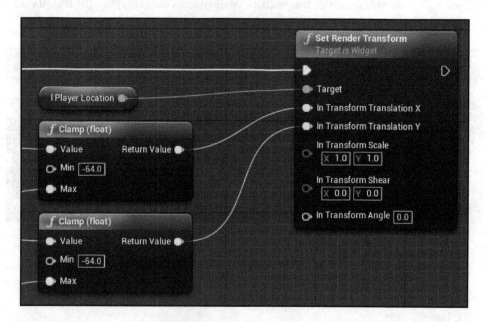

Now that our widget is all set up, we need to add the widget to the screen and make it visible. This is something we had already done in the previous recipe, when we created the compass, so let's do it again.

47. Go back to the level we are working on and open up its **Level Blueprint**.

48. Drag a wire out of the execution pin for the **Event Begin Play** and create a **Create Widget** node.

49. With that last node in focus, select the widget we just created for the minimap in the **Class** drop-down box.

50. Connect a **Get Player Controller** node to the **Owning Player** input pin of the Create Widget node.

51. Create an **Add to Viewport** node and wire both its execution pin and the **Target** to the appropriate output pins of the previous **Create Widget** node:

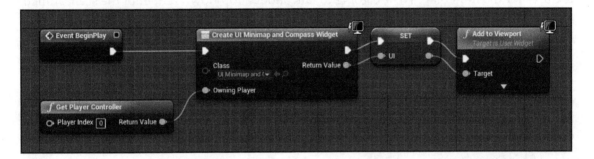

If you now hit play, you should be able to see a UI popup in front of you showing you where the player is! Of course, this can be a little bit obtrusive, but it helps prove a point. Something extra you could explore is to set up a button that would toggle the minimap visibility, enabling you to look at it only when necessary. We've done that for you, so feel free to open up **05_06_MiniMap_End** and look at the level blueprint to see how that was done alongside the widget itself, where we've also introduced certain changes. However, that's something extra, so make sure to test it out for yourself now!

How it works...

Even though this recipe included multiple different steps, the logic behind it all was quite straightforward. We focused on creating the minimap and the functionality that made it work—even though setting things in motion took a little bit of time, the underlying principles were simple.

The first step was, as always, to create the assets we would be working with. We are basically talking about two different elements at this stage: the image of the minimap and the icon for the player's location. They work together thanks to the overlay panel within the widget editor, which puts one on top of the other.

The second and last part of the process was to actually code that functionality into the event graph; we did that by comparing the real-world coordinates of our play area to that of the widget we were using. Having a way of translating what was happening in world coordinates to those used in the UI made it possible to update the player's location and show where it was within the minimap. And that enabled the whole system to work!

There's more...

As we said at the beginning of this recipe, here's a method you can follow to get your own textures for the mini map. We are going to talk about a top-down render of the scene, much like the one I captured for our scene, which you can use later on as the mini map itself. You can also take that to an image-editing program and tweak it there to make it more stylish or give it a different look. In any case, here's how you can start off doing this: drag a camera into the scene and make it look at the scene from above. Ensure that the camera rotation is right—this is, make sure that the top part of the image the camera is producing is effectively the North of our scene. Once that's done, head over to the little arrow located to the left of the projection drop-down menu. You'll be able to find an option in that menu called **High Resolution Screenshot** if you look toward the bottom.

Before you hit the button, make sure you are looking through the camera's view. Your final image should look something like a top-down projection of the level, so make sure that's the case. You can also print the screen an image, as seen from the position of the camera that covers the area that is going to be used as a mini map, which is a quick and dirty option. The point is that it shouldn't be difficult to get hold of this type of texture! One thing to keep in mind before we move on is to try to keep the edges of the image very close to the boundaries of our level, as they should match the playable area.

See also

Minimaps are a type of asset that can be greatly expanded upon in order to include many other different functionalities, beyond the ability to show the player's location within the world. Points of interest, navigational cues, and objective-based markers are but a few examples, and it would take us a long time to cover them all. That being the case, let me leave you with a good tutorial on how to create an advanced version of our mini map system: https://www.youtube.com/watch?v=EQgmt20knLo.

Advanced Material Techniques

6

If we look at the different input pins that a typical Unreal Engine 4 material has, we'll see that the first few entries are named like this: **Base Color**, **Metallic**, **Specular**, **Roughness**, and so on. We can already say that we've used most of them with the **Normal** node so far. This is no coincidence, as they are the most common features we'll need when creating a material. However, there are times when we need to move beyond those boundaries and use other more specific features within our materials in order to enable certain effects. This is what we are going to be focusing on in the next few recipes.

In this chapter, we will cover the following recipes:

- Painting a mesh with vertex painting
- Using decals to add granularity to our scenes
- Creating a brick wall with Parallax Occlusion Mapping
- A brick wall using displacement
- Proximity-based masking with mesh distance fields

Introduction

Even though we are still on our crusade to cover as many different topics as we can, it's time to get back to more normal materials and finish looking at some of the other techniques that can be used in combination with more traditional material setups. This will give us the opportunity to look at some very interesting features, such as vertex painting, and explore some of the material nodes we haven't used yet, like World Displacement or Parallax Occlusion Mapping. All in all, they should greatly enhance your ability to create any material that you so desire, so let's take a look at all of these new techniques!

Painting a mesh with vertex painting

As we said in the introduction to this chapter, we are going to learn and use some advanced techniques that we haven't seen yet. We'll start off by looking at an important and useful technique called **vertex painting**, which will allow us to assign specific values to the vertices that make up our models with the aim of reusing that information to drive the appearance of the materials we apply to them. This can be very useful under certain circumstances, such as when we don't want to use masks to define how materials look or to manually paint specific effects on an object. I'm sure you'll find this technique very useful once we take a proper look at it, so let's not delay that any further!

Getting ready

Vertex painting is a technique that is not very demanding in terms of the objects that you need to have in order to use it. You'll basically need a model and a material, which you can easily get hold of through the **Starter Content**, either by using your own models or the ones we'll be providing. In either case, there's no specific conditions that we need to talk about at this stage, so let me just point you in the right direction in case you want to follow along using the same resources: `Content Browser / UE4ShadersAndEffects / Maps / Chapter06 / 06_01_VertexPainting_Start`.

The assets contained in the previous level can be found, as always, in the `Assets` folder for the current chapter and recipe.

How to do it...

Vertex painting requires at least a couple of different elements that we'll need to set up – a material that can be used with this technique and the actual painting of vertex values on the meshes on which we are going to be operating. We'll take care of those two parts in that order, so let's start things off by creating a new material:

1. Create a new material anywhere you fancy within the **Content Browser** and give it an appropriate name. I've gone with `M_ VertexPaintingExample_End` for this particular example.

2. Assign the previous material to the model you want to work on. If you've opened the map we are providing, that will be the lamp in the center of the level.

3. Open up the material editor by double-clicking on the newly created material.

The next steps will probably make more sense if we briefly talk about what we want to achieve by using this technique and that is to assign different textures and effects to certain parts of our model. Taking the lamp as an example, we want to set the base of that object to look different to the rest of the body. To do that, we'll actually need to bring all of the necessary textures into the material itself so that we can choose which to use when we paint the vertices. Let's do that now.

4. Create two **Texture Samples** within the material graph editor.

5. Set the first of them to use the **T_ Lamp_ Color** texture. Apart from that, select that node and look at its **Details** panel, and change the **Sampler Type** from **Color** to **Linear Color**.

6. The second one should make use of the **T_ Lamp_ Base** asset.

7. Include a **Lerp** node and place it after the previous two **Texture Samples**, and connect the first of them to its **A** input pin. The second one should be connected to pin **B**.

8. Connect the output of the **Lerp** node to the **Base Color** input pin in our material.

Doing this will see us interpolating between both textures, which we'll use to define the look of the base of the lamp and its main body. However, we still need to assign something that can act as the interpolation value—this is going to be the key element of this recipe, that is, the **Vertex Color** node.

9. Create a **Vertex Color** node by right-clicking and typing that same name anywhere within the material graph.

10. Drag a wire from its **Red** output pin and connect it to the **Alpha** input pin of the **Lerp** node we created previously:

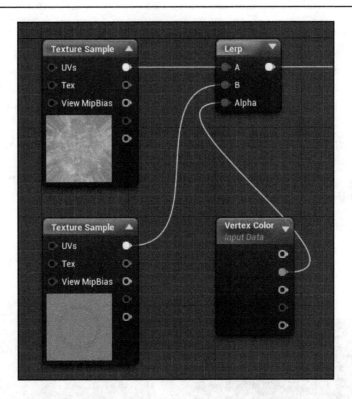

The **Vertex Color** node gives us access to the painted values of the vertices of the mesh on which the material is being applied. We can then use that information to drive certain functionality within the material, as we've just done in the previous step by feeding the red channel's output of the **Vertex Color** node into the **Lerp** that is blending between the two different textures. The reason why we are using that output of the channel is because that is where we are going to be painting the vertex values later on, but we could use any other channel if we wanted. Seeing as this is going to be a simple material, we'll only need one. With that done, let's make the material a little bit more interesting by connecting something to the Metallic and Roughness input pins of the main material node.

11. Add four constants to the graph—two that will drive the metalness of the material and another two that will affect the **Roughness** attribute.

12. Assign a value of 0 and 1 to the first set of two constants—the ones that will drive the **Metallic** property of the material. As you may recall, a value of 0 means it will not be metallic, and a value of 1 will mean the opposite—just what we want to differentiate between the body and the base of our model.

13. Give the second set of constants whichever value you fancy—I've gone with 0.5 for the body and 0.25 for the base.

14. Create a couple of **Lerp** nodes to make the interpolation between the previous constants possible.

15. Connect the red channel's output pin of the **Vertex Color** node to the **Alpha** of the new **Lerp** nodes.

16. Wire each of the previous constants to the **A** and **B** input pins of the new **Lerp** nodes, just like we did for the **Base Color**.

17. Finally, connect the output of those nodes to the **Metallic** and **Roughness** input pins of the main material node.

As you can see, this is quite a simple material, but one that will allow us to see the **Vertex Paint** tool in action. All of the previous steps have left us with a working material, one that we can already apply to the model in our scene. But we can't stop there, as we'll need to paint the areas where we want each of the textures we created previously to show up. Let's take care of that next:

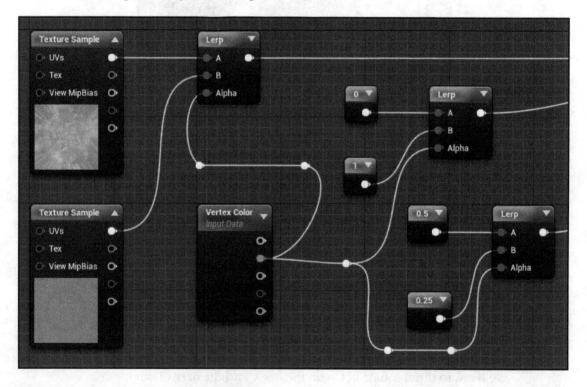

18. Select the model that we will be working on.

19. Assign the material we've just created in the **Materials** section of the model's **Details** panel.

20. Head over to the **Modes** panel and click on the **Paint** tab.

21. While in that panel, look at the **Brush** category and adjust the **Radius** so that you can comfortably paint on the model.

22. Focusing on the **vertex painting** area now, select the **Red** channel and deselect the rest. We want to be painting in that channel as that's what we chose to use within our material back in *step 10*.

23. Make sure that the **Paint Color** is set to white and that the **Erase Color** is set to black:

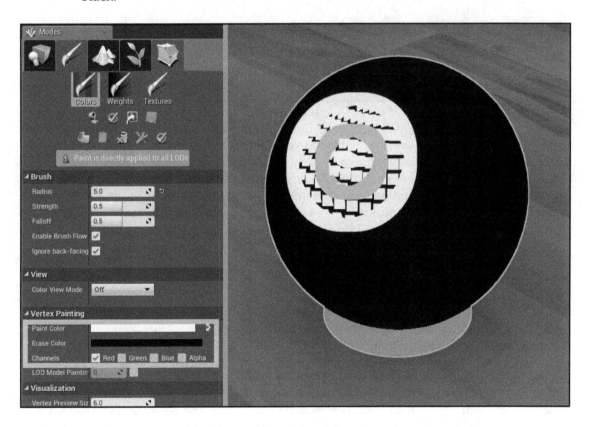

With that done, it's finally time to paint on our model! This can be done with your mouse, or with a pen device if you can get hold of one. Feel free to experiment and see how the appearance of our material changes with the different strokes we apply, blending between the different textures we set up in our material. At the end of this process, you should hopefully be looking at something like the following screenshot:

You can expand this technique by painting in multiple channels and using that information to drive the appearance of the material, and even play with the strength of the tool to create interesting blends between several assets. Something you could find very useful is the ability to slightly tweak the appearance of a large surface by using this method, just by creating different textures and blending between them. There are multiple possibilities, and you can benefit from them in multiple ways—sometimes to remove the use of masks, or perhaps to effect the appearance of large surfaces without using enormous textures. All in all, it's a handy and useful feature!

How it works...

Let's take a little bit of time to go over the **Vertex Painting** panel and the different options we can have access to thanks to it!

The first set of options allow us to tweak the brush we use when painting the vertex colors. The radius affects the size of the tool, letting us adjust how much of the model we cover at once. The strength signals the intensity with which we paint, and the Falloff lets us create an area where the intensity fades between 0 and the selected one, allowing us to seamlessly blend between adjacent areas. As an example, setting the **Intensity** to a value of **1** will fully assign the selected color to the covered vertices, whereas a value of **0.5** will assign half of the selected shade.

The last two settings in this section are called **Enable Brush Flow** and **Ignore back-facing** the first allows us to continuously paint across the surface (updating our strokes every tick), while the second one controls whether we paint over back facing triangles. This can help us in situations where we don't want to accidentally paint areas that we are not currently looking at.

Moving beyond the **Brush** section, we can find the **View**, the **Vertex Painting**, and the **Visualization** tabs. The first one lets us see the colors that we paint instead of the material that is being applied to the mesh. The **Vertex Painting** tab allows us to select which color we want to paint with and which channel we want to affect, as well as letting us paint multiple LODs at the same time. Finally, the **Visualization** panel contains a property that affects how big the vertices of the model are while we are painting:

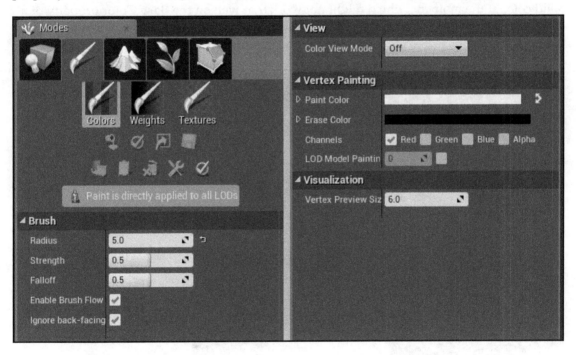

There's more...

Even though we centered our efforts in this recipe on the matter of vertex painting, there's more that we can talk about related to this topic. There are at least two things that I'd like to mention before we move on the different scenarios where we might benefit from using this technique and the possibility to not only paint vertices, but textures as well.

The first of these scenarios is the one where we use this technique to remove the visible tiling pattern that sometimes shows up on large scale surfaces. We can do that by blending between two very similar but different textures. Think of this as a way of adding variation to your levels in an interactive way, without having to blend between multiple different noise patterns and images within your material graph.

The second one relates to another tool that we can find within the **Paint** tab that works in a similar way to **Vertex Color Painting—Texture Painting**. This tool, which is located on the upper right corner of the **Paint** tab, allows you to modify any of the textures that are already applied to the mesh you have selected in your level. The only thing you need to do is select the texture where you want to be operating on from the **Paint Texture** dropdown menu. After that, start painting on top of it however you like! You can only choose from a solid color at the moment, which might not work that well on the **Base Color** property of a realistic textured asset—but be sure to try it out, as it can work wonders when you want to modify certain values like the Roughness or the Metallic properties:

See also

You can find more information on this topic through Epic's official documentation: `https:/` `/docs.unrealengine.com/en-US/Engine/UI/LevelEditor/Modes/MeshPaintMode/` `VertexColor`.

Using decals to add granularity to our scenes

Decals are a great thing as they allow us to project certain materials into the world. This opens up multiple possibilities for us, like having greater control over where we place certain textures or the ability to add variety to multiple surfaces without complicating our material graphs. They are also useful in a visual way, as they allow us to see certain changes without the need to move back and forward between the material editor and the main scene. Furthermore, Unreal has recently introduced a new type of decal that allows not only for planar projections but also mesh-based ones, which can be really useful whenever we want to project something into a non planar surface—as we are about to see. So without further ado, let's jump right into it and see what this is all about!

Getting ready

Just like we mentioned at the beginning of this recipe, we'll be making use of both the standard decals that Unreal has included since it launched and the new mesh-based ones. This means that we'll need to set up a scene that allows both of those techniques to show, ideally including a planar surface, like a normal floor or a wall, and a more complicated one, like a sphere where a planar projection just wouldn't work. Keep those conditions in mind if you want to set up your own scene!

If you just want to jump straight into the action, know that we've included a default scene for you, just like we always do. You can find it in the following folder: `Content Browser / UE4ShadersAndEffects / Maps / Chapter06 / 06_02_Decals_Start`. All that we've included in there is a plane and a hockey goal, with the intention of adding a little bit of flavor to this scene and making it a bit more interesting using decals. Let's see how!

How to do it...

There are two things that we'll be using in this recipe: the standard **Deferred Decals** and the new ones, known as **Mesh Decals**. The first type will work straight out of the box, but depending on which version of Unreal you are using, you might need to head over to the **Project Settings** and adjust a certain checkbox in order to use the latter type. Please also keep in mind that mesh decals are only available on version 4.13 or later, so don't try using an earlier version of the engine! Let's get started:

1. Head over to **Edit | Project Settings** and look for the **BDBuffer Decals** checkbox within the **Rendering | Lighting** category. Make sure that the box is ticked – it may be already, depending on your version of Unreal:

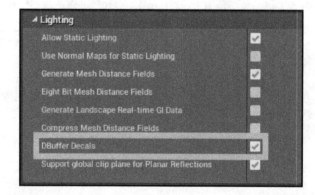

With that out of the way, we'll focus our attention on the creation of the actual materials that we'll be using alongside the Decals. You could think about this technique as a two-part process—the first being the definition of the material we want to project and the second one being the method that we want to use to project them.

2. Create a new material, and give it whatever name you think is appropriate. I've gone with M_ DeferredDecal_ HockeyLines as that's what I'll be using it for.
3. Open up the material editor for the new asset and select the main material node. With it selected, focus on its **Details** panel.
4. Set the **Material Domain** to **Deferred Decal** and both the **Blend Mode** and the **Decal Blend Mode** to **Translucent**.

The previous steps indicate to the engine how our new material should be used, which as we said will be as a decal. The next part we need to tackle is the creation of the actual material functionality that we want to include – displaying the hockey lines in our level.

5. Create a couple of **Texture Sample** nodes.
6. Assign the `T_ Hockey Lines_ Color` and `T_ Hockey Lines_ Normal` assets to the previous two nodes.
7. Wire the **Texture Sample** containing the normal texture to the **Normal** input pin of our material.
8. Connect the **Alpha** channel of the `T_ Hockey Lines_ Color` asset to the **Opacity** input pin in the main material node.
9. Multiply the main output of the previous texture sample times 500 and connect it to the **Base Color**. We do that to ensure that we get a clear white. Alternatively, you could wire a perfectly white color instead of using the **Texture Sample**:

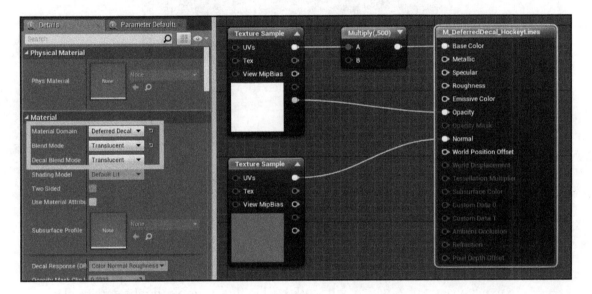

That's everything we need to do for the first decal, which will be projected as a standard one from Unreal. We now need to create a mesh-based decal material as well, so let's do that now before actually going back to the main editor.

10. Create another material and give it a name. I've gone with `M_ MeshDecal_ HockeyGoal` this time as I'll be affecting that object.
11. Double-click on the new asset to open up the material editor and select its main material node. Then, head to the **Details** panel as we'll be changing some properties, just like we did in the previous material.

12. Set the **Material Domain** to **Deferred Decal**, the **Blend Mode** to **Translucent**, and the **Decal Blend Mode** to the **DBuffer Translucent Color, Normal, Roughness** option:

The different options that start with the word DBuffer in the **Decal Blend Mode** dropdown menu allow the decals to work with lighting, such as the one you bake if you are using static lights.

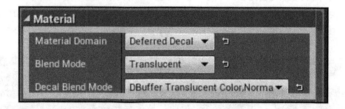

13. Create three **Texture Samples** – one each for the T_ HockeyGoal_ MeshDecal_ Color, T_ HockeyGoal_ MeshDecal_ AORM, and T_ HockeyGoal_ MeshDecal_ Normal textures.

14. We want to wire the output of the normal texture to the homonym input pin of the main material node.

15. After that, let's connect the green output pin of the T_ HockeyGoal_ MeshDecal_ AORM texture to the **Roughness** input pin of our material.

16. Connect the output of the color texture to the **Base Color** node.

17. Drag a wire out of the green output channel of the color texture and create a Cheap Contrast node at its end.

18. Create a Constant and connect it to the Contrast input pin of the previous node. Give it a value of 2, which will work well in this example, but be sure to play with that value once we finish creating this decal, as that will directly impact its opacity, as we are about to see.

19. Connect the output of the **Cheap Contrast** to the **Opacity** pin of our material.

We are almost done creating this second material, but something that we need to adjust at this point is the **World Position Offset** pin that we can see highlighted in the main material node. This is important in the case of mesh-based decals since we will be using a model to project a material into another model. This circumstance creates the need to adjust possible issues related to the depth calculations that Unreal will be performing – that is, we need to make sure that the geometry that projects the material is closer to the camera than the object where the effect gets projected. Let's do that now.

20. Create a **Camera Direction Vector** node by right-clicking and typing that name.

21. Add a **Multiply** node and place it after the previous **Camera Direction** one, and connect that to its **A** input pin.

22. Include a Constant and give it a negative value, something like −0.5, which will ensure that we achieve the effect that we are after. Connect it to the **B** input pin of the previous **Multiply** node.

23. Connect the output of the **Multiply** node to the **World Position Offset** pin of the main material node:

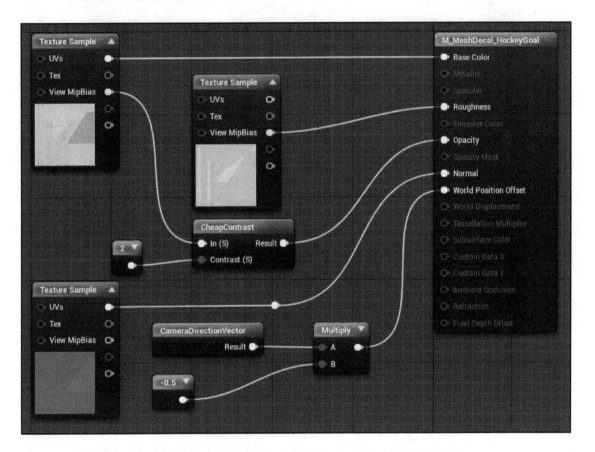

We'll have a working material once we click on the **Apply** and **Save** buttons that's ready to be tested within a live environment. That being the case, let's head back to the main editor and start creating the decals themselves.

24. Create a `Deferred Decal` actor by heading over to the **Modes** tab and searching for that name in the search box. If you don't wan't to type, you can also find it in the **Visual Effects** sub category. Drag and drop it into the main viewport.

25. With the new actor selected, focus on the **Details** panel and select the hockey lines material we created in the **Decal Material** section.

26. Play with the decal's scale and position until the lines show and align themselves with the world – take a look at the final picture to see what the expected result should be.

We've already taken care of the normal decal projection, so let's set up the mesh decal next. The steps to do this are even simpler than before, as you are about to see.

27. Duplicate the model that is acting as the hockey goal.

28. With the new actor selected, look at its **Details** panel and change the material that is being applied. Set it to the mesh decal material we have just created to see it in action!

As you just saw through the previous couple of examples, using decals is a great way to add details through projection methods, allowing us not to have to worry about the UVs of the object onto which we are projecting. You can read more about other cases where this technique is also useful, but as far as this recipe, goes we are already done with it. Take care and see you in the next one!

How it works...

Mesh decals are one of the elements I like the most inside of Unreal Engine, however strange that might sound. This is because they offer a type of functionality that I wanted the engine to include for a long time, and I couldn't have been happier when they finally added support for them. They give us the freedom to project textures based on any mesh that we select, and not just planes.

Something I always wanted to do was to project road markings based on real geometry, as using textures was a very expensive solution. Think for a moment about the following: you have a big set of roads that you want to texture, along with road markings. How would you do it? This could serve as a nice assignment to you, so challenge yourself and test this out if you want to master this technique!

You would probably be tempted to resort to some type of semi procedural technique to solve this challenge, as you can't possibly fit all of that big environment into a reasonably sized image. In spite of that, road markings can prove quite difficult to insert into that semi procedural methodology, as they often require specific care and attention that it's very difficult to achieve with those techniques. Using planar projected decals would also not solve our problem, as it would be difficult to adapt them to curved segments. Luckily for us, we can project them using meshes, as we've just seen.

There's more...

We always need to set up the appropriate type of material domain and blend mode, no matter what type of decal we use. Setting those options to **Deferred Decal** and **Translucent** is a one-two action we'll be doing any time we set up such a material. However straightforward that is, we regain control over the effect we are about to create in the next setting that needs to be specified—the **Decal Blend Mode**. There are multiple choices within the dropdown menu that we are presented with, and the exact number may vary depending on which version of the editor you are using. While we won't go into every single detail that makes them different, it's good to have an overview of when you should be using each.

That decision can sometimes be made just by reading the description of each of the options we see. The most common one will probably be **Translucent**, which lets us make use of most of the material inputs, such as the **Base Color**, **Metallic**, **Roughness**, and the **Normal** settings. Other modes remove the ability to affect certain channels, with the benefit of being lighter to calculate. Examples of that are the **Normal** or the **Emissive** blend modes, which remove certain properties, such as the **Base Color** or the **Roughness**.

Something important to note is that many of the different options we see don't work with baked lighting, as the tooltip itself states. If we want to have access to that option, we will need to choose one of the options that starts with the **DBuffer** word. Doing that leaves us with a similar decal behavior to what we've seen so far, with the notable exception that the metallic property has been removed in favor of using that channel behind the scenes to provide for the baked lighting solution.

See also

You can find more information on decals and mesh-based decals at the following sites:

- https://docs.unrealengine.com/en-us/Resources/ContentExamples/Decals
- https://docs.unrealengine.com/en-us/Engine/Rendering/Materials/MeshDecals

Creating a brick wall with Parallax Occlusion Mapping

In this recipe, we are going to explore one very useful way of adding detail without adding geometry. It might feel similar to using a normal map, but this technique actually pushes the pixels outwards or inwards, creating a real 3D effect that we just can't get with the previous type of textures. What's so special about this, then? Well, as we said, the geometry looks like it's there, but it actually isn't! It's a fake effect that looks real, and instead of making our CPUs work harder by using high poly meshes, we task the GPU with faking the image. This is something they are more efficient at since they were created for this purpose. Let's see what this is all about!

Getting ready

Something basic that you'll need to tackle this recipe is a good texture that contains depth information for the surface on which you want to apply the Parallax Occlusion Mapping technique. For instance, we are going to be talking about a brick wall in the next few pages, so a good brick wall depth texture will be needed. As always, you'll have access to the same assets we are using, so just open the scene named `06_ 03_ ParallaxOcclusion_ End` located within the following folder to start: `Content Browser / UE4ShadersAndEffects / Maps / Chapter06`.

As always, feel free to bring your own textures or even use some that are part of the Starter Content, such as the one called `T_ CobbleStone_ Pebble_ M` that comes bundled with it.

How to do it...

The first step we'll take in this recipe is going to be very similar to others we've taken before – and that means creating a material that we'll be applying different techniques to. Let's not dwell on this for long and get it out of the way quickly:

1. Create a new material and give it an indicative name something like `M_ Walls_ Parallax` if you are going to test it on a wall!

2. Apply it to whichever model you want, or on **Material Element 1** of the room walls if you've opened the same scene I'll be using.

   With that done, let's open the material editor for our new asset and start populating its graph with nodes that will bring our parallax effect to life. The first node we'll need to create is the **parallax occlusion mapping** one, which will act as a hub for many of the nodes we'll create after it. It is a function, as you can see if you double-click on it, and as such it expects several different inputs to work properly. Let's see how we can tackle it.

3. Right-click anywhere within the material graph and start typing `Parallax Occlusion Mapping`—select it and add it to our material. We refer to this node as POM for future reference.

4. By reading the different inputs it expects, we can see that the first one is a **Heightmap Texture**. Create a **Texture Object** and connect it to that node.

5. With the **Texture Object** selected, choose the **Depth Texture** you want to use in the details panel. We'll use the T_ Walls_ Depth in our example:

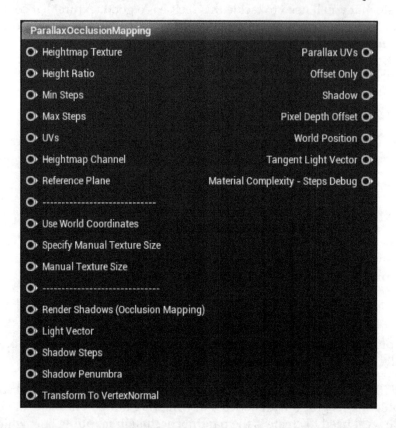

The next set of nodes we'll need to add are all going to be constants, which we can turn into scalar parameters if we so choose. We will interactively tweak them once we create a material instance. Even though we'll cover them briefly, you can visit the *How it works...* section for this recipe later on to learn more about them.

6. Create a **Scalar Parameter** and name it something like Height Ratio. We'll use this to affect how much our texture extrudes and intrudes in regards to the model we are applying the material on. Give it a value of 0.02, but make sure to play around with it later on to see how this affects the overall effect. Connect it to the appropriate input pin on the **POM** node.

7. The next **Scalar Parameter** we should create is the one that we'll hook into the **Min Steps (S)** input pin of the **POM** node, so give it a similar name to that and set it to something like 8. Both in this and in the next parameter we'll create, we will increase the quality of the final image.

8. Include another **Scalar Parameter**, name it something like Max Steps, but don't connect it to the **Parallax Occlusion Mapping** node just yet – we'll play with this one a little bit more in the following steps.
9. The fourth **Scalar Parameter** should be named something like Temporal AA Multiplier, and should be given a value of 2.
10. Create a **Lerp** node and connect its **B** input pin to the previous parameter we created, leaving the **A** input pin with a value of zero.
11. Right-click within the material graph and look for a node called **Dither Temporal AA**. Connect that to the **Alpha** channel of our **Lerp**.
12. Throw a **Multiply** node and connect both the maximum steps scalar parameter we created in *step 8* and the output of the previous **Lerp** to it.
13. Finally, connect the **Multiply** node to the **Max Steps** input pin on our **POM** node.

As we said previously, make sure to head over to the *How it works...* section of this recipe to learn more about how these last steps we've taken work inside the material. Just so you don't have to wait until then, what we've done so far effects the amount by which our material will seem to be extruded, as well as the quality of that extrusion, which is controlled through the minimum and maximum steps we created. The reason why we didn't just plug the **Max Steps** scalar parameter directly into the input pin of the **POM** node is because we want to smooth out the effect using the **Dither Temporal AA** node, as the end result might look a bit blocky otherwise.

With that out of the way, the next things we'll take care of are going to be the heightmap channel and the tiling of the texture itself. The second property is something we've already dealt with in the past, so it should be quite simple! However, you might find it strange to have to specify which texture channel we use for the heightmap. First, let's create the appropriate nodes—I'll come back to this later.

14. Create a **Vector Parameter** and give it a name, something like Channel. Give it a value of **red**, or 1, 0, 0, 0, as its final value.
15. Include an **Append** node and hook the output of the red and the alpha channel of the previous node to this one's input pins.

16. Wire that to the **Heightmap Channel (V4)** input pin of the **POM** node.

 The reason why we are appending the **Alpha** to the red channel is because the input pin of the **POM** node expects a vector of **4**, and the red channel by itself isn't such an asset.

17. Create a **Texture Coordinate** node and leave the default value of 1.
18. Add a **Scalar Parameter** so that you can contro tiling in case we create a material instance, and set it to 7.
19. Place a **Multiply** node after the last two and wire them up. Connect its output to the **UVs (V2)** input pin of the **POM** node:

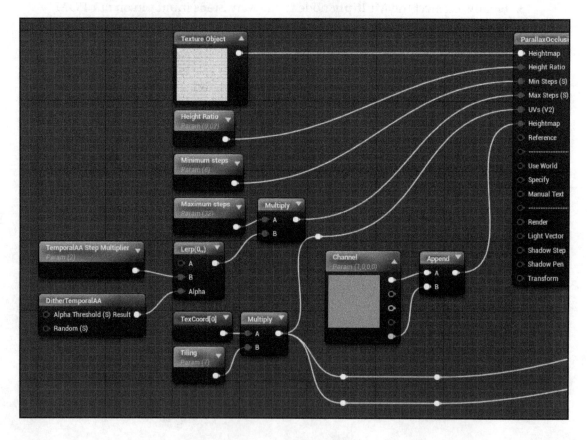

The reason why we needed to specify a texture channel for the heightmap is merely because of the way the **Parallax Occlusion Mapping** node has been set up to work. We used a **Texture Object** for the heightmap texture, and thus we didn't have access to any one particular texture channel. We don't mind which channel we are using; the texture we selected is a greyscale one. However, think for a second about what would have happened if you used a texture that contained the height information in a particular channel. You would need a way to tell the POM node which of the RGBA nodes you wanted to use! That's why we need to specify the heightmap channel, like we've done previously, since the engine needs to know that information.

Now that we have the **Parallax Occlusion Mapping** all wired up, we can use the calculations that it is doing as the base for the next set of textures that we'll use. Let's starting creating them!

20. Create three **Texture Samples** and assign them the following textures: T_ Walls_ Depth, T_ Walls_ AORM, and T_ Walls_ Normal.
21. Connect their UV input pins to the Parallax UV output pins of our **POM** node.
22. Wire the output of the first texture to the **Base Color** input pin of the material, the red channel of the second texture to the **Ambient Occlusion** input pin, and the green channel to the Roughness slot.

We need to tweak some settings before doing anything else with the normal texture, as we'll use a slightly different method than the ones we've seen before. This is due to the fact that we are using this POM technique, and if we want our normals to look good, we need to tweak a couple of settings in the material. Select it and look at its **Details** panel.

23. Select the **Texture Sample** for our normal map and look at its **Details** panel. Change the **Mip Value Mode** setting from **None** to **Derivative**.
24. Create a couple of nodes before the normal **Texture Sample**—in particular, the **DDX** and **DDY** nodes that you can find by right-clicking and typing their names.
25. Connect the output of the Multiply node we created in step 19—the one affecting the tiling to these new nodes.
26. Wire the output of the new nodes to the newly available **DDX** and **DDY** input pins in the normal map **Texture Sample**.
27. Finally, connect the output of the **Normal** map to the **Normal** input pin of our material. We are all done!

At this stage, all we need to do is to click **Save** and **Apply** our material to the appropriate model in our scene. You should be looking at a white brick wall that extrudes out of the plane in which it was originally applied, and that effect remains visible no matter the angle that you are viewing it at. All of this was achieved without us having to use any extra geometry!

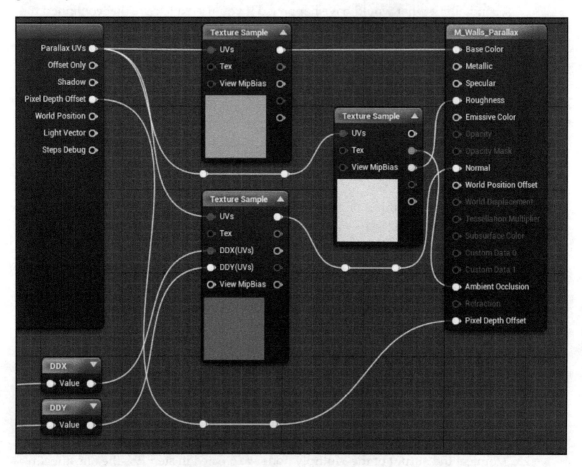

You can see the last set of nodes we created in the preceding screenshot, and the final result in the following screenshot:

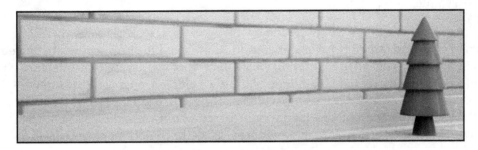

How it works...

As you saw, the POM node is quite a complex one, as it includes multiple different inputs that we need to properly set up for the effect to work well. However daunting that can seem, things will start to make more sense once we go into a little bit more detail on what they do and how each setting we create contributes toward building the final effect.

The first bit that we need to be aware of is how the effect actually works. **Parallax Occlusion Mapping** works on top of Unreal's standard rendering pipeline, which consists of the rasterization of the meshes that make up our level and which in turn assign a world position value to each pixel in our scene. In other words, each pixel that we see on screen is the result of a calculation made by the engine, which takes into account the position of our models and any other effects or materials that are being applied. **Parallax Occlusion Mapping** takes the world position of a given pixel, as calculated by the engine, and modifies its location according to the different settings that we specify in the node we saw in this recipe. The first of those options that we need to tweak is the heightmap texture, an asset that determines the difference in position of a given pixel in regards to the underlying model. In our example, a brick wall material was applied to a plane, and the white parts of the texture indicate that those areas are being extruded outwards while the black bits get pushed inwards.

The second setting that we tweaked was the height ratio, which serves as a modifier that increases or decreases the values of our previous heightmap, making the effect more or less notorious. On top of that, we added a couple of extra constants that affected the Min and Max Steps of the effect, which in turn decide the quality that we end up seeing. More samples mean that the effect will appear more realistic, while less means the opposite. The reason why we call them steps is because this effect is similar to what we see in splines or curved surfaces in a 3D package—the more subdivided they are, the more rounded they will appear.

It's also for that very reason that we used the **Dither Temporal AA** node, which increases the smoothness between the different steps we created. This makes them blend better and in a more seamless way.

Finally, the last two settings we needed to tweak were the UVs and the Heightmap channel. The former is quite a straightforward operation, as we need to specify how much we want our material to tile. The latter is quite curious – instead of specifying which texture channel we want to use in the original Heightmap texture we created, we need to do so here. This is a quirk of the **POM** node we are using, which expects a **Texture Object** as texture input rather than a Texture Sample. The type we are forced to use lacks the ability to specify the channel we want to use, therefore making these last settings necessary.

There's more...

As we've explained previously, Parallax Occlusion Mapping is a GPU-driven effect. This means that the CPU doesn't have access to what's being created there, and this is an important thing to have in mind. As with any game engine, there are many different processes happening at the same time, and some of those get taken care of by the CPU while others rely on the graphics unit. Such is the case of something that effects us in this case—the collision system. Whenever we use the POM technique, we usually apply it with the intent of adding detail and transforming the surface onto which we are projecting the effect. As a result, we end up with a different surface or model—one where its visible bounds differ from those of the original model. This is an important thing to consider when we need to have collisions in that same model, as those are computed by the CPU and don't know anything about what's happening GPU-side.

A possible workaround to this problem is to create a custom collision mesh that takes into account the end result of the parallax occlusion mapping technique—maybe by adding a collision volume that respects the new visual bounds we see after we apply the aforementioned technique. Whatever we decide to do in the end, make sure to keep the nature of this effect in mind in order to prevent any possible issues when working with other systems that are driven by the CPU.

See also

Parallax Occlusion Mapping can be a very interesting topic from a technical point of view, and learning more about it can give you a good insight into how computer graphics work. I'd like to leave you with a good link to a site that explains it well, and one that can gives you a into a bigger world if you want to read even more: `http://online.ts2009.com/mediaWiki/index.php/Parallax_Occlusion_Map`.

A brick wall using displacement

As you already know, this chapter is all about exploring some advanced material effects and also some of the material input pins we haven't used so far. Even though we've already covered many interesting new features, we haven't really explored the rest of the options that we get out of a normal material. Certain inputs, like the **World Displacement** or the **Tessellation Multiplier**, are still unknown to us. And here is where we remedy that by taking a look at those features in Unreal and comparing the new technique to the previous one we've seen, that is, Parallax Occlusion Mapping. These two can be quite similar, so it's also worth exploring the similarities and differences between them—we'll do that by using an almost identical scene to the one we used previously. In essence, **World Displacement** is the node that we want to use when we need to displace the triangles of a model according to a given texture. The **Tessellation Multiplier** subdivides the original triangles of our mesh in order to make the previous displacement operation more evident. We can achieve some very cool effects when we use both methods at the same time, so let's jump on board and see that in action!

Getting ready

The scene we are about to start exploring is quite similar to the one we used in the *Creating a brick wall with Parallax Occlusion Mapping recipe,* so all of the considerations we mentioned then will still apply here. However, there is one extra element we need to talk about, and that's the setup of the mesh that we will be applying the material we create in this recipe to. Even though the walls of our level might look identical to the ones found in the Parallax Mapping example, we are actually using a different mesh, and one that is more subdivided. This is actually very important if we want the tessellation effect to work well, as simple planes don't tend to behave properly when combined with this technique. Keep that in mind if you decide to use your own models! If you want to use the same I'll be using, feel free to open the level called `06_ 04_ Displacement_ Start` that's located within the `Content Browser / UE4ShadersAndEffects / Maps / Chapter06` folder.

How to do it...

The first thing we'll do in this recipe will be creating the material we'll be working on, as well as its initial setup, so that it makes use of the Tessellation feature:

1. Create a new material and give it a name. I've gone with `M_ BrickWall_ Displacement` this time.
2. Select the main material node and look at its **Details** panel as usual, there are a few things we'll need to tweak in here.
3. The first setting we need to change is called **D3D11 Tessellation Mode**, and it can be found under the **Tessellation** tab, a bit further down the **Details** panel (close to the bottom). Change the default value to **PN Triangles**.
4. There are some other settings in that same category that you can play with namely **Crack Free Displacement**, **Adaptative Tessellation**, and **Max Displacement**. I've left them in their default states this time, except for **Max Displacement**, which I've bumped to **100**.

 Ticking the **Crack Free Displacement** checkbox can remove the seams that appear in certain models when using Tessellation, especially around sharp changes in geometry. It has its limitations, but you might want to check it if you experience any issues.

Here's a screenshot of the previous settings in action:

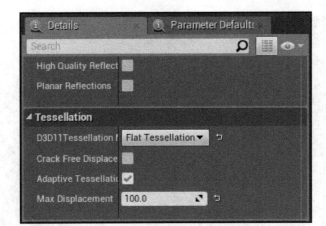

With those settings enabled, we are now ready to start implementing the nodes that will drive the displacement of the mesh. Let's see how.

5. Create a **Texture Sample** and assign the T_ Walls_ Depth asset to it.
6. Add a **Scalar Parameter** and name it Contrast Intensity, as we'll use it for just that. Give it a value of 1.

 The **Contrast Intensity** scalar parameter we just created will increase the contrast of the original Texture Sample according to the value we feed it. This means that the distance between the pushed and pulled areas of the material will be greater.

7. Include a **Cheap Contrast** node and place it after the last two. Connect the **Texture Sample** to the **In (S)** pin and the **Scalar Parameter** to the **Contrast (S)** pin.
8. Include a second **Scalar Parameter** and name it something like Height Intensity. We'll use it to control how far we push the displacement effect. Give it a value of 1, which will leave things the same as if we didn't use it, but feel free to play around with this value later to see the effect it has.
9. Multiply the previous **Cheap Contrast** and **Scalar Parameter** together.
10. Create a VertexNormalWS node, which is vital to drive this effect as we need access to the position of the vertices in world space.
11. Multiply the previous node times the output of the previous **Multiply** from *step 9* by creating a second **Multiply** node.

12. Connect the previous sequence to the **World Displacement** input pin:

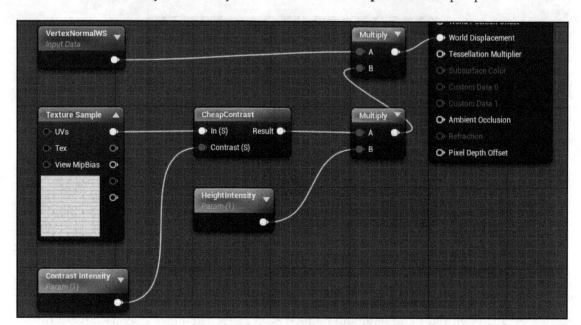

The previous set of nodes have given us the amount by which the surface where the material is being applied to will extrude, but we now need to specify how much we want to subdivide that surface. Greater numbers will make it appear more realistic, but at a greater cost. Furthermore, there is a limit on how subdivided a model can be, which can be checked by selecting the **Wireframe** view mode—so sometimes, greater numbers won't have an effect at all.

13. Create a **Scalar Parameter** and name it something like `Subdivision Amount`. Set it to something like 5.

14. Wire the output of that node to the **Tessellation Multiplier** input pin in the main material node.

Even though we've set up a fixed number in this instance, it might be useful to set up the material graph in such a way that it varies by that amount based on how close or far we are from the model—something that we've already seen in Chapter 3, *Opaque Materials and Texture Mapping,* in the *Distance-based texture blending* recipe. You can also see that for yourself by opening the scene called `06_04_ Displacement_ End` and looking at the material I've created for my displacement.

Finally, the last part we need to take care of is the rest of the material—that is, setting up the roughness, the **Base Color**, and the normal maps.

15. Create two **Texture Samples** and set the following assets as their default textures: T_ Walls_ AORM and T_ Walls_ Normal.

16. Duplicate the **Texture Sample** we used for the **Displacement**, since we'll use that for the color as well.

17. Create a **Texture Coordinate** node and set it to 7 in both the **U** and the **V Tiling**.

18. Connect the output of the previous **Texture Coordinate** to the **UVs** input pin on each of the four **Texture Samples** we should now have.

19. Connect the output of the T_ Walls_ Depth copy to the **Base Color**, the red channel of the T_ Walls_ AORM to the **Ambient Occlusion**, the green channel to the **Roughness** slot, and the output of the normal map to the **Normal** input pin of the material.

Performing those last few steps has left us with a material that we can already apply to the model in our scene. Let's head back there now and see it in action!

As you can see, the final effect is very similar to the one we got when using the Parallax Occlusion Mapping technique. However, you should be able to see some differences if you move the camera freely around the scene. One of the most immediate effects we should be able to see is how the tessellation method can feel a bit blocky, especially if we don't adjust the tessellation multiplier accordingly. Feel free to fine-tune the different settings now that we are done tweaking the material so that you can adjust it to your liking!

How it works...

Much like in the previous recipe, where we used the Parallax Occlusion Mapping technique, this new method allows us to add more detail to our models through the use of a properly set up material. This time, that detail isn't faked. Instead of using clever GPU-driven techniques, we are telling the engine to actually increase the number of polygons in a given mesh and modify the new vertex positions according to a texture that will give us the final look we want.

This is a feature that is tied to the DirectX API, and to the eleventh version in particular (DX11). It works on the Microsoft Windows ecosystem and other related products, so we need to keep that in mind when developing a product that might not be able to use those programming interfaces.

In spite of that, it can be a powerful technique to use under certain conditions. For example, even though the results are similar to the Parallax Occlusion Mapping example we saw earlier, it tends to work better on close-ups and it also generally presents less artifacts. It is an expensive tool, though, so it tends to work better on mid- to high-end computers rather than on other devices, such as consoles or tablets. It is best used when combined with distance-based toggles, so the tessellation amount can vary depending on how far we are from the material in question. All in all, both techniques need to be tested and optimized until you reach a point at which you are happy in terms of performance and visuals. Welcome to the great world of optimization!

There's more...

Something we did at the beginning of this recipe was set the **D3D11 Tessellation Mode** to **PN Triangles**. There's another setting that we could've chosen called **Flat Tessellation**. Both work in a very similar way by enabling the subdivision of the base mesh. However, there's a key difference in how these two methods operate. The one we used tends to subdivide and smooth out the mesh, acting in a similar—albeit more limited—way to how the **Turbosmooth** modifier works in Max or the smooth mesh preview in Maya. Flat Tessellation ignores that smoothing part and limits itself to the task of subdividing the mesh. Depending on the result that you are after, make sure to check both alternatives and see which one works best for your project.

See also

As always, here are some links to the official docs in case you want to read more about this technique!

- https://docs.unrealengine.com/en-us/Resources/ContentExamples/MaterialProperties/1_8
- https://docs.unrealengine.com/en-us/Resources/ContentExamples/MaterialNodes/1_11
- https://docs.unrealengine.com/en-us/Resources/ContentExamples/MaterialNodes/1_12

Proximity-based masking with mesh distance fields

You could say that each different recipe we've tackled so far has explored something new within Unreal's material creation pipeline. We sometimes talk about new material features, useful nodes, or smart shader creation techniques, and we even go as far as using other elements from outside the material editor to affect our creations. This is going to be one such example, since we'll be looking at a specific feature called **Mesh Distance Fields** that allows us to change the appearance of a material based on how close or far it is from other geometry in the scene. This, as you'll see, can be very useful, as it allows us to create dynamic effects such as distance-based masks or ambient occlusion-driven effects. Jump on board and let's take a look at one such example!

Getting ready

The scene we'll be using to demonstrate this technique is going to be very simple—in fact, we'll only use a plane and a sphere in terms of geometry. However, I'd advise against using the assets that are provided by the engine this time. The reason for that is that there will be a specific setting that we'll need to tweak within the static meshes that we use that we can't control if we use the assets provided by the engine. Any other model that you import into the engine will be fine, so if you want to use your own assets, feel welcome to do so. As we stated previously, our main concern is being able to freely tweak certain settings within our models that are protected in the ones included in Unreal.

If you want to follow along using the same scene I'll be showcasing, remember to open the level called `06_ 05_ Mesh Distance Fields_ Start`, located within the `Content Browser / UE4ShadersAndEffects / Maps / Chapter 06` folder.

How to do it...

Some of the most specific features that Unreal has to offer need to be activated per project—that is, we need to head over to the Project Settings and tick the appropriate checkboxes to enable them. This is going to be the first step in our journey. We will also set up our objects so that they work well with the new technique we are about to see. Let's get started:

1. Head over to **Edit** | **Project Settings** and look under the **Engine** | **Rendering** | **Lighting** section for a property called **Generate Mesh Distance Fields**. Make sure that it is ticked, as it might be already enabled, depending on which version of Unreal you are using.

   With the first step out of the way, look at the scene that you have in front of you. If we are using the same, you should be able to find a couple of models—a plane and a sphere, which are intersecting it. In order to use the Mesh Distance Fields technique appropriately, it's useful to know which models are going to be affected by it, as we'll need to treat those differently from the rest. In our case, we'll want to apply a material to the plane, which will take the **Distance Fields** into account, so let's tweak that model first.

2. Select the plane in our level and open its **Static Mesh** editor. Remember that you can do this by selecting the model in the level, looking at the Details panel, and double-clicking on the icon you see to the right of the **Static Mesh** section.

3. Once inside the new editor, look at the **Details** panel and scroll down to the **General Settings** category. Look for the option named **Generate Mesh Distance Fields** and make sure it's turned off.

4. With that done, head back to the main level and open the **Static Mesh Editor** for the sphere.

5. Look for the same setting we searched for previously the **Generate Mesh Distance Fields** and turn it on.

6. Scroll a little bit toward the top of the Details panel and find the setting called **Distance Field Resolution**, which is located toward the bottom of the **LOD0** section. Set it to **5** and click on the **Apply** button located immediately below it.

Doing this will have made sure that the sphere in our scene contributes to the creation of the **Mesh Distance Fields**, but not the plane. Removing the ability to create distance fields for the mesh on which we are going to work is an important step to carry out, as they would otherwise conflict later on when we create the material that will use that effect. An easy way of explaining this is as follows: you want to apply a material that is aware of the **Mesh Distance Fields** of other objects, but not of the object on which it is being applied, otherwise it would get confused as it would be also reading its own **Mesh Distance Field**. That's why we need to remove it! With that out of the way, we can now concentrate on creating the material that will make use of this engine feature:

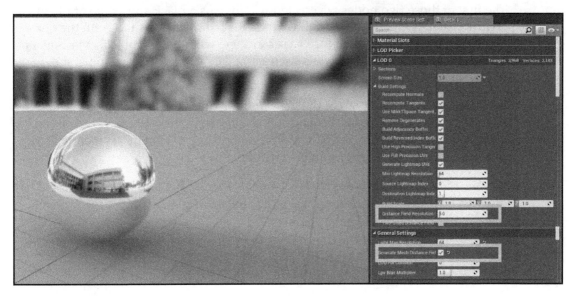

You can see the settings that we'll need to tweak in the preceding screenshot for the object that we need to generate mesh distance fields for. Tick those same properties off for the material that you'll apply on the material we'll be creating next.

7. Create a new material and give it a name. I've gone with `M_ SimpleOcean_ End` as that's what we'll be creating in this recipe if you've opened the same level.

> We are basically going to create a simple *toonish* ocean material that shows foam around the edges of the objects that it comes into contact with. You might want to use this technique on the more complicated material we created back in the *Animating a sea shader* recipe back in `Chapter 4`, *Translucent Materials and More*.

8. Open the new material and add the first node to our graph—one named **Distance To Nearest Surface**. Remember that you can look for it either in the **Palette** tab or by right-clicking and typing that name.

9. Add a **Scalar Parameter** and name it something like **Distance Offset**. We'll use this node to adjust the mask that gets created once we use the previous **Distance to Nearest Surface** node. Give it a value of `0.015`.

10. Create a **Multiply** node and hook the output of the previous two nodes to the input pins of this new one.

The first of those two nodes we created will give us a black and white gradient texture that gets created around the objects that come into contact with the one our material is being applied to. The second one will give us control over how far that gradient will extend, which is something we need in order to adjust the effects we'll be creating later on.

Now that we've got that out of the way, and seeing as this is going to be a simple material, something we can do is introduce a break in the previous gradient and make it look a little bit more like a toon shader. We'll do that by segmenting the gradient into smaller steps, which we will do now.

11. Create a **Scalar Parameter** and give it a name similar to `Number of Steps`. We'll use this value to fragment the gradient we have so far—the bigger the number, the more bands we'll have.

12. Include a **Multiply** node and use it to connect the previous **Scalar Parameter**, as well as the output of the **Multiply** node from step 10.

13. Add a **Floor** node. This will give you the bottom value of a float for example, if you have a value of 0.6, the result after the node will be 0. Connect it to the output of the previous **Multiply**.

14. Place a **Divide** node after the previous one and connect the output of the **Floor** to its **A** input pin. Connect the **B** input pin to the output of the Scalar Parameter we created in *step 11*. Refer to the following screenshot for more information:

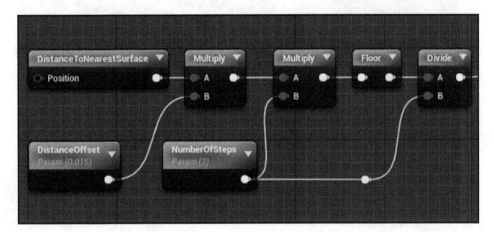

The previous set of nodes have given us a banded gradient, something which works well with toon-like shading techniques. The main reason why the **Floor** node can create gradients of this type is because it takes a color input and discards the decimal part of the color value. Because we have a gradient, each pixel has a different value, and thus the **Floor** node gets rid of the seamless variation in favor of a more stepped one since it gets rid of intermediate values—the ones between integers. Knowing this, let's get back on track with the creation of our material by putting the previous sequence to work as a mask.

15. Create a couple of different colors by placing two Constant 4 vectors in the material graph, and assign them different values. I've gone with blue and white.

16. Add a **Lerp** node and connect the previous Constant 4 vectors to its **A** and **B** input pins. The Alpha should be connected to the output of the **Divide** node from *step 14*.

17. Connect the output of the **Lerp** node to the **Base Color** of our material.

18. Include a simple Constant to modify the value of the Roughness. Something like `0.6` works well in this case!

19. Click on the **Apply** and **Save** buttons of the material, and assign it to the plane in our level:

Ta-da! Look at what you now have! This simple material, which is used in tandem with the Mesh Distance Field property of our models, can work well for any kind of distance-based effect. Things like ambient occlusion-based dirt, or water effects like the one we've just seen, are great examples of that. Furthermore, this technique is dynamic in nature, meaning that the effect will update itself in real-time as things move around your level. There are many possibilities, so make sure that you play around with it for a while to see how far you can take it!

How it works...

Mesh distance fields can feel a bit daunting at first, especially since they are something that not many artists come into contact with very often. We'll try to introduce the basis on which they operate and, more importantly for us, how to increase their quality whenever we need to.

Trying to simplify the concept as much as possible without going into too many technical details; we can think of these assets as the way that the engine stores the distance that the different parts of the model are apart from within a volume texture. Let's take a look at the following screenshot:

What you can see in the previous screenshot is the visual representation of the Mesh Distance Field for the sphere located in the middle of our level. You can enable this view mode by clicking on **Show** | **Visualize** | **Mesh Distance Fields**. As you can see, the sphere is contained in a surrounding volume, and the distance field is computed in regards to that. These calculations are done offline, and don't happen in real time as they would be too expensive. However, we can tap into this precomputed data to drive different effects, from the one we saw in this recipe to dynamic flow maps, just to name a few.

Something we need to keep in mind though, is how to effect the final quality of these fields we are creating. We can do so through the setting we saw at the beginning of this recipe the **Distance Field Resolution** multiplier. Going beyond the default one will make the volume texture heavier, but we sometimes need that extra quality in very detailed objects or other specific examples. Remember to tweak that whenever you need to!

There's more...

The quality of the Mesh Distance Fields depends on many different settings, some of which we've already seen. However, there's a handy console command that you might want to know more about, `r.AOGlobalDFResolution`. Typing that into the console and a number after it to change the quality of these assets. Try different values, like `128`, `256`, or similar to see what the results are in case you want to modify the defaults. Have fun with it!

See also

Make sure to check out Epic Games' official docs if you want to continue learning about Mesh Distance Fields: `https://docs.unrealengine.com/en-us/Engine/Rendering/LightingAndShadows/MeshDistanceFields`.

Using Material Instances

7

Instancing is where you take a parent material and make copies of it that have differences within them. This was already touched upon in the *Instancing a material* recipe in `Chapter 3`, *Opaque Materials and Texture Mapping*, but there are a lot of things that can be done with this concept.

In this chapter, we will cover the following recipes:

- Creating snow on top of objects using layering materials
- Changing from a sunny scene to a snowy one through parameter collection
- Changing between seasons quickly with curve atlases
- Blending landscape materials
- Customizing UVs

Introduction

As artists, we can provide tools to make it easier for others on the team to be able to tweak the aspects of a material, while designing the game or tweaking them at runtime. For instance, the game designers on your team may like to tweak how a material looks but may not have knowledge of how to use the material editor. Alternatively it may be your programmers want to support different weather types in the game. We can create the base material and then expose properties that can be modified to display things differently over time.

In this chapter, we will move away from the things we can do inside a material to those we can do once we have created it, such as quickly tweaking it using material instances, layering different shaders on top of each other, or affecting multiple material settings at once.

Creating snow on top of objects using layered materials

Introduced in Unreal Engine 4.19, Material Layers is a method of taking different types of materials and using an easy-to-use interface to put them together with no additional pixel shader instructions, thus improving performance.

To see just how easy it is to put this together, we are going to see how we can use this concept to add snow to the top of a material based on the world.

Getting ready...

Material Layers are an experimental feature, so unless you turn them on, you won't be able to use them:

1. From the Unreal Editor, go to **Settings | Project Settings**. From the top search bar, type in material layer and check the **Support Material Layers** option:

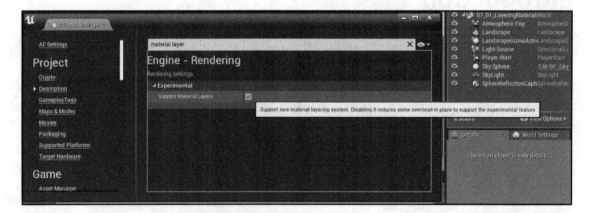

2. You may get a window pop up that says that you need to restart Unreal for changes to take effect. If so, click on the **Restart Now** option and wait for Unreal to open up again.

How to do it...

Now that we have the Material Layers feature enabled, let's actually make our first Material Layer:

1. Right-click anywhere inside of the **Content Browser** and under the **Create Advanced Asset** section, select **Materials Textures | Material Layer**:

2. Name it whatever you want—I'll go with **Layer_Base** for this particular instance. Double-click on the newly created material to open up the material editor:

This editor should look fairly familiar to you if you've used Material functions before, the only difference being that on the right-hand side there's a new node called **Output Material Attributes**. This result is what will be used within our material later on.

3. To the left of **Input Material Attributes**, right-click and create a **Make Material Attributes** node by searching for its name and selecting it.

This node should look similar to the other materials we created previously. We can create this material just like any of the ones we've created previously, but for the sake of simplicity, we will only use the **BaseColor** and **Normal** channels.

4. From the Unreal Editor, in the **Content Browser**, open up the `Content\StarterContent\Textures` folder. From there, select a Diffuse and Normal texture to bring into the Material Layer editor and drag and drop it into there. For this example, I used `'T_Brick_Clay_New_D.T_Brick_Clay_New_D'` and `'T_Brick_Clay_New_N.T_Brick_Clay_New_N'`.

5. Connect the textures to the **BaseColor** and **Normal** channels of the **MakeMaterialAttributes** node.

6. Connect the output of the **MakeMaterialAttributes** node to the **Preview** input of the **Input Material Attributes (Material Attributes)** node.

7. We want to be able to support having other objects covered in snow easily, so right-click on both **Texture Samples** and select **Convert to Parameter**. Name the diffuse texture `Base Diffuse` and the normal texture `Base Normal`. If all went well, you should have something that looks like the following:

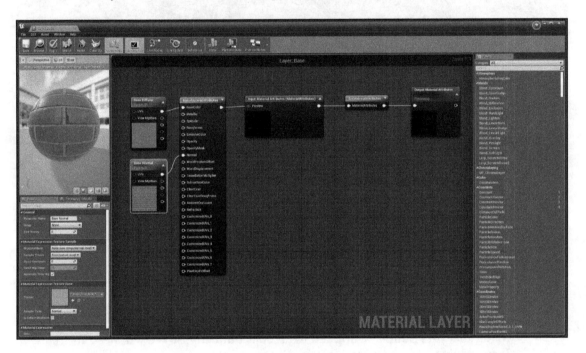

8. Click on the **Apply** and **Save** buttons from the editor and exit this layer.

Now that we have our base layer, we need another Material Layer for the snow.

9. In the same folder as your `Layer_Base` material layer, right-click on the **Content Browser** and create another material layer called `Layer_Snow`. Double-click on it to enter the **Material Layer Editor**.

10. This material will be built in the same way as the previous material layer, but instead of the brick texture, we will use something that looks like snow. In our case, the Starter Content does not include a snow texture, but it does have `T_Concrete_Poured_D.T_Concrete_Poured_D`, which looks pretty close to snow:

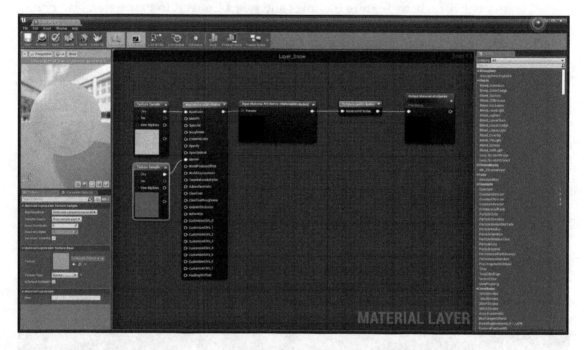

11. Click on the **Apply** and **Save** buttons from the editor and exit this layer.

Material layers cannot be applied to an object directly, so we will need to create a material that uses the material layers instead.

12. Create a material and name it `M_SnowLayeredMaterial`. Double-click on it to enter the material editor.

13. To the left of the default channels, right-click and add a **Material Attribute Layers** node and name it `Layer Stack`.

Since this is a normal material, you'll notice that the result node of the material contains all of the normal channels that we are used to using and that the Layer Stack is considered to be material attributes.

14. From the **Details** tab of the material, scroll down to the **Use Material Attributes** property and check it. You'll see all of the normal channels combine into one property, **Material Attributes**.

15. Connect the output of the **Layer Stack** to the **Material Attributes** property of the **M_SnowLayeredMaterial** node:

16. Now that we have the connections created, we can start adding to our Layer Stack. Select the **Layer Stack** node and from the **Details** tab, click the arrow next to the **Default Layers** property. Expand the background and from the **Layer Asset** dropdown, select our Layer_Base.

17. Afterwards, click on the + icon next to **Default Layers** to add a new layer to the stack. Select and expand the newly created **Layer 1** and set its **Layer Asset** property to Layer_Snow:

You should notice that the snow is now covering the original background. Layers work in a similar way to how Photoshop handles them, with layers being drawn on top of each other.

The **Blend Asset** property defines what parts of **Layer 1** should be drawn on top of the **Background**, so we will implement that next.

18. Hit **Apply** and **Save**. Then, close the editor.
19. Right-click inside of the **Content Browser** and under the **Create Advanced Asset** section, select **Materials Textures | Material Layer Blend**.
20. Name it whatever you want—I'll go with **SnowBlend** for this particular instance. Double-click on the newly created material to open up the material editor:

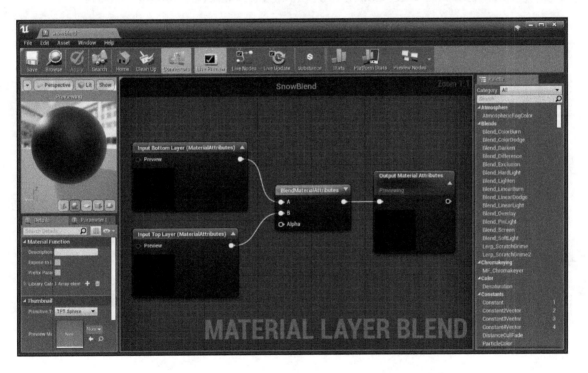

As you can see, on the left-hand side we have two inputs, the **Input Top Layer** (the snow) and the **Input Bottom Layer** (the bricks), which are being passed to a node called **BlendMaterialAttributes**. The **Alpha** property dictates whether the value should be the same (black) or if it should show fully (white). In our case, we want to blend based on the alignment of the vertices based on the world.

21. Below the inputs, add a **WorldAlignedBlend** node. Then, connect the **w/Vertex Normals** output to the **Alpha** property of the **BlendMaterialAttributes** node.

22. To the left of the **Blend Sharpness (S)** input, create a **Constant** with a value of 10 and assign it to the **Blend Sharpness (S)** input of the **WorldAlignedBlend** node.

23. Afterwards, create another Constant connected to the **Blend Bias**. Right-click on this node and select **Convert to Parameter**. Name this parameter Snow Bias:

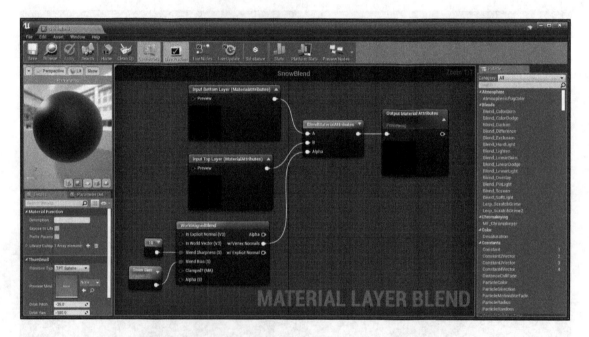

24. Hit **Apply** and then **Save** your material. Afterwards, you can exit the material editor.

25. Back in `M_SnowLayeredMaterial`, select the **Layer Stack** node and set the **Blend Asset** to the `SnowBlend` we just created. If all goes well, you should see the top half of the preview image covered with our snow layer!

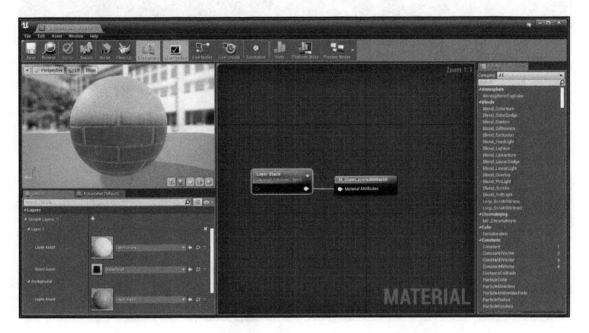

26. To make this easier to see with traditional assets, go ahead and create a scene with a more complex mesh, such as SM_MatPreviewMesh_02.SM_MatPreviewMesh_02, and drag and drop our material onto it:

Now that we have the basic material, we can instantiate instances of it very easily.

27. Right-click on `M_SnowLayeredMaterial` and select **Create Material Instance**. Name this new material instance `M_SnowLayeredGold`. Double-click on it to open the editor:

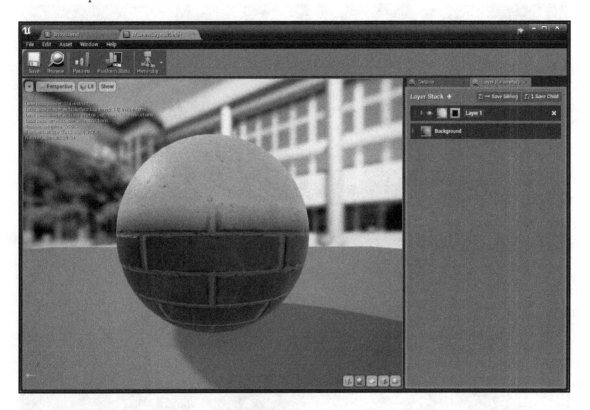

28. Unlike before, you'll notice that the menu has been streamlined. Open the **Background** property and click on the arrow next to **Layer Asset** and then **Texture Parameters**. There, you should see our previously created parameters.

As we discussed previously, this content is fairly experimental and I experienced crashing issues when enabling the checks in the next step. If the same happens to you first, clear the **Blend** by expanding the **Layer 1** option, clicking on **Blend Asset**, and then selecting **Clear**. Check the properties and then assign the **Blend Asset** back to **SnowBlend**.

29. Click on the checks for **Base Diffuse** and **Base Normal**. You should be able to set these to new texture values, such as those for gold:

30. From the Unreal Editor, drag and drop this material instance onto an object(s), for instance, the chair and table in the **Minimal_Default** layer:

31. Go back to the material editor and under **Layer 1**, open up the **Blend Asset** and **Scalar Parameters** arrows, and then check the `Snow Bias` property and tweak the value. Note that the chair and tables will be modified in real time:

32. Note that if we rotate the chair, the tops of them will always be covered in snow:

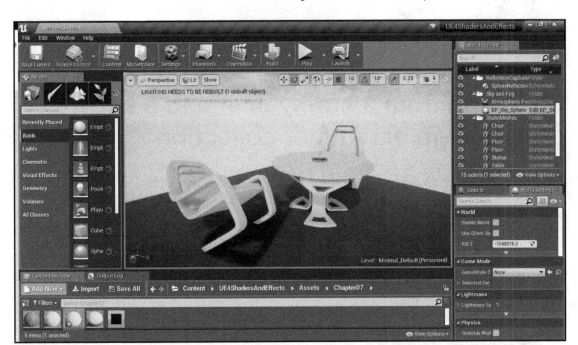

This idea can also be easily expanded so that you can work with any material that you would want to tweak often, such as color schemes for character skins.

How it works...

A material layer acts similarly to a material function, but has the ability to create children, just like when you create Material Instances.

The **Material Layer Blend** provides instructions on how to draw the different layers in the material on top of each other. In our instance, we used the result of the **WorldAlignedBlend** node to determine where the snow layer should be drawn, which is on the top of the surface it is placed on.

When we create an instance of the parent material, you'll notice that, when opened, the material opens to a **Layer Parameters** menu instead of the default editor. This menu is only shows aspects of the material that are parameters, with the idea of making it very simple to add and/or modify aspects of the material. It's important to note that you still can access the **Details** tab as well if that is what you'd prefer.

For more information on Layered Materials, check out the following link: `https://docs.unrealengine.com/en-US/Engine/Rendering/Materials/LayeredMaterials`.

Changing from a sunny scene to a snowy one through parameter collection

Another common issue that is seen in game development is that you sometimes want to have multiple materials change at the same time. We've already learned about parameters and how we can change them at runtime using Blueprints, but you have to change each material parameter individually.

Material parameter collections allow us to create special variables that can be referred to in multiple materials and then modified in an editor or at runtime through Blueprints or C++. To see just how easily it can be used, in this recipe, we will show you how we can make multiple materials in an environment so that it looks like it has snowed.

Getting ready...

To begin, you will need to create a material with two states: one state where it's completely dry and another for when it has snowed. You'll connect both states to a **Linear Interpolation** (**Lerp**) node. Alternatively, you may use a **LayerBlend** like we did in our previous recipe.

How to do it...

Instead of using a parameter, we will use a Material Collection. Let's get started:

1. Right-click inside of the **Content Browser** and under the **Create Advanced Asset** section, select **Materials Textures | Material Parameter Collection**. Name this whatever you wish; I went with `SnowCollection`.

2. Double-click on the new collection and you'll be brought to a window that contains two properties: **Scalar parameters** and **Vector Parameters**:

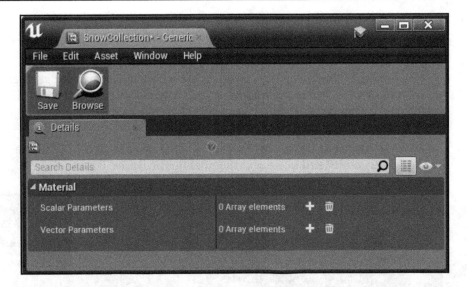

3. Click on the + button next to the **Scalar Parameters** option. Once this new option has been created, expand the **0** and you'll see two properties. Set the **Parameter Name** to Snow Amount:

4. Hit the **Save** button and return to the Unreal Editor.

5. Double-click on the **SnowBlend** material layer blend we created in the previous recipe.

6. Next to the **Snow Bias** property, right-click and add a **CollectionParameter** node. Once created, select the node and from the **Details** tab, set the **Collection** property to the **SnowCollection** we created. Afterwards, set the parameter to **Snow Amount**.

7. Connect the output of the **Snow Amount** property node to the Blend Bias (S) of the **WorldAlignedBlend** node and then delete the **Snow Bias** node:

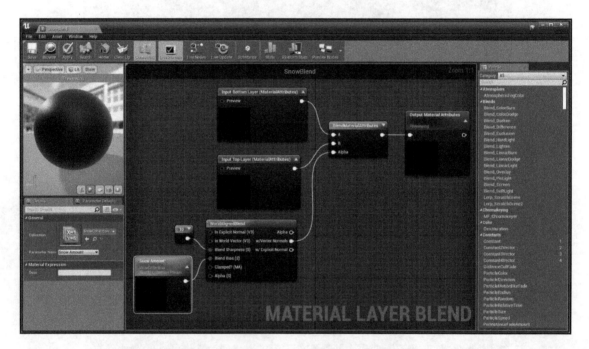

8. Hit the **Apply** button and then **Save** and exit the editor.

9. Create a scene where you can see both of the snow materials we created in the previous recipe. You can open an example in the `Content / UE4ShadersAndEffects / Maps / Chapter07 / 07_02_MaterialDisplay` file for this:

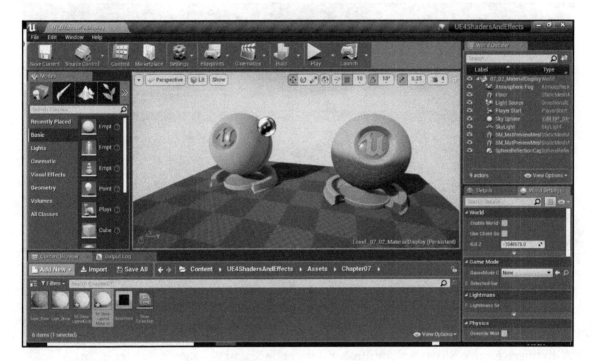

10. Now, return to the Unreal Editor and open up the **Snow Collection** once again from the **Content Browser**. Once there, modify the **Snow Amount** value and notice how we are able to change multiple materials without any need to recompile at runtime. For instance, here is the value at −3:

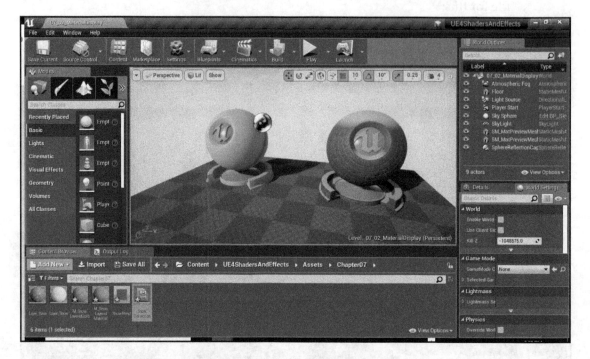

With this, we can easily tweak multiple things at once and use the parameter in any material and/or blend!

How it works...

Material collections allow us to modify properties on multiple materials at once. While this requires some time up front to set them up, it's well worth it.

Changing between seasons quickly with curve atlases

Curve atlases store multiple curves together and allow you to linearly interpolate between them. When used together with material instances, it is possible to create a wide variety of changes within your materials. In this recipe, we will see how we can use this concept to make materials change and reflect different seasons by making use of Blueprints and Material Instance Dynamics.

Getting ready...

This recipe will use the **Starter Content** that is optionally included in Unreal projects, but you may use any texture of your own.

How to do it...

In order to create a curve atlas, we will need to create some curves to use:

1. From the **Content Browser**, right-click and select **Miscellaneous** | **Curve**:

2. From the **Pick Curve Class** window, select **CurveLinearColor** and then click on **Select**:

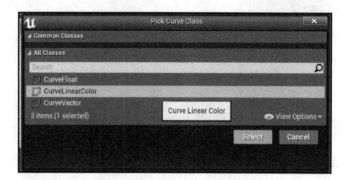

3. Give the curve a name (I used `SummerCurve`) and then double-click on it to open the editor:

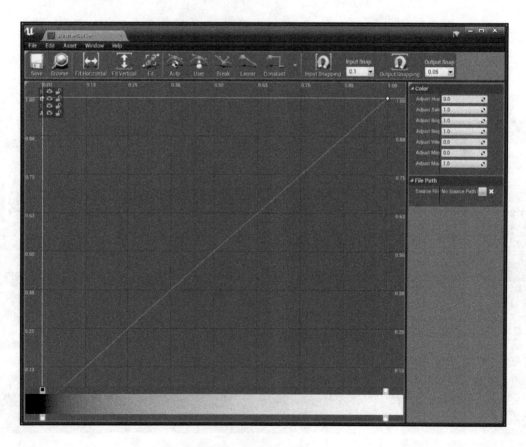

In our case, we care about the **Curve Gradient Result**, which you can see on the bottom part of the editor. Note that there are two keys on the top of the gradient and two below. The bottom section is the alpha of the color, while the top is the color.

4. Double-click on the black box to open up the **Color Picker** menu. Click on a green value in the color value and set the V value to 1. Afterwards, click on **OK**:

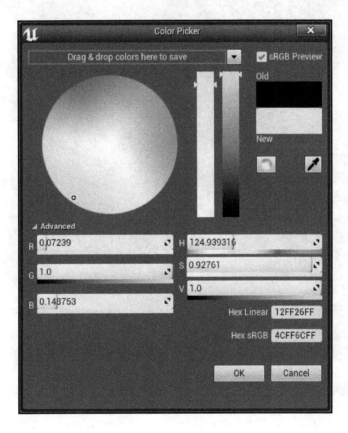

5. Notice that the gradient has been updated. Click on other points to add more variation to your gradient:

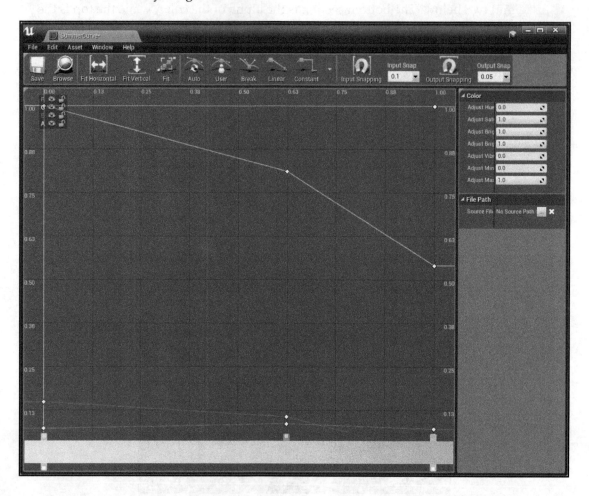

 For more information about the Curve Editor, check out the following link: https://docs.unrealengine.com/en-us/Engine/UI/CurveEditor.

6. Click on the **Save** button and return to the Unreal editor.

7. Afterwards, create three additional curves for the other seasons. Alternatively, you can use the ones we created in the example code for this book:

8. Now that we have our curves, we need to build the **Curve Atlas Asset**. From the **Content Browser**, right-click and select **Miscellaneous | Curve Atlas**.

9. Name the new **Curve Atlas** SeasonAtlas. Afterwards, double-click on it to open the editor.

10. From the **Details** tab, open the **Gradient Curves** property and click on the +
    button to add an element to your array. Afterwards, set the item to the first curve
    (**SpringCurve**). Then, click the + button and add the next curve (Summer), then
    Fall and Winter. Finally, set the Texture Size to 4:

11. Hit the **Save** button and return to the Unreal Editor.

Now that we have a **Curve Atlas**, we can create a **Material** that uses it:

1. From the **Content Browser**, right-click and select **Material**. When asked for a name, use **M_SeasonGround**. Double-click on the material to open the Material Editor.

2. From the Unreal Editor, in the **Content Browser**, open up the `Content\StarterContent\Textures` folder. From there, select a **Diffuse** texture to bring into the Material Layer editor and drag and drop it into there.

3. To the right of the Texture Sample that was just created, create a Desaturation node. Select the node and from the **Details** tab, open the **Luminance Factors** property and change **R**, **G**, and **B** to 1. Then, connect the pin from the Texture sample to the top pin of the **Desaturation** node.

4. Lastly, for demonstration purposes, connect the output pin of **Desaturation** to the **Base Color** property:

As you can see, we've removed the color of the texture. Now, we will add it back in using the **Curve Atlas**:

1. Right-click in the graph and add a **CurveAtlasRowParameter** node:

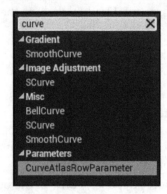

2. When asked for a name, use Season.
3. Under the **Details** tab, set **Curve** to SpringCurve. Afterwards, set the **Atlas** to SeasonAtlas.
4. To the right of the Season node, create a **Blend_Overlay** node.
5. Connect the output of **Desaturation** to the **Base (V3)** property of the **Blend_Overlay** node.
6. Connect the top pin of the **Season** node to the **Blend (V3)** property of the **Blend_Overlay** node.

7. Lastly, connect the **Result** of the **Blend_Overlay** node to the **Base Color** node:

8. Save the Material Editor and return to the editor.

At this point, we can assign the material, but it won't change. To do this, we will need to use Blueprints:

1. Open up the Level Blueprints for your project by going to **Blueprints** | **Open Level Blueprint**.
2. Create an **Event BeginPlay** event.

3. To the right of that, create a **Create Dynamic Material Instance** node. Uncheck the **Context Sensitive** option and ensure that you select the one that has `Target is Primitive Component` in the tooltip:

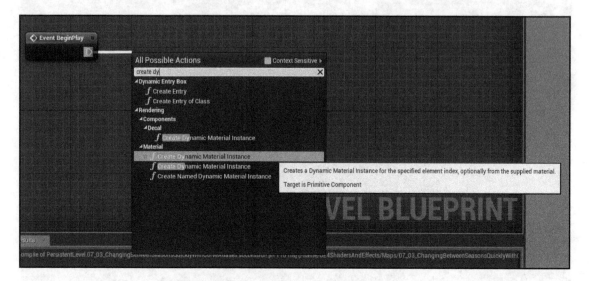

4. Select the node and under **SourceMaterial**, select **M_SeasonGround**.

5. Then, set **Target** to an object in your scene that has a Material. For instance, I selected the **Chair** object from the default scene. Drag and drop the object into the **Event Graph** and then drag and drop the pin to the **Target** property. A conversion from the object to the **Static Mesh Component** will be created:

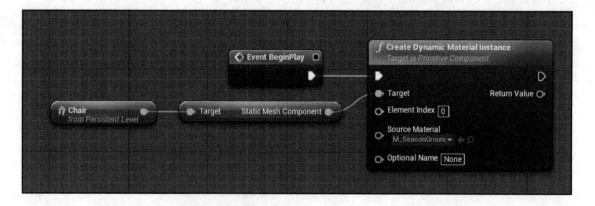

6. To the right of the **Create Dynamic Material Instance** node, create a **Set Scalar Parameter Value** node. Ensure that **Context Sensitive** is disabled and use the version that has the **Target** is **Material Instance Dynamic**:

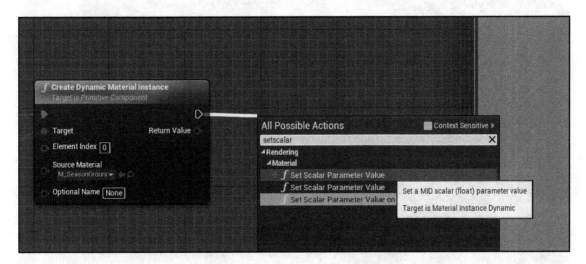

7. Under **Parameter Name**, use the name of the parameter we created previously (Season) and under **Value**, put 0.5. Finally, connect the **Return Value** of the **Create Dynamic Material Instance** node to the **Target** property of the **Set Scalar Parameter Value** node:

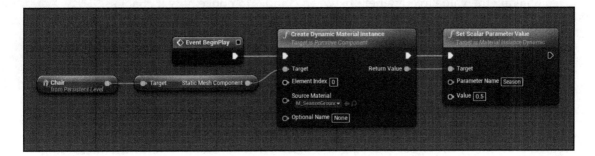

8. **Save** and **compile** the blueprint and start the game:

As you can see, the chair now has a new material and is modified by the curves! Try changing the value to anywhere between 0 and 1 to notice how it changes.

How it works...

When you create a **Linear Color Curve**, the **Content Browser** will display a preview of the gradient information of it.

In our case, the value between **0** and **1** will go through each of the season curves that we created previously, with 0 being spring and 1 being winter, and any value between going through each of the options presented.

Taking our base recipe, we can easily expand on this by starting at **0** and increasing the value gradually to see the changes it causes over time:

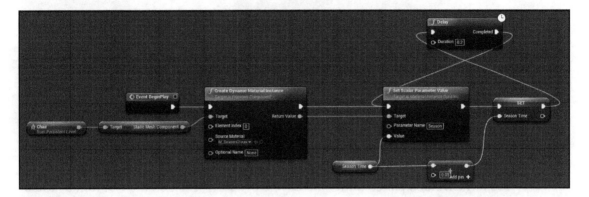

This can be done by creating a variable and then incrementing its value over time with a delay before calling the **Set Scalar Parameter Value** node again. You can see this in action in the 07_03_ChangingBetweenSeasonsQuicklyWithCurveAtlases map within the example code from this book.

Blending landscape materials

Another place where having instances of materials can be useful is when you're creating materials for landscapes. Unreal Engine comes with a very powerful landscape system built into it that allows you to have a single material that can blend between various textures through the use of the **Landscape Layer Blend** node. In this recipe, we will explore how to create and apply such a material.

Getting ready...

While this recipe will tell you what you need to know about landscapes to create the material and see it in use, it will not go into depth about how it works and how to create the landscape itself.

For information on creating landscapes, check out the following link: `https://docs.` `unrealengine.com/en-us/Engine/Landscape/Creation`.

How to do it...

Before we apply a material for the landscape, we need to create that material. Let's get started:

1. Create a Material and call it `M_Landscape`. Double-click on it to enter the Material Editor.
2. To the left of the default channels, right-click and add a **Landscape Layer Blend** node.
3. From the **Details** panel, under the **Layers** property, click on the + button to add a layer to your blend.
4. Click on the arrow next to the newly added **0** property and expand the options for the layer. Change the **Layer Name** to `Grass`.
5. Click on the + button again to add an additional later. Under the new 1 index, change the **Layer Name** to `Rock`.
6. Connect the output pin on the right-hand side of the **Layer Blend** to the **Base Color** property of **M_Landscape**.
7. Afterwards, connect a texture for each of the layers we created. This can be done by going to the **Content Browser** and opening the `Content\StarterContent\Textures` folder, and then dragging the `T_Ground_Grass_D` and `T_Rock_Slate_D` textures into the Material Editor.

8. Afterwards, connect the top pin of the **Texture Sample** nodes into their respective layer property on the **Layer Blend** node:

9. Select the three nodes we created. Afterwards, copy and paste them by hitting *Ctrl + C* and then *Ctrl + V*. Connect the output of the **Layer Blend** node to the **Normal** property, select the **Texture Sample** nodes, and change the texture to the normal images. When you're finished, you should have something like the following:

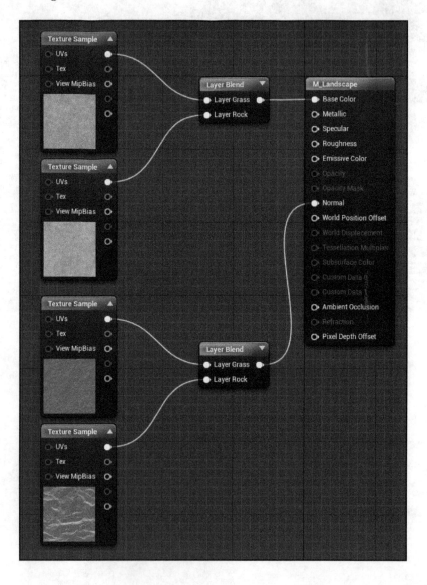

10. After this, click on **Apply** and **Save**, and exit the Material Editor.

11. Create a level if you haven't done so already. Afterwards, create a landscape, again, if you don't have one already. You can do this by going to the **Modes** tab and selecting the mountain icon or hitting *Shift + 3*:

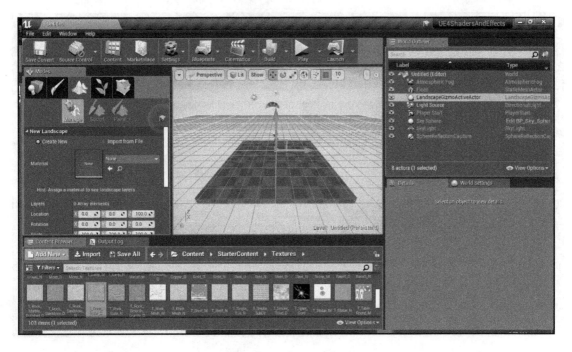

12. From the **Modes** tab, scroll down to set the **Material** property to the **M_Landscape** we created.

13. Below that, change the **Section Size** to **7 x 7 Quads** to make the map smaller for the purposes of this recipe.

14. Afterwards, click on the **Create** button and wait for the shaders to compile.

15. Next, click on the **Paint** button and scroll down to the **Target Layers** section. From there, open the **Layers** property and click on the + button to add a **Landscape Layer Info Object** instance for the layer. From the menu that pops up, select **Weight-Blended Layer (normal)**:

16. Select a folder to hold the information in. I'll be using
    `UE4ShadersAndEffects\Assets\Chapter07`. Once selected, hit the **OK**
    button.

    After waiting a few seconds, you should notice the landscape change so that it
    uses the first layer to fill the entire area:

17. Do the same thing with the **Rock** layer.
18. Now, with the **Rock** layer selected, click and drag within the scene window. You should notice the rock layer being painted on the scene wherever your mouse cursor goes over:

And with that, we have seen how we can blend between layers within landscapes!

How it works...

The Layer Blend node allows us to blend multiple textures or materials together so that they can be used as layers within the Landscape mode. Each layer has a number of properties that dictate how it will be drawn. We are using the default blend mode, **LB Weight Blend**, which allows us to paint layers on top of other layers.

You can learn about the other blend types here: `https://docs.unrealengine.com/en-us/Engine/Landscape/Materials#landscapelayerblendtypes`.

From the **Paint** menu, you can make use of the **Brush Size** and **Brush Falloff** properties to change how much is being painted at once. We can also add as many layers as we'd like to get whatever look we are looking for.

Customizing UVs

Games are generally computationally expensive, so it makes sense to improve performance whenever you can. With a computer's GPU, a vertex shader is run for every vertex on a model, and pixel shaders are run for every pixel on the screen. Unreal has a feature called CustomizedUVs that can give a performance boost if you run it on just the vertex shader instead of also needing to use a pixel shader. This gives us the ability to tile a texture more efficiently.

Getting ready...

To easily see the differences in UVs, you should have a texture where you can easily tell where the edges of it are. In this case, I will be using the `UE4_Logo` texture, which is included in the `Engine Content/VREditor/Devices/Vive/` folder in the **Content Browser**.

How to do it...

Before we can modify the UVs of a material, we need to create a material to use. Let's get started:

1. Create a material and give it a name of `M_CustomizedUVs`. Double-click on it to enter the Material Editor.
2. From the editor, create a texture sample by holding down the *T* key and then clicking to the left of the `M_CustomizedUVs` result node. Connect the top pin to the **Base Color** pen.

3. Then, with the **Texture Sample** node selected, go to the **Details** tab and set the **Texture** property to something that you can easily tell the edges of. I used the `UE4_Logo` texture:

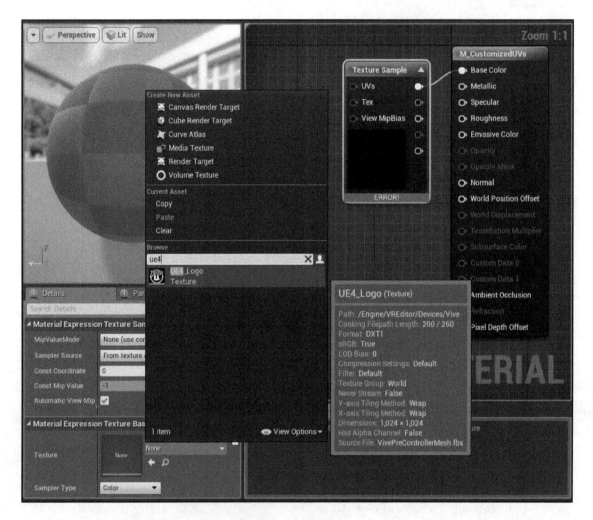

4. Afterwards, deselect the node by clicking elsewhere on the screen. The **Details** panel will fill with information about the material in general.

This information will also show up if you select the **M_CustomizedUVs** result node as well.

5. From the **Details** tab, click on the search bar and type in the word `custom`. You should see the **Num Customized UV** property. Set that to `1` and press *Enter* to commit the change:

If all went well, you should see from the result node that a new property was added to the bottom, Customized UV0.

Now that we have the ability to modify the UVs on the material, we need to create some UVs that we can modify. This is done through a node called **Texture Coordinate**.

6. To the left of the **Customized UV0** property, right-click and type in tex. From there, select the **TextureCoordinate** option:

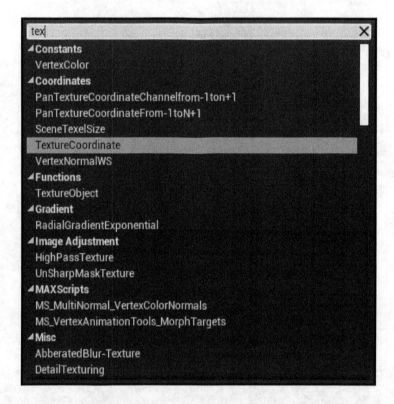

7. For the sake of demonstration purposes, connect the output pin of the newly added **TexCoord[0]** node to the **Customized UV0** node. Once connected, select the **TextCoord[0]** node and from the **Details** tab, set the **UTiling** and **VTiling** properties to 4:

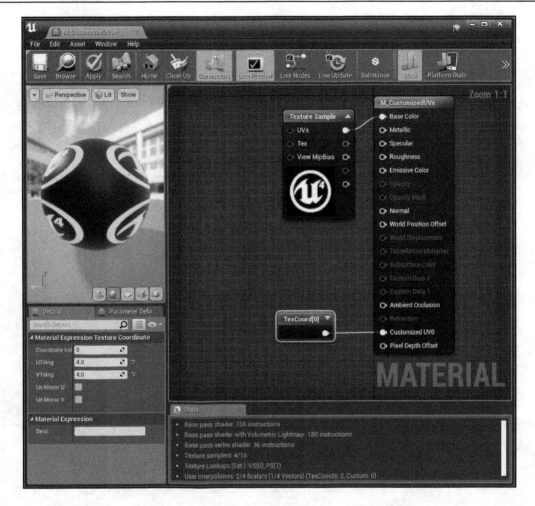

As you can see, this causes the image to tile four times in the **X** and **Y** axes, and is an easy way to zoom in or out of your material.

To show this concept being taken further, we can also modify the UVs in other ways.

8. Delete the connection of **TexCoord[0]** and the **Customized UV0** channel by holding down *Alt* and clicking on the connection.
9. Between the two nodes, create a **Panner** node. Afterwards, connect the output of **TexCoord[0]** to the **Coordinate** pin of the **Panner** node. Then, connect the output pin from the **Panner** node to the **Customized UV0** channel.

10. Select the **Panner** node and from the **Details** tab, set the **Speed X** property to 1. Afterwards, set the **Speed Y** to 2:

If all went well, you should see the material moving around the object without any modifications having to be made to the other channels!

How it works...

UV mapping is the process of taking a 2D texture and drawing it onto a 3D object. Generally, models have their own default UVs that can be created in modeling programs. In this recipe, we saw how we can modify them. We can use this example for something like a waterfall or lava and have a panning image that changes over time, but this can also be changed for other things such as shaking a hologram.

In this recipe, we saw how we can use Customized UVs to modify how our material is drawn. We added in the ability to customize our UVs through the **Num Customized UV** property. Customized UVs start counting at **0**, just like arrays do.

This default state of how to draw UVs on an object is referred to as the **Texture Coordinates** of the object, which is what we used as a foundation for modifying the UVs on this material (TexCoord[0]). By modifying the **Texture Coordinates**, we are able to modify the entire material in one spot with minimal performance costs.

Previously, we used the **Panner** node in the *A different type of translucency hologram* recipe in Chapter 4, *Translucent Materials and More*, but instead of panning the texture in the **Base Color**, we can also modify how an object is drawn by modifying the UVs.

 For more information on Customized UVs, check out the following link: https://docs.unrealengine.com/en-us/Engine/Rendering/Materials/ CustomizedUVs.

Mobile Shaders and Material Optimization

8

In this chapter, we will cover the following recipes:

- Creating materials for mobile platforms
- Using the forward shading renderer for VR
- Optimizing through texture atlases
- Baking a 3D model material into a texture
- Combining multiple meshes with the HLOD tool
- General material-optimization techniques

Introduction

Moving away from the most powerful gaming and computing platforms means that we, as developers, have to cater for less-capable devices, and demanding elements, such as shaders, have to be tweaked in order to maintain performance. We will take a look at how to bring our materials into a mobile environment and how to optimize them.

Creating materials for mobile platforms

When developing materials for mobile platforms, there are some things to keep in mind. Due to a number of hardware limitations, you can't expect to be able to do everything that you perhaps used to with the Material Editor. As you spend more time building materials for mobile devices, you will discover that there are often trade-offs that are required, reducing complexity for the sake of your application size or frame rate. This recipe will discuss the creation of materials with mobile platforms in mind.

Getting ready...

Any textures that you want to use on mobile platforms need to have a resolution of 2,048 x 2,048 or lower, preferably a square texture with a power of 2 (64, 128, 256, 512, 1,028, 2,048) as that is the most efficient use of memory.

For more information on creating textures for mobile platforms in UE4, check out https://docs.unrealengine.com/en-us/Platforms/Mobile/Textures.

How to do it...

To get started, we will first create a standard material, then see how we can tweak it for mobile platforms:

1. Create a material and name it M_MobileExample. Double-click on it to enter the Material Editor.
2. From the editor, create a texture sample by holding down the *T* key and then clicking to the left of the **M_CustomizedUVs** result node. Connect the top pin to the **Base Color** pin.
3. With the **Texture Sample** node selected, go to the **Details** tab and set the **Texture** property to something that also has a normal map. I used the **T_Brick_Cut_Stone_D** texture from the **Sample Content**.
4. Create another **Texture Sample** and assign the normal map texture to it (in my case, **T_Brick_Cut_Stone_N**). Connect the top pin of the newly created **Texture Sample** to the **Normal** pin:

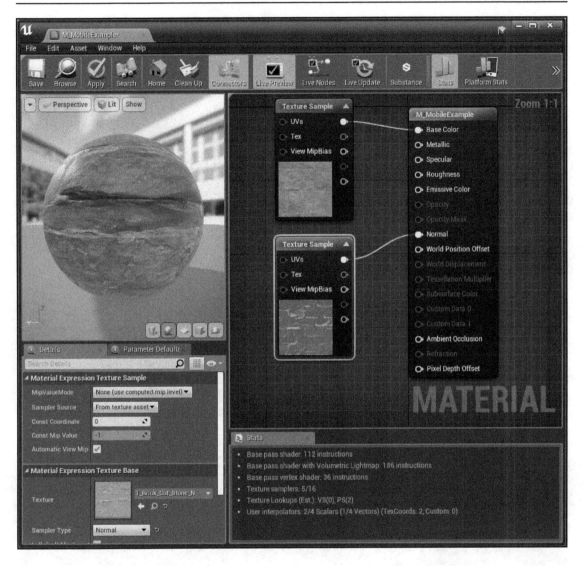

Notice that the **Stats** tab contains a list of the instructions used for this particular material. If you don't see the **Stats** window, you can open it by clicking on the **Stats** button on the top toolbar.

5. Select the **M_MobileExample** node. From the **Details** tab, go down to the **Material** section and click on the downward-facing arrow to open the advanced options. Once opened, enable the **Fully Rough** property:

As you can see, the **Stats** window now displays fewer instructions in both the **Base pass shader** and **Base pass shader with Volumetic Lightmap** sections!

How it works...

The Material Editor contains a section called **Mobile**, which has two properties: **Use Full Precision** and **Use Lightmap Directionality**. These are intended for mobile devices and to save performance. By default, Unreal will use less-precise math in order to save on memory and computation time. When enabled, the **Use Full Precision** property will use the highest precision available on a mobile device. This will solve certain rendering issues at the cost of being more expensive to use. Generally, you'll leave this property disabled unless you notice issues with how the material looks.

Use Lightmap Directionality, has an effect that is very apparent when using a normal map. Basically, it will use the lightmap to show the light at the top of the normal map and shadows at the bottom. You'll need to **Build** the project in order to see the lightmap information being used. If disabled, lighting from lightmaps will be flat but cheaper.

The **Material** section contains the **Fully Rough** property that, when enabled, will ignore the **Roughness** channel and instead force the material to be completely rough. This will save a number of instructions for optimization's sake and reduce one texture sampler.

The **Forward Shading** section contains the **High Quality Reflections** property which, when disabled, can increase the number of texture samples you can use by two. Turning this off will remove them to instead be used for cubemaps to display reflections.

While some of these properties will have less quality than the traditional fully-formed material, the settings can reduce the number of instructions on the **vertex shader** and the **Texture samplers** used, which you can see from the **Stats** toolbar from the Material Editor.

There's more...

Since there are so many mobile devices out there, there are a number of feature levels that can potentially be supported. To ensure maximum compatibility, the following channels can be used without any changes:

- **BaseColor**
- **Roughness**
- **Metallic**
- **Specular**
- **Normal**
- **Emissive**
- **Refraction**

However, you can only make use of up to five texture samples in your entire material. One of the ways to work with this limitation is to make use of Customized UVs, which we learned about in Chapter 7, *Using Material Instances*, to avoid needing to fetch extra textures.

You're also limited to using the **Default** and **Unlit** shading models and should limit the amount of materials with transparency or masks as they're very computationally expensive.

 You can find more information on creating Materials for mobile devices at https://docs.unrealengine.com/en-us/Platforms/Mobile/ Materials.

See also...

The *Customizing UVs* recipe in Chapter 7, *Using Material Instances*, discusses how to modify the UVs from a single texture. This concept can be used to effectively cut an image to only display parts of it.

In this chapter, the material quality system discussed in the *General material-optimization techniques* recipe is also quite helpful for ensuring that your materials can work on many different types of mobile devices.

Using the forward shading renderer for VR

Working with VR gives artists and designers a lot of interesting challenges. Even though VR experiences typically involve high-powered computers, often you can have performance issues due to the large screen size required. Unreal Engine 4 contains a different rendering system, called Forward Rendering, which will removes some rendering features, but gives a performance boost.

Getting ready...

In order to play your game in VR, you will need to have a VR headset that is plugged and able to be used. If you have a VR device plugged in and the option is greyed out, close the UE4 editor and restart it.

How to do it...

Forward Shading is disabled by default. We can enable it fairly easily though. Let's see how to do it:

1. From the Unreal Editor, go into **Edit | Project Settings**.
2. From the **Project Settings** menu, go to the left-hand side of the menu and scroll down until you reach the **Rendering** option, then select it.
3. Scroll down to the **Forward Renderer** section and then enable the **Forward Shading** property:

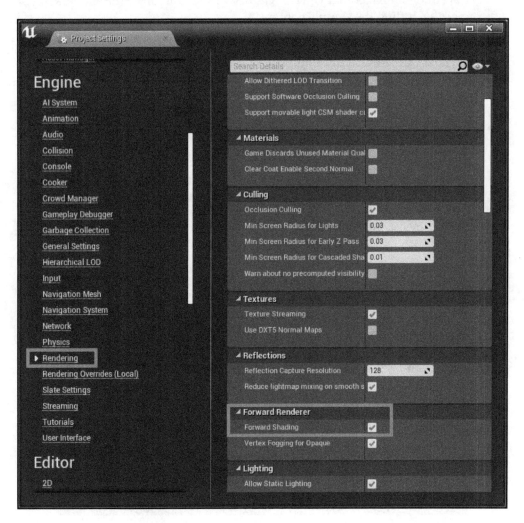

You will be prompted to restart the editor on the bottom right of the screen:

4. Click on the **Restart Now** button and wait for the editor to restart.

    Once the editor restarts, you'll be able to use the other **Forward Renderer** options and features. Do note that this may take a considerable amount of time to restart due to the fact that Unreal will need to rebuild all of the shaders in your project, including the sample content.

5. Open the **Project Settings** menu again by going to **Edit | Project Settings** and then select the **Rendering** option.

6. Scroll down the menu until you get to the **Default Settings** section. From there, change the **Anti-Aliasing Method** to **MSAA**:

7. You may be asked to rebuild your lighting. Do so, and then from the **Play** menu, click on the dropdown and then select **VR Preview**:

With that, you'll be able to play your game in VR, making use of the forward renderer!

How it works...

Unreal Engine 4 makes use of a deferred renderer, by default, as it gives artists and designers access to many more rendering features. However, those features are computationally expensive and may slow down games trying to run VR software. The forward renderer provides a faster experience on average, leading to better performance at the cost of losing some features, and has additional anti-aliasing options, which help visuals greatly in VR projects.

It is important to note that this feature is experimental and, as such, may change in future versions of UE4. You can learn more about the Forward Shading Renderer and any future updates to the system at `https://docs.unrealengine.com/en-us/Engine/Performance/ForwardRenderer`.

See also...

The majority of features talked about in the this recipe can are used to improve performance, not only for mobile projects but for VR ones as well.

If you are interested in learning even more about creating art with VR in Unreal Engine, check out Jessica Plowman's *Unreal Engine Virtual Reality Quick Start Guide*, also available from Packt Publishing.

Optimizing through texture atlases

Often referred to as a sprite sheet in the game industry, texture atlases are a great way to optimize game projects. The general concept is to have one image that itself contains a collection of smaller images. This is often used when there are smaller textures that are used frequently to reduce the overhead of the graphics card being used having to switch between different texture memory.

For more info on texture atlases, check out `https://en.wikipedia.org/wiki/Texture_atlas`.

Getting ready...

To complete this recipe, you will need to have a single texture what contains multiple smaller images inside of it. If you do not have one, you can make use of the flipbook texture from the `Engine Content/Functions/Engine_MaterialFunctions02/ExampleContent/Textures` folder.

How to do it...

One of the ways we can use texture atlases is through modifying the UVs on the object. Let's do that now:

1. Create a Material and name it `M_TextureAtlas`. Double-click on it to enter the Material Editor.
2. From the editor, create a texture sample by holding down the *T* key and then clicking to the left of the `M_TextureAtlas` result node. Connect the top pin to the **Base Color** pin.
3. With the **Texture Sample** node selected, go to the **Details** tab and set the **Texture** property to something that also has a normal map. As mentioned, I used the flipbook texture from the `Engine Content/Functions/Engine_MaterialFunctions02/ExampleContent/Textures` folder.

   To make it easier to see our cropping, we can change the preview display to show a flat plane.

4. From the preview window on the left side of the Material Editor, click on the
plane primitive button:

5. Move the camera so you can see the plane. You can click and hold the left mouse
   button to rotate the camera and then use the mouse wheel to zoom in and out:

6. To the left of the **Texture Sample** node, create a **Texture Coordinate** node. Connect the pin from the right side of the **TexCoord[0]** node to the **UVs** property of the **Texture Sample** node.
7. Select the **TexCoord[0]** node. From the **Details** tab, change the **UTiling** and **VTiling** properties to 0.5:

You should notice after the shader compiles that the material will only display the top-left half of the image (the **1** on the flipbook texture). To display a different image, we can offset the UVs being used by using an **Add** node.

8. Remove the connection between the **TexCoord[0]** and **UVs** pin by holding *Alt* and clicking on the connection. Move the **TexCoord[0]** node to the left to add some space between the nodes; in the new space, create an **Add** node.

9. Create a **2Vector** by holding down the **2** key and then clicking below the **TexCoord[0]** node. Connect the output pin from the **0,0** node to the **B** pin of the **Add** node.

10. Select the **0,0** node. From the **Details** tab, change the **R** value to **0.5**:

Once the shader compiles, you should see the **2** on the screen!

How it works...

To access the different aspects of the texture atlas, there are two steps that need to be performed: scaling the image and then offsetting it to the section you want to see.

First, you have to scale the image to display the portion of the image you wish to display. The **Texture Coordinates** node allows us to zoom in and out on the image by using the **UTiling** and **VTiling** values. A value of **1** means it will display 100% of the image, **0.5** means 50% of the image, and **2** would be 200% and duplicate the image. In this example, we want to only display one of the images at a time, so **0.5** is the value we want to use. In the case of each image being even, you can find this value mathematically by taking the number of parts you want to display divided by the total number of parts (in our case 1/2 or 0.5).

The second aspect is to decide what tile to use. In this case, by default, we see the one image. To see the others, we will need to offset the UVs. We can do this through the **Add** node. In this case, we are adding a **2Vector** that will offset the image in the X and Y axes. In this case, the **R** property is used for the X offset and **G** for the Y offset. The value we need to use is a percentage, just like the UV tiling properties. Using **0.5** in the **R** property moves the image 50% of the size of the image to the right. Using **0.5** in the **G** value would move us down 50%. So, for instance, (0.5, 0.5) would display 4.

You can see this concept being expanded on and used in greater detail with the **Flipbook** node, which includes variables to display images over time. You can see an example of this in the M_Flipbook material included in the example code for this chapter:

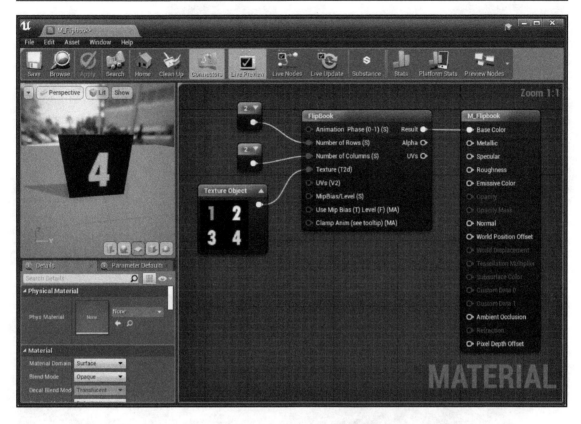

If you double-click on the **Flipbook** node, you'll be able to see each of the steps used to create it.

This type of behavior is often used in games, such as for spritesheets in 2D games to creating waterfalls by panning the UVs of an object. It's a great way to animate an object with a lower performance cost.

Baking a 3D model material into a texture

In this recipe, we will see that one of the possible ways to optimize your games is to bake your materials into textures. The main reason to want to do that is when your static meshes use many different materials on them, the more you have the more computationally expensive it will be to render them within your scene. It would be better if the mesh just had one material so there'd just be one draw call for each object. Effectively, we will be reducing all of the complex shader math being done to instead be baked into the texture.

If you are doing something using position offsets or animations, this will likely not work well. However, this could work well for props that will not change their structure.

There may be some precision things to take into consideration, as you may not have as high fidelity as the original meshes. For deploying your projects to mobile or other platforms that require you to optimize your materials as much as possible, it can be a very valuable tool for your work and can be really useful when you're trying to optimize everything that you can in order to hit your target frame rate.

Getting ready...

To get ready, you will want to have a mesh that has one or more materials attached to it placed within a scene you would like to use. If you don't feel like making one yourself, you may open the `08_04_MaterialMerge_Start` level located in the `Maps` folder of the example code for this book:

This example uses a **Material Preview** sphere with a **Cobblestone Material**.

How to do it...

One of the easiest ways to combine materials together is through the **Merge Actors** tool:

1. From the Unreal Editor, select the object with the model you want to bake. In this recipe's case, we'll select the **SM_MatPreviewMesh** object.

2. Go to **Window** | **Developer Tools** | **Merge Actors**:

3. From the menu that pops up, under **Mesh Settings**, set the **LODSelection Type** to **Use specific LOD level**.

4. Under **Material Settings**, check the **Merge Materials** option:

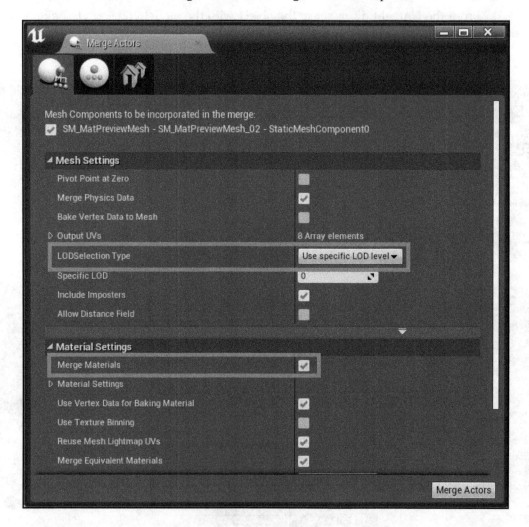

5. Click on the **Merge Actors** button and you'll have a menu ask you where you'd like to save our new mesh and materials. I selected the `Assets\Chapter08` folder and created a new folder called `MergeActors`. From there, change the **Name:** to `SM_Merged_Default`. Click on the **Save** button and wait for Unreal to do all the heavy lifting:

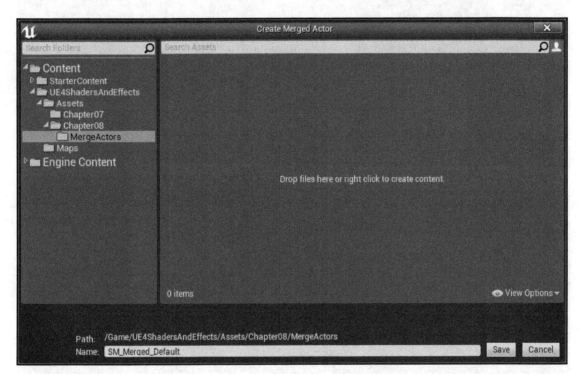

6. The **Content Browser** will immediately move to your new folder and will contain a number of new files, including a Static Mesh named **SM_Merged_Default**. Drag and drop the static mesh into your level:

As you can see, we have a new mesh with a single material instead of two, but we seem to have lost a lot of quality as well. This is due to the default parameters used heavily decreasing the number of texture samples and properties used for the sake of optimization. To get an example of something closer to the original, we can customize some additional options.

7. Select the original **SM_MatPreviewMesh** within the editor and return to the **Merge Actors** menu.
8. To add some additional details, click on the arrow to the left of the **Material Settings** option.
9. Under **Texture Size**, change the value to **2048** for both the **X** and **Y** properties.

10. Check the **Roughness Map**, **Specular Map**, and **Ambient Occlusion Map** options:

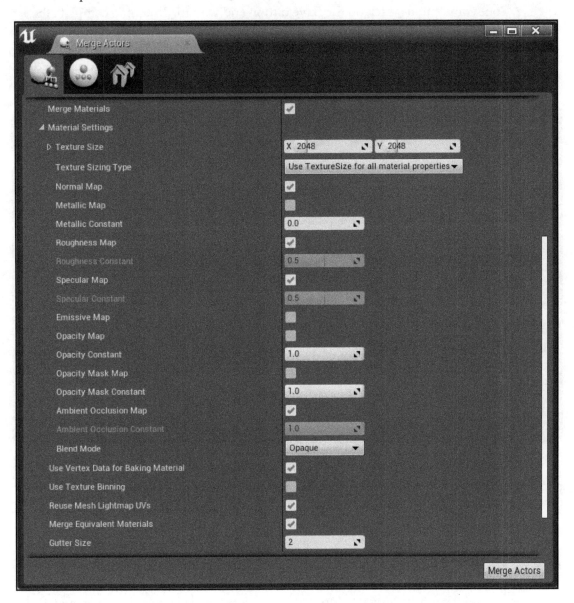

11. Click on **Merge Actors** and go to the folder where you'd like to place the files. I chose the same folder and used the name `SM_Merged_2048`. Once you've picked out your options, click on the **Save** button and wait for Unreal to complete the merge process.

12. The **Content Browser** will immediately move to your new folder and will contain a number of new files, including a Static Mesh named **SM_Merged_2048**. Drag and drop the static mesh into your level:

As you can see, this looks a lot more like the original material, but at the cost of performance. Tweak the **Material Settings** properties until you're content with the quality of your material.

How it works...

The **Merge Actors** tool is traditionally used to combine multiple static meshes into a single new actor. This is typically done later on in development after playtesting a level and ensuring that you are not going to move objects after the fact for the sake of optimization. We're using this tool in this recipe, because in addition to combining meshes, it can also have materials baked together into a single material with the UVs set correctly.

To find out more about the **Merge Actors** tool, check out `https://docs.unrealengine.com/en-us/Engine/Actors/Merging`.

The tool is non-destructive, so any of the changes you've made don't actually change the original materials. Once a merge occurs, it will automatically generate textures and materials based on your settings from the **Material Settings** option. In the default case, it made two textures for a Diffuse and Normal map and then a material that uses those two materials and a new static mesh.

 For more details on what each of the different aspects of the **Material Settings** menu means, check out `https://docs.unrealengine.com/en-us/Engine/Actors/Merging#materialsettings`.

The second time we created a mesh, we added three additional textures and doubled the resolution size. This gets closer to the max we can use in a single material for current mobile devices.

 Epic Games has done a video talking about a number of other ways to complete the process of baking materials into textures: `https://www.youtube.com/watch?v=WaM_owaUpbE`.

Combining multiple meshes with the HLOD tool

You may have noticed when playing AAA games that, as you get closer to an area of a map, a higher-detail version of what you've seen will come into play, or trees will suddenly start appearing. This is typically done in order to ensure that when a player is closer to an area it has the highest quality possible, but the further away it is, the less detail it needs to have. The **Hierarchical Level of Detail** (**HLOD**) tool allows you to take static objects within your levels and reduce your draw calls by having additional combined meshes to use in place of all of the individual ones.

Getting ready...

You should have a level that contains a number of static meshes within it. If you don't have one already, you can also open the 08_05_HLOD_Start map within the example code of this book:

How to do it...

Before we can use the HLOD tool, we must enable it:

1. Go the **World Settings** menu by going to **Settings** | **World Settings**.
2. From the **World Settings** tab, scroll down to the **LODSystem** section and check the **Enable Hierarchical LODSystem** property.

   You should notice that the **Hierachical LODSetup** property changes to now show **1 Array elements**.

3. Go to **Window** | **Hierarchical LOD Outliner**:

You should notice from the menu that pops up that the left hand side of the screen looks very similar to the **LODSystem** section of the **World Settings** menu. Open up the **Hierachical LODSetup** property and the **HLOD Level 0** and **Cluster generation settings** arrows and then change the Desired Bound Radius to a smaller number, such as **250**.

4. Go back to the **Hierarchical LODSetup** property and click on the + icon to the right of it to add an additional HLOD level. If you open up the newly-added **HLOD Level 1**, you should notice that it automatically will fill the **Desired Bound Radius** with a larger value than the previously-created HLOD:

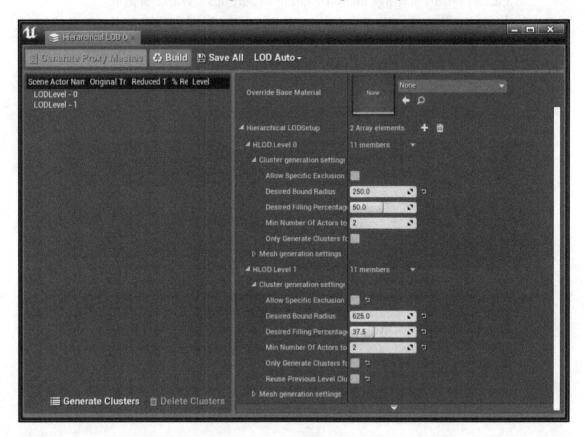

5. Click on the **Generate Clusters** button on the bottom-left of the screen. Unreal will automatically group your meshes into clusters:

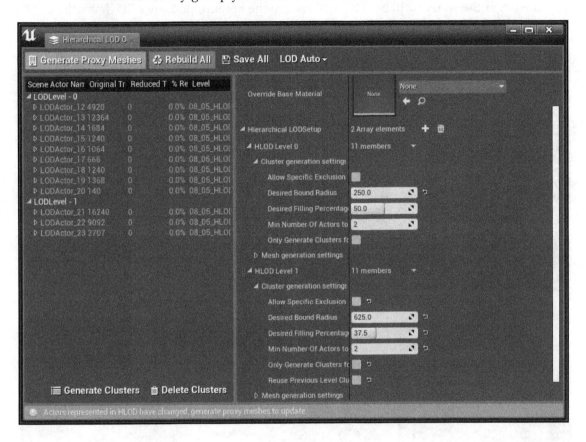

If you select any of the LODActors, you will see a sphere placed around what objects are being used. The higher the LODLevel, the more the actors are away combined and the larger the sphere will be. This will reduce the amount of draw calls that will be used the farther the user is:

6. Click on the **Generate Proxy Meshes** property to build the LODActors. This will typically take a while so you may want to take a break while your computer is working. When finished, you'll have something similar to the following:

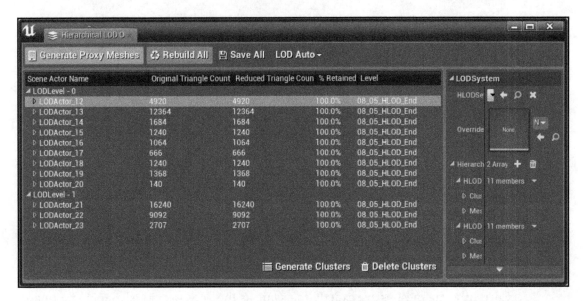

7. Click on the **Save All** option to save the generated proxy meshes. From the window that pops up, click on the **Save Selected** option:

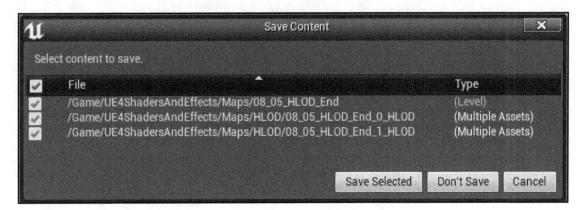

8. If you go to the HLOD folder that was just created, you should notice a number of new static meshes that have been created out of the pieces of the meshes that were created previously:

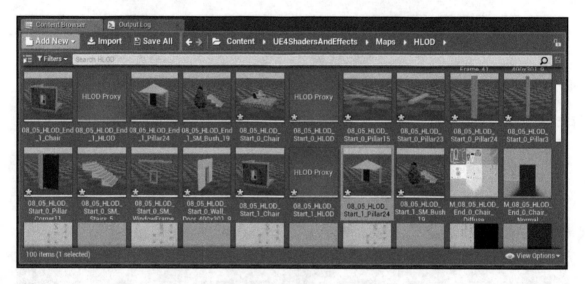

Currently, the meshes are exactly the same as the ones previously created, but are use a single texture for each of those objects, reducing the number of draw calls needed the farther we are from objects within the scene!

9. From the **Hierachical LOD Outliner** menu, select the **LODLevel -1** option and from the right side of the screen. Open the **HLOD Level 1** option and open up the **Mesh generation settings**. From there, note that there is a **Material Settings** property that can be expanded and used just like in the previous recipe. Alternatively, you can check the **Simplify Mesh** setting and then the **Proxy Settings** property will show up, which has its own **Material Settings** property. After making the changes you'd like to see, click on the **Generate Proxy Meshes** option and wait for it to complete:

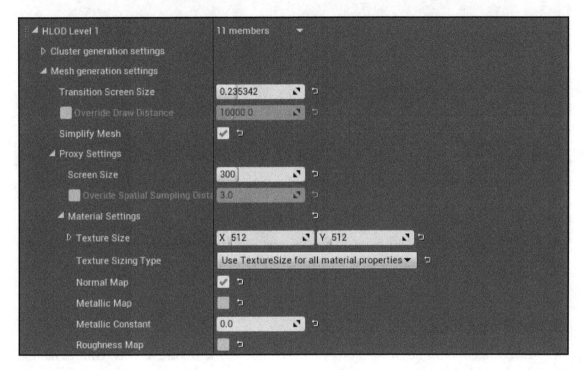

Now if you play the game you should notice that the meshes will fade between meshes based on the distance to the objects:

And, with that, we now have an understanding of how to work with the HLOD tool!

How it works...

The HLOD system must be enabled on every level that wishes to use it. This requires us to go to the **World Settings** menu to enable it. Once enabled, we have the ability to go the HLOD Outliner to set up how HLODs are generated.

 You can learn more about the HLOD tool here: `https://docs.` `unrealengine.com/en-US/Engine/HLOD/HowTo`.

The **Desired Bound Radius** notes how far to look for actors to combine together. The larger the radius, the more objects that can be combined. In levels that have sparse static meshes, such as deserts, the radius may need to be larger, but for complex and detailed areas, it may need to be smaller. The more levels that you have, the more possibilities of blending there are.

By default, all of the meshes will be exactly the same, but the objects will share a single material which contains the same properties and works exactly as our last recipe. However, if you have large levels, it makes sense to simplify meshes that are further away to improve performance, but you'll often need to spend time tweaking the properties to get something that feels right for your level.

It's important to note that HLOD objects can only be used with static meshes, so moving objects will not be able to use this tool. We are required to generate proxy meshes every time we make changes to our properties because the system works in a very similar way to how baking lighting works. We're doing work ahead of time in order to improve performance at runtime.

 The Unreal Engine team did a live training session that shows off the HLOD tool and some ways you can use it. Check it out at `https://www.youtube.com/watch?v=WhcxGbKWdbI`.

General material-optimization techniques

One of the ways that we can develop materials that can work on both low- and high-end devices is through the material quality-level system. This recipe discusses the creation of materials with quality settings in mind, allowing us to create one material that can be used on a variety of devices.

Getting ready...

In order to complete this recipe, you will need to have a material that you would like to look different depending on what quality level your game is running on.

How to do it...

To start, let's create a material that will display something:

1. Create a Material and name it M_QualitySettings. Double-click on it to enter the Material Editor.

2. From the editor, create a texture sample by holding down the *T* key and then clicking to the left of the **M_QualitySettings** result node.

3. With the **Texture Sample** node selected, go to the **Details** tab and set the **Texture** property to something that also has a normal map. I used the **T_Brick_Cut_Stone_D** texture from the **Sample Content**.

4. Create a **Quality Switch** node. Connect the top pin from the **Texture Sample** to the **Default** pin of the **Quality Switch**. Then connect the pin on the right side of the **Quality Switch** node to the **Base Color** node on the **M_QualitySettings** result:

To make it very clear that our material is being modified, let's use a color when we switch to the low-quality level.

5. Below the **Texture Sample**, create a **4Vector** by holding down the *4* key and then set it to a color of your choice; I used red, which is (1,0,0,0). Connect the pin from the right side of the **4Vector** to the **Low** pin of the **Quality Switch** node:

6. Create another **Texture Sample** and assign the normal map texture to it (in my case: **T_Brick_Cut_Stone_N**). Connect the top pin of the newly created **Texture Sample** to the **Normal** pin of **M_QualitySettings**:

7. Create a new scene. From there, go to the **Modes** tab and drag and drop a cube into your scene. Apply the material to the newly-created cube to see what the default material looks like at the default **High** quality level:

To see the material in action, we will need to actually set the **Material Quality Level** of our scene.

8. From the Unreal Editor, go to **Settings** | **Material Quality Level** | **Low**:

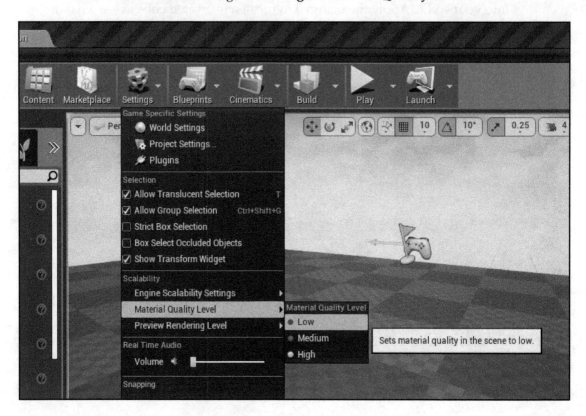

At this point, you'll have to wait for Unreal to compile all of the shaders for this quality level. Once finished, notice that the material is now using the **Low** channel from the **Quality Switch** node:

You can also adjust the quality level of the game during play through the console by pressing the ` key and then typing `r.MaterialQualityLevel 0` with 0 for Low, 1 for High, and 2 for Medium quality levels. For more info on this and other ways this can be set, check out `https://docs.unrealengine.com/en-us/Platforms/Mobile/Performance#settingmaterialqualitylevel`.

How it works...

The **Material Quality Level** property allows us to use less intensive mathematical operations on our shaders when we are targeting devices with less powerful graphics cards.

The **Quality Switch** node works much like a switch statement does in programming: based on the value of the **Material Quality Level**, it will run the relevant code. If nothing is provided to a pin, the default will be used. It is important to note that you are required to use the **Default** channel, as not doing so will cause an error.

You can find additional information about the **Quality Settings** system at https://docs.unrealengine.com/en-us/Platforms/Mobile/ Performance#mobilematerialqualitysettings.

You can add as many **Quality Switch** nodes as you'd like. In fact, you will need to have one for each of the channels that you want to act differently depending on what is being done.

You can also create materials that will do certain things depending on the Feature Level of the device, through the Feature Level Switch, which works almost exactly the same as this node. For more information, check out https://docs.unrealengine.com/en-US/Engine/Rendering/ Materials/ExpressionReference/Utility#featurelevelswitch.

With this in mind, you now have the knowledge to create materials that will support almost any kind of device and get the optimization that you're looking for!

Some more guidelines for performance for both level designers and artists can be found at https://docs.unrealengine.com/en-us/Engine/ Performance/Guidelines.

Some Extra Useful Nodes

9

Unreal has many different and useful nodes, some of which we've already seen, while others are still left to be explored. It would probably be over-ambitious to try and cover them all, given the huge amount of nodes and functionalities at our fingertips. However accurate that might be, it's also true that the more nodes and examples we see, the better prepared we'll be when we are tasked with creating a new material. That being the case, we'll take a final look at some of the useful nodes that we haven't had the chance to explore so far that can be immensely helpful under certain circumstances.

In this chapter, we will cover the following recipes:

- Adding randomness to identical models
- Adding dirt to occluded areas
- Matching texture coordinates across multiple meshes
- Adjusting material complexity through quality switches
- Using interior cubemaps to texture the interior of a building
- Using fully procedural noise patterns

Introduction

All of the nodes that we are about to cover can be described as very useful, but they are the types of asset that don't receive enough praise as they require a certain intent from the user. Think, for example, about one of the topics that we'll talk about in this chapter—adjusting the quality of the textures we use based on the camera focus. Examples such as this one are very specific, and they wouldn't make the cut for any introductory course for that same reason. However, they can become essential once our projects grow, and they can make the difference between a novice approach toward materials and a more professional one. They can help us at different levels, from achieving specific effects to making our projects more efficient. Whatever the case, it'll be great to have them as our allies as they can help us tackle problems from a different perspective:

Adding randomness to identical models

The first recipe we'll tackle in this last chapter is going to deal with a specific type of model instances. You might have heard about this type of asset before, as they are a common feature in many different 3D content creation packages. We use that name to refer to identical copies of an asset that get scattered throughout our scenes, where each duplicate is easier to render than if we were dealing with different models altogether. This can be a very cool technique to use when we deal with vegetation or whenever we want to place multiple similar meshes.

However, more often than not, we also want to change how each instance looks or at least add a little bit of variety to each of them—a task that isn't always easy. In this chapter, we'll explore a simple little node that will let us do just that, and assign a random value to each instance so that we can alter their look within our materials. Let's see how that's done:

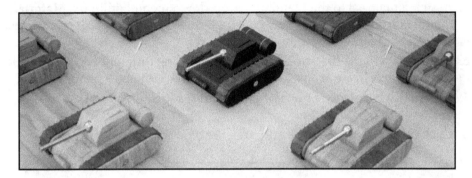

Getting ready

As we always say, you can either follow along using your own assets or by opening the scene that we'll be providing. The requirements this time will be simple in case you want to use your own creations—a simple model is all we'll need. We won't need much else apart from that, even though we'll be operating in some of the materials we've used in the past. In any case, the stars of the show will be a couple of new nodes that you can have access to through the material editor, so no special requirements are required there, either!

If you want to use the same scene you'll be looking at in the next few pages, open the level called `09_ 01_ AddingRandomness_ Start` located within the `Content Browser/ UE4ShadersAndEffects/Maps/Chapter09` folder.

How to do it...

Seeing as we want to add visual variety to multiple instances of the same model, the first step in this recipe will be the creation of those assets. Let's see how we can do that:

1. Create a blueprint somewhere within your **Content Browser**. Pick **Actor** as the parent class, and double-click on it to open the Blueprint Editor.
2. Click on the **Add Component** button in the top-left corner of the editor and select an **Instanced Static Mesh** component.

3. Drag and drop the new **Instance Static Mesh** component on top of the **Default Scene Root** and look at its **Details** panel.

4. With our new component selected, set the **Static Mesh** to whatever you want to use for this recipe. I've gone with **SM_Tank** in this case.

5. Assign a material to the **Element 0** drop-down menu within the **Materials** tab of the **Instanced Static Mesh** component. It doesn't matter which one you choose, as we'll be creating a new one later on.

6. Head down to the **Instances** tab and start adding different entries by clicking the + button. Create as many as you want, which will be **9** in our case.

7. Expand each instance's transform panel and adjust their location, as they would be overlapping otherwise.

8. Click on **Save** and **Compile** and drag the blueprint into our level:

All of the previous steps should have left us with a Blueprint that we can use to test the effect we are about to create. Make sure to drag and drop the new asset into the editor to see it in action! Now that we've taken care of that, it's time to start learning a little bit more about the nodes that will allow us to add variety to the models that we've just spawned.

9. Duplicate the original material we had applied to the toy tank in a previous recipe, called M_ ToyTank_ Textured. We created that material back in Chapter 3, *Opaque Materials and Texture Mapping*, so you can look for it in that chapter's Assets folder. Rename it something distinctive, such as M_ ToyTank_ Instances.

It doesn't matter if you duplicate the previous material or if you create a new one—what we'll be doing inside the material will be very similar. Using an existing material will save us time when we're setting up certain parameters, but you can ignore those and just focus on the new nodes we'll be creating later on.

We'll be focusing on a specific part of the material—the part that deals with the color of the main body of the tank. No matter what you choose—either using the same material or creating a new one—the steps we'll introduce here should be pretty straightforward to follow.

10. Create a **Per Instance Random** node and place it somewhere within the material graph.
11. Add a **Multiply** node and connect the previous **Per Instance Random** to its **A** input pin.
12. As for the **B** input pin, connect the output of the wood texture that drives the main color of the body of the toy tank to it. That's the one that's currently connected to the **B** input pin of the **Lerp** node.
13. Reconnect the output of the **Multiply** node to the **B** input pin of the **Lerp** node that was being previously driven by the wood texture. Refer to the following screenshot:

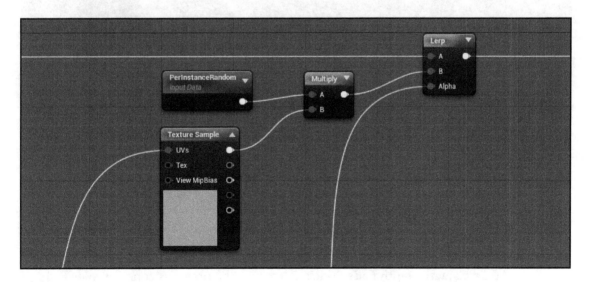

The **Per Instance Random** node can be directly connected to the **Base Color** input pin of our material, instead of being used like it was previously. Feel free to do that if you are using a new material instead of the duplicate we've already shown here. In essence, the new node will assign a random grayscale color to each item of the instance static mesh array. This isn't really a color as much as a floating-point value, which we can use for other purposes, for example, to modify the UV coordinates of the textures that we apply within the material. Let's see how we would go about that.

14. Head over to the **Texture Coordinate** node that is driving the T_ Wood_ Pine_ D texture and create another **Per Instance Random** node there.

15. Add a **Multiply** node after it, and connect both by plugging the output of the **Per Instance Random** node to the **A** input pin of the new node we've just created.

16. Unhook the **Texture Coordinate** wire from the **UVs (V2)** input pin node of the **CustomRotator** node and hook it to the **B** input pin of the previous **Multiply** node.

17. Reconnect the **UVs (V2)** input pin of the **CustomRotator** to the output of our new **Multiply** node. Take a look at the following screenshot:

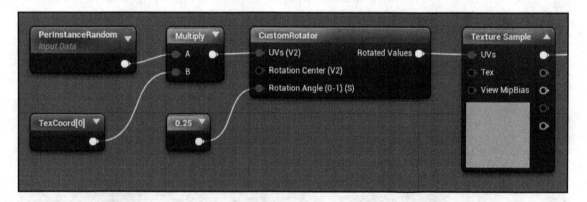

Another look that we can introduce that's handy whenever we work with instances is the **Camera Depth Fade** one. This will allow us to hide objects based on how far we are from them, which is sometimes useful if you have hundreds or thousands of the same object in the distance that you no longer want to see.

18. Create a constant and give it a value of **100**.

19. Add a **Camera Depth Fade** node and connect the previous constant to its **Fade Length (S)** node.

20. Connect the **Result** output pin of the **Camera Depth Fade** node to the **Opacity Mask** of our material:

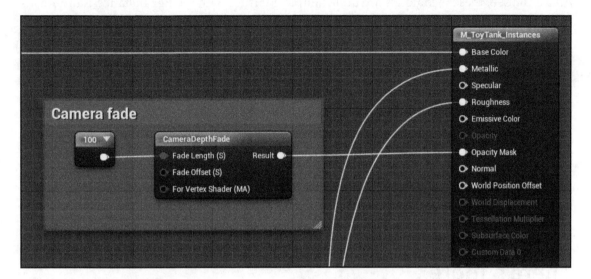

Now that we've implemented all of those changes, the last thing that we need to take care of is actually applying our new material to the instanced static meshes. Head back to the blueprint we created previously and assign it by selecting the instanced static mesh component and choosing our new material in the drop-down panel from *step 5*:

As you can see, this technique can be very useful whenever we want to differentiate between the different instances across our levels. It combines the performance boost that we get by using this component with the variability of the material node. Make sure to keep this in mind whenever you work with these types of assets!

How it works...

As we can see, these techniques are quite simple. Starting with the **Per Instance Random** node, this little helper assigns and exposes a random value to our Instanced Static Meshes, which we can use to drive different types of interesting functionality. The other node, that is, `Camera Depth Fade`, allows us to hide certain meshes, depending on the distance they are from us.

Apart from the last node we talked about, which is useful for hiding things that are close to the camera (such as when objects get in the way and might block our visibility), there are other nodes that you might find useful that work in a similar way. For instance, another cool node we could use is called **Per Instance Fade Amount**, which is very similar to the **Per Instance Random** node we previously used. Instead of assigning a random float value per instance, this time, the number we are given relies on the position of the instance itself in regards to the camera. We can use this to hide the models that are further from us, instead of the ones that are closer, like we did in this recipe. Be sure to check that out!

There's more...

Even though we've used nodes that only work when applied to instances of a mesh, it's good to note that the `Instanced Static Mesh` component isn't the only one that can take advantage of that. There's another component that can also benefit from the techniques we've shown in the previous pages, and that is the **hierarchical instanced static mesh (HISM)** component. It's good to learn about both of them as they can be used to increase performance in our games. They are especially helpful when we need to scatter multiple instances of the same mesh, such as railings or trees, as the computer only stores information about one and repeats it across the world multiple times.

They are both very similar, but the HISM allows us to pair the gain in performance given by the instancing feature with the creation of different levels of detail that we can get on normal static meshes. Be sure to check this very similar component out, as well as the next section, which contains some useful links to that feature.

See also

Links to the Epic documentation and a video tutorial on how to implement HISM components have been provided here:

- https://docs.unrealengine.com/en-US/Engine/Rendering/Materials/ExpressionReference/Constant
- https://www.youtube.com/watch?v=bOjYP-c4qhA

Adding dirt to occluded areas

I'm sure you know by now how powerful baked lighting can be in Unreal Engine 4. It makes our scenes look ultra-realistic if done well, as the computed shadow maps don't have any equivalent in terms of quality if we use dynamic lighting. However useful they are, calculating lighting for our scenes isn't only helpful for this process of baking shadows—we can reuse this information in other ways within our materials. We have one useful node at our disposal that lets us tap into that data to drive the appearance of our materials. One common use for that is to apply dirt to areas that are occluded, which we'll look at here! Take a look at the following screenshot:

Getting ready

The scene that you can open if you want to follow along using the same assets is called 09_ 02_ PrecomputedAoMask_ Start and can be found in the Content Browser / UE4ShadersAndEffects / Maps / Chapter09 folder.

As always, you can use your own assets and levels, but there are some things you should take into consideration when doing so. First, the level that you want to operate on needs to have computed baked lighting. This is crucial to this recipe, as the material node we'll use needs to tap into that information and won't work otherwise.

As a consequence, your lighting needs to be set to stationary or static, and the models you work with need to have properly laid out UVs. Keep that in mind before continuing with the following pages! You won't have to worry about these things if you decide to open the level we are providing though, as it already complies with the previous considerations and the lighting has already been calculated.

How to do it...

The very first step we'll need to take in this chapter is building the lighting in our level. As we stated previously, this is a crucial step in our journey before we attempt to create the material we'll be applying, as the new node we'll use this time relies on the existence of shadowmaps. You won't have to worry about this circumstance if you open the level we referred to in the previous section, but take that into account if you use one of your own.

With that out of the way, let's start creating our new material:

1. Create a new material and give it an appropriate name, something indicative of what we'll be creating—I've gone with M_ DirtyWalls as that's going to be the use of our material. Double-click on the new asset to open up the Material Graph.

2. Right-click anywhere within the Material Graph and search for a node called **PrecomputedAOMask**. Then, add it to the graph.

3. Include a **Power** node after the previous **PrecomputedAOMask** node and wire the **Base** input pin of the new node to the output of the previous one. Leave the **Exp** as **1**. Refer to the following screenshot:

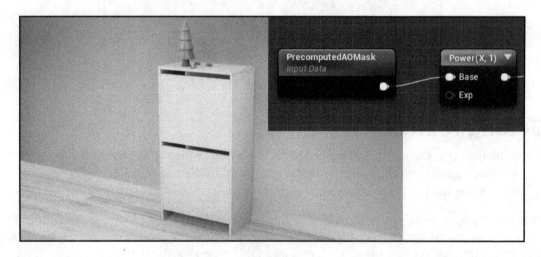

The **PrecomputedAOMask** node is going to be the star of this recipe, and is the node that will allow us to tap into the baked lighting information that we can use as we desire. A common practice when working with this node is to use it blend a dirtier version of a base texture in order to show the wear and tear that usually happens on occluded areas of our scene. We'll take that same approach in the following steps to show some dirt on those parts of the model where we'll apply this material.

4. Create a couple of constant 3 nodes and assign them two different values. Seeing as we are going to apply this material to the walls in our scene, we can go for the already familiar white and a brown, which we'll use to drive the appearance of the dirty areas.

5. Interpolate between the previous two nodes by creating a **Lerp** node after the previous two constants. Connect the white value to the **A** input pin and the brown color to the **B** input pin.

6. Connect the **Alpha** input pin of the previous **Lerp** to the output of the **Power** node we created in *step 3*.

It might be difficult to know which input pin we need to connect our constants to in the **Lerp** node. As a rule of thumb, think of **A** and **B** as *black and white*—**A** will affect the black areas of the texture and **B** will affect the lighter ones.

Seeing as the **PrecomputedAOMask** node assigns lighter values to the areas that are occluded—perhaps a bit counter-intuitively—the **A** input pin needs to be fed with the values that we want to have on the non-occluded areas, leaving the **B** input pin for the occluded ones. Setting the material to work in this way will leave us with a white and brown surface, which isn't what we expect to see on areas that are covered in dirt. We can fine-tune our results by introducing a second mask at this stage.

7. Add a **Texture Sample** and select the texture called T_ Water_ M as its value. This is part of the Starter Content, in case you also want to use it on your own projects.

8. Include a **Texture Coordinate** node and hook it to the previous **Texture Sample**. Set a value of 10 in both the **U** and the **V** tiling settings.

9. Create a new **Lerp** node and add it after the previous one we had in our graph.

10. Connect the output of the previous **Texture Sample** to the **Alpha** input pin of the new **Lerp**.

11. Hook the **B** input pin to the output of the previous **Lerp**.

12. Wire the **A** input pin to the output of the white constant.

13. Connect the result of the latest **Lerp** into the **Base Color** input pin on the main material node:

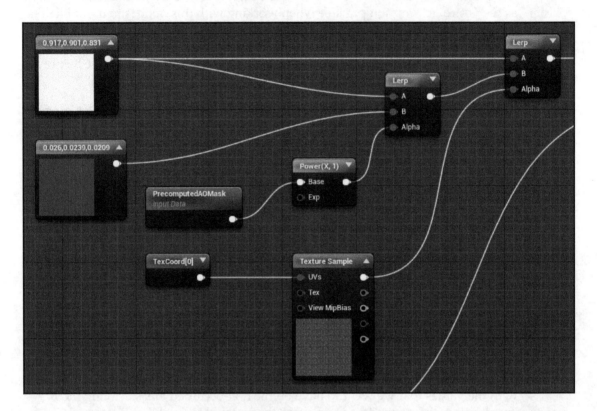

The previous steps have introduced another mask within our already existing mask that we were getting out of the **PrecomputedAOMask** node. This is a very common technique to use as it gives us greater flexibility in regards to how we want to place our textures without the need to create custom ones and add extra texture calls. The last steps we need to implement are the creation of the **Roughness** and the **Normal** properties. You can copy these over from the material that was originally applied to the model, M_ ColoredWalls, which we created back in Chapter 2, *Post-Processing Effects*. You can take a look at the two images that follow in case you want to copy the nodes.

14. Create a **Texture Coordinate**, a **Texture Sample**, a **Constant**, and a **Power** node to drive the **Roughness** of our material. The **Texture Coordinate** should have a value of 10 on both the **U** and the **V** tiling; we are using the T_ MacroVariation texture here, and the value of the Constant is 0.15.

15. Add another **Texture Coordinate** and a **Texture Sample** to effect the normals in our material. The **Texture Coordinate** should be given a value of 7, both on the **U** and the **V** tiling, and the **Texture Sample** should be set to `T_ Wallpaper_ Normals`.

Of course, feel free to assign other values and textures for the roughness and the normal properties if you are using your own material. The last step we need to take is actually applying the material to the model of our walls, so do that now and check out the result!

As you can see, our walls now look like they've seen some action in the past, with multiple marks of dirt along the surface; these are concentrated on the areas that are occluded! This is one of the most commonly used scenarios for this particular scene—one that can save you time from manually placing certain textures and that can be mixed with procedural creation techniques.

How it works...

The way the **PrecomputedAOMask** node works is very simple—it takes the lightmaps that have been calculated for our models and uses them as a value that we can tap into inside the material editor. Even though this is a very simple technique to grasp, we usually want to apply some kind of modification to the base texture we receive. This is because the texture that we are presented with usually turns out to be a very smooth gradient, something that might not be ideal when we want to apply it as a mask. More often than not, we'll want to apply some kind of transformation, such as the **Power** node we used in this recipe or a Cheap Contrast one. Both have the ability to alter the base texture, either by augmenting the contrast or by increasing the values of each pixel. This process leaves us with a more defined image, where the areas that are occluded and the ones that aren't can be easily differentiated—something that's usually good for our purposes.

There's more...

Even though we've managed to apply the material to the walls in the scene successfully, keep in mind that you'll need to build the lighting every time that you want to use this effect. As the node itself says, we are dealing with a precomputed effect here, so we won't be able to take advantage of it under certain conditions, such as when we have a movable type of light. Whenever we have a situation like that, we could resort to using other techniques, such as creating an ambient occlusion texture in external software or by using other similar nodes, such as the **Distance To Nearest Surface** one. While not identical, using mesh distance fields can prove useful, such as the masking material we looked at in `Chapter 6`, *Advanced Material Techniques*. Be sure to check that one out if you'd like to know more!

See also

Something that might be of further interest is how to control the whole light-baking process within Unreal. Here is the official documentation regarding that: `https://docs.unrealengine.com/en-US/Engine/Rendering/LightingAndShadows/Lightmass`.

Matching texture coordinates across multiple meshes

The way we apply materials and textures varies a lot, and is something that depends on multiple factors. Are we working on small props? Are we texturing large surfaces? Do we need to accurately depict real-life objects, or can we include procedural creation techniques in our workflow? Those are some of the questions that we need to ask ourselves before we begin working on an asset. So far, we've had the opportunity to work on both small and large props throughout this book, but we haven't yet had the need to apply the same material to two or more different models. This situation presents its own set of challenges, and it's one of those that we will be tackling next—how do we make sure that the material looks the same on all of the objects that we apply it to? Make sure to continue reading to find out how!

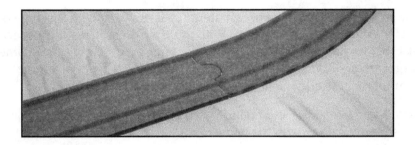

Getting ready

Something that we'll need in this chapter are at least two different meshes, with their own set of UVs that look substantially different. We set ourselves the objective to make two different models look as if they were textured together, so in order to prove that point, we'll be better off starting with very different assets. Keep that in mind if you plan on using your own resources.

If you want to follow along in the same environment we will be describing in this recipe, just open the level called `09_ 03_ TextureCoordinates_ Start` that's found inside the `Content Browser / UE4ShadersAndEffects / Maps / Chapter09` folder. You will find a couple of *toy rail tracks*, each with a different model, which we'll use to texture in a similar way.

How to do it...

The key to tackling this recipe is to have two or more different models that, when applying the same material on them, look different. You can see this behavior in the following screenshot:

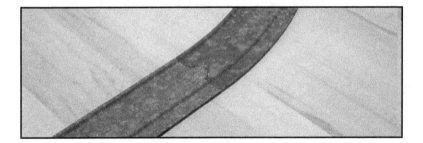

In the following pages, we'll create a new material that can cope with this type of situation, something that we'll probably have to deal with multiple times. Creating a specific material for every asset that we have is often neither efficient nor practical, so this is something that we should target when dealing with specific types of objects—especially large ones. The first step in our journey, as often, will be the creation of the material:

1. Create a new material and assign it to the two tank circuit tracks that we have in our scene. I've gone with the name `M_ Wood_ Track_ Start` this time.

2. Jump straight into the material editor and create the star of this recipe: the **World Position** node.

   It's important to know that the node itself is called **World Position**. That's what you should type in the search bar when you look for it, even though you'll see another name once you create it—**Absolute World Position**. That prefix depends on the actual properties defined on its **Details** panel, which can be changed.

3. Next up, create three component masks and set them to the following values: the red and green channel on the first one, green and blue for the second one, and red and blue for the third one.

4. Connect all of the previous masks input pins to the output of the **World Position** node.

5. Add a couple of **Lerp** nodes to the graph to interpolate between the previous three masks.

6. Connect the output of the red and green mask to the **A** input pin of the first **Lerp** node, and the output of the green and blue mask to the **B** input pin of the same **Lerp**.

7. After doing this, connect the output of that **Lerp** to the **A** input pin of the second one, and connect the output of the red and blue mask to the **B** input pin:

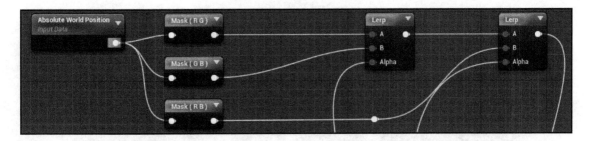

The previous set of nodes will allow us to use the World Position node on different surfaces of the models on which we apply this material. At its core, the World Position node acts as a planar projection method, and we need to specify different projection planes for the effect to work on all possible surfaces, not just on one. You can read more about this in the next section, *How it works...*. The next bit of logic we need to implement is the actual detection of which direction each pixel is facing so that we can apply the desired projection method correctly.

8. Create a **PixelNormalWS** node.
9. Include a couple of component masks next to the previous node, and select the red channel on one of them and the green channel on the other.
10. Connect the output of the **PixelNormalWS** node to the input pins of both of the previous masks.
11. Create a couple of **Abs** nodes and place each immediately after each of the previous component masks, connecting them appropriately.
12. Look for an **If** node and add it to the graph.
13. Add three constants and give them the values 0, 5, 0, and 1. The first one (0,5) should be connected to the **A** input pin of the **If** node, the second one (0) to the **A > B** input pin, and the third one (1) to both the **A == B** and **A < B** input pins.
14. Place the **If** node and the three constants next to the **Abs** node that's being driven by the red channel mask, and connect the output of the **Abs** to the **B** input pin of the **If** node.

15. Create a copy of the previous **If** node and the three constants, and place it after **Abs** node being driven by the green mask, just like we did in the previous step. Remember to connect the **Abs** to the **B** input pin of the **If** node:

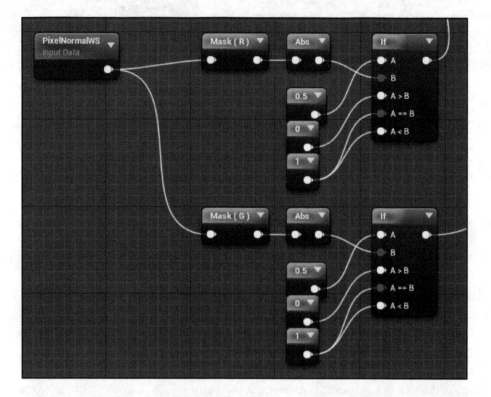

The previous sequence of the graph creates a conditional statement that will assign a specific value, depending on the direction the pixels on our models are facing, which is useful to drive the **Alpha** input pins of the previous **Lerp** nodes.

16. Connect the output of the **If** node being driven by the red mask to the first of the two **Lerp** nodes we created back in *step 5*, that is, the one being driven by the red/green and green/blue masks.

17. Connect the output of the other **If** node to the **Alpha** input pin of the remaining **Lerp**.

Now that we've set up that logic, we finally have a material that can detect the direction that each pixel is facing and assign a value according to it. We need to do a couple of extra things within our graph, that is, assign a texture and adjust its tiling. Let's do that now.

18. Include a **Divide** node and place it after the last **Lerp**, connecting its **A** input pin to the output of the interpolation node.

19. Create a **Scalar Parameter** and give it a name and a value. We've chosen `UVing` as the name, as that what it's controlling, and `5` as a default value.

20. Add a **Texture Sample** node and select any texture that you'd like to see on the tank tracks. Connect the output of that to the **Base Color** input pin on our main material node. I've chosen one sample from the Starter Content for this node, called `T_ Concrete_ Grime_ D`, and I've made it a bit darker by multiplying it times a constant set to `0,5`.

21. Finally, feel free to add anything to modify your material, such as some parameters to control the **Roughness** or any other properties. The material we are working with will include a Constant to drive the **Roughness**, set to a value of `0,7`:

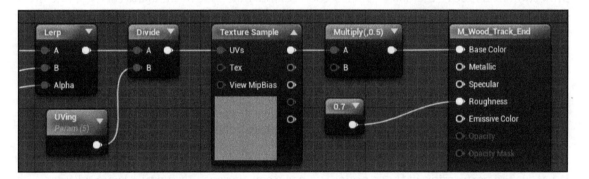

As you can see, this method is a very useful one whenever you want to match the material that's applied on surrounding surfaces. We can apply this to many different models from roads to pavements, to these toy tracks we've just created, and many others. It's also a good technique to employ when dealing with models that don't have nicely laid out UVs, saving you the time of adjusting those in an external software, or even creating them altogether!

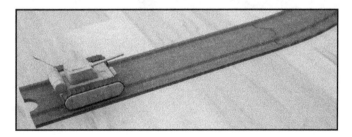

How it works...

The way the material we've just created works is a little bit hidden behind the network of nodes we've just created, so let's take a little bit of time to explain how everything works in tandem. To tackle that, we need to know that there's two basic parts to this material—the section where we specify how the projection works and the part where we determine the direction in which the pixels of our models are facing.

The first of those two is handled by the **World Position** node, which basically gives us the location of each pixel in a global coordinate system. Using that information instead of the UVs of the object is what allows us to planar project any texture that we later add, but we need to mask the node in order to get the specific plane in which we want that projection to happen. Selecting two channels means that we project along the third one—for instance, when we chose the red (x) and green (y) channels, that basically meant performing a planar projection from above the object (z). It's good to note that we can translate each channel into one of the coordinate's axes—red being the X, green being the Y, and blue being the Z. This is also indicated by the color-coded gizmo that Unreal uses when displaying this information.

The second part of our material dealt with the identification of the direction in which our pixels are facing. We checked whether they were facing in the X or the Y direction, as we need different projection planes for those cases. The pixels that are aligned mostly along the Z axis are also using a separate projection, but we don't check those as that's the base assumption. For the other two, X and Y (or red and green, using the material's terminology), we need to perform a detection that can be seen on the **If** nodes we place. What we are performing in those nodes is a basic comparison—if the pixels are within a certain threshold, we assume that they are facing in a specific direction and mask them. This is the skeleton of this part of the node.

As for the final steps, they are all quite straightforward. We use the information we've gathered so far to drive the appearance of a texture, which in turns defines the look of the material. A little bit of spicing in the shape of a **Roughness** property, et voilà—material created!

There's more...

Even though we've used our material in a three-dimensional object, planar projections are more often than not used on planar surfaces. We've mentioned roads and pavements already in this recipe, and those are two examples that see this technique being used a lot. The calculations and the complexity of the resulting material in those cases are usually much simpler than what we've seen, as we only need to take one plane into account. Take a look at the following screenshot to see the resulting graph:

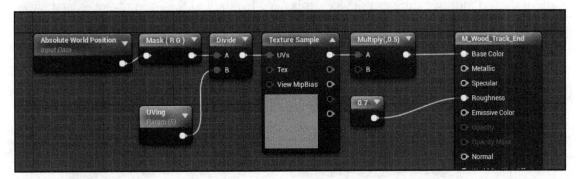

As you can see, things are much simpler and lighter, so make sure to use this option when you don't need to take all the axes into consideration!

See also

Here's a little thread on the Unreal Engine 4 forums about this node and how to use it: https://forums.unrealengine.com/development-discussion/rendering/78756-absolute-world-position-material-how-to-set-it-up.

Adjusting material complexity through quality switches

You are probably familiar with different quality settings if you've played computer games before. This doesn't happen very much on consoles, which are closed environments, but PC users often have to select between different quality presets to cater for their computer's specs. With the advent of cross-platform development, where the same project sees the light of day on multiple different devices, this need to adapt to the strengths of each device, has become more and more widespread. Not only that, but more often than not, those same devices can't support the same level of rendering features, so we need to take care of that too. You'll see how you can do this in the following pages!

Getting ready

The scene we'll be using in this recipe is quite similar to another we used back in Chapter 6, *Advanced Material Techniques*, when we dealt with tessellation. This is a good technique to bring back to this recipe, as that rendering feature isn't supported on every platform available to us as Unreal Engine 4 developers. You might want to take that into consideration if you plan on using assets of your own. It doesn't matter what you create, though—the nodes we are about to introduce are quite simple to understand, and you'll be able to try them out on any assets that you can get hold of, so don't feel limited to using tessellation as well.

In any event, if you want to use the same assets you'll be looking at in the next few pages, feel free to open the level called 09_04_QualitySwitch_Start located in the Content Browser / UE4ShadersAndEffects / Maps / Chapter09 folder.

How to do it...

Let's start this recipe by creating the material that we'll use throughout, and also setting up some settings in it:

1. Create a new material and give it a name. We've gone with M_ Walls_ QualitySwitch this time. Double-click on it to open up the material graph.

   Just like we did in a previous recipe, we'll want to use tessellation in this material, so select the main material node and look at the **Details** panel to change certain parameters.

2. Head over the the **Tessellation** panel and choose **PN Triangles** instead of the default **No Tessellation** option under the **D3D11 Tessellation Mode** setting.

3. Turn **Adaptive Tessellation** on and set the **Max Displacement** to 100.

   Doing that will allow us to use the tessellation technique we've seen before, which will be a good feature to turn on and off, depending on whether the hardware we run our apps and games on supports it. Let's create the actual node graph.

4. Begin with the creation of a **Texture Coordinate** node, and set both the **U** and the **V** tiling parameters to 7.

5. Create four **Texture Samples**, and set the first one of them to use the asset called T_ Walls_ Depth. Connect all of the **UVs** input pins on **Texture Samples** to the previous **Texture Coordinate** node.

6. Multiply the first texture times a color (Constant3 node), as we'll use that to modify the tint that our material will show. I've selected a purple shade, but feel free to choose whatever you fancy!

7. Connect the output of the previous **Multiply** node to the **Base Color** input pin of our material.

   The previous set of nodes will affect the color that our material displays, but so far nothing is new in our workflow. We'll change that soon.

8. Set the second **Texture Sample** to use the T_ Walls_ AORM image.

9. Create a **Quality Switch** node by right-clicking a little bit to the right of the previous node and searching for that name.

10. Add a Constant and set it to something like 0, 7. Connect it to the **Low** input pin of the previous **Quality Switch** node.

11. Connect the green channel output pin of the **Texture Sample** containing the T_ Walls_ AORM texture to both the **Default**, **Medium**, and **High** input pins of the new **Quality Switch**.

12. Wire the output of the **Quality Switch** to the **Roughness** material input pin:

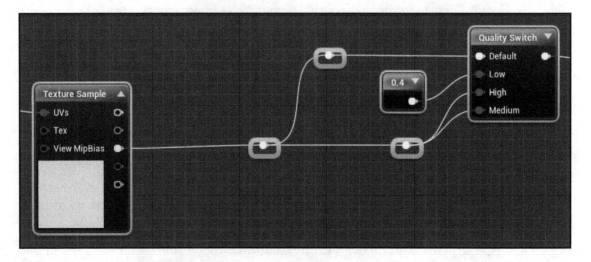

And there you have it—the first new node of this recipe! We are talking about the **Quality Switch** node, which we haven't seen yet. This is the one that allows us to toggle between different quality presets within our materials, something that we often see in computer games. Having the choice to choose from between a texture and a constant allows the user to choose between saving up on texture memory or increasing the realism of the reflections. We'll see how to visualize this setting later on, once we finish setting up the material.

13. Set the third **Texture Sample** to use the T_ Walls_ Normal texture.

14. Create another **Quality Switch** and connect the output of the previous **Texture Sample** to its **Default**, **High**, and **Medium** input pins.

15. Add a Constant 3 vector and assign it a value of 0,0,1. This is a default texture that, if applied, leaves the normals of the objects as they are. Connect it to the **Low** input pin of the previous **Quality Switch**.

16. Connect the **Quality Switch** to the **Normal** input pin in our material:

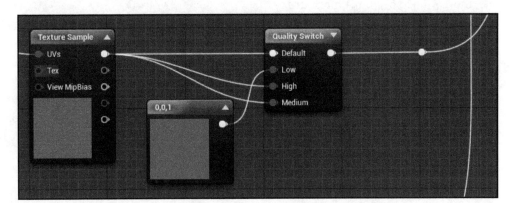

We have another example of the **Quality Switch** node being used in the previous set of steps. We have affected the normals of our material thanks to those nodes, which allows us to use a texture in the higher settings and a constant in the lower ones. With that done, let's continue building our material!

17. Create a couple of **Scalar Parameters** and assign them names similar to `Subdivision Amount_ High` and `Subdivision Amount_ Low`. These will control the tessellation factor of our material. Set the first one to `5` and the second one to `0`.

18. Right-click and look for a node called **Feature Level Switch**. Connect the output of the **Subdivision Amount High** parameter to the pin called **SM5**, and the output of the other one to the other inputs.

19. Connect the output of the **Feature Level Switch** node to the **Tessellation Multiplier** input pin of our main material node.

And there you have it—the second new node of this recipe! We are talking about the **Feature Level Switch** this time, which even though may sound similar to the **Quality Switch** one, it's meant to be used in a different context. Whereas the **Quality Switch** lets us change between different quality presets, the **Feature Level Switch** node deals with the type of features that different hardware supports. For instance, Android phones don't support the same techniques that a Windows computer does, regardless of how powerful they are. You can learn more about this in the *How it works...* section of this recipe, so make sure to head over there once you're finished here! At the moment, let's concentrate on finishing up the material.

20. Add a **VertexNormalWS** node into the graph.

21. Set the fourth **Texture Sample** to use the same asset as the first one, that is, the `T_ Walls_ Depth` texture.

22. Connect that to a **CheapContrast** node, and create a **Scalar Parameter** to drive the **Contrast (S)** input pin of our new node. Give that a value of 1.

23. Multiply the result of the **Cheap Contrast** node by a **Scalar Parameter** with a value of 1. You can name it something like `Height Intensity`.

24. Create a **Multiply** node to carry that operation between the previous Vertex Normal WS node and the result of the **Multiply** node from the previous step.

25. Add another **Feature Level Switch** after all of those nodes and connect the output of the previous **Multiply** to the **SM5** input pin.

26. Include a Constant, give it a value of 0, 5, and hook it to the **Default**, **ES2**, **ES3_1**, and **SM4** input pins of the previous node.

27. Connect the output pin on the **Feature Level Switch** node to the **World Displacement** input pin in our material:

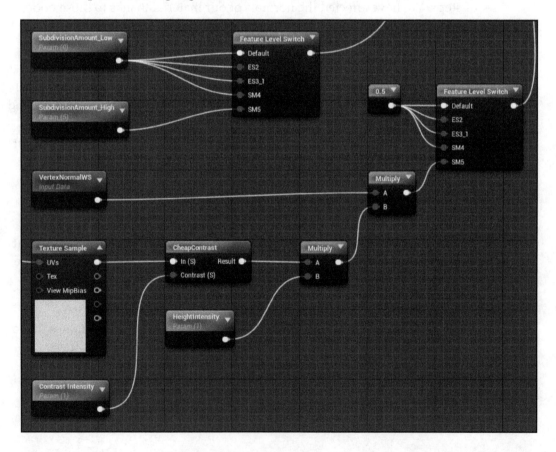

Completing the previous step has seen us finishing the material. The last thing we need to do is apply it to the walls in our scene and visualize what we've done.

28. Select the walls (**SM_Walls_Corner**) and apply the material we've been working on. You should be looking at the material in all of its glory, with tessellation being applied and all of the nice features we've decided to include.

29. Click on the **Settings** button on the main toolbar and expand the **Material Quality Level** section. Select the **Low Preset**. This will allow you to see the features we plugged into the **Low** input pin of the **Quality Switch** node.

30. Click on the **Settings** button again, head over to the **Preview Rendering Level** section, and select the **Shader Model 4**. This will hide the tessellation effect on the material, just as we decided to do when we created the **Feature Level Switch** node:

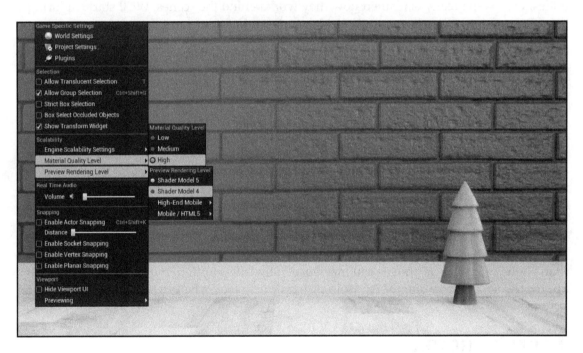

And that's how it works! Of course, we've only customized the material in order to make things easy for us to see and visualize, but you can use this technique according to the needs of your project, which might be different to what you've seen before. It's always a good idea to include some of these switches in your creations, especially in those that are more demanding. Knowing the devices that your project is targeting is another good thing to consider, as you need to know what feature levels those terminals support in order to be able to include some of the more advanced techniques that the engine supports. Welcome to the world of material optimization!

How it works...

Even though we've worked with both the **Quality Switch** and the **Feature Level Switch** nodes, we haven't really explained how they work behind the scenes. We'll start exploring the first type initially, as that is quite straightforward to understand. In essence, a **Quality Switch** is a node that lets us choose which branch of the material graph we want to process. This is something that we might decide to use whenever we want to give the user a choice between graphic fidelity and performance, for example.

Unlike them, the feature level switch is used to fill in a similar but different gap: it is there to let the developer choose which branch of the graph gets executed according to the features that a given machine can support. For example, a smartphone might not support the same graphical techniques that a modern PC does—not just because of the difference in computing power, but also due to their architecture, OS, and other different elements that have a role to play in that equation. This doesn't just happen between smartphones and computers, though, as we also see differences within each of those groups. For example, most modern PC hardware can support the core capabilities of Direct X 11's Shader Model 5, while older models might only go as far as using Direct X 10. The realm of mobile devices is even more diverse, and Unreal offers the ES2 and ES3_1 feature levels to accommodate that. High-end mobile terminals can make use of the latest option, but be sure to check the appropriate documentation for Android or Apple developers before going down that route!

There's more...

If you use these type of nodes in your projects, you probably want to be able to change between the different material quality options at runtime and not just on the editor. That would only be logical! We'll make sure not to leave you wondering how to do that. The answer is simple, and it comes in the shape of a console command.

All you need to do to implement this system is to enable a console command that goes by the name of `r.MaterialQualityLevel`, and then a number from 0 to 2. With that notation, you would input the following lines to change between the different quality levels: `r.MaterialQualityLevel 0` for the low quality preset, `r.MaterialQualityLevel 1` for the high quality preset, and `r.MaterialQualityLevel 2` for the medium present. You might find it weird that the notation goes from low to high and then to medium, but this is just the way that it's currently set up. It's probably a historical thing within Unreal, as initially only low and high were available to us. Medium is a preset that was introduced later on, hence its position in that list.

See also

Quality switches and feature level toggles are here to help you optimize your apps and games, and they go hand in hand with the optimization tools that Unreal provides. I'd like to leave you with some useful links, should you want to check them out:

- Engine performance: `https://docs.unrealengine.com/en-us/Engine/Performance`
- Materials for mobile platforms: `https://docs.unrealengine.com/en-us/Platforms/Mobile/Materials`

Using interior cubemaps to texture the interior of a building

We've come a long way since we started this journey, following a path that took us from very introductory concepts to more advanced ones. We've covered many different techniques along the way, and that's something that will not change, even as we near the final pages of this book. This second to last recipe will showcase yet another new technique that is very useful when working with exterior scenes filled with buildings, where windows are a prevalent element and seeing what's inside is sometimes a difficult thing to tackle.

You can probably think of many different video games where the windows of the buildings are shown as a static texture, with no sense of depth or of what's inside. In the following pages, we'll take a look at a more contemporary technique that brings those elements to life, adding realism to our levels.

Getting ready

Unlike most of our previous recipes, where we could almost jump into them straight away, you'll actually need to have a specific type of asset if you want to follow along using your own resources. We are going to be working with a texture commonly known as a cubemap, which doesn't come bundled in Unreal. You can get one from their official docs, which is the same one we'll be using, or create your own according to Epic's guidelines. You can find more information on this topic in the *There's more...* and *See also* sections of this recipe.

However, know that you can use the resources we'll be providing you with if you so desire. They can be found in the Content Browser / UE4ShadersAndEffects / Assets / Chapter09 folder. If you follow this route, you can also open the 09_ 05_ InteriorCubemap_ Start level, which contains the map we'll be working on as an example.

How to do it...

The first thing we'll do in this recipe is going to be taking a look at the map we have in front of us, which will help us understand what we are trying to achieve—plus which elements you'll need to have if you want to use your own textures and assets. Let's take a look at the scene:

As you can see, we have a basic block, which we'll use as a house of sorts—our goal will be to have some windows in its walls and show what's inside without actually creating any more geometry. If you want to bring your own models, something like a building without an interior would work great. Let's start working on the material that will allow us to achieve this effect:

1. Create a new material and give it a name—something like M_Interior Cubemap could work well!

2. Double-click on it and add your first node to the material graph, a **Texture Sample**. Choose T_ House_ Color as its parameter.

The textures that we are placing in this recipe have been created specifically for the model that we are applying them on, so make sure to bring your own images if you use your other models.

The previous texture has given us the look we are going to be applying to the exterior of our model, which you can check straight away if you compile, save, and apply the material to our model. The next step we'll need to take will be the creation of the looks of the interior, and the blending between those and the exterior we've already created.

3. Create a **Lerp** node after the previous **Texture Sample** and connect its **A** input pin to the output of the previous node.

4. Add another **Texture Sample** node and set it to use the T_Default Interior Cubemap image.

5. Connect the output of the previous node to the **B** input pin of the **Lerp**.

6. Right-click and look for a specific node named **Interior Cubemap**, and place it before the **Texture Sample** hosting the cubemap. Connect its **UVW** output pin to the **UVs** input pin of the texture.

7. Add a **Constant 2** node and connect it to the **Tiling (V2)** input pin of the **Interior Cubemap** node. Give it values of 2 and 4 on the **R** and **G** channels, respectively.

8. Throw another `Texture Sample` to use as a mask, and assign it the `T_ House_ Mask` texture. Connect its output to the **Alpha** input pin of the **Lerp**.

9. Finally, connect the output of the **Lerp** node to the **Base Color** input pin on our material:

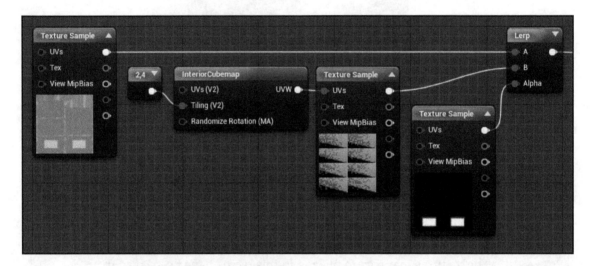

The previous set of nodes are the implementation of the cubemap logic inside the material. Everything is condensed in the **Interior Cubemap** node, which is a handy function that packs a much larger set of nodes inside. You can check how that logic is constructed if you double-click on the node itself, or learn more about how it works in the next section. In any case, we've already established the base logic that we need to implement when we use these type of assets within a material by taking a cubemap, applying it on a specific area that we have masked, and blending between that and the other parts of the material. The next bit we need to tackle is the masking and the creation of the rest of the nodes.

10. Add two more **Texture Samples** into the graph, as we'll need those to drive the normals and the Metalness of our material.

11. Assign the `T_House_ AORM` texture to the first of them, and the `T_ House_ Normal` texture to the second one.

12. Connect the output of the normal map straight into the **Normal** input pin of our material.

13. Create a **Lerp** node and hook the output of the blue channel in the `T_House_ AORM` texture to its **A** input pin.

14. Create a constant and give it a value of 0, and plug it into the **B** input pin of the material.
15. Connect the same texture we used as a mask to the **Alpha** channel of the new **Lerp**.
16. Wire the output of the **Lerp** into the **Metallic** input pin on our material.

All we've done in the previous steps was assign some extra information to our material—in particular, to the Normal and the Metallic channels. The Constant we've used could have been replaced with the actual roughness values for the interior cubemap, via a texture, just like we did in the **Base Color** section of the graph. This is the same setup that we would follow should we decide to add any other information, such as Roughness attributes. The emissive channel is one that gets used quite often in interior cubemaps, as there are often lights within the rooms that we see—especially at night time. The last thing we need to do is assign the material and see how it looks!

How it works...

The inner workings of the interior cubemap node can be seen if we double-click on it, as that opens the actual scripting that powers this function. Even though it's quite a long chain of different nodes, we'll try to go over them briefly as understanding them can give us some good ideas about how to create other, similar effects.

The first thing that we need to know is that this interior cubemap node is a camera-driven effect that affects the UVs of our models. That's why we see a **Camera Vector** node if we open up the function. Something that also affects the node itself are the three values we can give it through its input pins—the **UVs (V2)**, the **Tiling (V2)**, and the **Randomize Rotation (MA)** values. Those are different function inputs that come into play at different stages within the function's own node graph, all of which affect the logic that is written inside. So, what actually happens inside them? In essence, we can boil that answer down to UV calculations being made based on the camera view.

We start by taking the vector defined by the camera view and transforming it from **World Space** to **Tangent Space**. That data needs to be mirrored, as that's the effect we are emulating when viewing a fake 3D environment on a flat surface. All of this information gets affected by how much we want to tile the texture we use and the UVs that we are applying. We'll get a grid-like structure by inputting that information, where each cell of the grid shows the desired effect. This is something important to take into consideration as it's easy for us to apply this function on planar surfaces, but we tend to encounter different types of issues if we move away from those. One typical example would be the effect that we can see on adjacent faces of a cube, where the illusion we are trying to create breaks if there's an obvious discontinuity in the effect. In those circumstances, it's always a good approach to create different interior cubemaps to account for the rooms of a building that are at the corners instead of trying to use the same one. Be sure to test this technique on your specific models to see how to best tackle these possible issues!

There's more...

As we saw previously, this technique can prove very useful when dealing with building interiors. That being the case, the cubemap we'll probably want to use will be our own instead of the default one that we've used in this recipe. So, how would you go about creating one?

The key is to create a texture that fits within Unreal's expected formatting for cubemaps, which you can learn more about through the links found in the *See also* section of this recipe. The basics that we need to know is that the texture needs to adjust to a specific pattern that you can see in the following diagram:

As you can see, that texture is made up of six different pieces, each matching a specific camera direction. This is the key to capturing cubemaps—making sure that we align the camera appropriately. If we translate that into a real-world scenario, this means that you need to point the camera in each of the possible axis directions—Positive X-axis, Negative X-axis, Positive Y-axis, Negative Y-axis, Positive Z-axis, and Negative Z-axis and render the scene like that. You would then bring those six images into an editing program, such as Photoshop, and arrange the pictures from left to right according to the order that Unreal expects, as shown in the previous diagram.

Saving that file into the correct format is another matter, one that you need specific tools for, as provided by different vendors, such as Nvidia or AMD. You can find more information on that in the following section.

See also

- Link to the cubemap creation process in general through Epic's official docs: `https://docs.unrealengine.com/en-US/Engine/Content/Types/Textures/Cubemaps`
- Specific cubemap tools section: `https://docs.unrealengine.com/en-US/Engine/Content/Types/Textures/Cubemaps/CubemapTools`

Using fully procedural noise patterns

We wanted to end our journey with this last recipe, which talks about a technique that is both powerful and flexible, but also quite demanding in terms of computing power. It is best used as a means of creating other assets, and isn't really directly employed in real-time apps and games. We are talking about the noise node—a fully procedural, mathematical system that allows you to create many different non-repetitive textures and assets based on it. Similar to the semi-procedural material creation techniques we saw in earlier chapters, this node takes things a bit further and enables you to use an effect that's very widespread in offline renderers, giving you the ability to create materials where repetition is not a concern. Let's see how it's done!

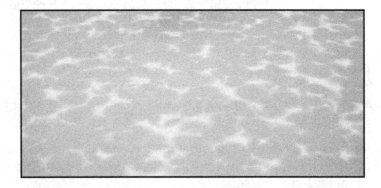

Getting ready

Unlike in the previous recipe, we won't need anything else apart from what the engine offers us to tackle this recipe. However, we've prepared a small scene that you can use should you choose to do so—its name is `09_ 06_ Noise_ Start` and you can find it in the `Content Browser / UE4ShadersAndEffects / Maps / Chapter09` folder.

If you want to use your own scenes and assets, feel free to bring anything you want. The only things we need to have are a model that we can apply this effect on and some basic lighting in place so that we can see it. Anything else is optional!

How to do it...

As always, let's start by creating the material that we are going to apply to the plane in our scene. In this case, we'll create one to use as a toon shader example, with animated waves driven by the noise node we'll be introducing. Something good to note before we start is the fact that this material is going to have several different parts—one for the sea foam, one for the normal sea color, and another for a slightly darker variation on this last parameter just to spice things up a bit. We'll be referring to these different parts throughout this recipe, which will be good to remember. Let's get started:

1. Create a new material and give it an appropriate name, something like M_Toon Shader. Assign it to the plane in our scene and double-click on it to bring up the material editor.
2. The first section we'll tackle is going to be the different sea color variation. Start by creating two constant 3 nodes and adding them to the graph.
3. Assign the previous two nodes slightly different blue colors, as we'll use them to paint our sea.
4. Create a **Lerp** node and connect both of the previous nodes to its **A** and **B** input pins.

   The next part that we need to create is the mask that is going to be driving the **Alpha** input pin of our previous **Lerp**. Instead of relying on a static texture, we'll use this opportunity to introduce our new procedural friend—the **Noise** node!

5. Add a **Texture Coordinate** node to our node graph.
6. Include an **Append** node after the previous one and connect them.
7. Create a Constant and add it to the **B** input pin of the previous node.
8. Right-click and look for the **Noise** node. Add it to our graph, and hook the output of the previous **Append** node into its **Position** input pin.
9. Select the new procedural node and set the following parameters in the **Details** panel—choose the **Fast Gradient - 3D Texture** method as the function, and set the **Output Min** to -0.25. All of the other other values should be left as default.

10. Connect the output of the **Noise** node to the **Alpha** of our **Lerp**:

 The reason why we are adding a Constant with a value of 0 to the **Texture Coordinate** node is because the **Position** input pin of the **Noise** node expects a three-dimensional vector.

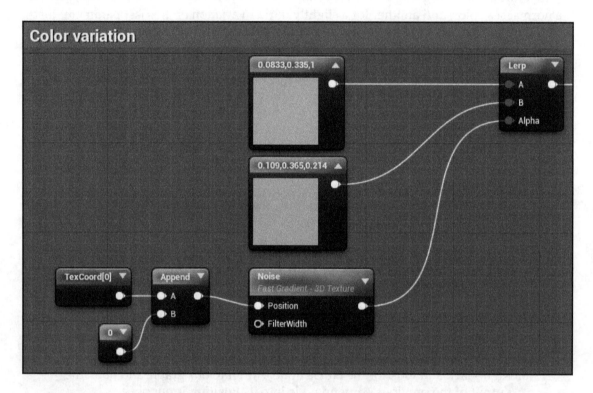

The previous steps have left us with a non-repeating pattern that allows us to mix two different colors without any kind of repetition. Of course, this first part—which we'll call color variation just for future reference—is just a very small color variation—a subtle effect that's used to randomize the look of the final shader. Let's continue and create the other parts of the material.

11. Create a third constant 3 and give it a value close to white—we'll use this to color the sea foam.

12. Add a new **Lerp** node and connect the previous constant 3 to its **B** input pin.

13. Wire the output of the first **Lerp** we created back in *step 4* to the **A** input pin of the new one.

With that done, we can now start creating the noise pattern that we'll use to mix between the normal color of the sea and the sea foam. We'll use the **Noise** node again, but we'll also want to animate it so that it looks even better in motion.

14. Create a **World Position** node.
15. Add a **Panner** node and change the value of **Speed X** to 5 and **Speed Y** to 15.
16. Throw an **Append** node and a Constant with a value of 0 after the **Panner** node. Connect the Constant to its **B** input pin and the **Panner** node to the **A** input pin.
17. Create an **Add** node and plug the output of the World Position into the **A** input pin and the result of the previous Append to the **B** one.
18. Include a **Noise** node and adjust the following settings in the **Details** panel: **Scale** to 0.015, **Quality** to 5, **Function** to **Voronoi**, **levels** set to 1, and **Level Scale** set to 4.
19. Connect the output of the previous **Add** node to the **Position** input pin of the new **Noise** node.

Before we continue, it might be a good idea to go over some of the most recent nodes we have created. As we stated previously, the **Noise** node is creating a non-repetitive pattern that we can adjust through the **Details** panel. However, we haven't really talked about what each of those settings do or effect, which we'll cover in the next section, *How it works....* However, it's good to know at this stage that the **Function** parameter is a very important one, as it defines the shape of the noise that we get. We can further effect that shape through many other different parameters – for instance, we are animating said shape with the **Panner** node sequence we created previously. Pay attention to the nodes we'll be creating in the following steps, as those will adjust it as well.

20. Create a **Constant** and set it to 0.3, and connect it to the **Filter Width** input pin of the previous **Noise** node. This will basically make the result of the noise node *leaner*, as it would be in a more defined grayscale mask.
21. Include a **Power** node immediately after the **Noise** node, which we'll use to push the black and white values apart. Connect the output of the **Noise** node to its **Base input** pin.
22. Add a Constant to drive the **Exp** input pin of the previous **Power** and give it a value of 4.
23. Multiply the result of the previous output by three to increase the lighter values in our mask.
24. Connect the output of the previous **Multiply** to the **Alpha** input pin of the **Lerp** node we created back in step 12.

These last set of nodes have helped us define the **Noise** node we are using to drive the position and appearance of the sea foam color. We will call this section of the graph **Sea Foam Variation**, just for future reference, and with this done, we are almost finished tweaking the material. However, we can still adjust it a little bit more – after all, the sea foam pattern we've created is only being animated in one specific direction, which isn't great in terms of the final look it gives us. Let's add a bit more variation to that:

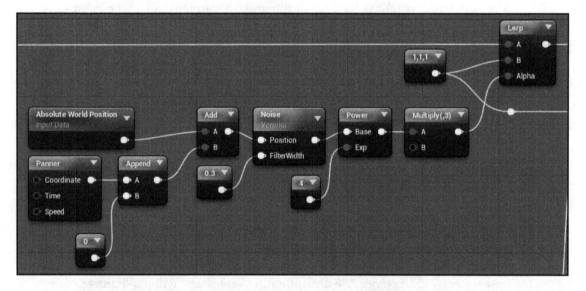

25. Copy the previous set of nodes we created, from steps 14 to 23, and paste them elsewhere—we'll use them as the base to create a little extra variation on the sea foam front. Let's comment and call this part Extra Variation for clarity.
26. Change the values of the new **Panner**—**Speed X** should be set to 10 and **Speed Y** should be set to 5.
27. Modify the **Scale** of the new **Noise** node to 0.0125.
28. Set the Constant driving the **Exp** input pin of the **Power** node to 3.
29. Create a new **Lerp** node and connect its **A** input pin to the output of the previous **Lerp** node from step 12. Connect its **B** input pin to the output of the Constant 3 vector driving the sea foam color.
30. Connect the **Alpha** to the output of the duplicated **Multiply** node that ends the set of nodes we just duplicated, that is, the Extra Variation part.

31. Connect the output of this last **Lerp** node to the **Base Color** of our material:

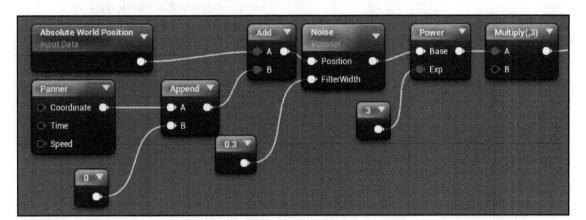

And there you go! That's what our material looks like in the end, without any sort of repetition going on, no matter where you look. This is a very powerful technique that you can use to get rid of that problem, given that you are aware of the cost that it introduces to the rendering pipeline. That cost is something that you can check, either by looking at the shader instruction count or by relying on the tools that Unreal provides to test how well your app or game performs. As always, stay tuned for the next two sections, where we'll talk a little bit more about what's going on beyond this node's surface.

How it works...

Even though we've already used the **Noise** node a couple of times, it won't hurt us to take another look at it and see what we can accomplish by tweaking the different parameters that are exposed on the **Details** panel. The first of them, if we look at the different options in order, is the **Scale**.

This is quite a straightforward node – the bigger the number, the smaller the noise is going to be. This can be a bit confusing at first, as we will usually need to type in really small values if we want to use the noise more as a masking technique and not as a small grain effect. Values such as **0,01** and lower usually work better than the default **1**, so be sure to remember this when you are on your own and can't figure out what's going on with your node!

The second parameter we can tweak is the **Quality** one, which will affect the end result in a subtle way – mostly by getting a smoother effect where the areas that show transition between different values are displayed a bit better. The third parameter, the **Function**, is probably the most important one, as it controls the logic that generates the final pattern. We'll talk about these more in the next section, as this is where the meat of the node is.

Turbulence is the next option we can enable, and that determines how many frequencies get combined to produce the final result. Using more frequencies means that the end result presents more variation—you can think of turbulence of variation as being inside an already varied source material. The next setting, **Levels**, also increases the variation of the end result that we get, making it richer in terms of finer detail. Further down, you can find the **Level Scale** setting, which will let you adjust the size of the levels. You can increase this value when you have a low number of levels in order to fake the detail that you would get were you using more levels, effectively faking the effect to make it more efficient.

Now, we can control the **Output Min** and **Output Max** settings—these control what the minimum and maximum values are, with 0 being black and 1 being white. The default values are set to negative and positive, and it's useful to tweak them as though we had a scale: if we have a minimum of -6 and a maximum of 1, we'll have a greater range of values located in the negative, darker tones than lighter ones.

The final set of settings are for **Tiling** and **Repeat Size**. Checking the first option will make the pattern repeat over the size that you specify, allowing you to bake a texture that you can then use as a noise generator at a much lower rendering cost. It's a handy feature when you want to create your own assets!

There's more...

The most important settings that we need to select within the **Noise** node are probably for the functions that drive this feature. They are different in many levels, but mainly in terms of their rendering cost and their final looks. Even though you might have seen them implemented in other 3D packages, one of the important things to note when choosing between the different types within Unreal are their limitations and the cost that they incur.

As an example, Epic's documentation tells us that certain types are better suited for specific situations. For instance, the `Simplex` function can't tile, and the `Fast Gradient` one is bad for bumps. That already signals to the user which one they should choose when creating a specific effect. Apart from that, the number of instructions is a really important element to keep in mind: for example, the `Gradient` function packs 61 instructions per level in its non-tiled version, whereas the `Fast Gradient` option peaks at around 16.

Beyond that, an expensive but very useful function is the `Voronoi` function, which is the latest function to be added to the engine. It is a really useful one when you're trying to recreate many different elements that we see in nature, as it comes close to reproducing stone or water, to name two examples. This is what we've used to recreate the ocean shader, but given different inputs, we could have just as well created a cracked terrain. Examples of this can be found in the documentation we've left in the following section.

See also

You can find more information about this node on a blog post by Ryan Brucks, one of the guys at Epic Games who worked on making that node a reality: `https://www.` `unrealengine.com/en-US/tech-blog/getting-the-most-out-of-noise-in-ue4`.

Other Books You May Enjoy

If you enjoyed this book, you may be interested in these other books by Packt:

Hands-On Artificial Intelligence with Unreal Engine

Francesco Sapio

ISBN: 9781788835657

- Get an in-depth knowledge about all the AI Systems within Unreal Engine
- Create complex AIs, understanding the art of designing and developing Behavior Tree
- Learn how to perform Environmental Queries (EQS)
- Master the Navigation, Perception, and Crowd Systems
- Profile and Visualize the AI Systems with powerful debugging tools
- Extend every AI and Debug system with custom nodes and functions

Unreal Engine 4 Virtual Reality Projects
Kevin Mack

ISBN: 9781789132878

- Understand design principles and concepts for building VR applications
- Set up your development environment with Unreal Blueprints and C++
- Create a player character with several locomotion schemes
- Evaluate and solve performance problems in VR to maintain high frame rates
- Display mono and stereo videos in VR
- Extend Unreal Engine's capabilities using various plugins

Leave a review - let other readers know what you think

Please share your thoughts on this book with others by leaving a review on the site that you bought it from. If you purchased the book from Amazon, please leave us an honest review on this book's Amazon page. This is vital so that other potential readers can see and use your unbiased opinion to make purchasing decisions, we can understand what our customers think about our products, and our authors can see your feedback on the title that they have worked with Packt to create. It will only take a few minutes of your time, but is valuable to other potential customers, our authors, and Packt. Thank you!

Index

CPSIA information can be obtained
at www.ICGtesting.com
Printed in the USA
LVHW041923091222
734911LV00001B/68